ENTITY MODELING:
Techniques and Application

RONALD G. ROSS
Editor/Publisher, *Data Base Newsletter*

DATABASE RESEARCH GROUP, INC.
Boston, Massachusetts

ENTITY MODELING: Techniques and Application
Ronald G. Ross

Printed in the United States of America.

10 9 8 7 6 5 4 3 2 1

ISBN 0-941049-00-0

To Maria

PREFACE

One of the most serious difficulties facing data professionals has been the lack of any text that was both comprehensive as well as readable for one of our foremost analytical tools, entity modeling. An additional problem—made all the more urgent by the recent emergence of powerful PC workstations—has been the lack of coordinated, rigorous conventions for graphic notation. For those of us working daily in the planning and building of large-scale database systems, these deficiencies have become increasingly intolerable.

To my knowledge, this will be the first practical book that attempts to correct those crucial deficiencies. For that reason, writing this book has been something of a pioneering effort in both the best and worst sense.

It's fair to say that the experience has been both rewarding and humbling. The rewarding moments have come in seeing many clear solutions emerging for data analysis problems that have troubled both myself and many other practitioners in by-gone projects stretching back over many years past. I now feel very confident that the "static" side of data design is firmly under control. The moments that have humbled have come in not being quite able to pull out from the mist a complete description for some newly perceived opportunity—but knowing that one nonetheless surely must exist and that it would probably pop out right after publication. Maybe this is what really makes the subject of information design both so interesting and so challenging—that gut feeling that perhaps there can *never* be any truly last word on "data." But alas, sooner or later the time does come to publish.

In any case, this work started out to be a simple, readable reference book on all aspects of the entity modeling approach. I hope that it did turn out to be readable, but parts of it are certainly not simple. One myth that I hope will finally disappear is that the design of data is somehow the "easy" part of systems analysis. Frankly, I wish it *weren't* so complex, but the real world, after all, is itself complex. Entity models are nothing more than simply its reflections. Looking at it that way, why *should* entity modeling be simple?

In point of fact, the book didn't really turn out to be entirely about "data" either. Perhaps the most exciting part of exploring so powerful a tool as entity modeling is that it leads unexpectedly in completely new directions, toward areas in particular where traditional distinctions between "process" and "data" become fuzzier and fuzzier—and may ultimately break down altogether.

Part III of this book introduces something I've called *Behavior Modeling*, which I believe establishes a whole new frontier for data-driven design. It's not simple, and it's definitely not for the newcomer to entity modeling, but its purpose is clear. In essence, Behavior Modeling is an attempt to extract so-called business rules out of applications—i.e., the "process" side—and to move them to more fertile ground, namely the entity model itself. To my knowledge this book is the first practical work that covers this important area in comprehensive and rigorous fashion following consistent graphic conventions.

This is not to say that practitioners haven't known intuitively about such business rules before, and that they even haven't tried to capture some of them as best they could using natural English with occasional graphic notation. But as I have told students in my seminars many times, the more and more you believe in "data," the less satisfying this approach will gradually become. One problem is the lack of rigor; the other problem is the lack of direct connection to the graphic entity model itself.

Perhaps just having written a book on entity modeling has made me overly biased toward graphic solutions in general, but think about this. In all, the book contains over 200 diagrams. (Producing that many diagrams is no small chore, incidentally, even using a state-of-the-art graphics and design workbench like Index Technology Corporation's Excelerator.) How much longer would the book have been if I had stuck exclusively *to the English language* to try to explain all the details? The correct answer is definitely too long for me to write, and almost certainly too long for anybody to read. English is good, but pictures are always worth a lot of words. Business rules work better in graphics!

In any case, Behavior Modeling was just the first inkling that entity models might possess far more potential for the "process" side than I had personally ever expected. To be frank, I have always been somewhat nervous that entity modeling, even given Behavior Modeling, would make the gap that currently exists between "process" and "data" (both politically and methodologically) even worse than ever before. Call it a tiny lack of due faith in a powerful approach.

What I discovered was the concept of entity life cycles and the idea of examining state changes for comprehensively identifying the transactions necessary to drive an information system. (Many other people have "discovered" this too, so I claim no special credit.) But the difference comes in unification—I am finding that the very same graphic notation can be used to pursue this area of analysis as used for basic entity and behavior analysis. In other words, with very little in the way of new diagramming conventions—and nothing at all in the way of new diagram types—entity modeling can be extended into the crucial area of transaction analysis, permitting "process" to be re-integrated with "data" in a fundamental way. I find this to be a very large, unexpected bonus.

What I now see emerging is an approach I'm calling data-*controlled* design, a powerful new and integrated way to pursue the analysis of information systems. This is leading-edge stuff, and frankly still in the shakedown stage, so I will carefully avoid making any wild and unprovable claims about it. If it turns out to be as good as I think, it will speak for itself anyway. In any event, I did think that it merited delaying publication of the book until I could get at least a brief chapter in on it at the end, even if woefully incomplete. So you'll find this material in a Supplement at the end of the text. I suspect my next book will cover this exciting area in much greater and certainly well deserved detail. Fortunately, I am already able to teach a good measure of it in some of my seminars.

Incidentally, for those of you to whom I promised the book would be available sooner, I apologize. *I* wish it had been out a whole lot sooner too. I could catalogue all the reasons for the delay, but it wouldn't serve any real purpose. My defense is that I wanted to do the best job possible.

What I can do, however, is thank all the people who have helped breathe life into the project along the way. I want to especially thank Ms. Linda Murphy of Database Research Group in Boston MA, who has gone beyond all call of duty in helping me produce the manuscript. Also of the *Data Base Newsletter* staff (present and past), Ms. Karin Watkins, Ms. Cynthia Jeffers, and Ms. Katherine Sing deserve special thanks. I also appreciate the labors that Chris and Archie Browne of Princeton, NJ have put into the production of the manuscript.

I also want to thank Index Technology Corporation for its assistance in producing the diagrams using their CASE tool, Excelerator. At Index Technology, Dick Perkinson has been instrumental in building support for the graphics. Production of the diagrams themselves has been monumentally assisted by Valerie Hatch, Mr. Doug Henning, and Ms. Nan Solomons.

My thanks also to colleagues in entity modeling and Data Administration too numerous to name for their suggestions and critiques along the way.

Finally, I wish to thank my wife's family in Lima, Peru (where the bulk of the original draft was written) for putting me up, and putting up with me, during that special time.

RONALD G. ROSS
Editor/Publisher
Data Base Newsletter

The diagrams in this book were created using
a customized version of Excelerator®

Excelerator is a registered trademark of Index Technology Corporation, Cambridge, MA.

CONTENTS

PRELIMINARIES

PART 1: OBJECTS

PART 2: DOMAINS

PART 3: BEHAVIOR

DESIGN SUPPLEMENT

PRELIMINARIES

Entity modeling may be used as a purely intuitive tool; however, as experience with it grows, a more formal framework for use of the technique is often desired. This Preliminary Section offers some concepts relevant in this regard. The beginning reader should skip this material and proceed directly to Part I.

0.1 Objects and Connections

Objects are the things in a real-world enterprise about which information is recorded in a database system. This information generally takes the form of conventional "data," but sometimes may also include specifications and/or rules for that data. An entity model may contain numerous types of objects—of these, entity types are the most basic. A complete list of objects is given in Appendix I.

An entity model represents these objects graphically. It also encompasses meaningful connections between the objects, which reflect interactions between them in the real world. These connections are indispensible in capturing the "meaning" of the objects and indeed are in some sense properties of the objects themselves. As with objects, an entity model may contain several different kinds of connections. Of these, relationship types are the most basic. Appendix I also gives a complete list of connections.

Objects and connections give an entity model substance and meaning. Meaning is often referred to as "semantics."

At a basic level, objects and connections correctly convey the sense that the entity model is static (i.e., does not provide a dynamic or functional view of the enterprise). This static view is the subject of Part I of this book, which discusses basic objects and connections.

At a more advanced level—especially in the areas of integrity and measurement—there is considerable overlap with what in conventional implementation would be considered "procedural." This more advanced interpretation is discussed more fully in Part III, on behavior.

The purpose of defining the objects and connections of a data resource is both to understand the enterprise in its full complexity, as well as to create a sound, stable and flexible database structure. To achieve these goals, one additional piece is necessary—the definition of domains, the atomic units of the entity model. This additional piece is fully discussed in Part II.

0.2 Levels of Detail

As suggested above, there are various types of objects useful in modeling a real-life enterprise. Some are basic, whereas others are detailed and highly refined. Use of object types (and associated connections) is therefore highly selective.

Generally, the selection of appropriate objects should be based on the following criteria.

- To whom knowledge about the enterprise is being presented. (Managers and end-users should be presented only basic objects; whereas systems implementors naturally require more refined objects.)
- How much is currently known about the particular enterprise. (Until the "big picture" emerges, it is important to concentrate on basics.)
- How close to implementation the project stands. (As the project draws closer to implementation, the more detailed objects are naturally necessary for complete specification.)

At least five distinct levels of detail are useful in building an entity model for any enterprise. These levels suggest what objects (and connections) are appropriate given the current level of understanding.

The five levels, enumerated below, are cumulative. Any object appropriate at a higher level is also available at a lower level. (The reverse, of course, is not true.)

Even as a model reaches a lower level of detail (i.e., greater complexity in terms of objects and detail), the need for communication with non-professionals remains critical. A model at a lower level of detail, however,

DETAIL LEVELS FOR ENTITY MODELING

1. **Presentation**—This is the simplest and most basic form for any entity model of an enterprise. Besides first-cut analysis of the enterprise, it is generally used only for communication with non-professionals—i.e., for *presentation*.
2. **Professional**—This second level of detail provides the richness in object types and connections necessary for professionals to fully capture the meaning and subtlety of a data resource, and to move toward its implementation.
3. **Integrity**—This level provides for additional rules to be specified that control the behavior of the data resource, as prescribed by business policy in the enterprise, in order to maintain correctness in the data managed during updating.
4. **Attributes**—Additional "detail" necessary in creating an entity model is specification of the complete set of properties (i.e., attributes), including "keys," that certain objects may have. Such definition may also extend the precision with which behavior and measurement may be specified.
5. **Measurement**—In any data resource, higher forms of information are inevitably synthesized from lower forms of data. Special objects are sometimes desirable to define such synthesis faithfully. Measurement also includes before-the-fact estimates of frequency for the data resource itself, a type of pseudo-measurement useful for performance tuning.

is generally too detailed for such communication to be effective. Consequently, there is a need for conversion of such a model to some higher level, where only more basic objects (and less detail) are represented.

Such transformation of an entity model to a higher level is called **ascending conversion**. Without careful management of object use by level, such transformation (and communication) would be difficult or impossible.

The five levels of detail are listed opposite. Part I of this book concentrates primarily on the first two of these, Presentation and Professional. Part III covers the remaining three. (For a complete list of object and connection use by level of detail, see Appendix II.)

0.3 Naming

Many, but not all, object types in an entity model must be given names meaningful to the enterprise. Those that cannot be named as such are given arbitrary identifiers. Certain connections between objects may also be named. This is generally optional.

Appendix I indicates which objects may have names. (As discussed below, any namable object or connection may also have aliases.) Appendix I also specifies which objects must be *uniquely* named.

0.4 Annotation

Meaningful textual description may also be desirable for any object (apart from graphic representation in the entity model itself), whether named or not. This is accomplished as follows.

Diagram 1.1

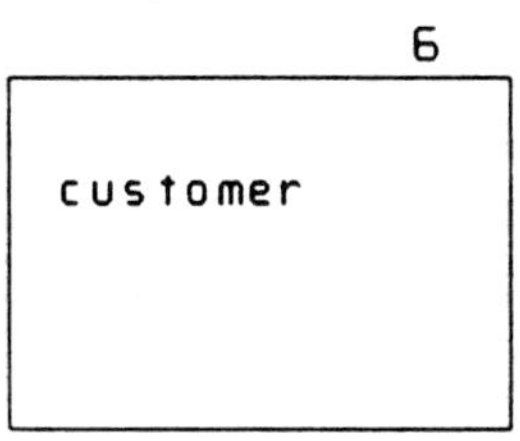

6 Any person or organization that may purchase our products.

Comprehensive annotation of a graphic entity model is strongly recommended. This permits the business policies directly reflected in the entity model to be stated in a form comprehensible to everyone within the enterprise.

0.5 Aliases

Any object or connection that can be named may also be given one or more **aliases**. These aliases are simply other names by which the very same object may be known. Since an entity model represents generally sharable or "integrated" data, recording aliases faithfully can offer substantially enhanced communication and comprehension. In order to avoid clutter in the entity model, however, excessive use should be avoided. Aliases for namable objects and connections are shown as follows.

Diagram 1.2

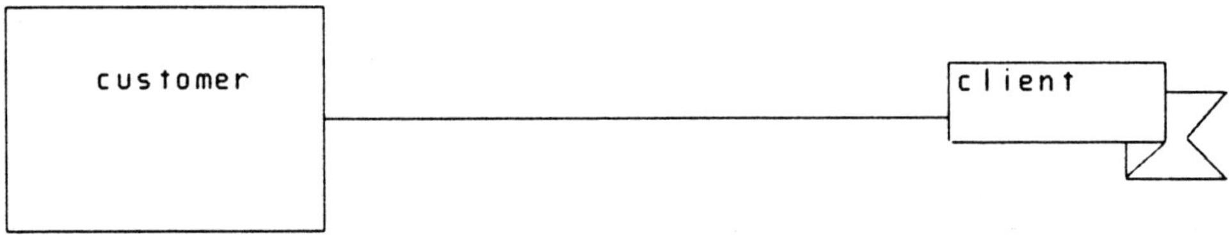

By use of the alias symbol (the banner at right), this enterprise shows it considers "customers" and "clients" to be exactly the same. "Customer" is the generally preferred or *primary* name for this object, whereas "client" is an acceptable alias.

Caution should be exercised in defining aliases. Often, upon closer inspection, an "alias" proves to be a more specific or more general class of the object in question (rather than *exactly* the same), having its own distinguishing properties, relationships, and/or behavior. (Refer to Section 1.2-3). The key lies in deciding whether or not the alias in question really refers to *exactly* the same thing as the specified primary name.

Sometimes it is desirable to show that the organization finds certain aliases unacceptable for some object or connection. (This is especially common for ambiguous abbreviations.) Naturally, such *prohibited* aliases should be used only cautiously as a primary name for any other object or connection. Prohibited aliases are shown as follows.

Diagram 1.3

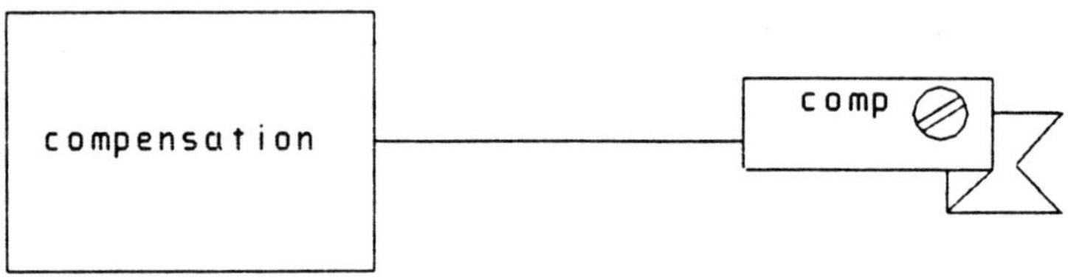

0.6 Zones

Any enterprise is really a dense interconnection of many individual components. To some extent, any division of these components will always be arbitrary and imprecise.

The entity model for an enterprise, or any piece thereof, is thus also tightly interconnected. An entity model is therefore essentially indivisible, and should always be developed and managed as a whole.

There are, however, sometimes reasons for defining certain selected portions of the entity model (called **zones**) in order to satisfy certain purposes, including those below. Note that such zone definition is *independent* of "level of detail" as previously discussed.

Referencing zones. A common problem in creating shared database systems is that different people or departments in the enterprise often call the very same objects by different names (i.e., by aliases). In order to enhance communication with diverse groups, it is often desirable to specify preferred aliases by each group within some portion (i.e., a zone) or even all of the shared model. This permits generation of a presentation model with specially tailored vocabulary.

Implementation zones. In actual implementation, an entity model may be split apart, or even pieces of it replicated, in order to accommodate geographical distribution, performance or other practical considerations. Each such portion of the entity model becomes a specific "zone" for implementation.

Window zones. Selective "windows" carve out special segments of an entity model in order to satisfy some special presentation or specification need. These special "windows" into the entity model (also called "**zoom**" diagrams) permit focused presentation of some specific portion of a larger (and probably highly complex) entity model, and/or allow additional specifications (e.g., for behavior) to be made that would otherwise hopelessly clutter the source model. The reader will notice that most of the sample models in this book are actually "zoom" diagrams—that is, replicated subsets of some larger model selected for the purpose of discussion and/or additional definition. The regular use of separate "zoom" diagrams—especially for behavior specification—is a practice strongly recommended for practitioners.

PART 1: OBJECTS

SECTION 1
Presentation-Level Objects and Connections

The most basic level of an entity model is simply the identification of what things, or entities, exist in the enterprise, and what the important relationships between them are. These are things about which information will be collected and stored in the database system. All further specification in an entity model is simply an elaboration of these basic data resource components.

1.1-1 Entity Types

Entities are the things (or objects) that make up the world. They are the things about which the enterprise must keep (i.e., generally "store") data in order to coordinate and support ongoing activities. There are an infinite number of entity types in the real world; the entity model consists of that subset that is of interest to the enterprise.

The word "entity" is confusing because it may refer either to the *type* of the thing (e.g. product) or to actual occurrences of that type of thing (e.g. nuts, bolts, screws, etc.). In this discussion, therefore, the term "entity" will never be used by itself. Instead, "entity type" or "entity type occurrence" (or simply, "occurrence") is used as appropriate. Sometimes the word "instance" is substituted for "occurrence"—both words mean the same.

In general, an entity type is simply something that exists and that has describable characteristics. It is meaningful to the business, and one or more of its specific functions or processes; this is why it is included in the entity model. Such inclusion means the enterprise either keeps information about the thing or is likely to do so sometime in the future.

An entity type is represented in an entity model by a rectangular box giving its name. Such an entity type name should *always* be a noun in the singular form.

Diagram 1.4

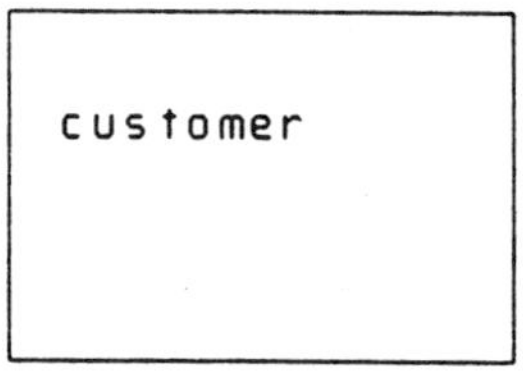

1.1-1.1 Identification and Properties of Entity Types

An entity type must possess a set of one or more identifiers, called **determinants** which are fields (or more precisely, **domains**) that uniquely and unambiguously distinguish between occurrences. For example, customer-no may be used as the determinant for the entity type, customer.

An entity type generally also has other fields (or domains) called **attributes**, each of which documents some *property* of the entity type. For example, a customer may have the attributes, customer-name, address, credit-rating, etc. Each customer may have some particular value for each of these attributes. Unlike the determinant values, however, other attribute values need not be unique across all occurrences of the entity type. For example, two different customers may have exactly the same value of credit-rating.

1.1-1.2 Classes of Entity Types

Entity types may be classified into *people, places, things, organizations, concepts,* and *events.* Examples are shown in the table opposite. Whereas this classification is useful in illustrating what variations may exist among entity types—and therefore in understanding a data resource more fully—*it really serves no formal purpose in entity modeling or database design.*

The classification, incidentally, is not necessarily exhaustive. For example, as Part III will show, there is reason to consider *measurement* as perhaps a seventh and distinct type of entity type. Indeed, a special object symbol will be introduced for that purpose.

Several questions about this classification of entity types are worth investigating.

What is the difference between a "thing" and a "concept"?

A thing is something that tangibly exists. This existence can be directly verified by one of the human senses (e.g., a vehicle can be seen and touched and often heard and smelled.)

A concept does not exist in that way. It is merely an idea or principle used to organize and/or control the activities of an enterprise. The only thing "tangible" about such a thing may be a "printout" of its contents. For example, a "customer account" is not recognizable by any human sense—at least until its current status is "output" on paper or "accessed" by a screen.

What is the difference between a "concept" and an "event"?

A concept may have some beginning and some end, but this is not its primary aspect. Also not primary is its chronological relationship to other occurrences of the same type. The primary intent of the concept is to organize the enterprise in some meaningful fashion.

A "customer account," for example, serves this function. Of less interest, is the chronological relationship of an "account" occurrence with other occurrences even for the same customer.

The primary focus of an event type entity type, in contrast, is not that individual occurrences exist over some continuous period, but rather that a *series* of occurrences will occur, usually specifically denoted (i.e., determined) by time. The orderly repetition or sequence of the event occurrences is of paramount importance. For example, the serial movements of a vehicle may represent an event type entity type.

Unlike concepts, events usually directly involve some other entity type (e.g., a vehicle in the example above) and merely add some time dimension to it. For this reason, events usually have two or more determinants, at least one of which refers to an entity type of some other type, and at least

CATEGORIES OF ENTITY TYPES

1. **PEOPLE** . . . HUMANS THAT CARRY OUT SOME FUNCTION(S).
   EMPLOYEES   CUSTOMERS   CONSULTANTS
2. **PLACES** . . . AREAS OR LOCATIONS SET ASIDE FOR PEOPLE OR THINGS
   OFFICES   WAREHOUSES   ROUTES
   CITIES   STATIONS   TERRITORIES
   REGIONS   LOCATIONS
3. **THINGS** . . . PHYSICAL OBJECTS, OR GROUPS OF OBJECTS, THAT ARE TANGIBLE
   EQUIPMENT   ITEMS
   BUILDINGS   VEHICLES
   PRODUCTS   PARTS
4. **ORGANIZATIONS** . . . FORMALLY ORGANIZED COLLECTIONS OF PEOPLE, RESOURCES, FACILITIES AND CAPABILITIES HAVING A DEFINED MISSION WHOSE EXISTENCE IS LARGELY INDEPENDENT OF INDIVIDUALS
   SUPPLIERS   ORGANIZATIONAL UNITS
   VENDORS   TEAMS
   AGENCIES
5. **CONCEPTS** . . . PRINCIPLES OR IDEAS NOT TANGIBLE PER SE USED TO ORGANIZE, OR KEEP TRACK OF, BUSINESS ACTIVITIES AND/OR COMMUNICATIONS
   PROJECTS   PRODUCTION CYCLES   SHIPMENTS
   ORDERS   INVOICES
   COMPLAINTS   ACCOUNTS
6. **EVENTS** . . . THINGS THAT HAPPEN USUALLY TO SOMETHING ELSE AT A GIVEN DATE AND TIME, OR AS STEPS IN AN ORDERED SEQUENCE.
   VEHICLE MOVEMENTS   PRODUCTION CYCLE STEPS   EMPLOYEE PROMOTIONS
   CHANGE REQUESTS   PROJECT PHASES

one of which involves time. (For example, the determinants for "vehicle movement" might be vehicle-no and date-time.)

Event entity types are one important way in which a time dimension is added to an otherwise "static" entity model.

CONVENTIONS AND GUIDELINES FOR ENTITY TYPES

- Entity types are things in an enterprise or its environment about which a business must record information. In a database design entity types often, but not always, become record types.
- Entity types may correspond to people, places, things, organizations, concepts, or events.
- There are usually many instances or occurrences of each entity type; however, an entity model shows only types, not occurrences.
- An entity type must have one or more identifiers, called determinants, which are domains whose values uniquely and unambiguously distinguish between occurrences. Each occurrence has one and only one value for its identifier(s).
- An entity type may have other attributes whose values document its properties. Attribute values need not be unique across all occurrences of the entity type.
- Entity types are named using a noun in the singular form that clearly identifies the object.
- Entity types are represented by rectangles in an entity model diagram.

1.1-2 Relationship Types

Relationship types are connections between entity types and sometimes other object types of an entity model. (See Appendix III for precise rules.) They reflect interactions between the corresponding things in the real world. They are always represented by lines connecting exactly two objects, with either single or double-headed arrows on both ends.

Diagram 1.5

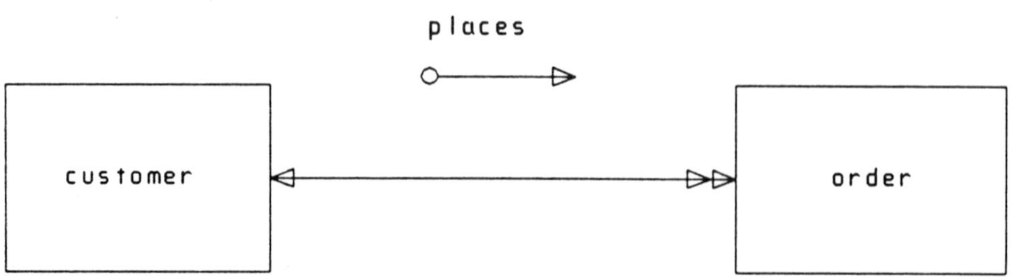

Especially at the "presentation" level of detail, a relationship type may be viewed as a **business action** between the associated entity types. In an English-language description of the relationship, this business action can always be designated by some verb called an **action name**. For, example, the business action could be described as "customer *places* order." "Places" is the action verb, designating the name of the business action, and "customer" and "order" (naturally nouns) designate the interacting entity types. The best way to discover relationship types for an entity model is generally to seek such verbs of action in natural language discussion (e.g., user dialogues or interviews) and/or text pertaining to the enterprise and its mode of operation.

1.1-2.1 Action Names for Relationship Types

The business action of any relationship type, as described in English, always has one entity type as the subject of the action, and another as the object of the action. For example, in the business action "train runs to destination," "train" is the subject and "destination" is the object. In diagramming this relationship type, the action is shown as follows.

Diagram 1.6

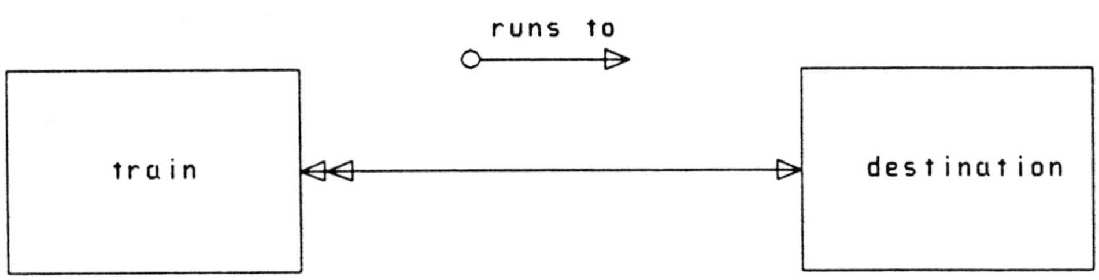

By convention, the action name is placed nearest the subject of the action, with a small directional indicator pointing toward the object. This directional indicator avoids any ambiguity in reading the "direction" of the action.

Showing action names is not only important in designating the meaning of relationship types, but also in distinguishing different relationship types that might otherwise appear as ambiguous or redundant. For example, without action names, the clarity and trustworthiness of the following model might be impaired. (In this model, the enterprise both buys and sells its products to the same group of companies.)

Diagram 1.7

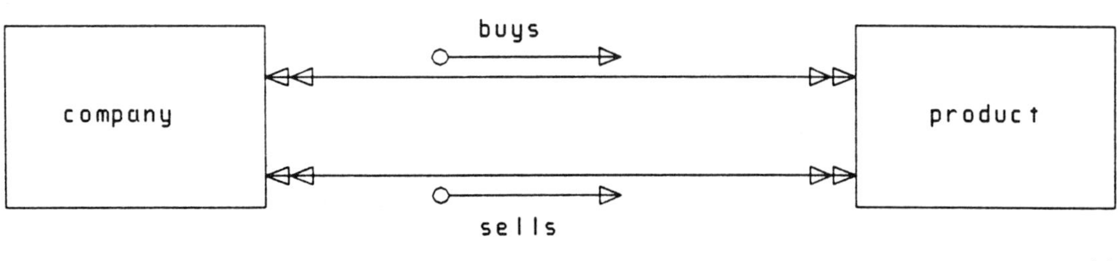

Action names should be used wherever the meaning and/or purpose of a relationship type may not be obvious to everyone who may eventually view the model. Liberal use is therefore recommended.

All relationship types, without exception, in an entity model are naturally "bi-directional." In other words, the interaction between the objects of the relationship type can always be traced in either direction.

However, one "direction" of given action name is normally "**active**," whereas the other is "**passive**." For example, the connection between customer and order may be described in the active form by "customer *places* order;" whereas the passive form would be described by "order *is placed by* customer." Note the transformation of the action verb from the active to the passive form. (Not all transformations, incidentally, are either this trivial, or even possible. Refer back to "the train runs to destination" example for an illustration. Try the transformation there!)

Both forms of a relationship type action verb can be shown for a relationship type, as illustrated below.

Diagram 1.8

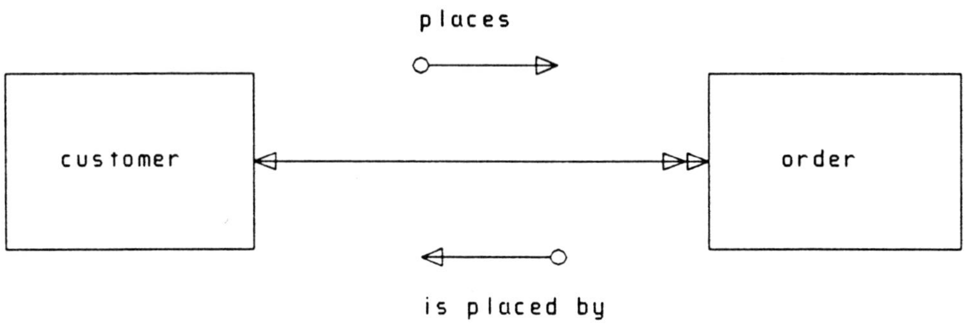

By convention, however, only the *active* form of an action name should generally be used (assuming that it is meaningful). This avoids clutter and keeps the language of the model crisp and nonredundant.

Also, whereas there are sometimes multiple active action names for the same relationship type pointing in the very same direction, the alternatives should generally be treated as aliases of some primary choice.

Diagram 1.9

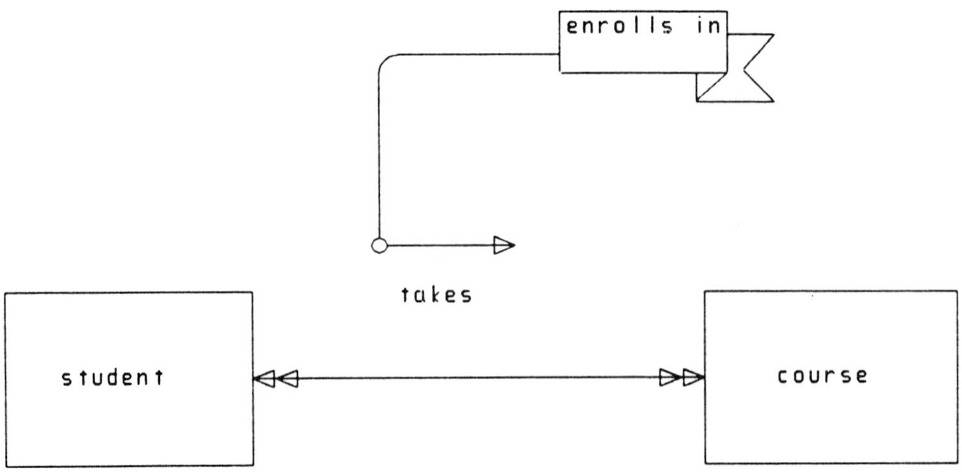

> **CONVENTIONS AND GUIDELINES**
> **FOR NAMING RELATIONSHIP TYPES**
>
> - Pick a verb of action, describing the business interaction of the related entity types.
> - Avoid passive forms of the action name where possible.
> - Choose one action name (in the active form) as the principle name; treat others (pointing in the same direction) as aliases.
> - Place the active form of the action name nearest the "subject" of the relationship type.
> - Use a small directional indicator to "point" toward the "object" of the relationship type.
> - Use action names liberally, especially where ambiguity or loss of clarity might otherwise result.

1.1-2.2 Single vs. Multiple Headed Relationship Types

As mentioned, every relationship type in an entity model is "bi-directional." This simply means that the business action so represented can be "traced" starting on either side. Given an occurrence of the entity type on one "side," the related occurrences of the entity type on the "other" side can therefore always be determined, and vice versa. This is illustrated in the following representation of actual entity type occurrences.

Diagram 1.10

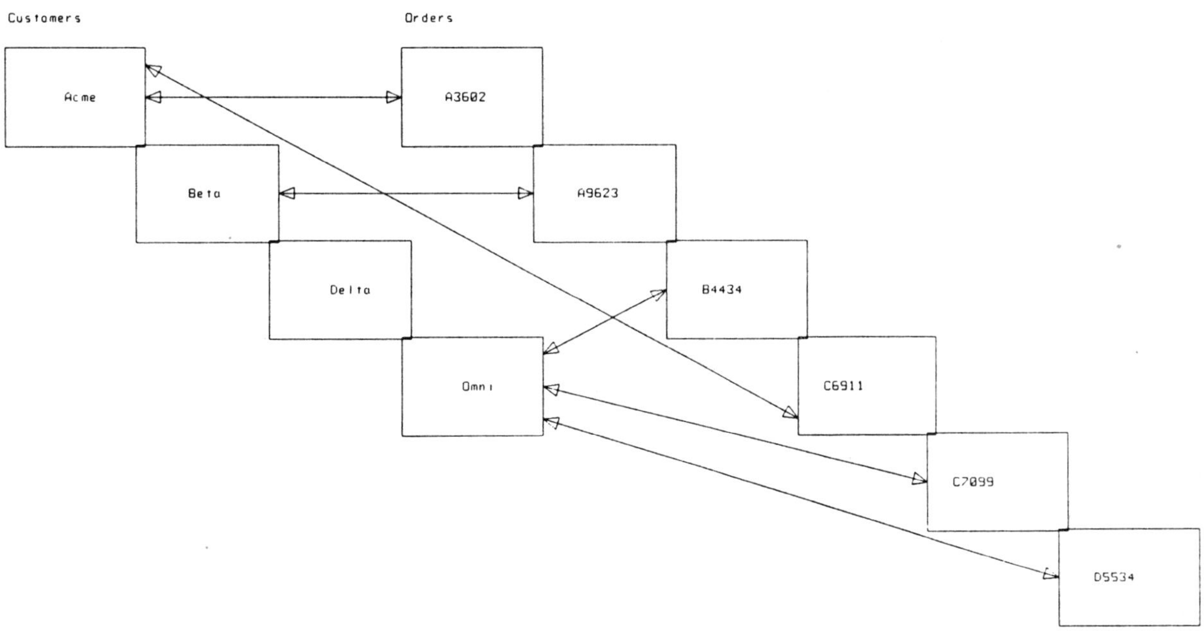

Note that any given customer may be related to zero, one or more orders, whereas no order (at least shown) is ever related to *more* than one customer.

When such "counts" can be stated as an abiding rule for the enterprise, the "type" or **cardinality** of the relationship is established. In the case above, this rule would apparently be stated as "one customer, many orders," and would be shown diagrammatically as follows.

Diagram 1.11

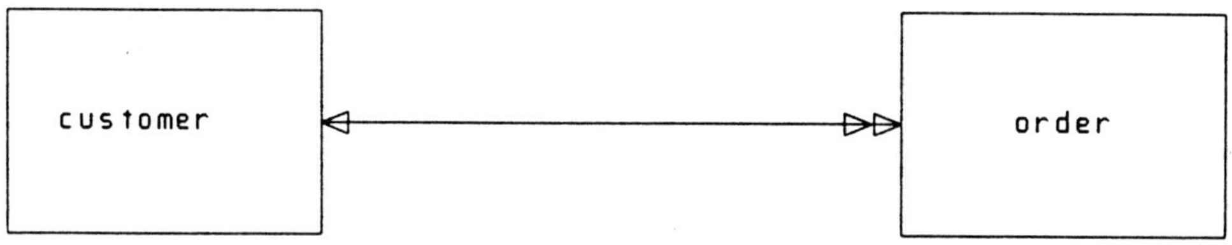

As stated, this rule becomes a *business policy* that no business transaction would ever be allowed to violate.

This model, upon implementation, would preclude any order from ever having more than one customer because of the *single-headed* arrow into "customer." However, it would allow each customer to place multiple orders, because of the *double-headed* arrow into "order."

In general, relationship types may be **one-to-one (1:1), one-to-many (1:M), many-to-one (M:1),** or **many-to-many (M:N).** A 1:M relationship type is exactly the same as a M:1 relationship type "drawn" as a mirror image (i.e., the other way around). Selecting the correct specification for any relationship type is a matter of carefully examining the relevant business policy and defining the most appropriate rule. For obvious reasons, a wrong or inappropriate choice once locked into an implemented database, can seriously hamper business operations. Post-implementation migration to the correct choice may be expensive and difficult, owing not only to DBMS restrictions but because the choice may become deeply embedded in application program logic. (The latter is probably the worse of the two.) Correct specification, therefore, is of most crucial concern.

1.1-2.3 Recursive Relationship Types

Both ends of a relationship type are permitted to enter the very same object type. This does not violate the previously stated rule that the relationship type always connects two objects, but merely says the two objects happen to be the very same.

Such a relationship type is called **recursive** because the object essentially points "back" to itself. Another way of saying this is that instances of the object may be made up of other instances. Because of this, recursive relationship types are also called **bill-of-material** relationship types.

Diagram 1.12

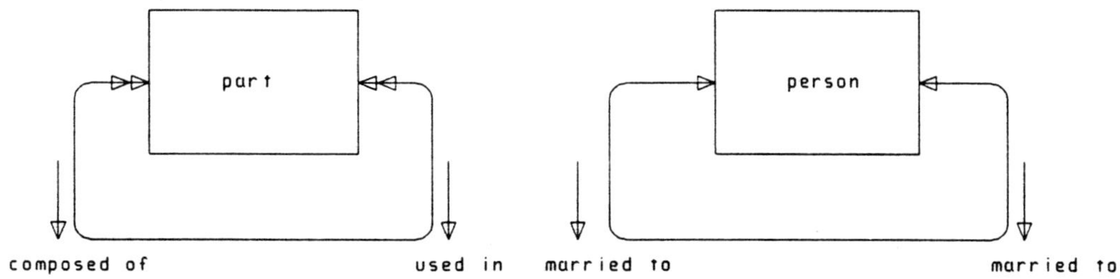

CONVENTIONS AND GUIDELINES FOR RELATIONSHIP TYPES

- Relationship types represent business interactions between entity types (or certain other objects).
- Relationship types are represented by thin, solid lines in an entity model diagram.
- A relationship type should *not* be looked upon as an "access path," even though upon implementation of the data resource, it may indeed support inter-object access.
- A relationship type always connects exactly two objects. (Sometimes it may be necessary to connect more than two objects to represent some business interaction; however, this requires an additional object type called an *association type*.)
- Each end of a relationship type must have either a single-headed arrow or a double-headed arrow. The single-headed arrow indicates a "one" relationship type, whereas the double-headed arrow indicates a "many" relationship type.
- In a recursive relationship type, both ends of the relationship type connect to the same entity type.

1.1-3 Sample Presentation-Level Entity Model

A complete entity model for some enterprise, or part thereof, contains only boxes and arrows at the Presentation Level. A simple example of such a model is shown below.

Diagram 1.13

SAMPLE ENTERPRISE ENTITY MODEL
(Presentation Level)

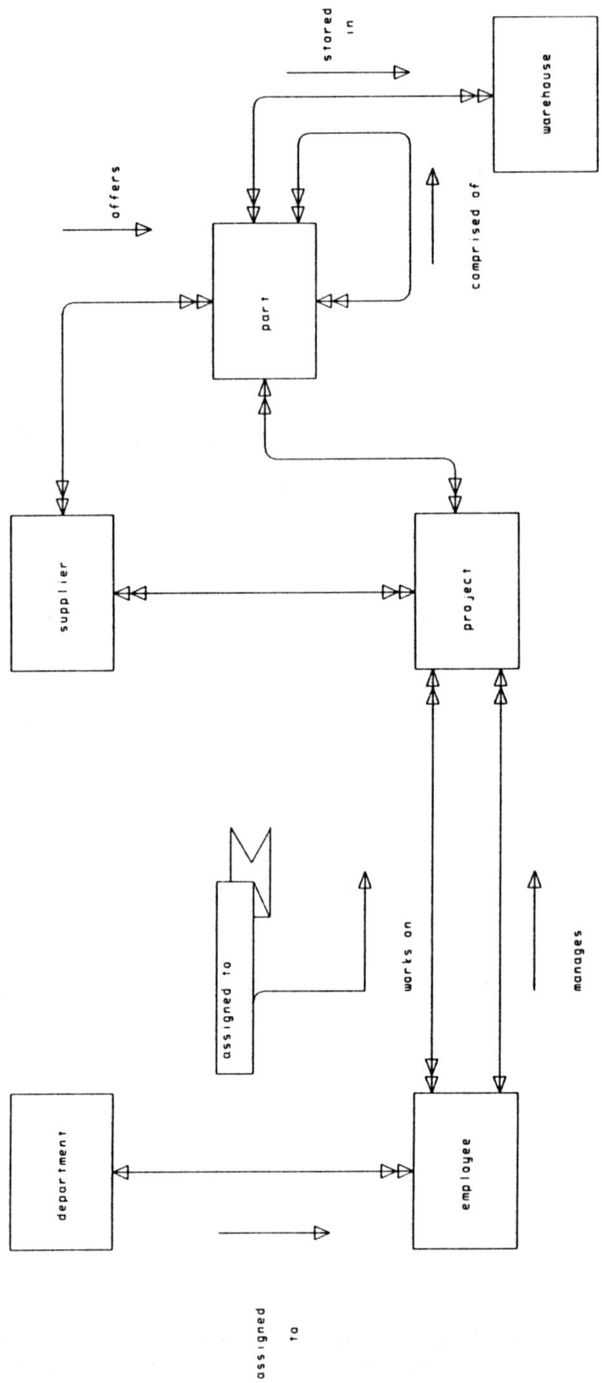

SECTION 2
Professional-Level Objects and Connections

A presentation level entity model must be substantially enhanced if it is to serve either as a precise representation of the enterprise or as a blueprint for physical implementation of the corresponding database. Such completeness is made possible by the additional objects and connections provided within the professional level of detail. In this section, four new general types of such objects and connections are examined in detail: **association types, characteristics, entity types hierarchies,** and **aggregates.** Each is very important in its own way.

1.2-1 Association Types

An **association type** is an object that gives additional substance to a relationship type. This additional substance generally means providing a place for properties (i.e., attribute types) that really describe or belong to the relationship type itself rather than to either of the related entity types (or other objects) individually. Such information is often called **intersection data**.

Suppose, for example, that the following relationship exists.

Diagram 1.14

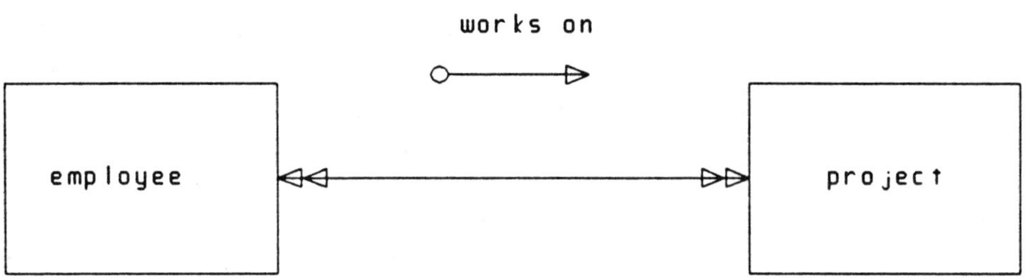

Employees themselves possess certain properties, as do projects.

There are certain other properties, however, that pertain strictly to the connection between them. For example, assignment-date provides a date when an individual employee was assigned to a particular project. Every combination of employee and project could have a different value of assignment-date; thus, there could be many such dates for either an individual employee or an individual project. In the model above, there is no satisfactory place to "put" this special employee/project information. The introduction of an association type (by convention a diamond-shaped object) solves this problem, as follows.

Diagram 1.15

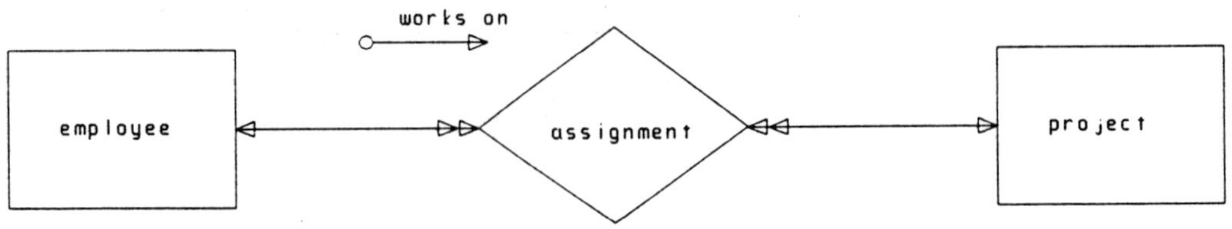

The new assignment object (an **association type**) now permits each combination of employee/project to have its own value of assignment-date. This also incidentally solves certain problems in implementation—namely that there is generally no way to implement M:N relationship types directly under most DBMSs (especially without violating beneficial normalization rules). Note that instead of the single M:N relationship type, there are now two relationship types that are both 1:M. This "splitting apart" always occurs when an association type is introduced.

1.2-1.1 Identifying Association Types

Like an entity type, an association type should be named using a noun (not a verb) that describes the meaning of the connection. Also like an entity type, it may possess its own properties (i.e., attributes), as illustrated above.

An association type differs, however, from an entity type in one very crucial respect: it *never* possesses its own unique determinant. Instead, the association type always "borrows" the determinants of the objects it interrelates and reuses them as its own.

For example, in the diagram above, if employee-id determines employee, and project-no determines project, then the determinants of assignment would necessarily be employee-id, project-no (no significance in the order listed). *There is no other choice.* Naturally, association types therefore always have more than one determinant.

This "borrowing" of determinants in an association type is crucial for an additional reason. Namely, because its determinants are merely the set of all those for the related things, if any of these other things go away (i.e., are deleted), the instance of the association type must also disappear (i.e., be deleted). This is a more or less "hidden" rule or consequence, but one nonetheless critical for the *integrity* of the operationally implemented database. It is the first such integrity rule thus far encountered in this discussion, and becomes *general* **Integrity Rule #1.**

Integrity Rule #1

An occurrence of an association type can only exist if the object occurrences it relates exist.

Association types also differ from entity types in that they need not necessarily be named uniquely in a single entity model. ("Assignment," for example, might easily appear more than once.) However, two association types with the same name *must* have a different set of determinants.

If two association types happen to have the same set of determinants (this is not altogether uncommon since the same two objects may be related in several different ways), then the association types must, of course, have different names. In other words, there must always be some way to tell association types apart from one another.

1.2-1.2 Using Association Types

Association types are often used for relationships strictly between entity types, but they may also be used for relationships between certain other types of objects (which may be different on either end), even including other association types. In other words, they can be used anywhere a relationship type can be used. (See Appendix III for exact rules.) The rule of "borrowed" determinants, however, always remains in force for an association type, no matter what it may join.

Diagram 1.16

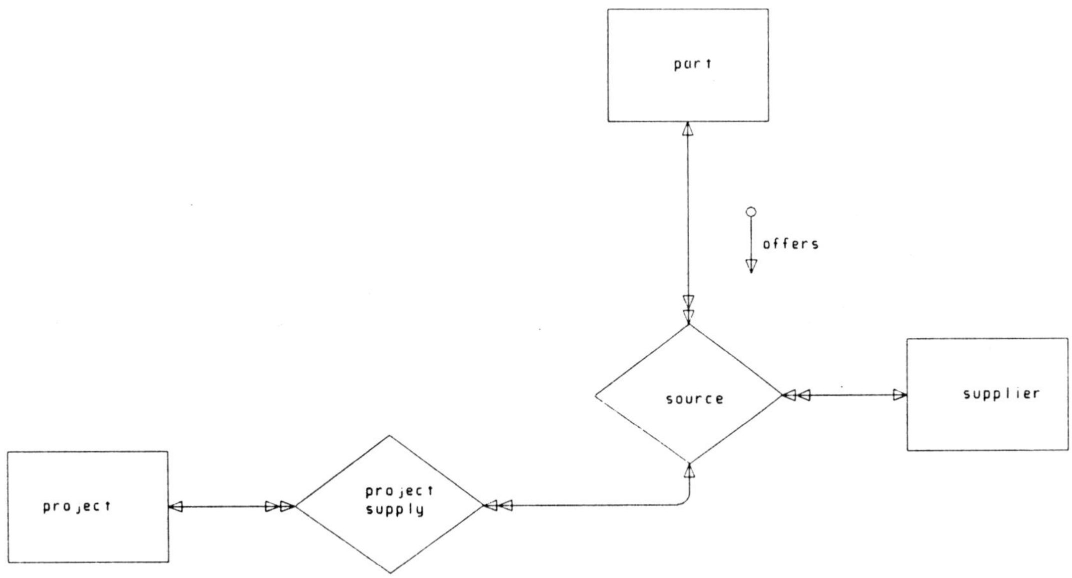

In this example, two association types appear. One of these, "project supply" connects "project," an entity type, with "source," another association type. Whereas "source" defines which suppliers supply which parts (in general), "project supply" defines which suppliers supply which parts to *particular projects*. Its set of determinants would consist of those for all three entity types (i.e., project-no, plus part-no and supplier-id, the determinants for "source").

Although association types are most commonly used for "breaking apart" M:N relationship types (note examples up until this point), they may also be used for 1:M relationship types, or even 1:1 relationship types.

For example, suppose the relationship type between customer and order is as follows.

Diagram 1.17

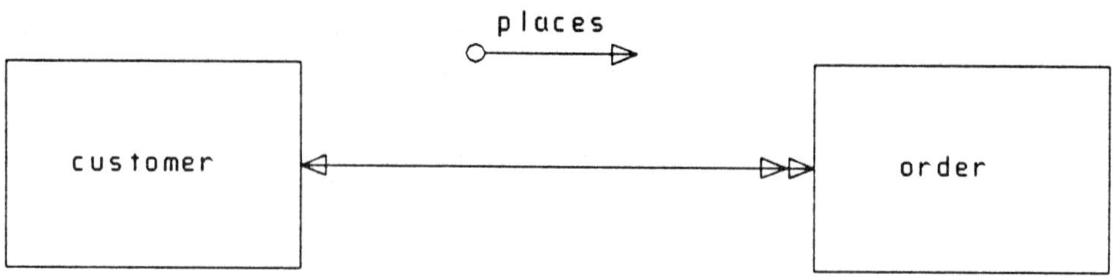

Suppose also that in this enterprise, a customer may receive a discount each time an order is placed. This discount may be treated as intersection data, to be supported by an association type inserted between customer and order, as follows.

Diagram 1.18

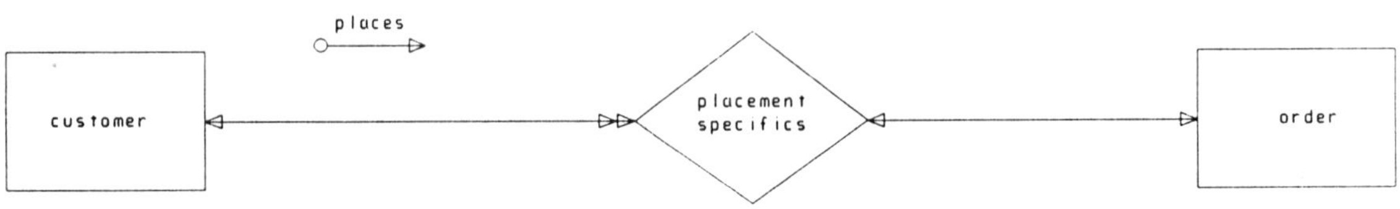

Note that the original relationship type has still been broken apart into two new ones, as was previously the case.

Inclusion of an association type into a 1:M or 1:1 relationship type is not generally considered as critical as in the M:N case. In the first place, in the former cases there is already somewhere to "put" intersection data; it may be treated merely as a property of an entity type on one side. (For example, discount may be treated as a property of order, since there will be only one discount value per order.) There is no violation of beneficial normalization principles in doing this. (For the reader: Why wouldn't placing it on the "customer" side work?)

Secondly, many DBMSs support 1:M and 1:1 relationship types directly (e.g., using a "foreign key" concept or equivalent), so the need for the association type is not so great an implementation concern. Generally, association types should therefore be used in 1:1 and 1:M relationship types only where they specifically help improve clarity.

Some counterpoints to the above include the following. Some DBMSs simply do not directly support either 1:M or 1:1 relationships (e.g., in IMS, a logical child is always needed in *any* logical relationship between roots). Also, it has been suggested that more flexibility to meet future business changes may be gained by always pre-allocating association types. Proponents of such a strategy also often recommend that *both* sides of all association types be treated as 1:M, even if currently 1:1. (The current, more restrictive rule can be specified using a "limit" integrity constraint with an upper limit = 1. See Section 3.1-1.4.) This approach, however, may not prove worth the trade-offs necessary to implement it.

1.2-1.3 Headed Arrow Migration

Insertion of an association type into a relationship type has one perhaps nonintuitive consequence—the original heads of the arrow migrate from the related objects "back" into the association type.

Diagram 1.19

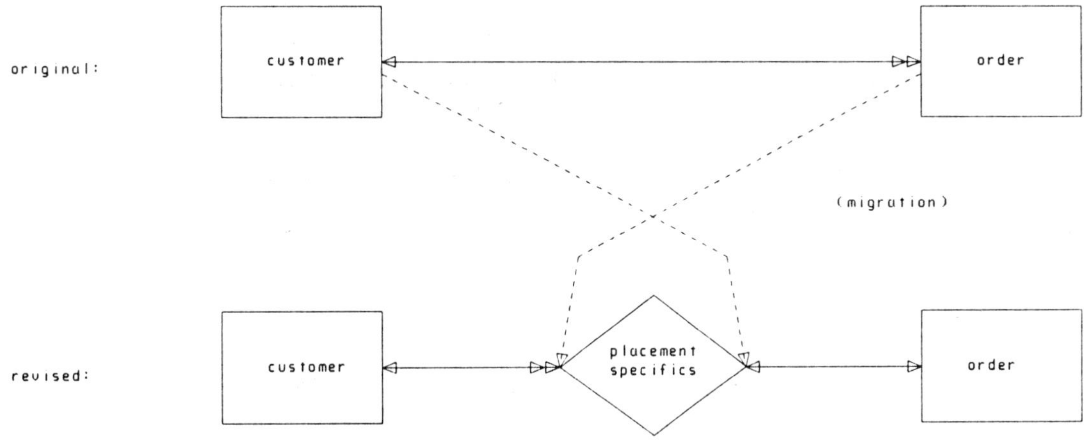

It should be noted that even after this migration occurs, the overall connection still "reads" exactly the same (i.e., "customer places order" and "order is placed by customer"). In other words, action names always read "through" association types.

Careful examination shows why this migration is necessary. This examination requires inspection of a segment of actual database content and some thought about actual implementation and field values.

Diagram 1.20

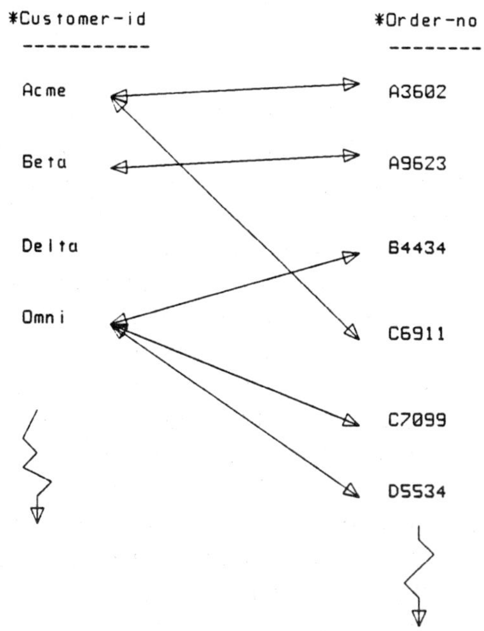

Note that in this original data (no association type yet inserted), some customers have multiple orders, but no order has more than one associated customer. (To be completely rigorous about establishing the relationship instances, a "foreign key" for customer-id would be desirable in orders.)

Diagram 1.21

Revised Version (association type inserted):

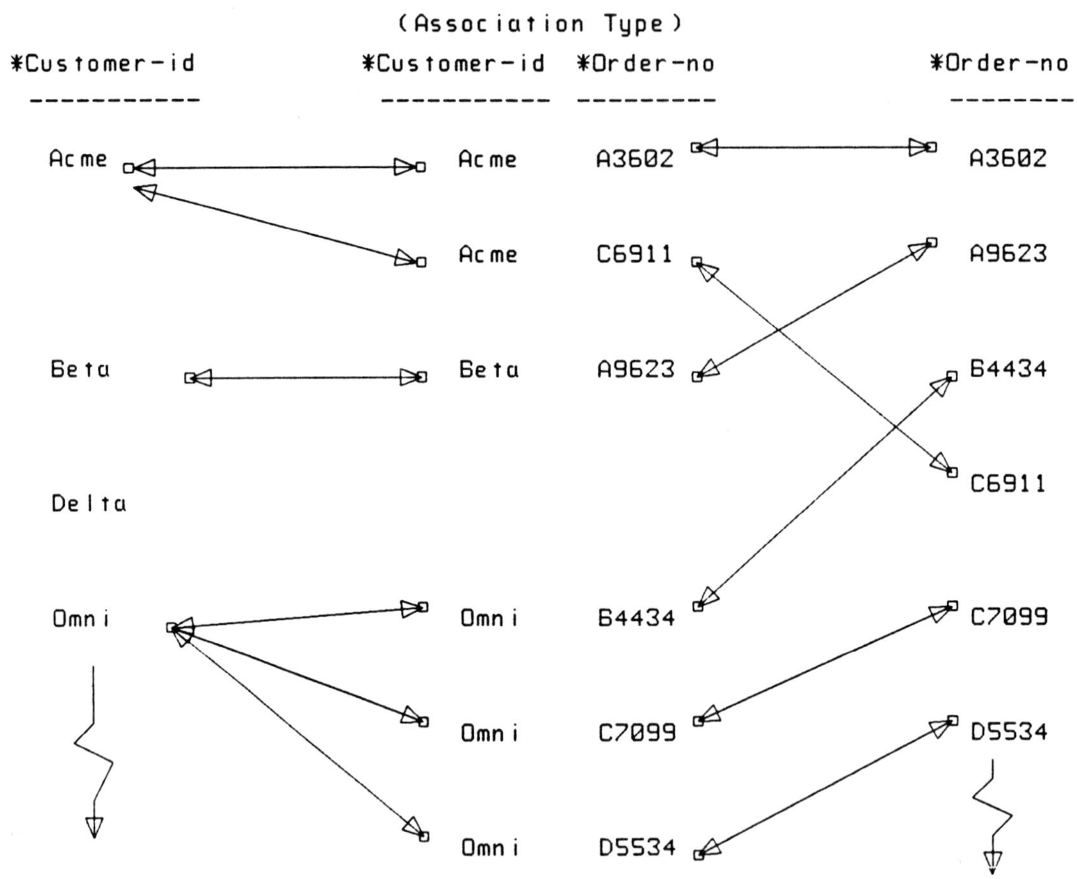

In this revised version, with the association type now inserted, note that each association type instance (i.e., table entry) points (outward) to one and only one customer, and to one and only one order. (These are the two new "heads.") Now, however, each customer entry may point to "many" association type entries (note the case of Omni). The old "many" head has migrated back from "order," and now goes into association type.

Likewise, the other old "head," once entering customer from order on a "one" basis, has also migrated back and now enters the association type from the other side. This is less obvious, of course, since this "head" is also a "one." (The reader should try the same exercise on a M:N relationship type—for example, on the earlier employee/project connection.)

In general, every association type must have at least two single-headed arrows pointing away from it, toward the objects being associated (specifically the ones whose "determinants" have been "borrowed"). Care should be exercised in this regard since there is a natural tendency to overlook proper "migration" of relationship type heads.

1.2-1.4 Binary vs. N-ary Association Types

The association types examined thus far have always associated exactly two objects. They can therefore be called **binary**. An association type that relates *more* than two objects (picking up all their determinants in the process) is called **N-ary**. Some practitioners prefer to use only binary association types insofar as possible since N-ary association types are often hard to interpret and difficult to implement. Sometimes, however, N-ary relationship types are necessary. The following provides an example of an N-ary relationship.

Diagram 1.22

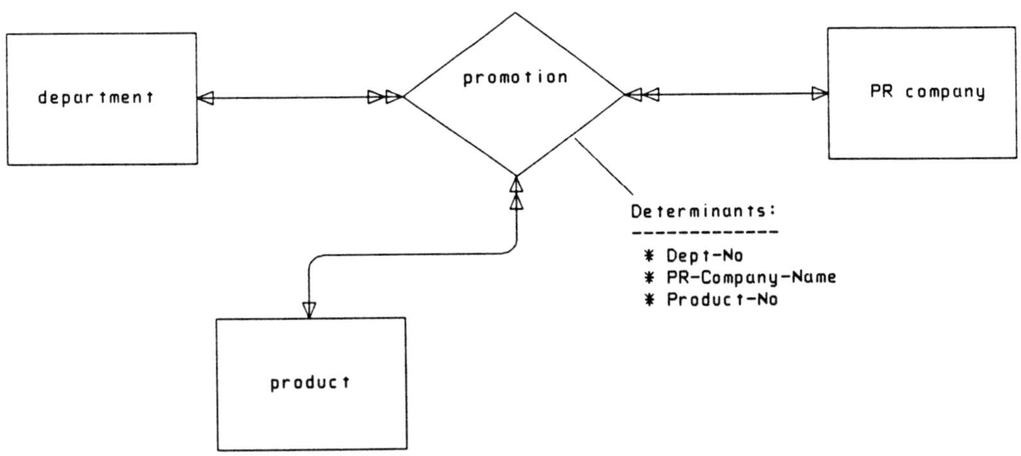

In this example, "promotion team" is a tri-nary association type because it picks up the determinants of all *three* things it associates. (It is possible, as "source" in the earlier example showed, for an association type to be related to more than two objects, but *not* pick up the determinants of all the related objects. It could thus still be binary, even though related more than twice. The key lies in which determinants have been "borrowed.")

The above tri-nary association type could be eliminated by substituting a series of two *new* association types (as in the earlier "source"/"project supply" example). One of the new association types would have two determinants. The second would have three determinants (but still be binary) and would associate the first association type with one entity type. (The reader should try this transformation as an exercise. What are the determinants? According to Integrity Rule #1, what will now go away when?)

The original tri-nary association type could also be eliminated by substituting a regular entity type (naturally with its own identifier), retaining all three original relationship types. (How does this change the deletion consequences?)

Both of the above modification approaches to the tri-nary relationship type, it should be noted, alter the relevant business policies associated with the entity model. This may or may not be desirable and must therefore be weighed very carefully.

GUIDELINES AND CONVENTIONS FOR ASSOCIATION TYPES

- Any relationship type may have "intersection data." An association type is inserted into the relationship type to accommodate this intersection data.
- An association type is always represented by a diamond.
- When an association type is inserted into a relationship type, two new relationship types are created.
- The association type must always have at least two single-headed relationship types leaving it. (It may optionally have more than two. The others need not be single-headed on the other end.)
- Relationship types coming into the association type may be either single or double-headed. They may connect to entity types, other association types, or certain other kinds of objects.
- The association type "borrows" the determinants of at least two related objects to also use as its own. It *never* has its own identifier.
- The association type instance must disappear if any of the related object instances are deleted (Integrity Rule #1).
- The association type should be named using a singular noun.
- Different association types in the same entity model may have the same name, so long as their determinants are not exactly the same.
- N-ary association types should be avoided insofar as possible.

1.2-2 Characteristics

Certain entity types are fundamental to an entity model as well as to the corresponding enterprise. Because they can essentially stand alone in providing information of interest, they are called **kernel**. Orders, vehicles and employees are examples of such entity types. Naturally, kernel entity types should be the initial focus for any newly initiated entity modeling process. Kernels are the only kind of entity type ever present in a presentation-level entity model.

Other entity types are less central to an entity model and basically only exist to provide some additional dimension to another object. This additional dimension may record a timed repetition of some event in which this other object is involved or document some multivalued property (actually, usually a set of properties) that it may have.

Such entity types are called **characteristic entity types** because they are tightly coupled to this other object (called the **characterized object** or simply "**CO**"), which they serve to describe in greater detail. Characteristics are thus highly dependent entity types.

Diagram 1.23

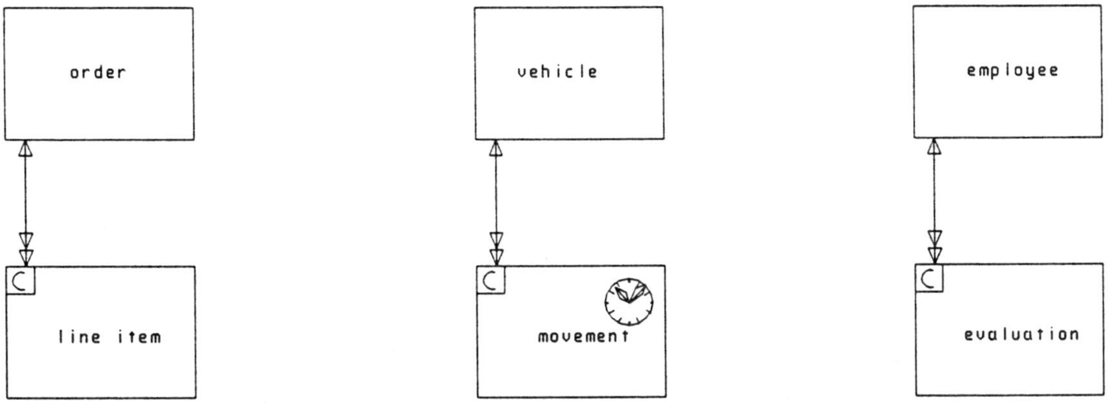

Like any entity type, a characteristic is denoted by a rectangular box, but with a small boxed "C" (for "characteristic") inside. It generally makes no sense to show a characteristic without also showing the object characterized, as above.

Only one relationship type may enter the small boxed "C" of the characteristic entity type (since any given characteristic may only characterize one object), and it must proceed (generally "upward") directly to the characterized object. (This object may naturally have other characteristics as well.) The head of this characterizing relationship type at the end entering the characterized object must be "single" because each instance of the characteristic entity type may only characterize one instance of the characterized object. (Naturally, each instance of the characterized object could be related to "many" instances of the particular characteristic.) The characterizing relationship type is naturally mandatory for the characteristic.

An association type is never permitted for a characterizing relationship type. In general, a characteristic entity type may characterize an entity type (common), an association type (somewhat rare), or another characteristic (not uncommon). Naturally, attribute types (and relationship types) are available to characteristic entity types just the same as for regular (kernel) entity types.

The purpose of the characteristic entity type is to provide some repetitive set of properties (and possibly relationships) for the characterized object. Sometimes this is as simple as say, providing for multiple "addresses" for each employee. Such use hardly gives a flavor of "entity type" at all, at least until it is recognized that "addresses" often come with some effective-date, perhaps giving the sense of some repetitive "event."

Other examples, including the ones above, are more concrete as objects, albeit dependent ones. For example, line items for an order provide information about how much of each item has been ordered. "Movements" of a vehicle describe where a vehicle has gone (or is scheduled to go), when it went (or is going), and what has happened (or may happen) along the way (i.e., real "events"). Evaluations for an employee (a repetitive event just like movements of a vehicle) may provide rating values and other evaluation details of interest.

As the examples above suggest, it is very common for characteristics to represent events, giving the corresponding entity model an important dimension of time. (Although it may seem contradictory to maintain that a "static" model such as the entity diagram can have a "time" dimension, it must be realized that the treatment of time is in a purely static fashion—i.e., as a discrete, repetitive event.) Effective accommodation of time is so

GUIDELINES AND CONVENTIONS FOR CHARACTERISTICS

- A characteristic entity type is portrayed as a rectangular box, just like a regular entity type, but with a small boxed "C" inside.
- The characteristic can only characterize one other object.
- This other object may be a kernel entity type, another characteristic entity type, or an association type. It may have other characteristics as well.
- The characteristic must share at least one relationship type with this other object. (No action name is necessary.) This is called the characterizing relationship type.
- This relationship type must enter the characteristic at the small boxed "C" area (only one such relationship type is permitted) and be single-headed at the other end.
- No association type is permitted for this relationship type.
- A characteristic may be related in normal fashion to many other objects.
- A characteristic must have at least one partial determinant of its own.
- The characteristic must also "borrow" the determinant(s) of the object characterized to also use as its own.
- Two or more characteristics may be named the same but if so, they must have a different set of determinants (and vice versa).
- An occurrence of the characteristic can exist only so long as the corresponding occurrence of the object characterized continues to exist. (Integrity Rule #2.)
- Characteristics are used to provide some repetitive or multivalued set of properties (and possibly relationships) for the characterized object.
- Characteristics are frequently used to document repetitive events, and thus capture a time dimension for an entity model.
- A characteristic is preferred over an association type in establishing a relationship between two objects wherever instances of these two objects may be related more than once, or where the "intersection data" should be retained even if a related object instance is deleted.

important to many data resources, that practitioners may wish to denote explicitly certain objects (usually characteristics) as supporting "time." This may be signalled by use of a "clock" symbol, as in the "movement" characteristic above.

1.2-2.1 Identifying Characteristics

Kernel entity types have a determinant whose values, by themselves, can uniquely distinguish among all occurrences. No reference to anything else—for example, some other determinant—is necessary for that purpose. Such determinants are said to be **kernel**. The determinants for "order," "vehicle," and "employee" are all of this type.

The determinant associated with a characteristic is different. By themselves, the values of such a determinant cannot distinguish uniquely and unambiguously between occurrences. Instead, they must always be coupled with the values of some other determinant in order to distinguish between occurrences of the characteristic. Determinants of this type are said to be **partial**, because they always only "partially" identify occurrences of the object of interest.

For example, suppose the determinant for line-item is line-item-no. By themselves, the values of line-item-no (say 1, 2, 3, 4 . . . etc.) really mean nothing unless coupled with some value of order-no (say D6321). Only when values for both determinants are given (say order D6321, line 21) can an occurrence of interest be identified.

This fact has several consequences. First, the determinants for a characteristic always include one partial determinant, plus all the determinants of the object characterized. In other words, the characteristic "borrows" the determinants of the object characterized to use, along with the partial determinant, as also its own.

A second consequence has to do with integrity. Obviously, for an occurrence of a characteristic to exist, the corresponding occurrence of the object characterized must already exist. Similarly, if the occurrence of the object characterized goes away (is deleted), any associated occurrences of the characteristic must also disappear automatically.

This can be stated as a second general integrity rule for entity models.

Integrity Rule #2

An occurrence of a characteristic can only exist if the corresponding occurrence of the object characterized exists.

1.2-2.2 Using Characteristics

A characteristic can naturally be related to other objects of interest using relationship types. In fact, in some cases this is an integral part of what the characteristics are all about. For example, it is difficult to conceive of a "line-item" on an order not referring to some product being ordered.

Diagram 1.24

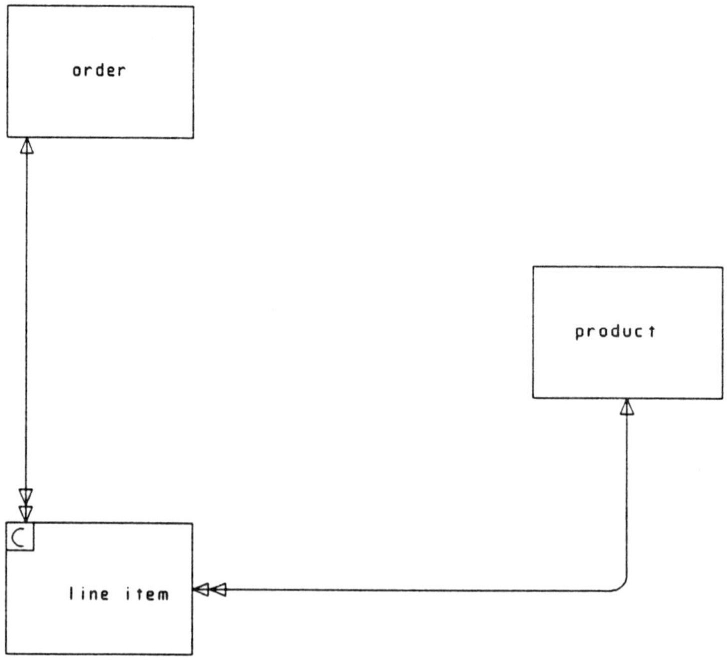

The natural question to ask, therefore, is why not use an association type for this "relating" to "product," rather than a characteristic tied to "order"?

In general, there are two basic reasons why characteristics may be preferable to an association type in establishing some given relationship. The first has to do with repeated relationships with the very same occurrence of a related object. For example, the former model would permit the same product to be ordered on the same order more than once. This is because line-item-no can be used to distinguish between the different instances (e.g. the product might first be referenced on line 6, then on line 13, etc.).

If, however, an association type is used in the place of the characteristic on the entity model, this would not be possible because there would consequently be no such way to distinguish between the multiple instances. With an association type, product-no would essentially substitute for the characteristic's determinant line-item-no, which would disappear. If the value of product-no were the same in two different instances of the association type for the same value of order-no, then the instances themselves would have to be considered identical. There would be no way to tell them apart. (The reader may wish to draw an "implemented" portion of the database—i.e., show relevant determinant values—to convince himself/herself this is so.) With an association type, therefore, two instances of the related objects can never be related to each other more than just once. This important fact can often lead to a kind of unintentional "tunnel vision" in actual entity modeling practice.

The second reason for using a characteristic instead of an association type in establishing a relationship type between two objects has to do with deletion. This can be illustrated using the following sample case.

Diagram 1.25

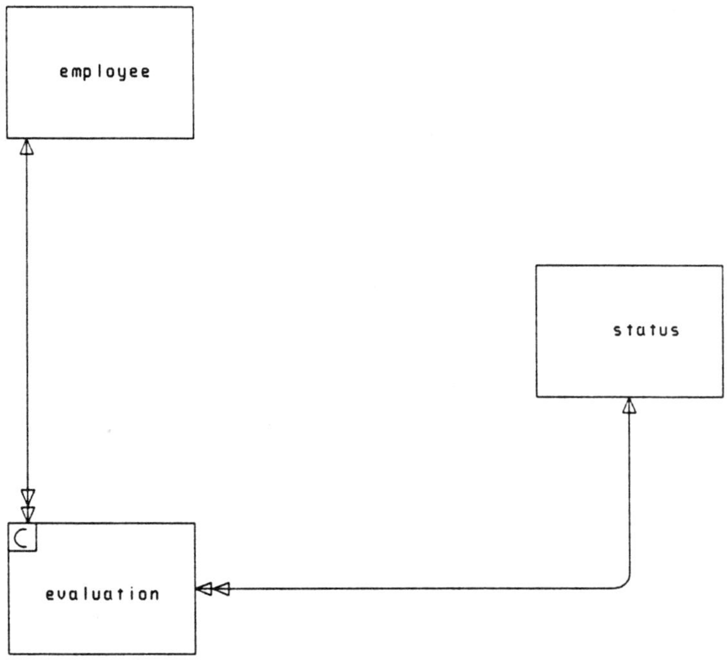

During each evaluation, an employee is given some relevant value of status, for which there is an official set of occurrences (i.e., a "status" entity type).

By using a characteristic to establish the relationship to this other object, the continued existence of any particular evaluation depends only on the associated employee, *not* on status. If the associated value of status goes away, (i.e., is discarded as an official evaluator), the employee's evaluation is unaffected (at least as shown above).

This result is probably what the enterprise would intend. However, had an association type been used instead of the characteristic, then the continued existence of an employee's evaluation would depend on both the employee and status instances—and would thus necessarily disappear should the related occurrence of either go away. This would probably not be the most desirable result. Avoiding this second type of "tunnel vision" is another important use of characteristics.

1.2-3 Entity Type Hierarchies (ETH)

Not all entity types are created equal. Some are merely special types of other, more general entity types. The purpose of **entity type hierarchies** (also called **generalization** hierarchies) is to understand and express such connections as succinctly as possible. This is useful for both analysis as well as implementation.

One of the most difficult practical problems that entity modeling practitioners have historically faced is entity overlap. Not all (or perhaps even most) entity types can be neatly boxed with unique identities, each completely separate and distinct from all others.

The most prevalent and troublesome question in actual practice has probably been, "Are entity types X and Y different, or are they the same?" There are numerous variations of this same question as the list below documents. (The reader can get some sense of this issue by trying to model the sample problem below using only conventions discussed thus far. A solution using entity type hierarchies is presented on page 34.)

Such debates frequently run on ad nauseam—consuming valuable time and resources in the process. Eventually, they are usually curtailed by some more or less arbitrary decision handed down by an understandably overwrought project manager that leaves no one totally satisfied. The uncomfortable feeling usually persists, "There must be some simple insight that was missed."

Fortunately, for many such cases a solution does exist which comes in the form of a new set of conventions, the entity type hierarchy. This solution is relatively simple, yet surprisingly powerful.

SAMPLE ENTITY MODELING DEBATE ISSUES

- "Some but not all of X do (Business Action)."
- "Some but not all of X have special properties."
- "An X is a special type of Y."
- "All X are Y, but not all Y are X."
- "Certain things hold true for both X and Y, which are otherwise different."
- "There is significant overlap between X and Y."
- "Y may be classified into types."
- "X is just a special type of Y."
- "Y is the more general case of X."
- "X is a category of Y."

ENTITY OVERLAP
A Sample Modeling Problem

In a given enterprise, vehicles may be owned either by companies or individuals. Vehicles may be either trucks or cars, each of which has certain specific properties, as well as other important properties in common. A given vehicle may have more than one owner, and an owner may own more than one car.

(Solution on page 34)

The basis for this solution is simply recognition that in dealing with the world, humans mentally classify things—and what makes sense for humans might also be useful for database design.

For example, in first introducing the concept of entity types earlier in Part I, even entity types themselves were classified—namely into people, places, things, organizations, concepts and events. All of these special types or things are still entity types, just special classes thereof. Anything that holds true for entity types in general, would also hold true for each specific kind. (The reverse, of course, is not necessarily true.) The real world abounds with classifiable entity types. Some additional examples are shown below.

Diagram 1.26

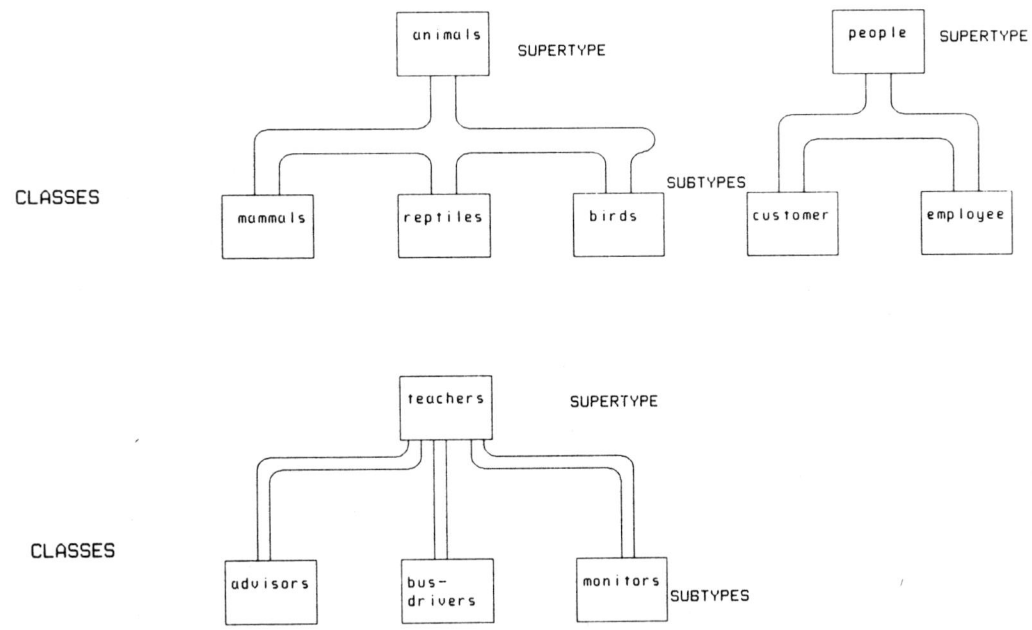

Whenever such **classification** occurs, the result is naturally a hierarchy, with something on the top and one or more things on the bottom. The thing on the "top" is the most general thing (or idea) and is called the **superior entity type**, or simply **supertype**. The word "**generalization**" is sometimes used to connote identification of this more general thing in a classification. "Generalization" is thus more or less the inverse of "classification."

The things on the "bottom" of a classification are the more specific things (i.e., special kinds, types or classes of the more general thing on the top) and are therefore called **subordinate entity types**, or simply **subtypes**. (They are also sometimes called **roles**.)

Appreciating the ETH concept fully requires holding in mind two seemingly contradictory ideas simultaneously. First, the thing on the bottom is the same as the thing on the top. But looking closer at the thing on the bottom, it is found to have special properties that make it a special and unique case. In other words, it's the very same thing, but nonetheless, has its own private and distinguishing properties. Some additional sample classifications are portrayed in the diagram below.

Diagram 1.27

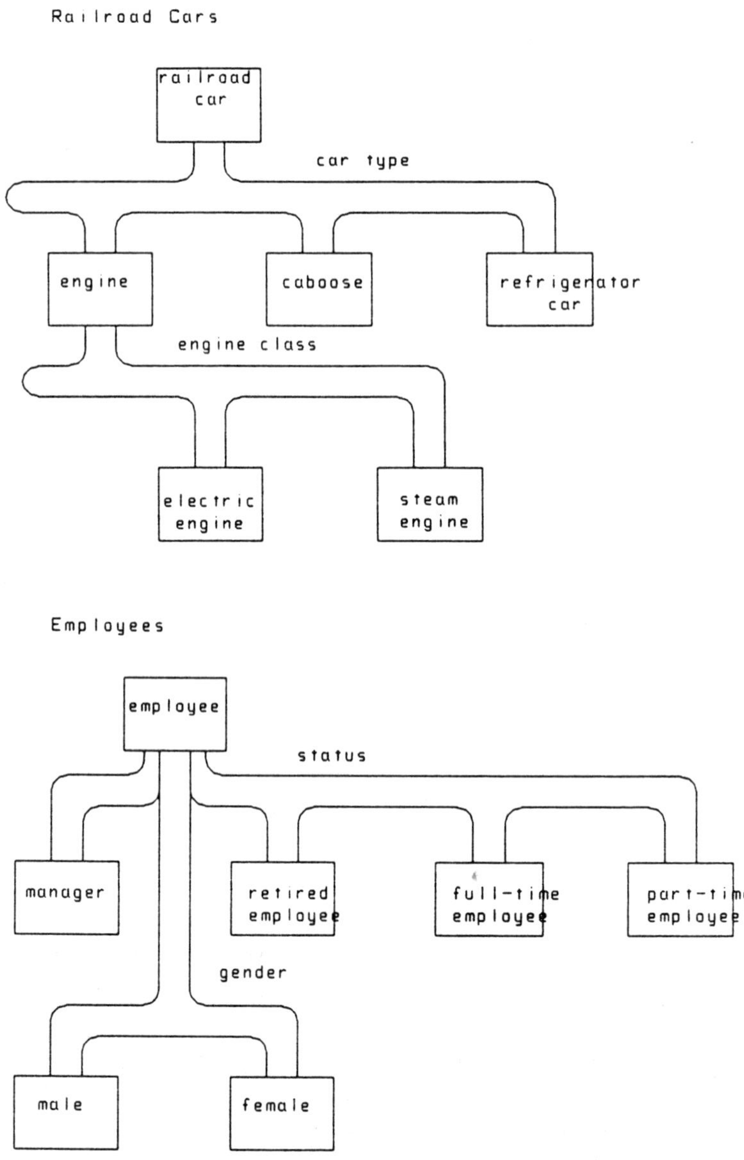

Several points are worth noting.

- Classification can be repeated to as many "levels" as are meaningful to the enterprise. In other words, even a special case can have its own special cases. In the case shown above, for example, engines are a special case of railroad cars, but they also have special cases—namely, electric engines, steam engines, etc.

- A given classification (i.e., ETH) is often named—e.g., "car type," "status," etc. (Such naming is useful and is encouraged.)
- Classifications may or may not be exhaustive, as shown. For example, "gender" is exhaustive (there are no other legitimate subtypes); whereas "car type" and "engine class" apparently are not (at least as shown).
- Several different classifications may be useful or necessary for the same supertype. (Note, for example, the various employee classifications. These are completely independent of one another.)
- A classification with only one subtype is legitimate and may be useful or necessary (e.g., "manager").

Although the examples above give classifications for kernel entity types, classifications for characteristics are also possible and often useful, as the following example illustrates. Classifications for other types of objects, including association types, are generally less meaningful except in the context of entity lifecycles (see Section S.1).

Diagram 1.28

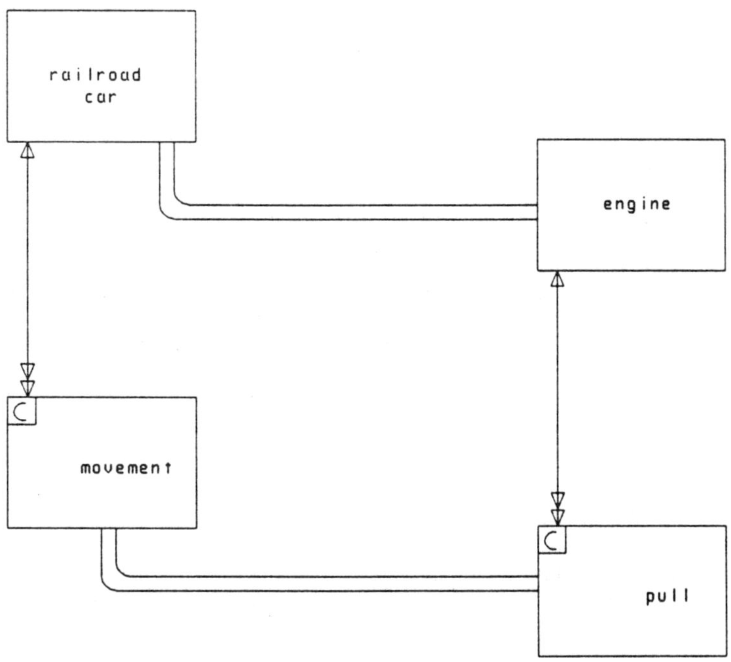

In this example, railroad cars move over time, as denoted by the characteristic. One special type of car is an engine. Sometimes when an engine "moves," it is actually "pulling" (other cars). Thus a "pull" (also a characteristic) is a special type of "move."

1.2-3.1 Classification Relationships

By convention, a classification of entity types is indicated using heavy dark lines or by headless parallel lines, as illustrated in the previous examples. Use of either convention to establish a connection between objects always indicates the presence of an ETH. Denoting these special classification relationship types carefully is important since special rules apply to ETH, as described below.

Apart from these special rules, a classification relationship type basically functions like a regular 1:1 relationship type. For each occurrence of the supertype, there can exist at most one and only one occurrence of the subtype. The relationship type could never be 1:M (or M:1 or M:N). This fact makes an ETH different from more conventional forms of hierarchies (e.g., as in IMS), where each occurrence on the top (the "parent") can possess multiple occurrences of the thing on the bottom (the "child").

Instances of a classification relationship are illustrated in Diagram 1.30. Note that each occurrence of the more general entity type (i.e., "animal") is related at most to only one occurrence of the more specific entity type on the bottom (i.e., "mammal"). For example, the animal "cow" is found to be related to a corresponding occurrence of "cow" as a mammal. (Obviously, a cow cannot possibly be a mammal more than once—thus there is only one occurrence.) The same is also true for the animal "deer." The animal "lizard," however, is not related to any corresponding occurrence of mammal. This is for obvious reasons—a "lizard" is not a mammal, but rather a reptile!

Diagram 1.29

Solution to the entity overlap exercise on page 30.

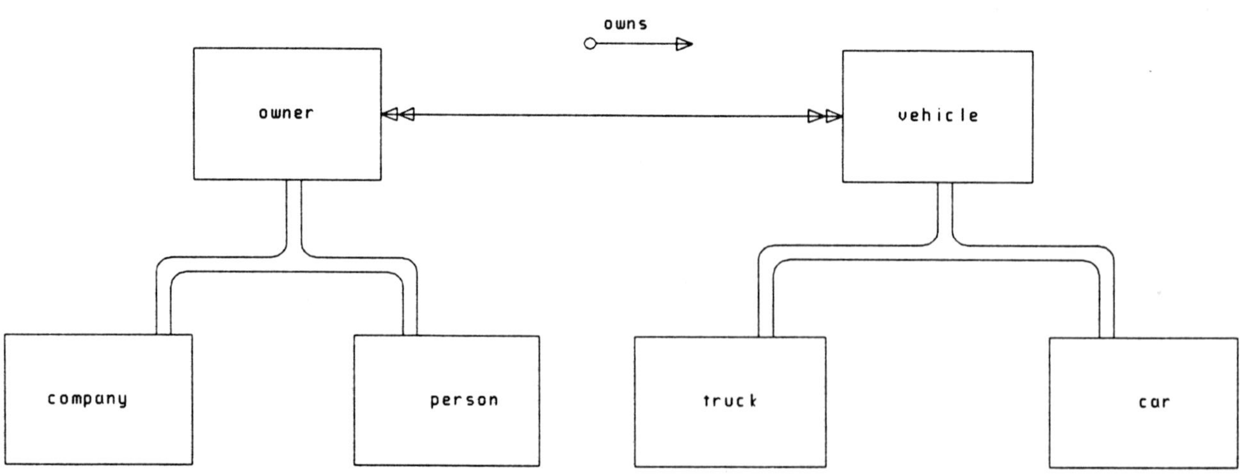

Diagram 1.30

Sample Classification Relationship Type Instances

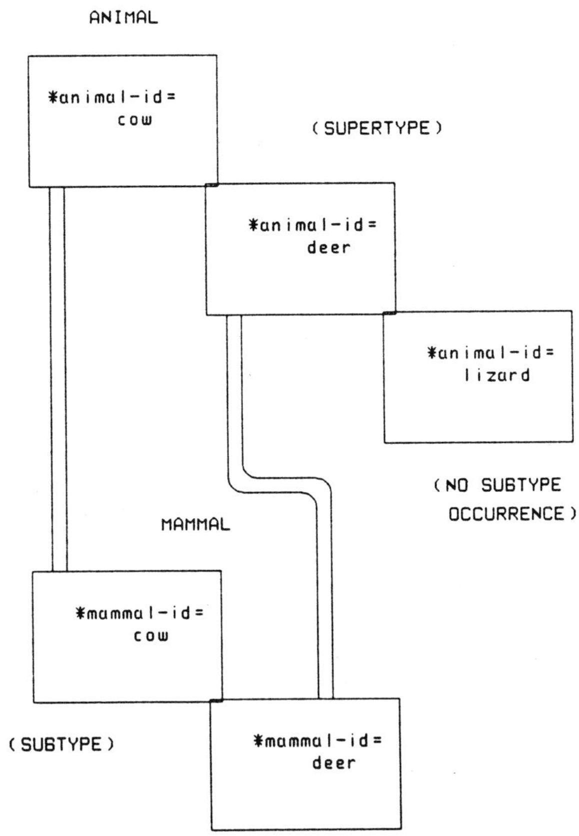

In general, a classification relationship, with its 1:1 form, simply answers a yes/no question: Is the thing on the top also a thing on the bottom, or is it not? If so, one (but only one) relationship instance will appear to the corresponding occurrence on the bottom; if not, none appears. Classification relationship types are also sometimes called **ISA** relationships. By the above reasoning, "ISIT?" might be a better label!

Because of this simple yes/no function, association types are never allowed for classification relationship types. In any event, the idea of "intersection data" (a major purpose of association types) is really meaningless in the classification case. (The reader may want to review the previous examples to verify this intuitive fact.) This is another important reason, incidentally, for the use of special conventions rather than 1:1 relationship types in the usual form to designate classifications.

1.2-3.2 Rules for ETH

Classification has several inevitable and, to some extent, commonsense consequences. Since these consequences apply to all ETH, and always act consistently in their coordination, these consequences can be stated as general ETH rules. Keeping these rules in mind will assist the practitioner in using the ETH concept effectively.

1.2-3.2-1 Rule of Precedence

Updating in an ETH can only operate in certain ways. Otherwise the whole notion of classification would be illogical.

Specifically, when an occurrence of an object on the "bottom" of an ETH is added to the database, an occurrence of the corresponding object on the "top" must also be added automatically. Reference to the previous example shows why this must be so. It is logically inconsistent, for example, to talk about a cow as a mammal without simultaneously implying that a cow is also an animal (a mammal is just a special type of the more general thing, animal). So the "animal = cow" occurrence must be added to the

GUIDELINES AND CONVENTIONS FOR ENTITY TYPE HIERARCHIES

- Classifications generally apply to entity types and characteristics.
- The object on the bottom is always a special case (i.e., type, kind, or class) of the object on top.
- The object on the top must be exactly the same thing as the object on the bottom, just a more general version.
- All subtypes in a classification of an entity type must be of the same type (i.e., person, place, thing, etc.) as the supertype.
- By convention, classifications are rendered using either heavy dark lines or pairs of parallel, headless, thin lines.
- No association types are permitted for a classification relationship type.
- The same object may be classified in multiple ways.
- In each classification, there may be one or more subtypes, but only one supertype.
- There can at most be one occurrence of each subtype for each associated supertype occurrence (i.e., the basic form of the relationship type is 1:1).
- The occurrence of the supertype must exist for the subtype occurrence to exist. (Rule of Precedence)
- Relationship types and properties of a supertype apply downward, but relationship types and properties of subtypes do not apply upward. (Rule of Inheritance)
- A classification may be exhaustive or nonexhaustive, mandatory or optional, and/or mutually exclusive or not mutually exclusive.
- A mutually exclusive classification may be vectored (by convention, always to the right), with named state changes.

database at the same time "mammal = cow" is asserted. Because of this, the object on the "top" is said to have *precedence*.

Furthermore, if an occurrence of an object on the "top" of an ETH is deleted from the database, any corresponding occurrence of an object on the "bottom" of the ETH must also automatically be deleted at the same time. (Again, the object on the top has *precedence*.) This follows logically.

For example, if "cow" is no longer of interest to the enterprise as an animal (i.e., is deleted), then there is no way "cow" could logically continue to be of interest as a mammal, because a mammal *is* an animal, albeit a special type. Continued existence of the "mammal = cow" occurrence would be simply inconsistent.

The notion of precedence is a simple, yet powerful idea as translated into actual database operation. Since it prescribes conditions for the "correctness" of database content during updating, it can be stated as a general integrity rule, as follows. Any implementation strategy for classifications should universally guarantee this rule across (and apart from) all applications.

Integrity Rule #3 (Rule of Precedence)

An occurrence of a subtype can only exist if the corresponding occurrence of its supertype exists.

1.2-3.2-2 Rule of Inheritance

All properties and relationship types of a supertype automatically apply to any subtype. In other words, anything that can be said about an object in general must also apply to any special case thereof (i.e., to any subtype). (If this is not true, then what has been said is not truly "general.") This is called **Inheritance**.

Another way of looking at this is that any relationship type or property that belongs to all subtypes really belongs to the supertype since that relationship type or property is apparently "general." In fact, its "ownership" by the supertype should be denoted carefully in the entity model, without any repetition with or among subtypes, in order to avoid "redundancy." (Normalization theory might talk about the potential for update "anomalies" in this connection. However, normalization theory per se provides no "normal form" that resolves this particular situation.)

Properties or relationship types *legitimately* belonging to subtypes, however, do not apply to the supertype. They are precisely what make the subtype a special case of the supertype. Another way of saying this is that inheritance always works "downward" in an ETH, but never "upward."

An example illustrating inheritance follows. In the particular school whose partial entity model is illustrated below, all bus drivers and advisors are apparently also teachers. All people who teach always have "teaches" (a relationship type) and a teacher-name, address, and pay, even when driving buses or advising students. The more general thing (i.e., "teacher") will automatically "supply" this information when and as needed in the context of these special subtypes. This is their "inheritance."

Properties and relationship types of subtypes, however, do not apply upward. For example, not all teachers have an assigned bus, or values for years-experience, license-no, or renewal-date, only those who are also bus-drivers. Similarly, only those teachers who are also advisors will have students advised, or values for office-hours or grade-advised. These special properties do not apply "upward." This is the flip-side to the Rule of Inheritance. "Supplying upward" simply is not meaningful in the same sense as "supplying downward."

Diagram 1.31

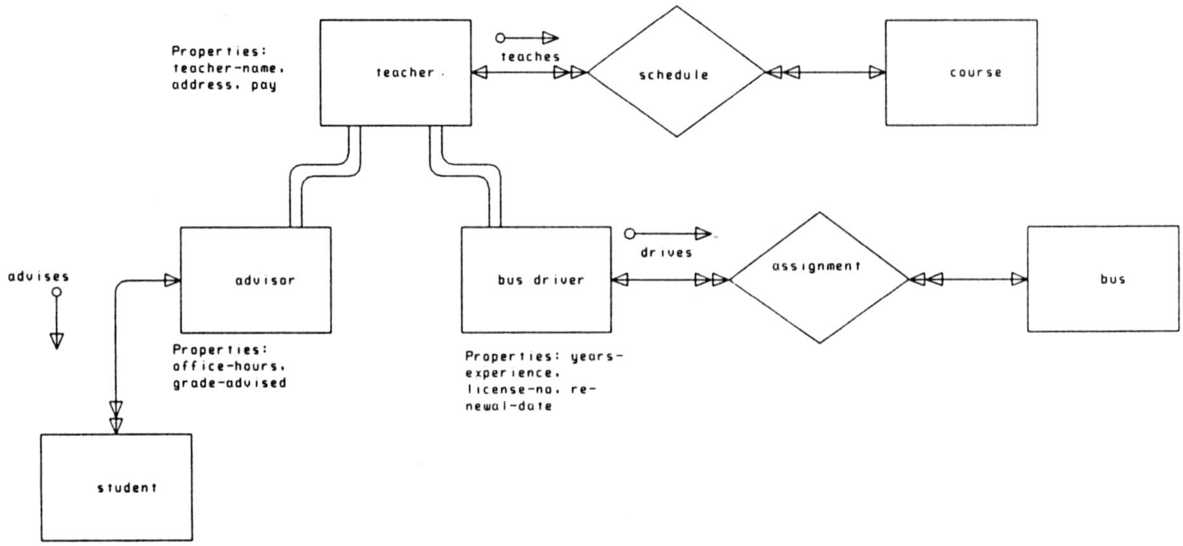

1.2-3.3 Prescriptions for ETH

There are several additional types of specifications for ETH permitting more refined modeling of the associated enterprise.

1.2-3.3-1 Exhaustive Classifications

Sometimes an ETH enumerates all possible subtypes in the classification, and sometimes it does not. One where all subtypes are shown is called **exhaustive**. A classification of people by gender into "male" and "female" subtypes would be exhaustive.

Reasons for omitting subtypes from a classification (making it **non-exhaustive**) include the following:

- They are unimportant or unnecessary for elaboration of the entity model.
- They have no significant special properties or relationship types that need to be managed (i.e., stored).
- They are unknown or ill-defined at the time of classification.

Examples of nonexhaustive classifications included "car type" and "engine class" in the railroad car ETH presented earlier.

1.2-3.3-2 Mandatory Classifications

Depending on the enterprise's business policy, some classifications may be mandatory, whereas others may be optional. In a mandatory classification, an associated occurrence of a subtype *must* exist for each supertype occurrence. (This specification is actually a type of integrity constraint, as discussed in Part III.)

Diagram 1.32

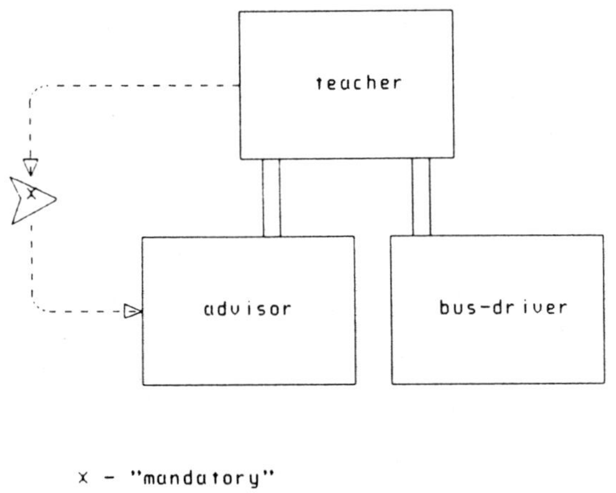

In this example, every teacher will also appear as an advisor because of the specified "mandatory" integrity constraint. An occurrence of bus-driver, however, is apparently optional (i.e., not all teachers are also bus-drivers), since no integrity constraint has been defined. (Note: For convenience, the "X" for mandatory is sometimes placed *inside* the subtype box (e.g., inside advisor) at the point where the classification relationship type connects. This shorthand form avoids use of the special integrity constraint symbol and connections as above.)

Diagram 1.33

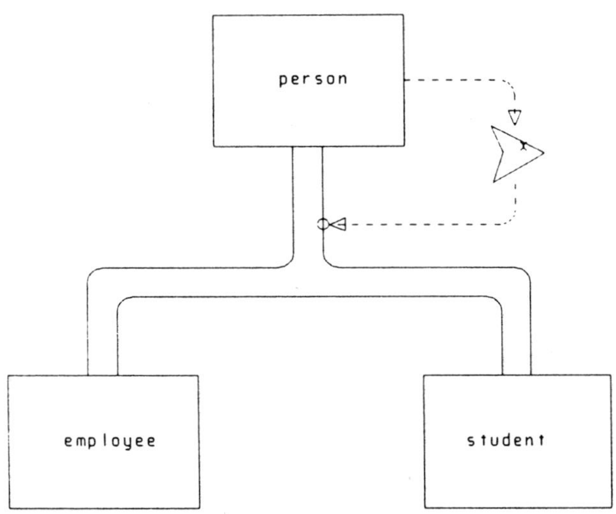

In this example, the classification itself is indicated as "mandatory," showing that every person (in the database) must be either an employee or a student. Note, however, that there is no specific "mandatory" prescription specifying that a person must be an employee or that the person must be a student. (Either subtype could be made individually mandatory by placing it specifically on the "receiving" end of an "X" integrity constraint, as before.)

1.2-3.3-3 Mutually Exclusive Classifications

Depending on the enterprise's business policy and the make-up of the real world, some classifications may be mutually exclusive. Others may not be. In a mutually exclusive classification, there can at most exist only one subtype occurrence for the whole classification, no matter how many subtypes that classification may have. (Like mandatory classifications, this specification is also a special type of integrity constraint, as discussed in Part III.) A natural example of mutually exclusive specification is the gender classification, where a person may be male or female but not both.

The classification discussed above can be assumed *not* mutually exclusive (no integrity constraint was shown). Thus the same person might be both an employee and a student at the same point in time. In other words, occurrences for *both* subtypes may exist simultaneously.

Diagram 1.34

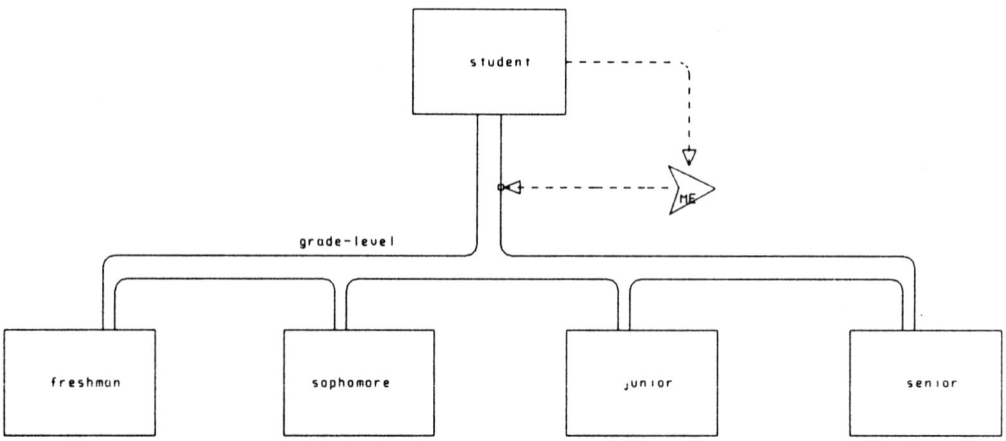

This classification indicates a student can have only one of the indicated grade-levels (i.e., only one occurrence among the four subtypes). Note that this does not preclude a new subtype occurrence from being created—for example, when the student is promoted—but in such case the old subtype occurrence must be deleted (or archived).

1.2-3.4 State Changes

The classification above is actually not only mutually exclusive, but **vectored** to the right as well. This simply means that because of the way in which the enterprise is organized, the single subtype occurrence is restricted to moving toward the right, never to the left. A student is always "promoted" to the next higher grade—only in highly unusual and exceptional circumstances would a student ever move "backward."

The classification above can be refined to represent these ideas as follows. The prior "mutually exclusive" integrity constraint has now been enhanced to indicate "vectored."

Diagram 1.35

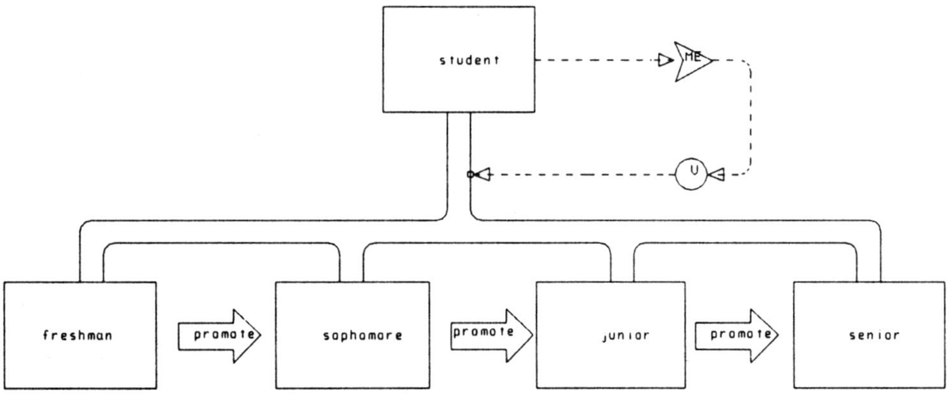

Also introduced in the diagram above is a special new symbol used three times in between each pair of subtypes. In this example, this symbol (which is actually the automatic action object type) designates a **state change** that occurs in moving from one subtype to the next. In all three cases, these have been named "promote" as appropriate in describing the relevant enterprise activity.

In general, a state change reflects some specific business event or response to a given set of conditions. (It does not, however, connote any type of proper "relationship" per se between the subtypes.) Any state change may be named, as above, and may also have aliases.

State changes are quite useful for modeling certain types of controlled changes in an enterprise's database (especially in conjunction with "triggers" and "archives") to express when and why certain actions take place. This topic is more fully explored in Part III. They are also quite useful in transaction discovery and process analysis, as discussed in the section on "entity life cycles" in the Design Supplement.

1.2-3.5 Pro forma

In many instances, classifications provide insights into an enterprise that are not necessarily meant to be implemented exactly as shown. In essence, such specifications merely provide a formal way to talk about the enterprise succinctly. **Pro forma** permits this distinction.

1.2-3.5-1 Pro forma Classifications and Subtypes

Classifications provide a very useful and convenient way to analyze and model certain complex aspects of an enterprise. Because they permit precise and meaningful naming, they are also a valuable way to help capture, communicate and standardize business terminology. They are therefore quite useful in a number of respects.

Beyond modeling, analysis, and naming, however, an entity model must also serve as a blueprint for database implementation. Since there are usually practical limitations on how much can be actually implemented in any given database, "important" classifications need to be distinguished from those less so. Classification for any complex enterprise, after all, is usually quite extensive.

The issue of which classifications should be implemented as such is a very complex one, and is not one to be taken lightly. The reader should refer carefully to Part II (on type-codes) and fully understand the limitations of alternatives before drawing any final conclusions in this area.

In general, careful consideration should be given to implementing a subtype as a discrete record type if, and only if, it already possesses, or is likely to acquire, any or all of the following.

- Unique properties (i.e. attributes).
- Special relationship types.
- Distinct integrity constraints.

The purpose of a subtype, after all, is to provide optimal handling of such "special" considerations.

Upon careful analysis it may be decided that the subtype or classification should not be implemented (i.e., stored as such). Still, it may be desirable to retain the subtype or classification in the entity model in order to exploit its special insight or vocabulary and the explicit specification opportunities they provide.

This is accomplished using "pro forma" designation. This designation simply says "here is a way to understand or talk about some component of an enterprise or data resource, but not one to be implemented in the database in this exact form." (Pro forma simply means "a formal way to talk about something.")

Diagram 1.36

This classification will not be stored in this form.

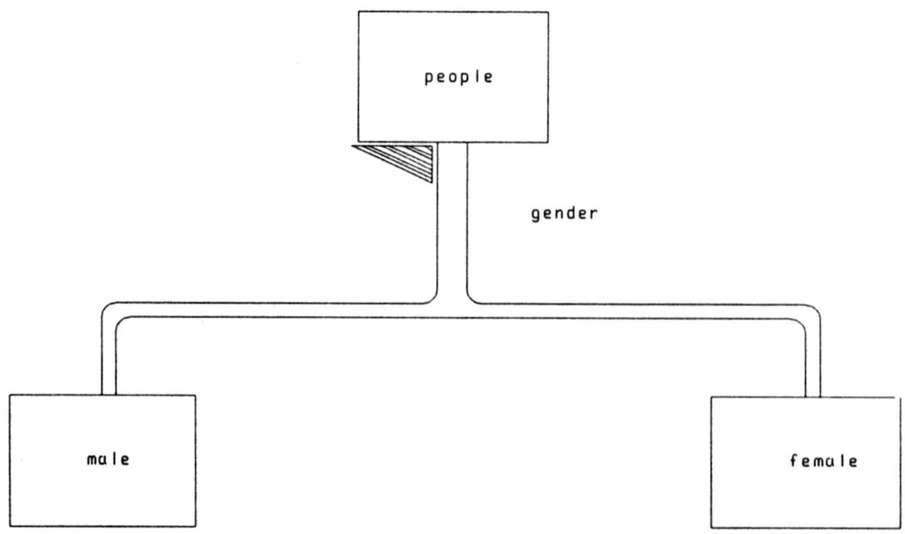

Diagram 1.37

The subtype consultant will not be stored in this form.

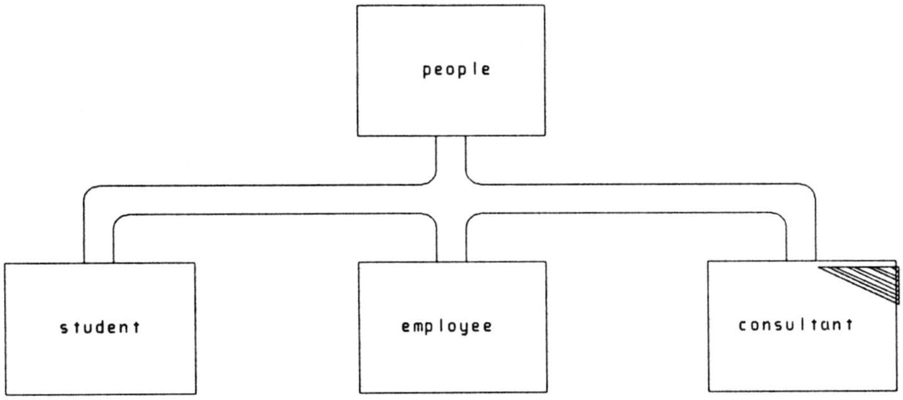

1.2-3.5-1 Pro forma Classification "Source"

As discussed in Part II, one alternative to implementing a classification directly is by use of a **type-code** attribute within the supertype. This strategy is modeled as follows.

Diagram 1.38

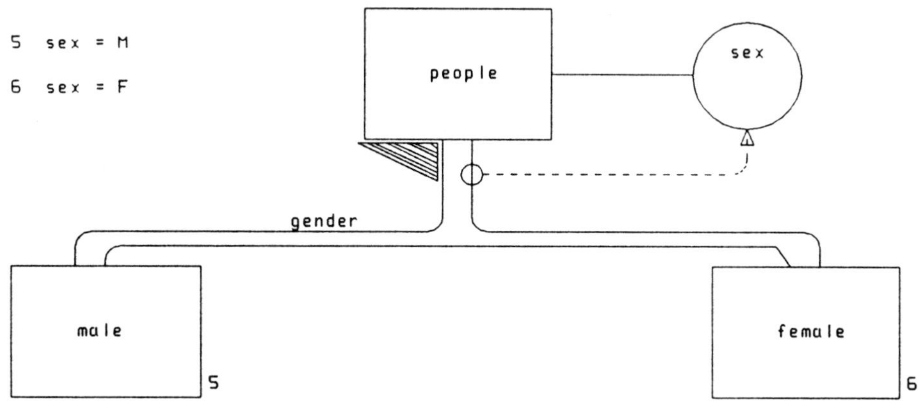

In this example, a special "source" connector is introduced, leading to the attribute of "people" sex. This establishes sex as a *type-code*, whose values will be used to distinguish between subtypes of this pro forma (not stored) "gender" classification.

1.2-3.5-2 Pro forma Relationship Types

By the Rule of Inheritance, all relationship types (and properties) of a supertype are also available to all subtypes. These relationship types should generally not also be actually implemented for each subtype, since this might introduce anomalies into updating of the database. As previously discussed, the supertype will "supply" this general information whenever needed in the context of the subtype.

Sometimes, it is nonetheless desirable to express the availability of the relationship type directly to the subtype, either because this enhances intelligibility or simplifies explanation, or because different terminology is associated with it when used specifically for the subtype. When also shown for the subtype, the relationship type is naturally considered to be "pro forma." ("Pro forma" again simply means it is there only to permit "talking" about it in a formal way.)

In showing the relationship type for the subtype, of course, the twin ideas "same as that of the supertype" and "not to be stored per se" must be carefully expressed so as to avoid any ambiguity. Two symbols, a new pro forma directional arrow for the relationship type, and a pro forma "source" connector are introduced to permit the necessary specification.

Diagram 1.39

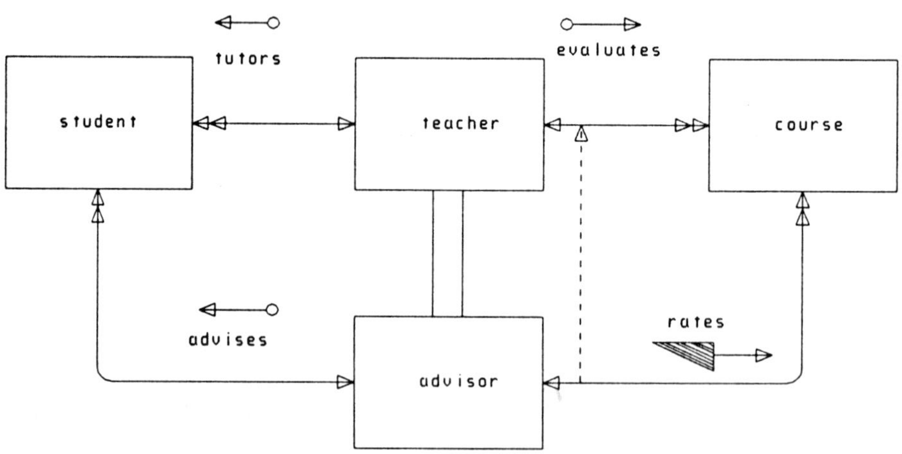

In this example, the "rates" relationship type is shown to be pro forma, with the "evaluates" relationship type as its inheritance source. It actually offers no occurrences different from those of "evaluates" and would not be implemented per se.

The "advises" relationship type, on the other hand, is not signified as pro forma, even though the "tutors" relationship type connects to the same entity type, teacher. In this enterprise, a teacher can apparently tutor students different from those the same teacher advises.

1.2-3.5-3 Pro forma Attributes

The "pro forma" concept may also be applied to attributes in a classification.

Diagram 1.40

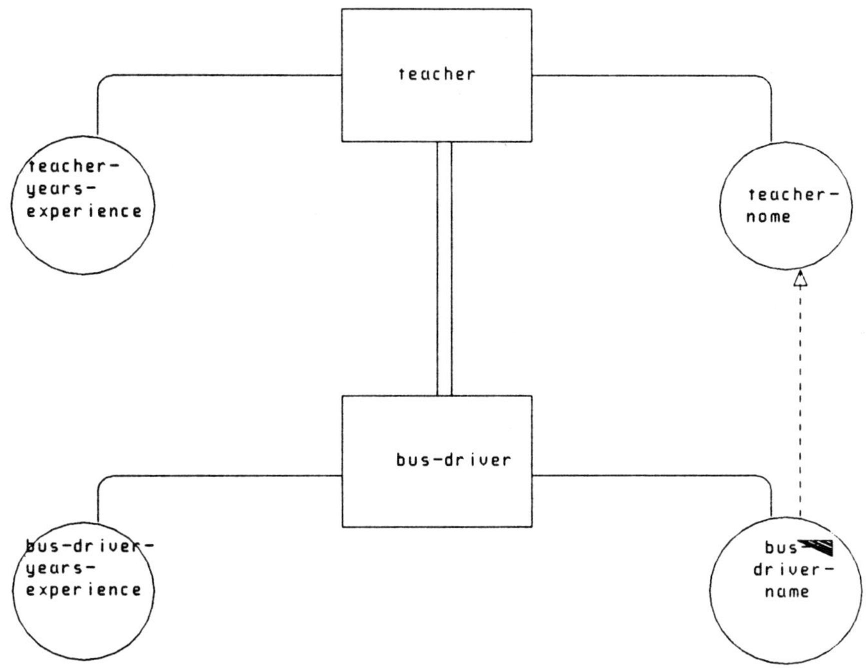

In this example, bus-driver-name is indicated to be pro forma, with teacher-name as its "source." Since the name of the person is exactly the same whether teaching or driving buses, this attribute would not actually be stored in the subtype, but rather its values would always be "inherited" from the supertype. Bus-driver-years-experience, in contrast, apparently refers to some different value than teacher-years-experience, and gives some special property of bus-drivers. It is not defined as pro forma.

1.2-3.6 Types of ETH

There can logically be three different kinds of classifications, as discussed below, depending directly on how determinants are used to identify the respective entity types. These differences, discussed more fully in section 2.1-1.1, have important consequences for implementation. (A given DBMS, of course, may provide or necessitate a physical implementation distinct from any one of these.) The Rules of Precedence and Inheritance naturally hold for all these types.

- **Domain-Based ETH.** In this type of classification, the determinant used for the subtype is either exactly the same as the determinant used for the supertype, or is a named subset thereof. In either case, the attributes establishing the relationship between the subtype and supertype are simply their respective determinants.
- **Abstract ETH.** In this type of classification, the determinant of the subtype and supertype are completely different, and represent completely distinct domains. To create the classification relationship, the determinant of the supertype is generally included as a "foreign key" among the other attributes of the subtype.

► **Imaginary ETH.** In the process of generalization, an entity type may be discovered for which the enterprise, for whatever reason, can provide no legitimate or controllable determinant whatsoever. ("People" in some of the examples above is probably like this.) This entity type is therefore "imaginary." There may be no doubt about its real existence (people "exist"), but it violates the basic rule that all entity types must have a unique identifier. Any classification of such an entity type, by implication, must also be "imaginary." Generally, it is difficult (but not impossible) to store an imaginary supertype. Because of this, it is important to identify which entity types are imaginary, and of these, to specify which should be stored.

Diagram 1.41

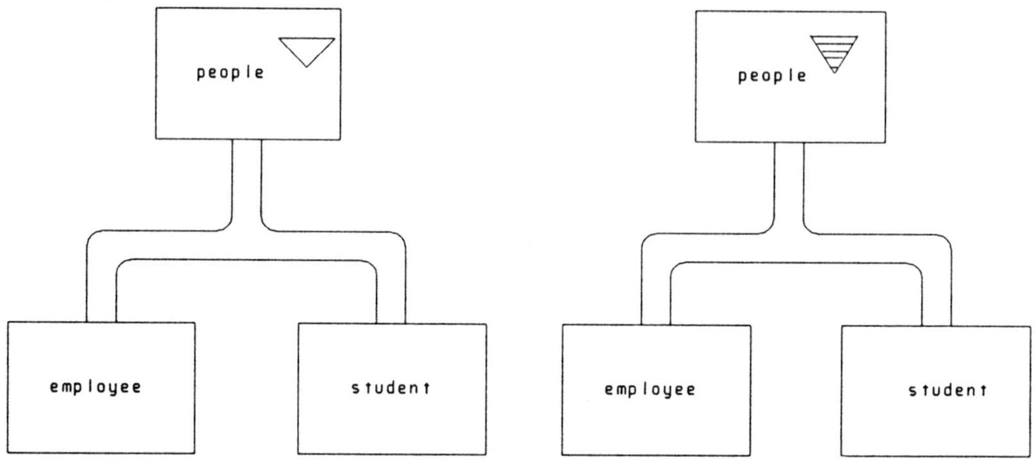

Two examples of imaginary supertypes are marked above. The symbol in the people box on the left indicates "store as such," whereas the one on the right indicates "not to be implemented per se."

1.2-4 Aggregates

In any enterprise, certain objects or connections, upon closer inspection, actually break down into a collection of several other objects and/or connections that possess more specific and well-defined implications for the entity model. Such objects and connections, called **aggregates**, may be viewed as essentially molecular (i.e., made up of smaller individual pieces), in contrast to the more basic objects and connections of an entity model, which are atomic (i.e., defined and implemented as individual units). It is often desirable to identify and define such aggregates (also sometimes known as aggregation hierarchies), either to fully accommodate business terminology or to provide a means to simplify an entity model for the purpose of communication.

1.2-4.1 Aggregate Objects

An **aggregate object** is simply a named collection of other objects, and their connections. These objects may be completely different from one another.

Diagram 1.42

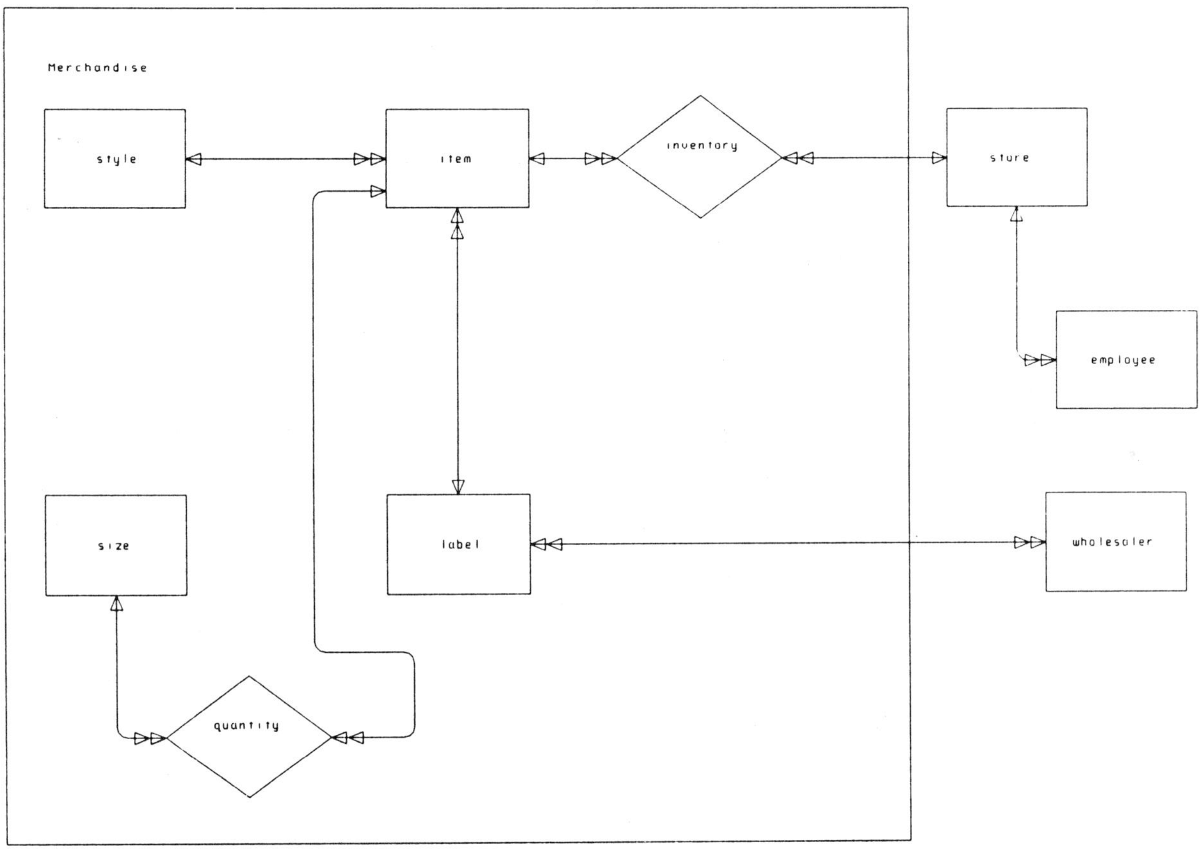

In this example, an aggregate object called "merchandise" has been defined and is shown to consist of a number of other objects and their connections. The aggregate object has been named using a noun, as is appropriate for objects of all types.

Note that an aggregate object differs significantly from a supertype in a classification:

- Unlike a supertype, the aggregate object may be broken down into completely dissimilar objects, not merely different objects of the same type. (Note in the diagram above, for example, "size" and "item" are not merely special types of "merchandise," but rather distinct components with individual identities.)
- An aggregate object may contain altogether different *types* of objects (e.g., both entity and association types as above), whereas an ETH must always consist only of entity types. (This makes showing aggre-

gate objects as hierarchies, whereas not inappropriate, nonetheless somewhat awkward.)

- The composition of an aggregate object can be defined in one and only one way, whereas the same supertype may be classified in many ways.
- An aggregate object is never actually implemented per se, whereas a supertype often is.

An aggregate object serves several major purposes for an entity model. First is simply to define some (aggregate) business term (e.g., "merchandise") in a meaningful and consistent fashion, even though the term itself does not possess any real "physical" implications.

Second, aggregate objects may be used to group entity types that are essentially different, and otherwise unrelated, but which have common participation in some given business process. For example, "cost center," a meaningful object for certain accounting processes, may actually be defined as an aggregate object consisting of the more basic entity types, employee, contractor, and location. These entity types have nothing in common except that they all receive payments from the enterprise. (Note that employee is a "person" type of entity type, contractor is an organization type, and location is a place type. The practitioner should view this as solid evidence that any grouping will produce an aggregation, rather than a generalization into an ETH supertype.)

Finally, the aggregate object also permits easy and precise simplification of an entity model for presentation purposes. Specifically, an aggregate object is reduced during such ascending conversion to a single box, which otherwise looks and acts exactly like an entity type. The "reduction" of the above model during ascending conversion, for example, would result in the following revised version. This alternative might be more suitable for presentation to end-users or management than the previous.

GUIDELINES AND CONVENTIONS FOR AGGREGATE OBJECTS

- An aggregate object is named using a noun.
- It may consist of any subset of the entity model, including dissimilar objects and entity types of different types.
- Aggregate objects may be nested (i.e., completely contained within one another) or overlap in any manner.
- In simplification of an entity model (e.g., for presentation purposes), an aggregate object "reduces" to a box, which otherwise looks and acts like a regular entity type.
- Relationship types are not permitted to aggregate objects per se.

Diagram 1.43

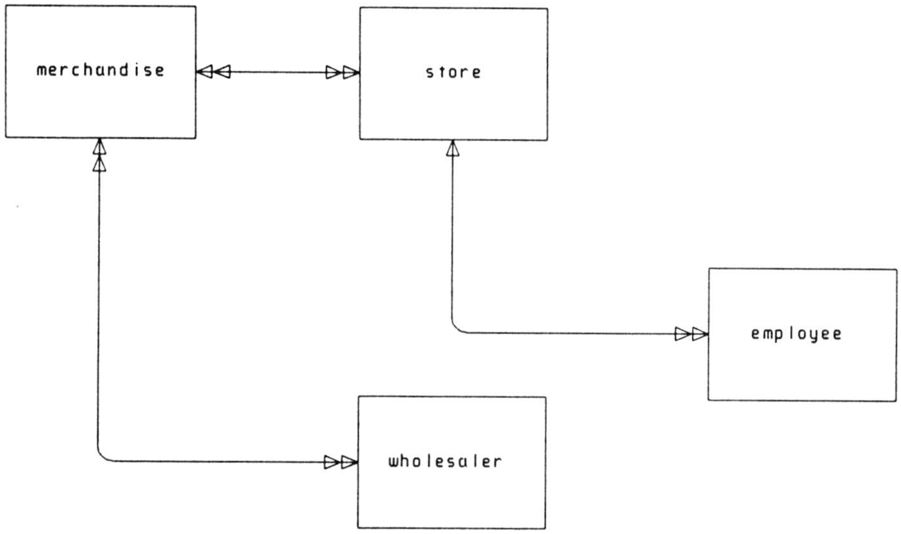

Aggregate objects may be defined in such manner that they are nested (one is completely contained within another) or that they overlap. Naturally such definition complicates reduction. Aggregate objects may also be used to prevent certain objects from disappearing during reduction—for example, nonstored, imaginary supertypes.

1.2-4.2 Aggregate Relationship Types

An aggregate relationship type is a named collection of other relationship types. Aggregate relationship types serve several principal purposes:

- To permit consistent and accurate definition of certain business "action" terminology that would not otherwise be discretely represented in the model.
- To support simplification of the entity model, especially for presentation to persons outside the professional group. (This is especially true for the first type of aggregate relationship type discussed below, those strictly defined between classifications.)
- To enable certain types of "behavior" specification (see Part III).

1.2-4.2-1 Classification Aggregate Relationship Types

The defined relationship types comprising an aggregate relationship type often exist strictly between the members of one or two specific classifications. This first type of aggregate relationship type is called a **classification aggregate relationship type**.

Diagram 1.44

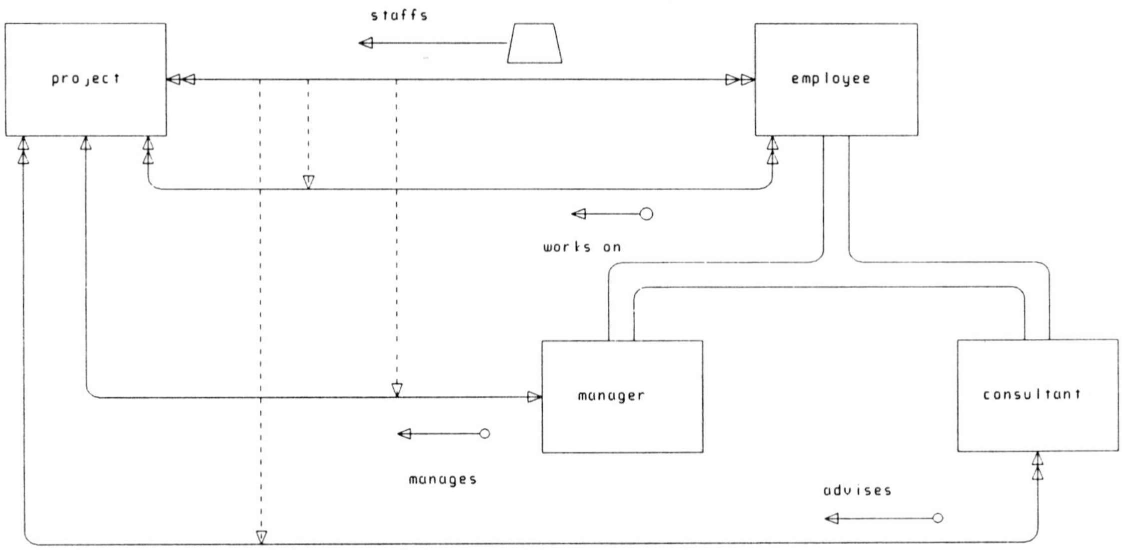

In this example, the relationship type designated by the action name "staffs" is defined as an aggregate relationship type, consisting of three other more specific relationship types, "works on," "manages," and "advises."

Several new symbols, an "aggregate" action directional arrow and "source" connectors to the other relationship types, are introduced to permit this specification.

The presence of "source" connectors also indicates that the aggregate relationship type is not actually stored or implemented per se. (This can be reinforced, if desired, by use of the "prohibited" or "not" symbol introduced in Part III.) Such implementation would be redundant with the other three relationship types and thus invite possible update anomalies. (In Part III, several "stored" alternatives to this configuration, where the resulting "redundancy" is automatically controlled, are also discussed.)

Simplification (i.e., reduction) of the above example (without additional specification) would result in the following.

Diagram 1.45

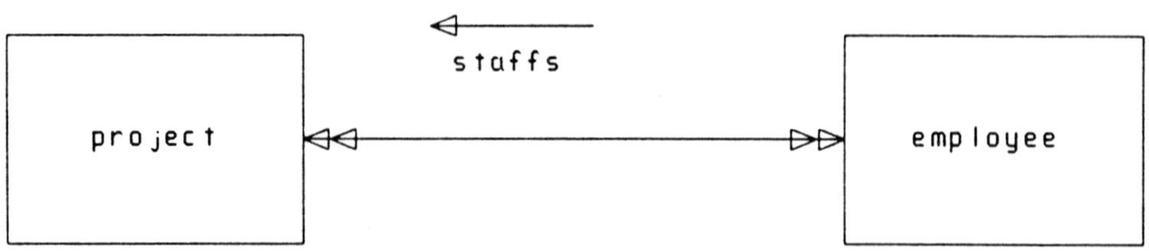

Communication using this alternative would be far simpler than under the former.

1.2-4.2-2 Series Aggregate Relationship Types

A second important variation of aggregate relationship type is one that identifies a more "direct" path through a series of other relationship types. This is called a **series aggregate relationship type**.

Diagram 1.46

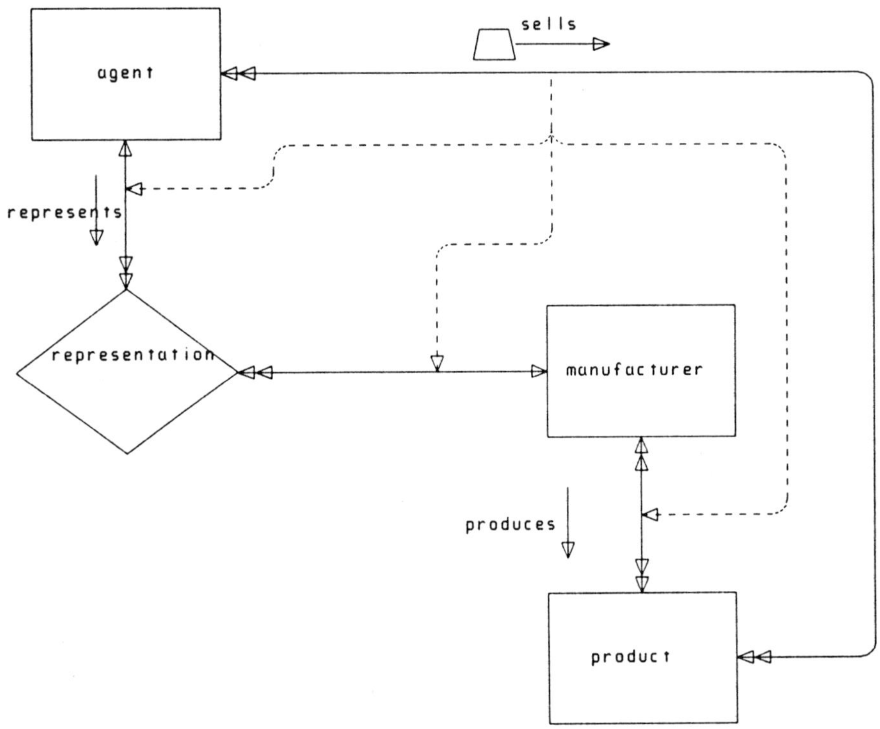

In this example, agents represent manufacturers, which in turn produce products. The relationship type "sells" has been defined as an aggregate relationship type, denoting that by virtue of this series of connections, agents ultimately "sell" products.

The actual information designated by "sells," of course, essentially just replicates that already inherent in the indicated series. To avoid redundancy and the consequential potential for anomalies, the above solution (by use of the "source" indicators) prescribes not actually storing "sells." (The controlled storage of series aggregate relationship types is again an important database implementation topic. Refer to Part III, on automatic actions, for alternatives to the above.)

1.2-4.2-3 Hybrid Aggregate Relationship Types

Hybrids between classification and series aggregate relationship types are naturally possible. Aggregate relationship types defined using other aggregate relationship types are also possible. Like any relationship type, of course, an aggregate relationship type must always be defined between two, and only two, individual objects.

PART 2: DOMAINS

2.0 Domains

Entity types and certain other kinds of objects possess properties which describe something about them or provide relevant information. Entity types literally have no substance without such properties.

Each property is represented by an attribute type (roughly, a "field") that may possess some particular value for each occurrence of that object type. These values must be named, formed, and interpreted in a uniform and consistent fashion. This is the purpose of defining domains, sets of like-defined values.

Domain definition has much the same connotation as "data element" definition in conventional usage. However, as typically employed, this latter term does not provide the full richness needed for effective entity modeling, especially in conjunction with classification. The term "data element" is therefore avoided in this text.

In part, domain definition is about naming, and how to integrate that task with analysis of the enterprise during entity modeling. In other words, it is about building a corporate vocabulary for data.

It is also about logical definition of the basic units of the entity model itself. Since all entity types must ultimately have properties to be meaningful, in some sense domains are the real underlying "stuff"—the real substance—of the entity model.

Furthermore, since implementation of the data resource is the ultimate goal—and normalized form is the optimal blueprint for that—domains also must ultimately provide the "glue" (via shared domains or foreign keys) that holds the entity model together. Look closely "underneath" any relationship type, and supporting domains must ultimately be found.

As Part III demonstrates, domains and their values also even control much of the defined "behavior" of a data resource—that is, rules that govern updating. It should be noted, however, that many such rules do not actually require details about attributes, which can therefore be considered as falling into a lower level of detail. (See Section 0.2.) *The practitioner primarily concerned with defining business rules should proceed directly to Part III.*

For all of these various reasons, domain definition is a critical complementary activity of entity modeling and deserves careful attention in its own right. The purpose of Part II of the book is to explore this important topic in detail.

2.1 Showing the Properties of Objects

Where desired, the properties of an entity type may be shown in either of two ways, as illustrated by the following examples. The first involves use of a circle to designate each property. The second, in which the properties are simply listed, is preferable where conservation of space, avoidance of clutter, and ease of definition are important. It is generally the recommended form.

Diagram 2.1

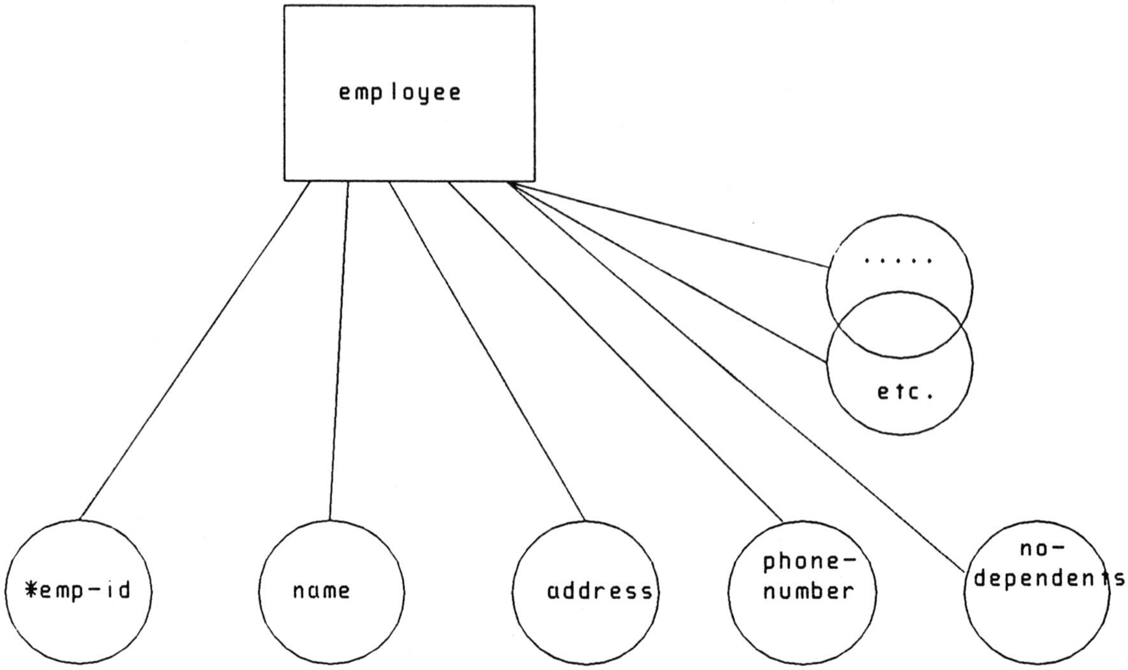

Diagram 2.2

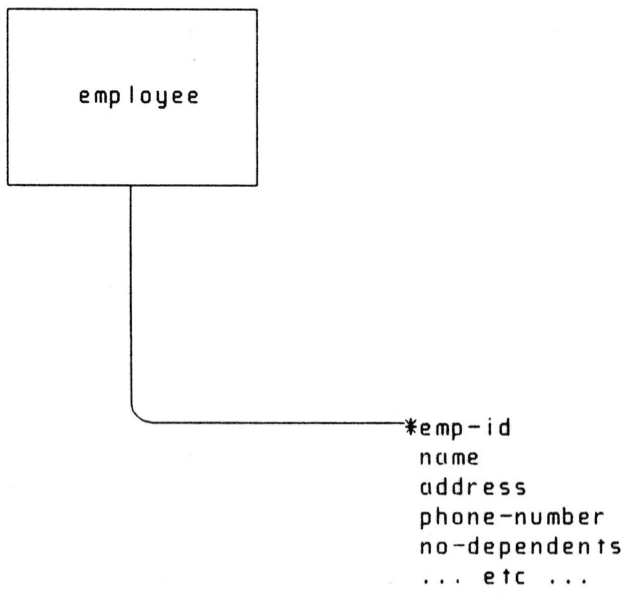

In both the above approaches, properties are identified by name, and connected by a single line (without heads) to the object type they describe. The determinant(s) of the object type are designated by means of an asterisk.

Upon specification in this fashion properties officially become **attribute types** of the object, capable of holding an actual value for the property in each object occurrence. As discussed below, each attribute type corresponds to some defined set of values—i.e., some domain.

Attribute types may be defined for any of the following object types.

- kernel entity types
- characteristic entity types
- association types
- aggregate association types
- measurement points

Although not really proper, attribute types are also sometimes shown for aggregate objects. This is simply shorthand notation for specifying that certain attribute types defined in uniform fashion belong to *each* of the object types within the given aggregate.

An example of attribute types defined for an association type (giving "intersection" data) is shown in Diagram 2.3.

Diagram 2.3

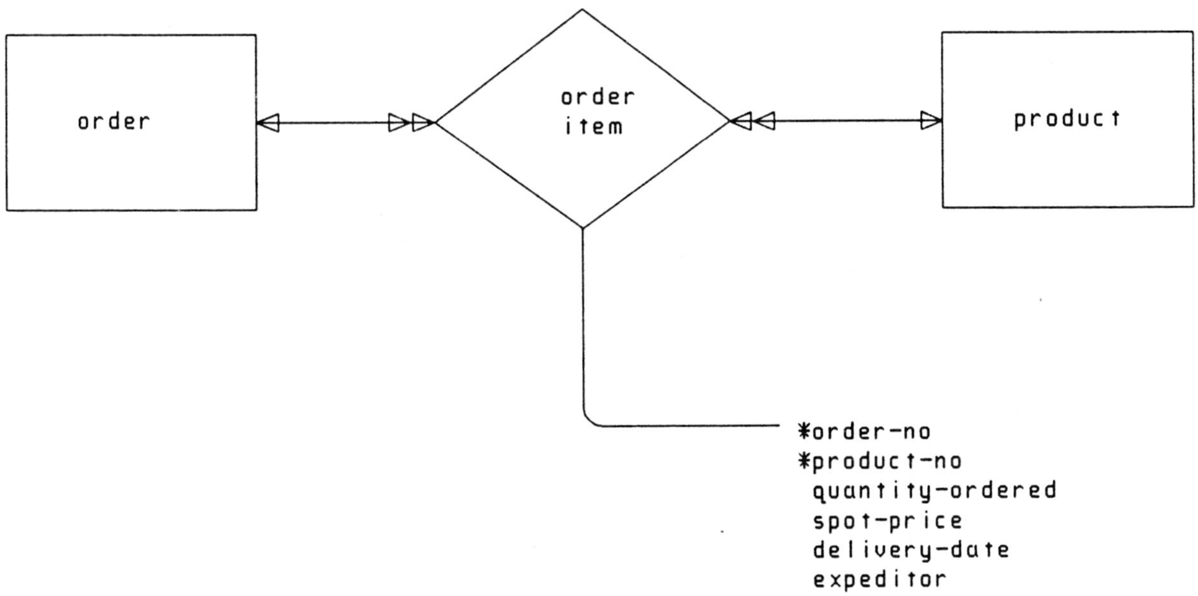

Note that the determinants of the related objects appear among the listed attribute types, as is logically proper for all association types. The nondeterminant attribute types represent properties individually describing the business connection between the two related objects. For example, quantity-ordered permits recording the number ordered of each product for every order.

In general, it is assumed that each attribute type possessed by an object will contain one and only one value for each occurrence of the object type. For instance, in the earlier example, each employee has only one value for address. (Since address is not a determinant, however, several employees may in fact share the very same address value.)

Although departure from this convention is not recommended, two or more values for each occurrence of an object can be indicated by either of the following methods.

Diagram 2.4

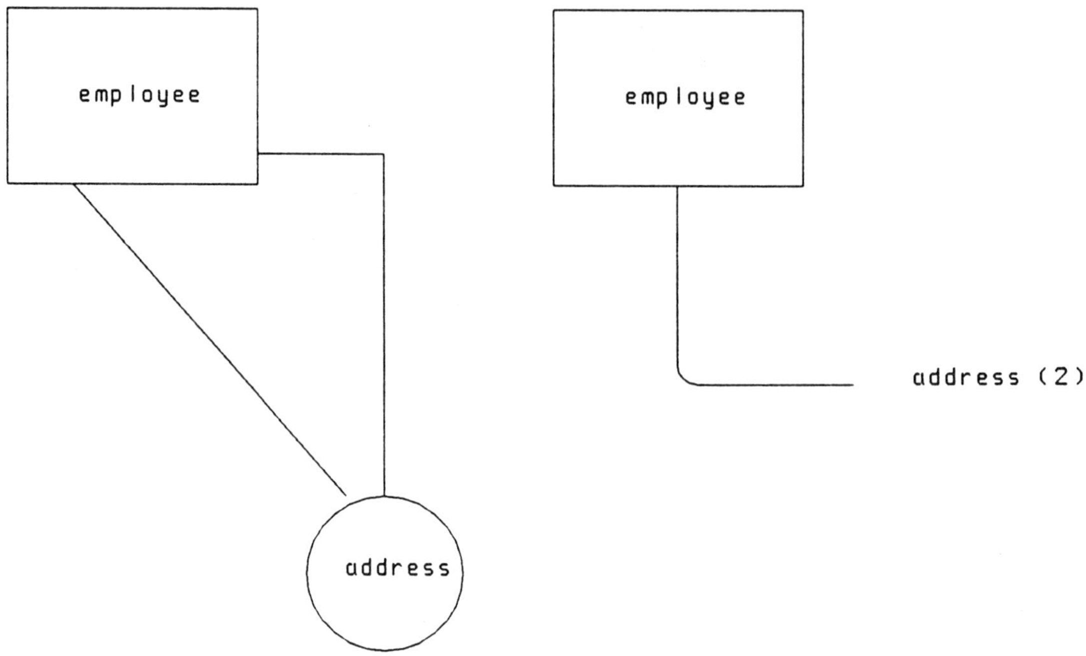

In these examples, each employee is indicated as having two addresses. In the model on the left in Diagram 2.4, this is indicated by the presence of two connecting lines to the attribute type address. The alternative on the right specifically permits two distinct values for this same attribute type. Whereas these conventions are sometimes convenient for producing more compact entity models, the practitioner should consider two representational alternatives; namely characteristics, which are used to support multivalued properties directly, or named domain subsets which, as discussed below, can be used to distinguish the meaning of multiple values. Both of these alternatives are formally more proper than the above.

In general, before implementation of an entity model, all entity types (and measurement points) must be given one or more attribute types, including at least their determinants. Otherwise, there is quite literally nothing about them that can be implemented. (The determinants of association types and aggregate association types, however, need not necessarily be shown since the identity of these determinants can be derived from the model itself. This is not true, of course, for the other attribute types of association and aggregate association types.)

Especially early in entity modeling for some unfamiliar data resource, inclusion of attribute types should be kept to a bare minimum—or to none at all. This is because attribute types often tend to clutter entity model diagrams, diminishing or obscuring object types (and behavior) of more

GUIDELINES AND CONVENTIONS FOR ATTRIBUTE TYPES

- The properties of entity types are represented in an entity model by attribute types. Each attribute type corresponds to some defined set of values (called a domain).
- The attribute types of an object may be shown either using circles "underneath" the entity type, connected by thin, headless lines, or simply by listing them nearby.
- Especially early in the entity modeling activity, only properties of objects essential for understanding or defining the object itself should be included in the model. This means most objects will have very few attribute types, or none at all.
- Use the "list" format for attribute types to conserve space, especially in more detailed models.
- An asterisk is used to show which attribute type(s) serve as determinants for defined objects.
- Attribute types may be used to give properties of kernel entity types, characteristic entity types, association types, aggregate association types, and measurement points.
- Attribute types connected to an aggregate object are assumed to belong to each object within it.
- Consider using either characteristics or named domain subsets for multivalued properties.

central importance. Greater detail also makes revision and iteration more cumbersome and time-consuming.

To ensure that a model first achieves a substantial measure of comprehensiveness and stability, the early focus should be centered on entity types and other basic object types, rather than on their individual properties. In general, only those properties absolutely necessary in defining or clarifying a given object type (or behavior) should be included. Completion of attribute specification should be considered the very last step in entity modeling, the final activity just before conversion to implementable form.

2.1-1 Showing Foreign Keys

In the relational model, all relationship types are supported by (and in fact created by) domains held in common by different objects. (The very same object can be related to itself, of course, by holding the same domain twice or more.) Without such commonly held domains, there can be no relating (i.e., "joins") of different information. The presence of such commonly held domains is therefore vital for successful conversion of an entity model to normalized form and to subsequent "physical" implementation. (Refer also to Section 3.2-3 on Referential Integrity.)

As an entity model's detail increases, it is sometimes desirable to designate explicitly which attribute types actually support given relationship types. This may be accomplished by designating foreign keys among the attribute types of some given object type.

A **foreign key** is an attribute type corresponding to some domain that serves as a determinant for any object type in the entity model. (The case where the foreign key and the determinant are actually the very same attribute of the very same object type is trivial and can be ignored. For the purpose of entity modeling, it is also appropriate to restrict foreign keys to determinant domains only.) Since the foreign key attribute is defined on the same domain as the other object's determinant, values potentially held in common provide the basis of relationships between the actual object occurrences.

Diagram 2.5

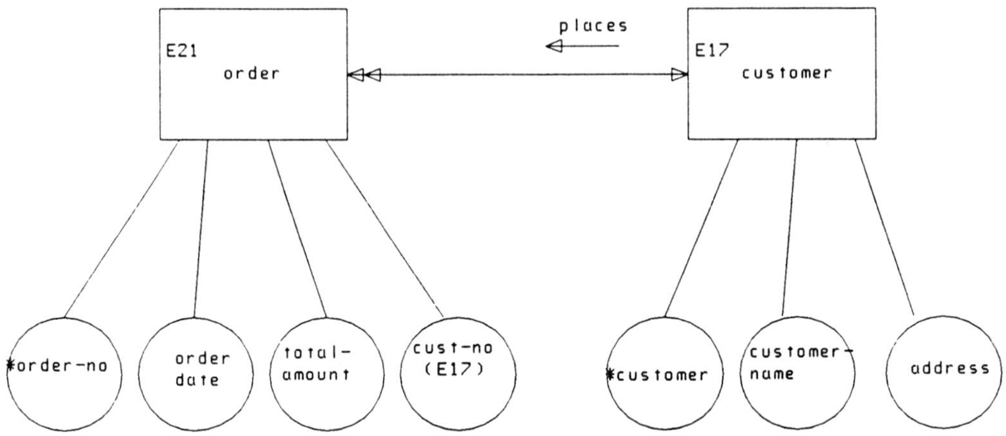

In this example, a relationship exists between an order and the customer who places the order. The order's cust-no attribute type has been designated as the foreign key basis of the relationship type. (The specification scheme above requires that object types in an entity model be coded or numbered—this is recommended practice especially as the model matures and stabilizes.) For each individual order occurrence, a value for cust-no (the foreign key value) will identify the particular customer who placed that order. This value should be equivalent to some value for customer, the determinant for customer.

As the above example illustrates, there is no requirement that the foreign key attribute type be named the same as the determinant attribute type at the other "end" of the relationship type. However, both attribute types must be defined on the same domain (e.g., the domain containing all identifier values for customer).

Notice also that the other end of the relationship type (entering customer) is single-headed. In general, foreign keys can only be specified where the opposite end of the associated relationship type is of a "1" type. This is because each occurrence of the first object type has at most one and only one value of the foreign key, and thus can refer or "point" to only one occurrence of the object type on the far end. (Remember that the

GUIDELINES AND CONVENTIONS FOR FOREIGN KEYS

- Use foreign key specification only in a relatively stable and complete entity model where explicit clarification of relationship types is deemed important.
- Every foreign key specification in an entity model should be associated with some explicitly documented relationship type. Foreign keys must be present to transform an entity model to normalized form.
- Designating foreign keys requires that object types be numbered or otherwise identified in coded form. Use the number or code of the other related object type in a relationship type to identify the attribute type(s) among those of the first object type that serve as its foreign key(s).
- Each relationship type may have foreign keys defined only on one end or the other—never both ends.
- The "end" of the relationship type opposite the foreign key specification must be single-headed.
- An attribute type designated as a foreign key must be defined on a determinant domain.
- Multiple foreign keys may be designated as supporting a relationship type.
- The opposite "end" of the relationship type for which a foreign key is defined must point to an object determined by the corresponding determinant(s).
- All of the determinants of this other object must be represented as foreign keys within the first object. The match must be exact.
- A foreign key attribute type need not be named the same as the corresponding determinant.
- The foreign key sets supporting two different relationship types may overlap.
- Avoid composites as attribute types if they make foreign key definition unclear or error-prone.
- Exercise caution in dropping relationship types from the entity model once foreign keys have been specified.

foreign key represents the determinant of the opposite side object type, and each value of a determinant can refer to one and only one occurrence of the object type it determines.) It would also be inappropriate for foreign keys to be designated on *both* ends of a relationship type. (For the reader: the only case where this could happen without violating the above rule is in a 1-to-1 relationship type. Why would specification of foreign keys on both "ends" of a 1-to-1 relationship type be unnecessary? Why would it probably be undesirable? Hint: What about possible loss of integrity during updating?)

Diagram 2.6

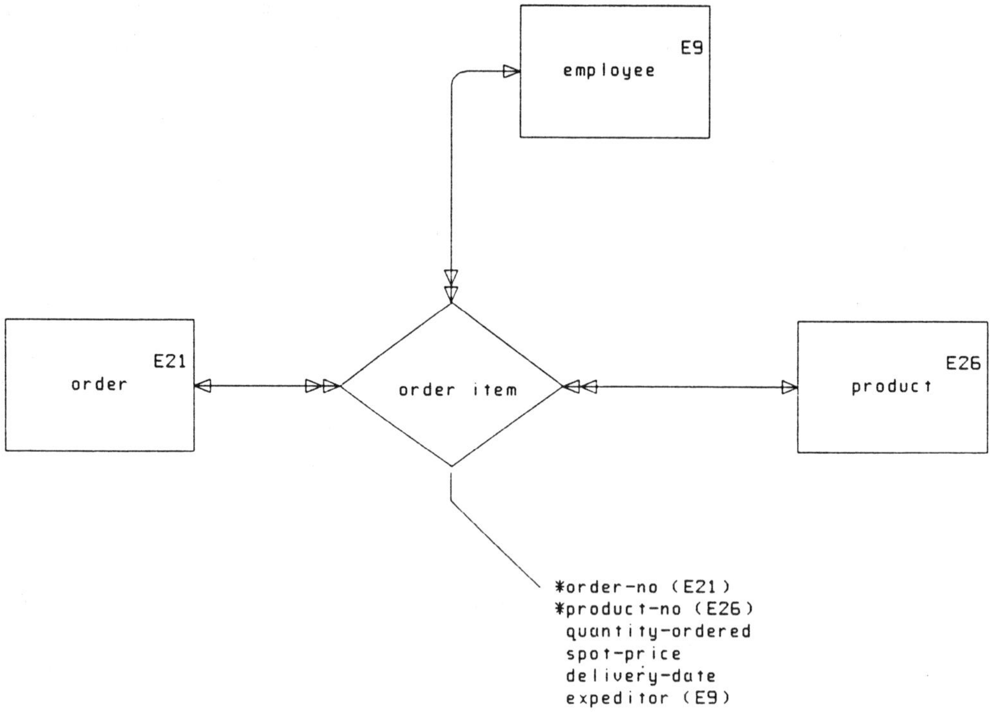

In this example, the association type order-item is involved in three relationship types, as shown. Two of them are with the object types (order and product) that order-item actually associates. Three distinct foreign keys have been designated, one for each of the three relationship types in which order-item participates. Two of these foreign keys (order-no and product-no) are also the determinants of order-item.

Diagram 2.7 specifies that multiple sections of a course are offered each semester, with multiple seats in each. Each seat may be assigned to one student.

The characteristic determined by seat-no has two sets of foreign keys defined. The first (designated by "CO"s) supports the relationship type to the characterized object, section. The second set supports the relationship type to the assigned student.

This example illustrates several important points about foreign keys. First, the foreign key set supporting different relationship types may partly overlap, as above. Second, it may take two or more attributes as foreign keys to support any given relationship type. This naturally depends on the determinants of the related object. All of the determinants of the related object, of course, must always be covered by foreign keys in the first object type. The match must be exact. (Note: Where composite domains have been used as attribute types, inexact matches may occur inadvertently between foreign keys and the associated determinants. Caution should be exercised to avoid such mismatches. In certain cases, it may be advisable to prohibit the use of composites for multi-part foreign key and determinant specification altogether.)

Diagram 2.7

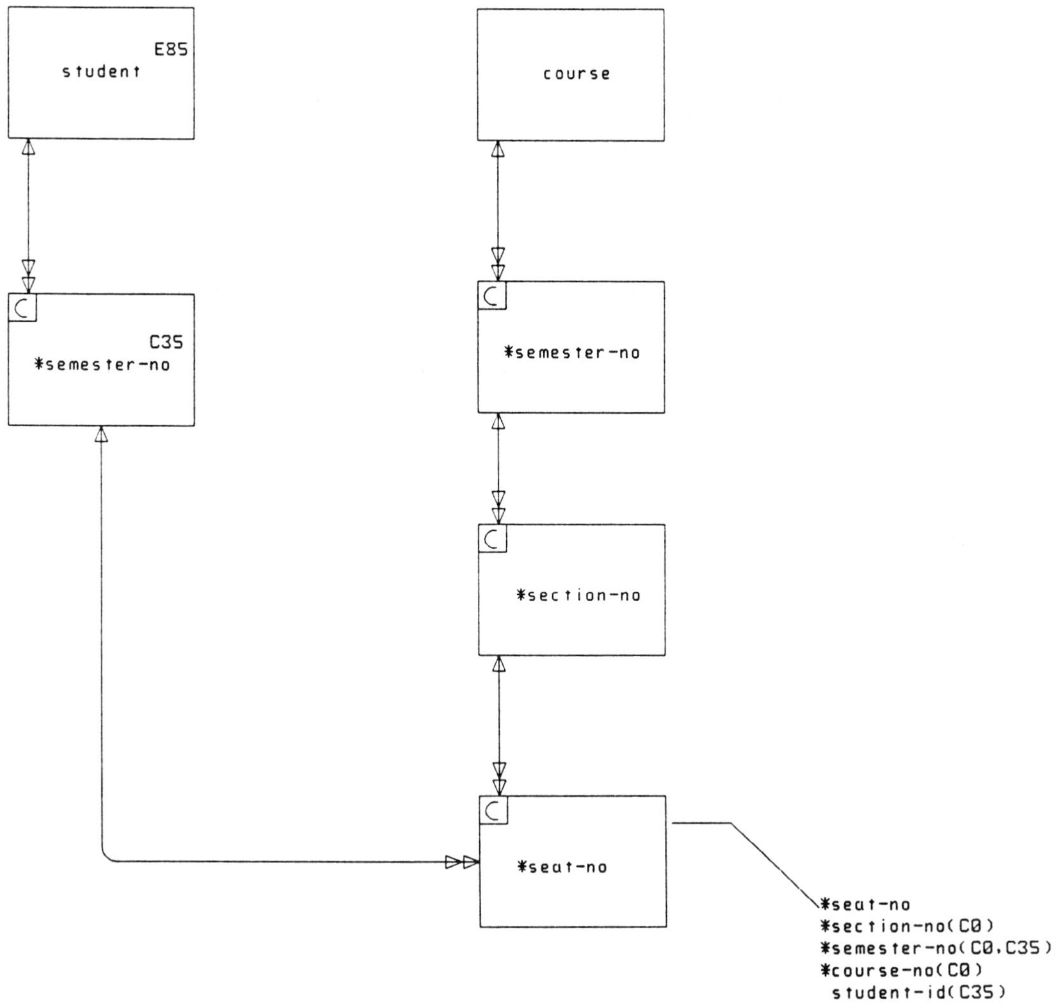

Note that once a foreign key specification has been made, the associated relationship type could actually be erased from the entity model since its existence is now implicit. (This "dropping" of relationship types is sometimes done to reduce visual clutter.) Caution should be exercised in this regard, however, since foreign key specifications alone effectively hide important business actions taking place between object types, thus reducing communicated knowledge. (Consider how the diagram above would look, for example, with the relationship type connections missing.)

Note also that foreign keys can always be ascertained and defined procedurally through formal inspection of an entity model in which determinants have already been specified. (Proving this is left as an exercise to the reader.) Therefore, whereas foreign keys are indeed an important test of "implementability," practitioners should generally only explicitly designate them where detailed exactness in the model is desirable (e.g., to assist with conversion to normalized form). Designation may also be desirable where objects already possess a defined complement of attribute types (possibly with irregular naming), and the need exists to identify explicitly the foreign keys among them.

2.1-1.1 Showing the Foreign Keys of Classifications

To remain consistent with the spirit of the relational model, all relationship types must be supported using foreign keys, including those involved in entity type hierarchies (ETH). These special classification relationship types, of course, are always 1-to-1.

In Section 1.2-3.6, three distinct types of entity type hierarchies were identified. The problem of foreign keys is examined below for each of these cases.

2.1-1.1-1 Domain-Based Entity Type Hierarchies

In this type of classification, the determinant(s) of both supertype and subtype, even if not named identically, are defined on the same domain. The determinants themselves thus establish a straightforward basis for the relationship type—in other words, they act as foreign keys.

Diagram 2.8

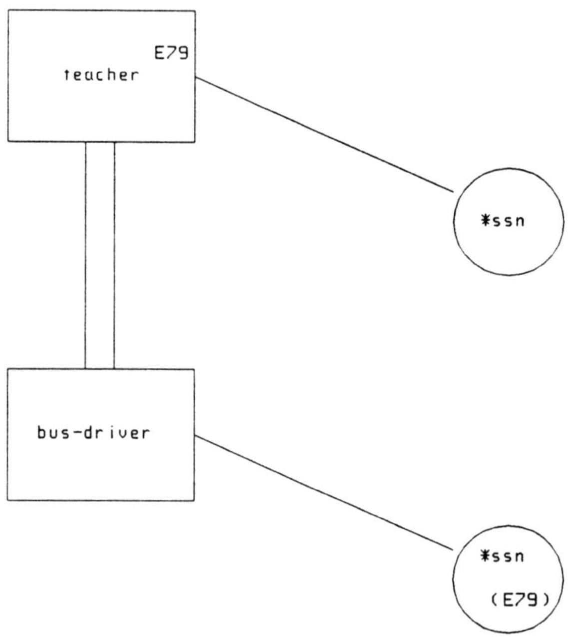

Social security numbers (SSN) are used to determine both teachers and bus-drivers (a strict subtype in this school). SSN has been defined as the foreign key for the classification relationship type.

Sometimes more consistent naming is desired than in the above. An alternative would be to define teacher-id and bus-driver-id as named domain subsets of SSN and to use these more selective names in establishing the classification relationship type.

Diagram 2.9

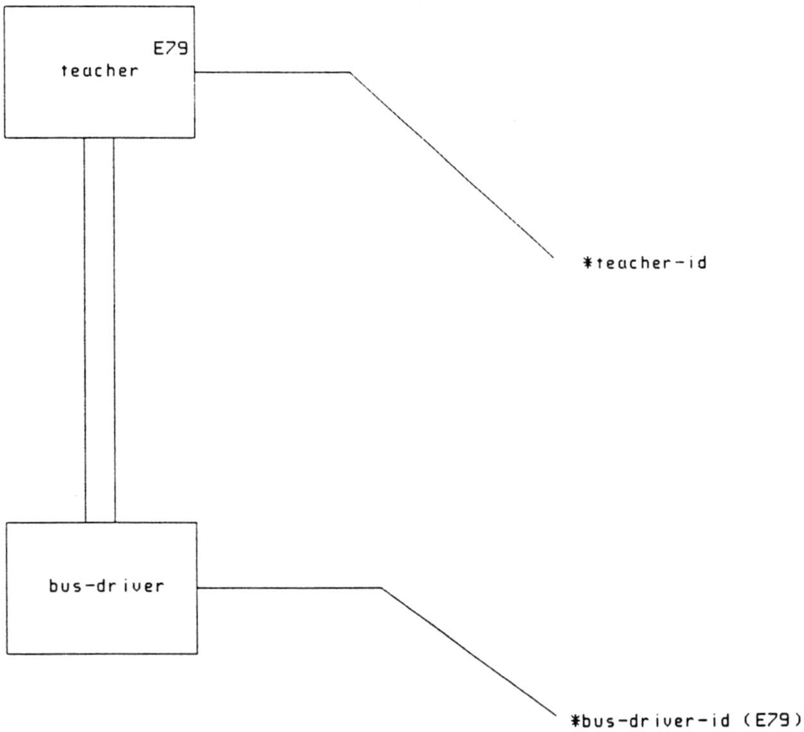

This approach is obviously valid only if both determinants are defined on the same domain (i.e., SSN).

2.1-1.1-2 Abstract Entity Type Hierarchies

In this type of classification, the determinants of supertype and subtype are completely different. Even though the Rules of Precedence and Inheritance still apply, the determinants of the supertype and subtype are defined on completely different domains.

In this type of ETH, a different basis than the previous must be used to support the classification relationship type. The preferred method is for the determinant(s) of the supertype to appear as attribute type(s) of the subtype, thereby acting as foreign key(s). Note that values of the foreign key(s) will always be present for every subtype occurrence that actually exists—in other words, no null values will ever be needed. [Why? Hint: Review the Rule of Precedence. Would this necessarily have been the case if the determinant(s) of the subtype had been used as foreign key attribute(s) in the supertype?] The avoidance of null values in this particular case is probably very desirable.

Diagram 2.10

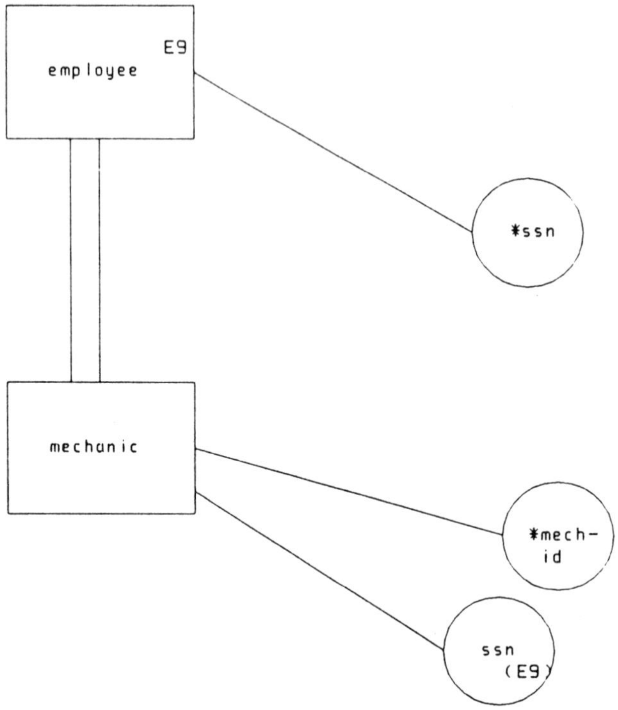

In this example, mechanics have their own identifier, mech-id (perhaps an industry identification standard) even though the only mechanics this enterprise records information about (by policy) are those who are also employees of the enterprise. The determinant of employee, SSN, has been included among the attribute types of mechanic to establish a basis for the classification relationship type (i.e., to act as a foreign key into the supertype). (Note: this attribute type cannot be defined as "pro forma" since "pro forma" essentially says "don't actually store values," and values here are definitely needed.)

A specification such as the above, incidentally, clearly indicates that this classification is "abstract" (i.e., not either domain-based or imaginary). No additional specification or symbol is required.

2.1-1.1-3 Imaginary Entity Type Hierarchies

Imaginary ETH are those defined as having a supertype with no (real) determinant whatsoever. (Since all entity types should have determinants, such a supertype is therefore "imaginary.")

Imaginary ETH may be specified as either "not to be stored" or "store as such." The "not to be stored" specification eliminates the need for the classification relationship type and thus for foreign keys. It need not be considered further. (Note: Any properties of an imaginary supertype are *physically* inherited by all next-level subtypes, where values will be recorded redundantly for corresponding occurrences. Any desired relationship directly among these subtypes can be represented using regular relationship and foreign key conventions.)

The "to be stored as such" specification is more problematic. Obviously, the first choice is to find or invent some domain that *can* serve as the determinant for the supertype.

If this proves impossible, the only remaining choice is to pick up the determinant(s) of each subtype and to include them as foreign key attribute types in the supertype, as below. Without an identifier, however, it is unclear exactly how this supertype might be implemented.

Diagram 2.11

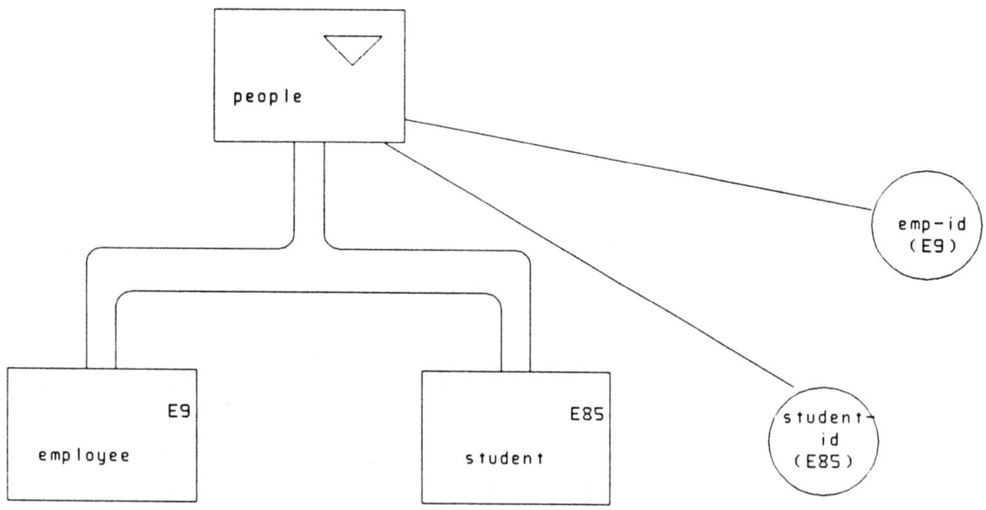

Note: This example assumes that emp-id and student-id do not share the same domain. If they did (e.g., they shared SSN), then only that one foreign key would be needed in the supertype.

2.2 Logical Definition of Domains

Defining domains, or sets of values, independently of those objects using them as properties ensures a high degree of consistency and uniformity in their usage across an entire entity model. Also, because the entity model itself is free of all "physical" and DBMS bias, purely logical definition of all the domains that complement it is possible as well.

Entity modeling therefore provides a basis for developing a corporate vocabulary for data. The entity model—with its full load of meaning and business policy—provides the optimal framework for such development to occur.

2.2-1 Name, Definition and Rules of Formation (Format)

Every domain requires a name so that it can be identified and referenced. In the case of determinants, this name wherever possible should closely reflect the name of the associated entity type. For example, the entity type student is preferably identified by the determinant student-id.

Every domain should also be described and documented by some brief textual explanation giving its meaning (i.e., semantics). Aliases, of course, normally do not require such documentation since their meaning cannot differ in any way from the domain name for which they can be substituted. Any domain name may have one or more aliases.

A domain is really just a set of uniformly created values, each unique and distinct from all others. To achieve such uniformity, specified rules (called **Rules of Formation**) are necessary. These rules are in some sense like format statements—for example they may give length—but they should never give any purely physical specification (e.g., "packed"). For example, valid rules of formation for teacher-id might say "all values must be seven positions in length, all numeric except the first position, which must be alphabetic."

Every domain has one and only one set of rules of formation. If the domain seems to require more than one set, then it is not a single domain and needs to be separated into two or more domains.

Taken together, the description of a domain (the semantics) and the rules of formation for the domain (the syntax) are sufficient for deciding whether or not any given value is a legitimate member of that domain. In other words, to be a legitimate member, a value must conform to the same meaning as all other member values of the set, and it must look like them as well.

Some domains contain values that are derived—that is, there is some explicit procedure, algorithm or set of calculations that actually produce the member values. Whereas it is not usually feasible or desirable to document the derivation formula in the domain definition itself (the entity model may provide an alternative—see Part III on measurement), it is sometimes desirable simply to specify that the values of the given domain are in fact derived. This may be accomplished as follows.

Diagram 2.12

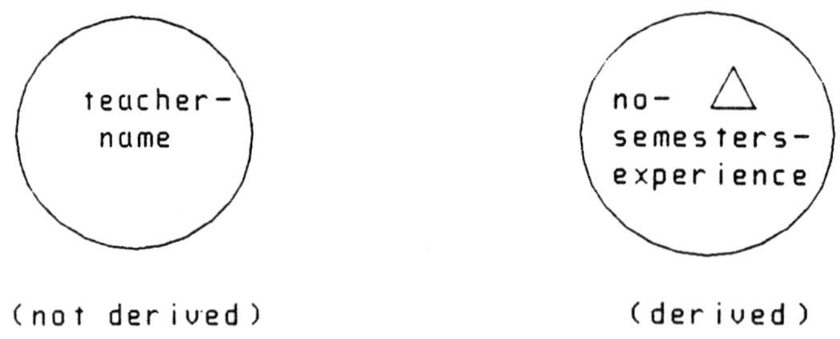

Any domain may also be either **open** or **closed**. In an open domain it is not feasible or meaningful to list all the possible values beforehand (i.e., prior to implementation of the database). If all goes well—in other words, if all possible values are not used up—the domain will always remain open so as to allow for growth. In this type of domain, the rules of formation are extremely important in order to maintain ongoing consistency. Teacher-id would be such a domain.

In a closed domain all the values are known beforehand and may be individually enumerated. The objective is actually to disallow, or rigidly control growth. Since all the values in a closed domain can be listed beforehand (and usually are), the rules of formation are relatively less important than for open domains. Hair-color, with pre-defined valid values (e.g., brunette, blond, black, etc.), would constitute a closed domain.

Closed domains are often used for editing, validation and control purposes. Since closed domains often imply "type-codes," and type-codes in turn have significant structural implications for an entity model, the reader is advised to review Section 2.3 on type codes below before aggressively standardizing closed domains for his or her enterprise.

2.2-2 Logical Domain Definition Basics

Besides the above, there are three essential components in the logical definition of any domain: *determinance, composition* and *subsetting*. These three components are discussed individually below.

2.2-2.1 Determinance

If the values of a domain may be used to distinguish uniquely and unambiguously between occurrences of some entity type, one value per occurrence, and one occurrence per value in all cases—then the domain may be designated as a **determinant**. If not, then it must be defined as a nondeterminant. Those domains that are determinants are distinguished by means of an asterisk in front of the domain name.

Diagram 2.13

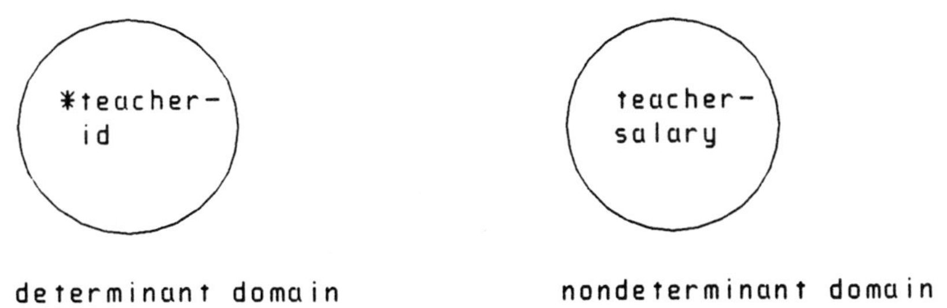

2.2-2.1-1 Kernel versus Partial Determinants

Some determinants can be used to distinguish between occurrences of some entity type, but only in conjunction with one or more other determinants. Such a determinant is said to be **partial**, because its values can only "partially" distinguish uniquely and unambiguously between occurrences of the given entity type.

For example, line-item-no might be defined as a partial determinant because its values (e.g., 01, 02, 03, etc.) cannot be used alone to reference anything meaningful. The determinant value of an order must always also be given (e.g., order-no = A62051) in order to refer to some particular data (i.e., a order line) of interest.

A partial determinant may be identified by use of a double asterisk in front of the domain name as below.

Diagram 2.14

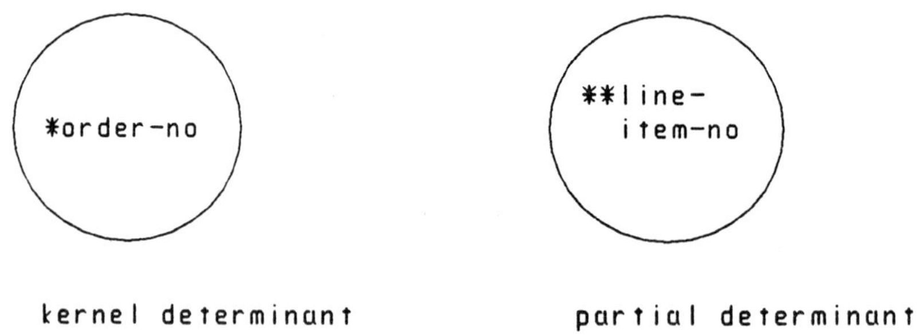

Determinants that are not partial are called **kernel determinants** since they are used to determine kernel entity types. Partial determinants are used for the identification of characteristic entity types (see Section 1.2-2). The entity type determined by line-item-no as above is an example of a characteristic. Once defined as partial, a determinant must be used to determine only characteristic entity types, never a kernel entity type. This represents a rather strong restriction on its use.

2.2-2.2 Composition

Some domains do not really possess their own rules of formation, but rather simply assemble two or more other domains into some larger unit. Such domains are said to be **composite** because they are made up of other domains (called **partitions**) as component parts.

Diagram 2.15

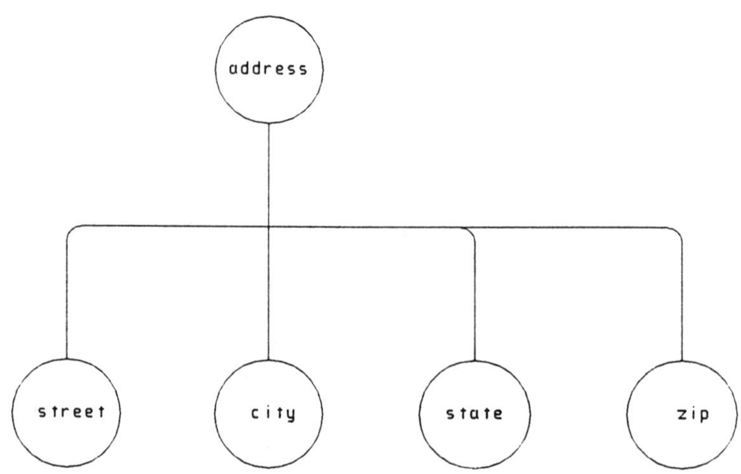

Address is shown to be a composite domain composed of four other domains as partitions: street, city, state, and zip. (By convention, a hierarchy of thin lines is used to define the partitions of a composite domain.) A valid value of address is formed by juxtaposing values for each of the four partitions.

Any of the partitions of a composite domain may also be composites themselves. For example, in Diagram 2.15, street might actually itself be a composite consisting of street-no, street-name, and unit-no. Note that when forming valid values of street, the unit-no partition might often be null. There is no sense of "mandatory" in giving values for each partition unless explicitly specified in the composite domain definition.

Any domain that has no partitions whatsoever is said to be **atomic**. Atomic domains naturally require rules of formation since they have no partitions from which such rules can be "borrowed." Good database design practice dictates that all determinant domains should always be atomic.

2.2-2.3 Subsetting

The real power of the domain concept in building a powerful corporate vocabulary for data arises through the subsetting notion. This notion permits definition and rules of formation to be kept to an absolute minimum, while nonetheless permitting the manageable number of meaningful and consistent names to expand significantly. This notion is explained below.

Since domains are simply sets of values, it is often meaningful to name and identify subsets within them—other sets whose values are fully within the original set. These subsets are generally smaller than the original set—that is, they have fewer values—but they may also sometimes be "improper" (they may actually contain all the values in the original set). Subsets, of course, can also be defined for other subsets.

In defining and identifying a subset of values (i.e., a **named domain subset** or **subdomain**), it is not necessary to list all the member values. Indeed, for "open" domains (the majority) this would usually not even be possible. Furthermore, whereas a subdomain has special meaning (i.e., unique semantics) that must be documented, it cannot have its own individual rules of formation. This is because all the subset's values are necessarily "borrowed" from the original domain (called the **superdomain**). No additional specification is therefore generally required.

2.2-2.3-1 Determinant Subsets

An example, Diagram 2.16, illustrates. Suppose that in a particular school, all bus-drivers must be teachers, and all teachers in turn must be employees. In terms of classification, the situation is conceptually as follows.

Diagram 2.16

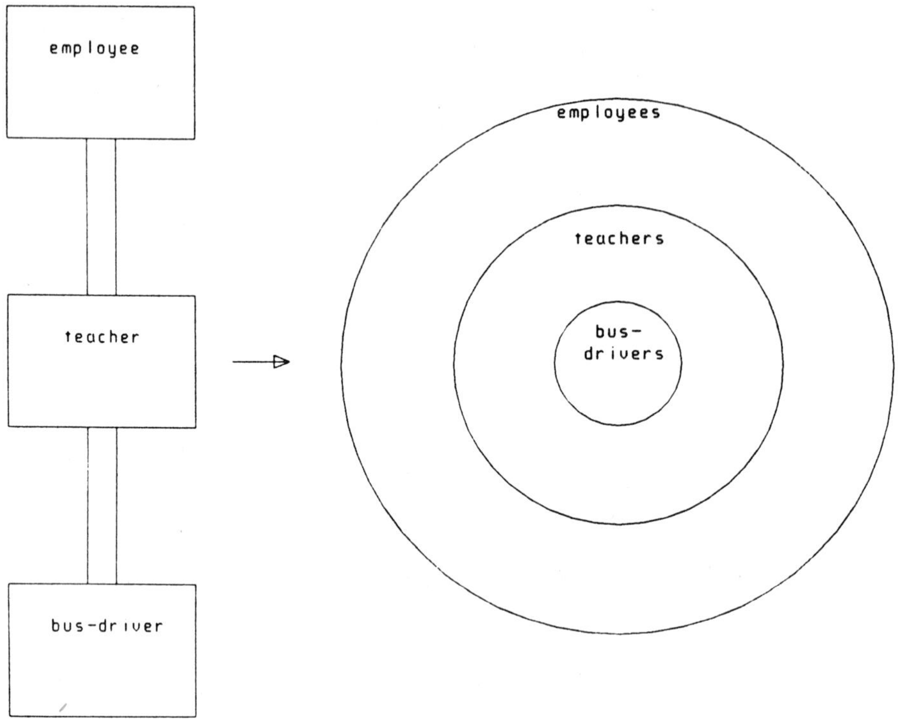

Drawn as sets, as on the right, the subsetting of people in this school is apparent.

Now imagine that the actual people filling these positions are identified. Their SSN might be used to do this. If all the values at a particular point in time for this school could be listed, something presumably like the following would be found.

Diagram 2.17

bus-driver-id	teacher-id	employee-id	SSN
286-51-3801	286-51-3801	286-51-3801	275-75-1669
452-60-2211	321-28-1919	321-28-1919	286-51-3801
486-33-3219	452-60-2211	329-92-8231	299-38-7210
579-21-3624	458-53-6805	452-60-2211	321-28-1919
	486-33-3219	458-53-6805	329-92-8231
	579-21-3624	459-51-4426	401-80-2193
	821-23-6622	486-33-3219	452-60-2211
		499-91-6541	458-53-6805
		579-21-3624	458-54-2816
		621-23-6622	459-51-4426
		633-26-9990	486-33-3219
			499-91-6541
			552-28-2963
			579-21-3624
			621-23-6622
			629-25-8859
			633-26-9990
			635-42-1168

subset

subset

subset

Four domain names have been provided to refer to the columns of values. Note that subsetting has been carefully preserved among these columns, as consistent with the earlier specifications. Note also that the subset names are not merely aliases—they each individually refer to truly distinct ideas (i.e., special classes of something larger).

The associated domain definitions should accurately reflect these facts. The following specification makes the necessary definition graphically.

Diagram 2.18

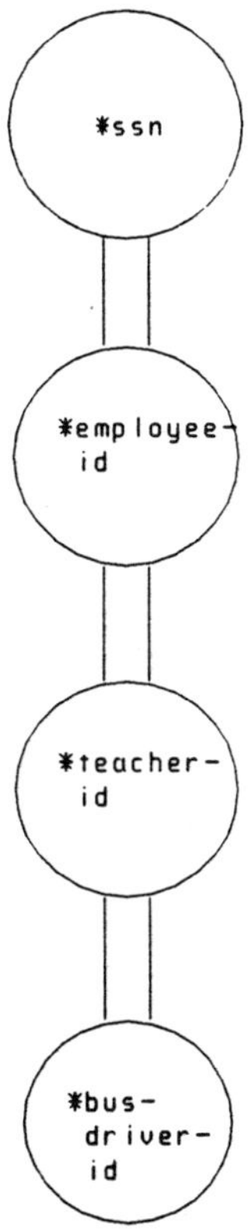

A pair of parallel, solid, thin lines (previously used for the subsetting of entities into subtypes) is used here to provide for the subsetting of the given domains. (Heavy dark lines may be substituted.)

In the above domain model, SSN is shown as the highest domain (i.e., the largest set of values) even though no corresponding entity type for this greatest generalization was included in the earlier entity type hierarchy and entity subsetting analysis. This presumably means that such an entity type falls beyond the scope of this data resource; however, it may also mean that the corresponding supertype has simply been "missed" in modeling to date. In either case, continuing correspondence between determinant domain subsetting and the corresponding entity type hierarchies should be carefully monitored.

In the example above, each of the domains within the subsetting has been specified as determinants. Such consistent marking is recommended. It should be noted, however, that if *any* of the domains within a subsetting is designated as determinants, then *all* of the domains are determinants automatically.

Only the highest superdomain in any domain subsetting needs complete rules of formation. All subdomains must comply with these rules faithfully. The only departure permitted (not generally relevant to determinants) is where a subdomain has rules of formation more restrictive than those of the superdomain. For example, suppose speed-limit is a subdomain of miles-per-hour. In general, an enterprise might permit measurement of miles-per-hour using five digits on either side of the decimal point. Speed-limit, however, might be restricted to positive integers less than 100, a much more restrictive measurement.

Note finally that there is no sense of "mandatory" in any domain subsetting (unless explicitly defined). Any subset may be empty, or a partial copy, or a full copy of its superdomain.

2.2-2.3-2 Nondeterminant Subsets

Subset domains for determinants are relatively easy to visualize because they correspond to subsets of real things (entity types) in the enterprise. Subdomains for nondeterminants may also be defined but these, of course, do not manifest themselves as subsets of real objects in the enterprise. In that sense, they are somewhat more abstract.

The following example helps illustrate the idea of subsetting for nondeterminant domains. Suppose that office-hours is a domain defined as any valid period during the school day that a person commits to being available in his or her office for consultation. Also, suppose that in this school all advisors are also teachers, but not all teachers are necessarily advisors. Furthermore, suppose that a person at this school may select values of office-hours that are different for their teaching role than those for their advising role.

Diagram 2.19

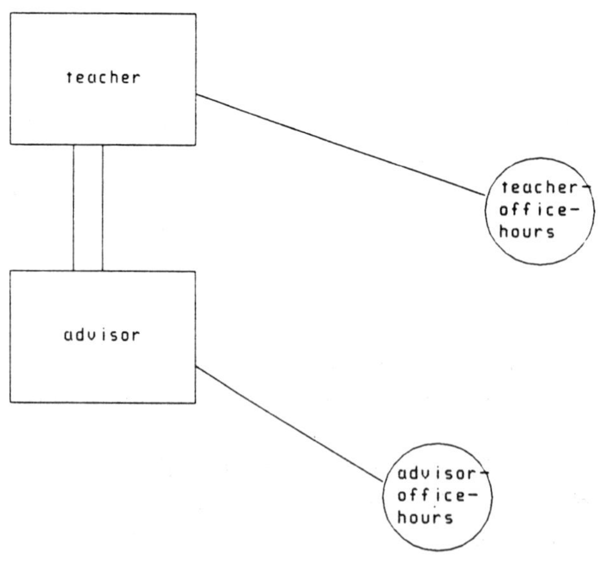

These indicated domains are similar in that they draw values from some common superdomain (i.e., office-hours) and thus need no individually defined rules of formation. They cannot simply be defined as aliases of that domain, however, because they connote distinct ideas as well as distinct values for occurrences of the respective entity types. Since their meanings are somewhat different, they require their own definition.

The appropriate graphic domain definition for these nondeterminant domains would appear as follows.

Diagram 2.20

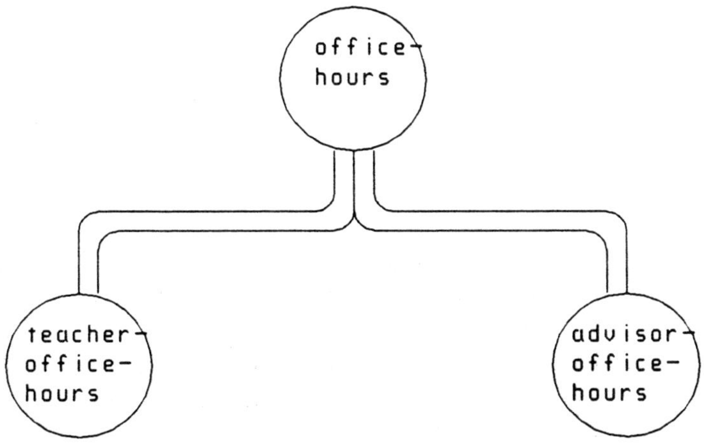

Both teacher-office-hours and advisor-office-hours are defined as named domain subsets (subdomains) of office-hours. It would not be surprising to find that both these subdomains are improper—that is, all the values of office-hours would be available for selection as advisor-office-hours and as teacher-office-hours. Note also that advisor-office-hours has not been defined as a subdomain of teacher-office-hours. This is simply a way of saying that all the values of office-hours are available to advisor-office-hours, not just those appearing as teacher-office-hours.

Because these domains are not determinants, the above domain diagram does not correspond to some ETH in an enterprise entity model. In these domain definitions, the sets of parallel lines simply imply subsetting.

Many other subsets of office-hours might be necessary in modeling this enterprise, as the following example suggests. Incidentally, this is an example of a "mixed" model, where domain definitions appear in the very same diagram as an entity model to help clarify some aspect of the enterprise. Mixed diagrams are generally useful only for segments ("window zones") of an entity model—not for the entire model.

In Diagram 2.21, each course may have a value of office-hours independently of teachers; each teacher may have a value of office-hours independently of courses; and each teacher/course combination may have some unique value of office-hours independently of the other two values. All three cases represent specific subdomains.

Diagram 2.21

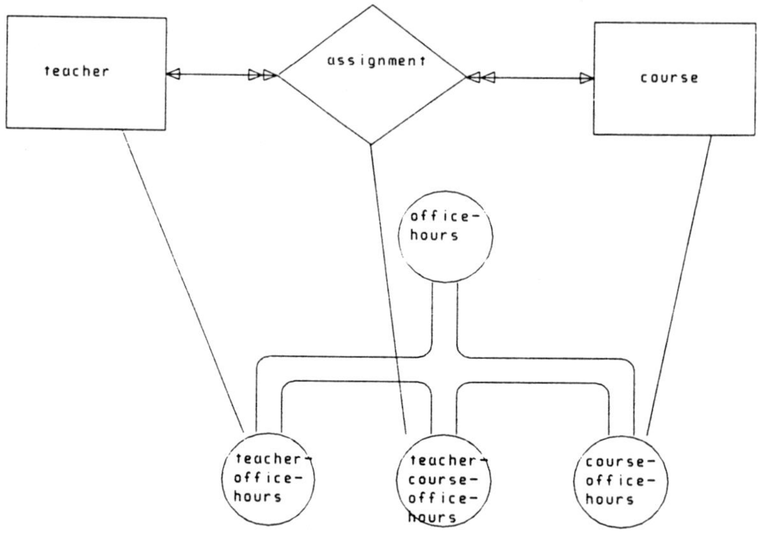

One additional point is worth noting. Definition of subdomains for composite nondeterminant domains is very common. Since all subdomains must follow the rules of formation of the superdomain, this means the partitions of a subdomain must always be equivalent to those of the superdomain. If explicitly named, these partitions become subdomains in their own right, as the following example illustrates.

Diagram 2.22

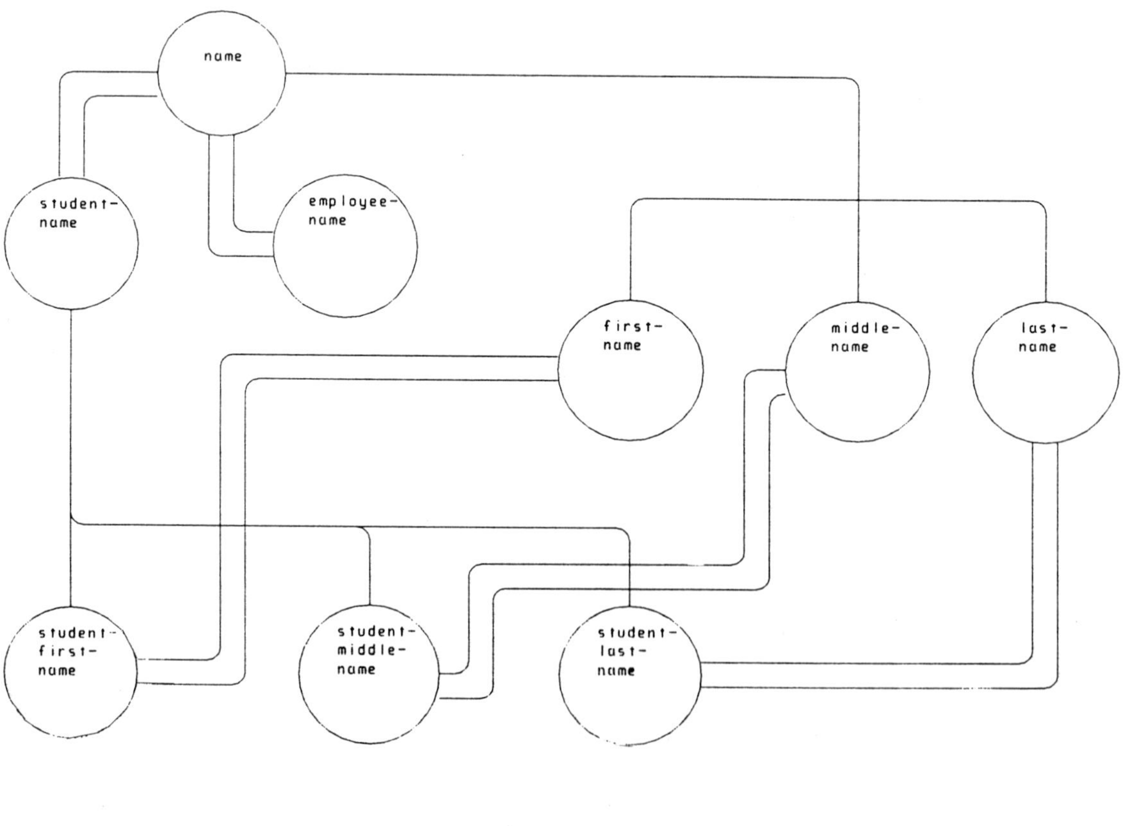

In Diagram 2.22, student-first-name, student-middle-name, and student-last-name (partitions of student-name, a subdomain of name) become subdomains of the partitions of name (first-name, middle-name, and last-name), respectively.

2.2-2.3-3 Pro Forma Subsets

In any enterprise, there is virtually an infinite number of classifications that could be defined. Whereas most of these classifications are never actually "stored" as such in a database, it is often nonetheless important to accommodate their terminology in building corporate data vocabularies, intelligible entity models, information directories, and/or user-friendly systems. It is thus important to define and accommodate the associated names. The pro forma concept permits this to be accomplished. (Refer also to Section 1.2-3.5.)

Consider, for example, the following pro forma classification.

Diagram 2.23

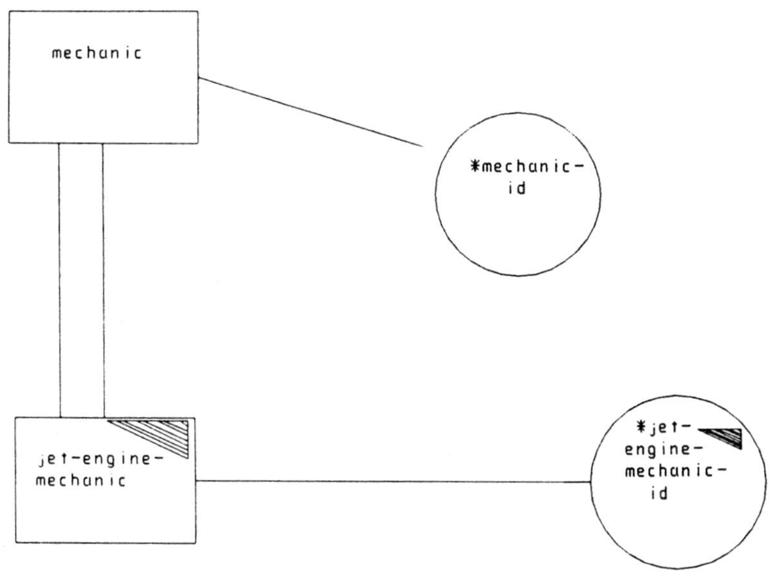

Jet-engine-mechanic is a pro forma subtype of mechanic. This dictates that its determinant (if defined) jet-engine-mechanic-id, is necessarily a pro forma subdomain of some other domain (presumably mechanic-id). It is an understandable name even though it will never represent a real stored field in the database.

Of greater interest and usefulness are pro forma nondeterminants. Consider the following example.

Diagram 2.24

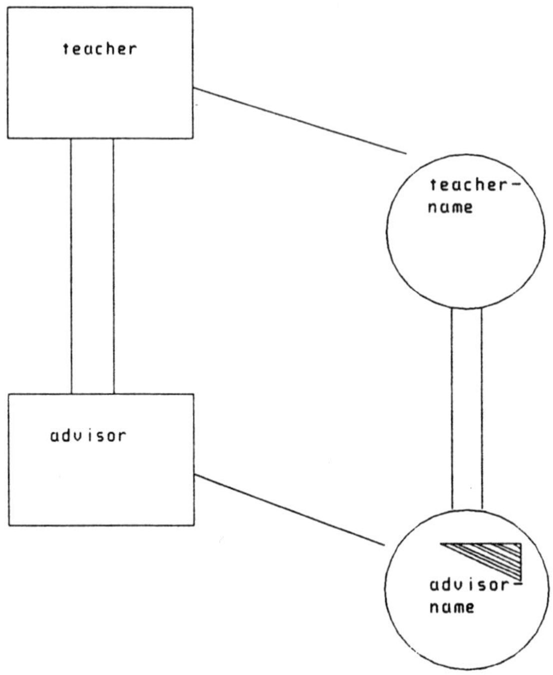

This classification is not pro forma—the subtype advisor will actually exist as such in the future database. Yet advisor-name (a "user-friendly" name) never refers to any value different from the corresponding value of teacher-name. In other words, the person performing these jobs has the same name even when acting as an advisor. (This makes it different from the earlier case of office-hours, where the respective values for the same person could be quite distinct.) Advisor-name is therefore defined in this mixed diagram as a pro forma subdomain of teacher-name. (In a nonmixed diagram, teacher-name would be shown as the "source" of the pro forma attribute advisor-name.)

The implication is that advisor-name is not a field to be stored as such in the future database because such storage would invite update anomalies. Instead, whenever any user asks for advisor-name, it is understood that the relevant value will be extracted from the corresponding teacher-name field. Teacher-name is therefore designated as its source. (Incidentally, the "view" concept under relational DBMS provides a straightforward mechanism to support a nonstored advisor-name field in this fashion for an implemented system. The subtype is simply joined with the supertype, and advisor-name is mapped to teacher-name.)

2.2-2.3-4 Subsets and Derivation

Subset domains often differ from their superdomain in terms of how (or whether) values are derived. The superdomain, for example, may be considered as not derived, even though values of the subdomain itself are.

Diagram 2.25

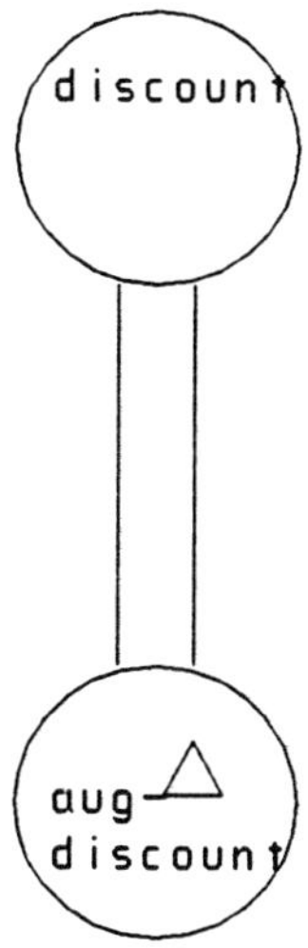

Discount is a domain whose values include all possible discount percentages. It is not considered to be derived. Avg-discount is a subdomain, whose values are calculated by some given formula. It is a derived subset of domain.

2.2-3 Domain Definition Decision Chart

Given any attribute type name appearing in an entity model, the following is a complete conceptual review of the domain definition actions that should be taken. (Ranging and reflective domains are discussed later, in Section 2.4.) This conceptual review is diagrammed in standard flowchart format.

Diagram 2.26

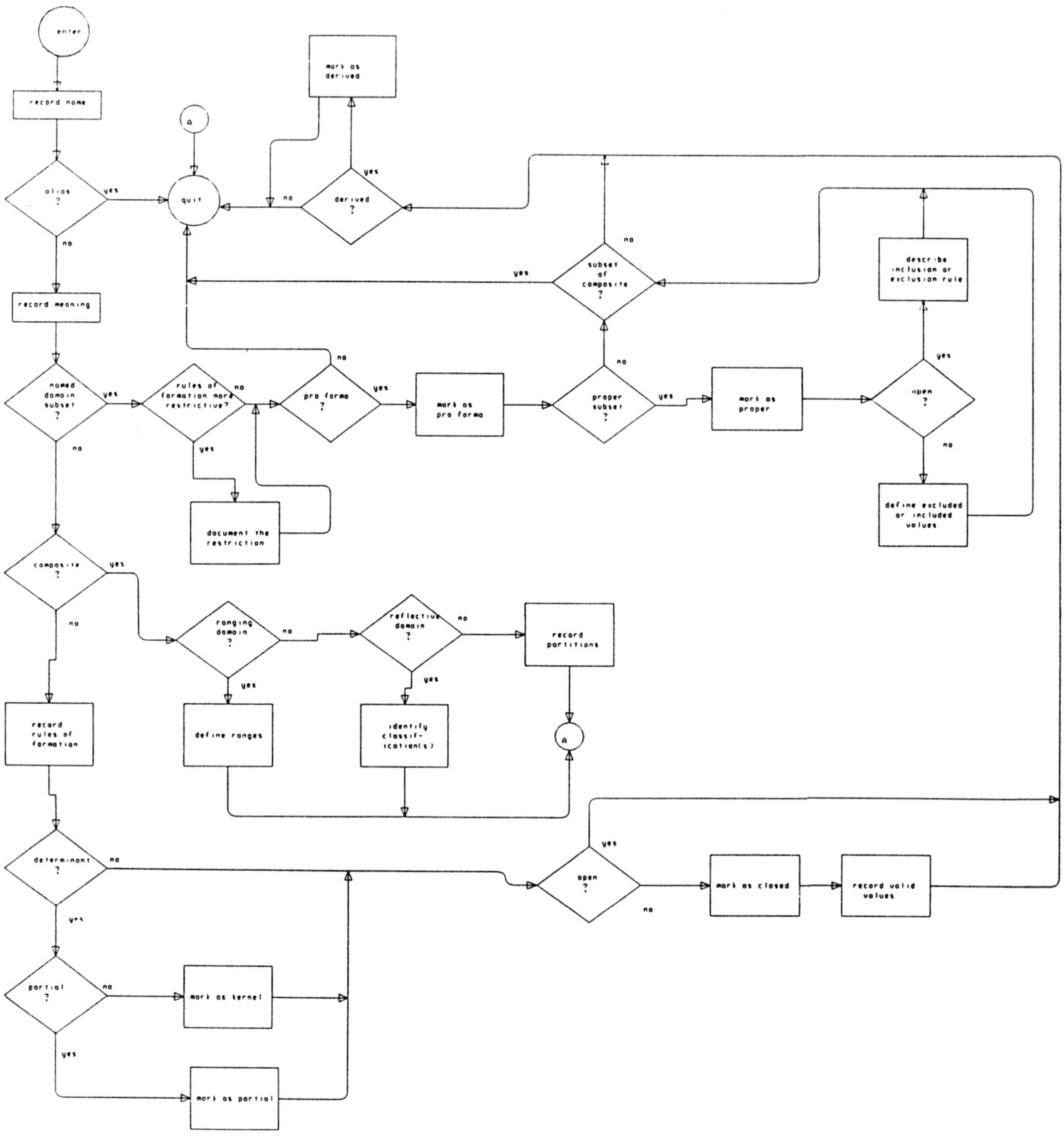

enter
record name
alias ?
yes
no
quit
A
mark as derived
derived ?
yes
no
record meaning
named domain subset ?
yes
no
rules of formation more restrictive?
no
yes
document the restriction
pro forma ?
yes
no
mark as pro forma
proper subset ?
yes
no
subset of composite ?
yes
no
mark as proper
open ?
yes
no
describe inclusion or exclusion rule
define excluded or included values
composite ?
yes
no
ranging domain ?
no
yes
define ranges
reflective domain ?
no
yes
identify classif- ication(s)
record partitions
A
record rules of formation
determinant ?
no
yes
open ?
yes
no
mark as closed
record valid values
partial ?
no
yes
mark as kernel
mark as partial

GUIDELINES AND CONVENTIONS FOR DOMAINS

- Comprehensive domain definitions substitute for data elements in a purely logical entity approach.
- Every domain type should have a name and brief textual description.
- A domain type may have aliases, but these should never require any additional semantic definition.
- A domain may have only one set of rules of formation (i.e., format); if more than one is required, then more than one domain exists.
- A domain may be derived or not derived, and open or closed.
- A domain or subdomain is graphically represented by a circle.
- The logical definition of every domain must include the following three essential components: determinance, composition, and subsetting.
- Kernel determinants are marked by a single asterisk; partial determinants may be marked by a double asterisk. Partial determinants must always be paired with at least one kernel determinant in an entity model to identify any object type of interest.
- A composite domain is made up of two or more partitions, each also a domain, and cannot have its own rules of formation.
- The partitions of a composite domain are graphically represented by thin-lined hierarchy. Each partition may also be composite.
- A composite domain can have no component value that is not among the values of the corresponding partition.
- Subsetting of domains is indicated using either pairs of parallel, thin, headless solid lines, or heavy dark lines.
- All values of a subdomain must be included among the values of its superdomain. Unless some restriction is specified, all superdomain values are deemed automatically available to the subdomain.
- A subdomain has special semantics (meaning) that should be documented, but it cannot have rules of formation that are incompatible with its superdomain. (They may, however, be more restrictive.)
- The values of a subdomain may be derived whereas the values of the superdomain are not.
- Defining any domain as a determinant automatically means all superdomains and subdomains are also determinants.
- Consistent marking of all subsets as determinants in graphic representation of the subsetting of a determinant domain is recommended.

(Continued)

GUIDELINES AND CONVENTIONS FOR DOMAINS
(Continued)

- The correspondence of subsetting for determinant domains should be continually monitored against any corresponding entity type hierarchies within the entity model.
- Subdomains may be defined for any domain, even those that are composite.
- The partitioning of a composite subdomain must exactly follow the partitioning of the superdomain.
- Show a subdomain as pro forma if its values are not to be actually stored in the database.
- Composite domains may be determinants; however, because of adverse implications for flexibility, growth, and change, this is not recommended.
- Use mixed diagrams (joint domain/object graphs) to clarify details of the enterprise. These should generally be presented in separate "windows" or zoom diagrams.
- Every attribute type in an entity model should have a corresponding domain definition

2.3 Type-codes

Type-codes are closed domains with carefully controlled values. Their purpose is to distinguish the type, class, or state of each occurrence of some particular object type. It is often desirable or important to define what values a type-code domain may have within the context of an entity model. It is also important to understand what problems the use of type-codes may produce.

2.3-1 Defining Type-code Domains

The values of any closed domain, whether or not a type-code, may be indicated by simply listing them, as in the following diagram. (Office-hours is defined as the start of 1-hour time slots.)

Diagram 2.27

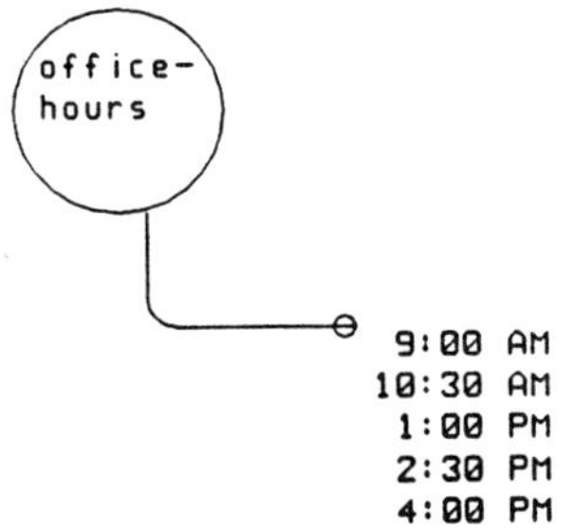

A subdomain is always defined as some subset (proper or improper) of a superdomain's value set. If no specification is given, then all the values are deemed available (i.e., the subdomain is an improper subset). Otherwise, the actual subset values may be indicated by list, or by restriction. The following two definitions, indicating a restricted domain for advisor-office-hours, illustrates. The two are exactly equivalent.

Diagram 2.28

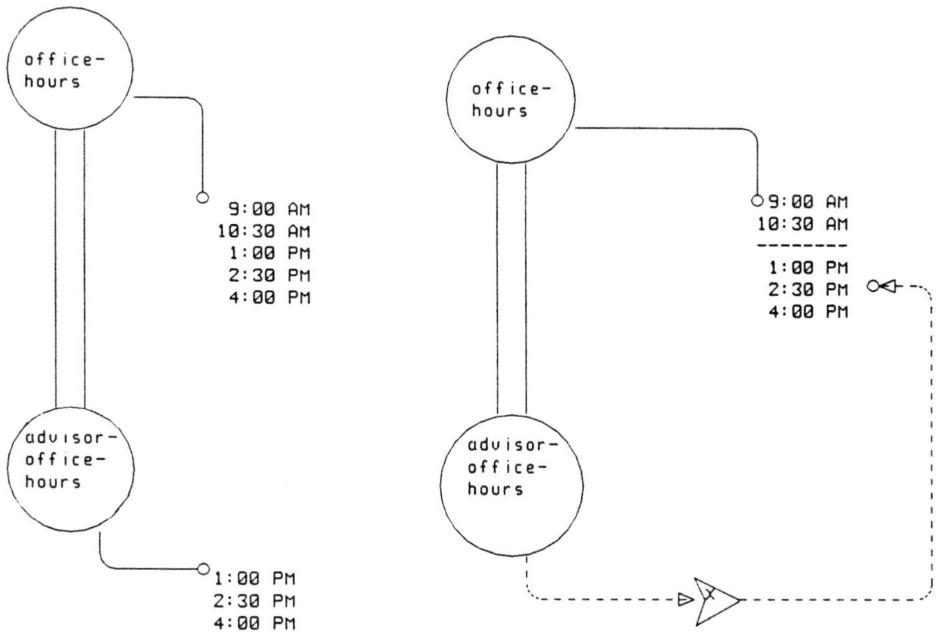

As shown, valid advisor-office-hours are only those office-hours values falling in the afternoon. Instead of a list, the alternative on the right uses a "mandatory" integrity constraint to define the restriction on included values. (*Excluded* values could be shown using a "not" integrity constraint qualifier. See Section 3.1-1.1-1.)

In many cases, closed domain or type-code values have both abbreviated and longer forms. The 1-to-1 equivalence of these forms can be shown as in Diagram 2.29.

Diagram 2.29

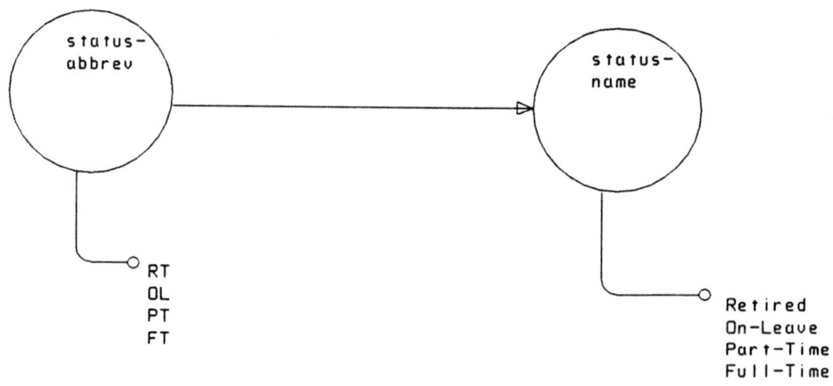

2.3-2 Type-codes and Classifications

Type-codes provide an alternative means of expressing a classification of some object type. From a purely conceptual point of view, the following two models are therefore equivalent.

Diagram 2.30

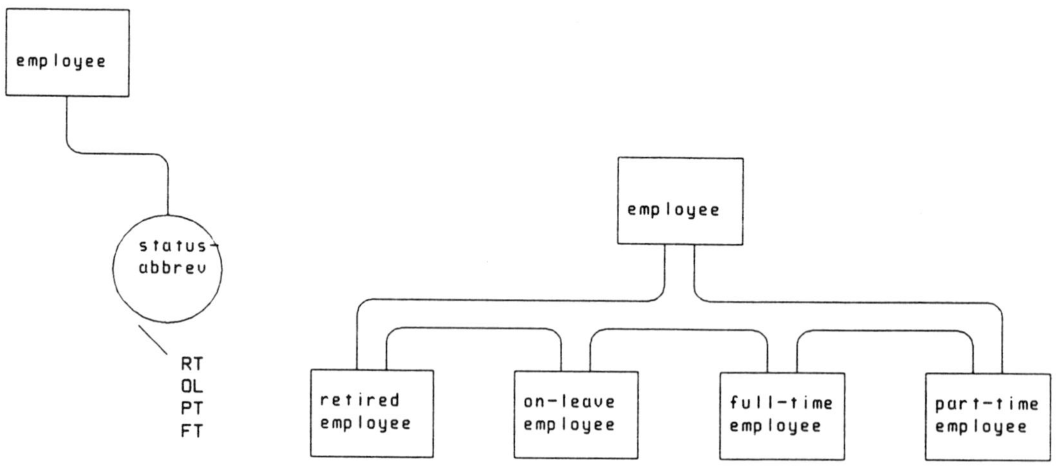

Of these alternatives, the version on the right is clearly preferable for communication and presentation. For this reason, type-codes should be avoided as much as possible until relatively late in the entity modeling of some data resource.

From an implementation point of view, of course, the version on the left may be preferred. For the benefit of implementors or others, the equivalence of the two versions can be shown as follows.

Diagram 2.31 indicates that the classification is pro forma (the subtypes are not to be stored as such). The given type of any particular employee occurrence within this breakdown can be ascertained through the values of status-abbrev, which acts as the "source" of the classification in the actual implementation. The correspondence of the status-abbrev values to the pro forma subtypes is shown explicitly.

Diagram 2.31

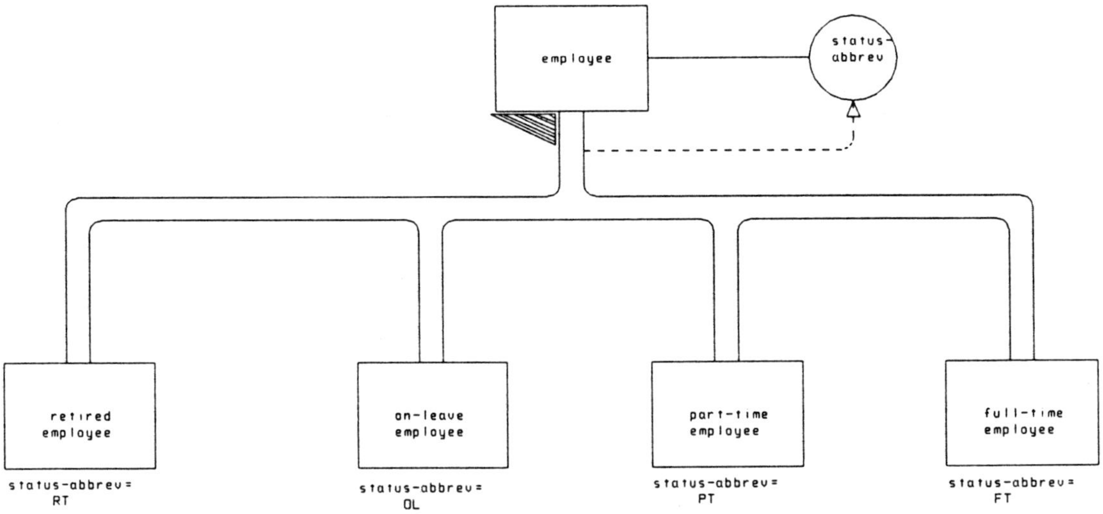

Use of type-code "source" indicators as above is recommended only in the following circumstances.

- As an entity model nears completion and decisions are being made about implementation.
- Some domain is recognized as a type-code, and thus with classification implications, and the need exists to explore or illustrate these implications more fully. (This should normally be done using a separate "window" zone diagram.)
- Full graphic definition of the type-code values, or precise definition of the associated business terminology, is desired.

An additional example illustrates further.

Diagram 2.32

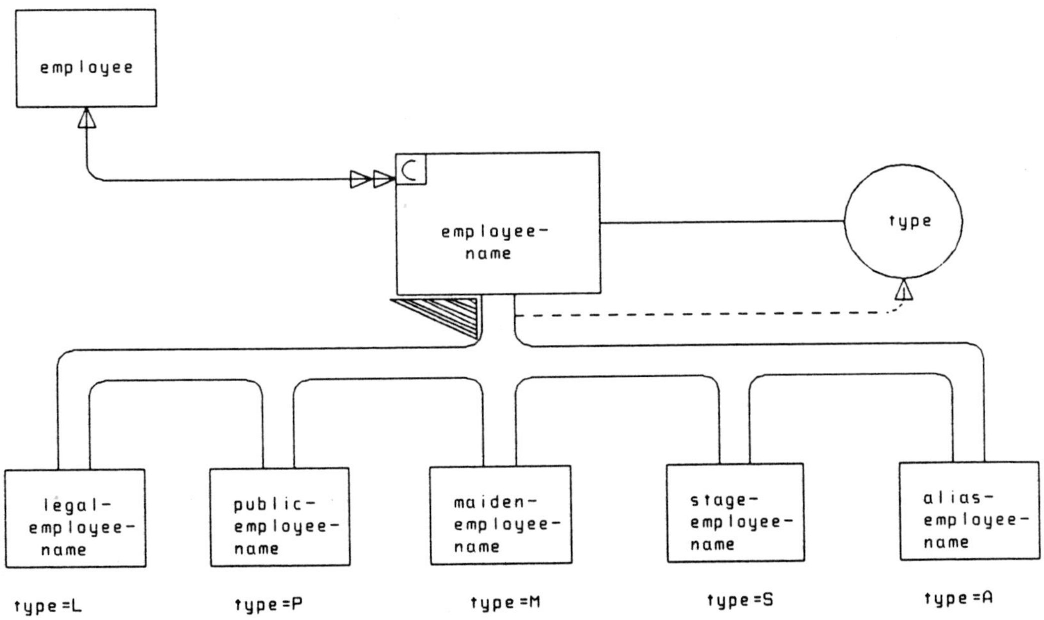

Multiple names may be associated with any employee. Each has some specified value of type, which distinguishes the names in this pro forma classification.

2.3-3 Type-codes and the Implementation of ETH

As the above examples illustrate, type-codes present one means of physically implementing any classification of an object. For lack of better implementation alternatives, they have traditionally been considered a "convenient" mechanism for that purpose.

They are also often intuitively perceived as being more performance-efficient than any alternative. Upon closer inspection, however, this argument holds up only marginally or not at all. Specifically, most DBMSs offer physical paging or blocking options that can be used to reduce significantly the I-0 impact of the additional record types needed to implement a classification without a type-code. I-0 overhead, of course, is generally held as one of the most critical factors in DBMS performance.

As the following illustration points out, there are many negatives associated with type-codes. Although the actual trade-offs are complex and subtle, serious consideration should always be given to the alternative that DBMSs offer. This alternative is elimination of the type-code and "direct" representation of a classification in pure form using the system's data structuring capability.

Diagram 2.33

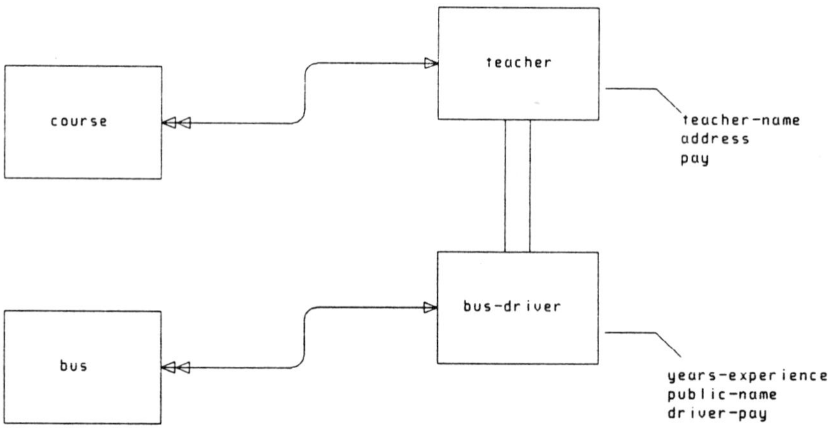

The business facts represented by this model are as follows. First, the classification reflects the business policy at this school that all bus-drivers must be teachers (the reverse is not necessarily true). Only bus-drivers can be related to buses, or given values of years-experience, public-name and driver-pay. Teachers in general, however, have a relationship to courses, and may be given values for teacher-name, address, and pay. (The entity types also have determinants, of course, but these have not been shown.)

The implications of this model are clear. Only bus-drivers can be assigned to buses and given values of years-experience, public-name, and driver-pay—not all teachers. It is logically impossible for such information to exist unless the person is truly a legitimate bus-driver. If that role for a given teacher is discontinued, all the related information simply must be deleted (or archived). Implementing the model in this exact form would ensure that all these rules would be faithfully enforced. (Most DBMSs provide the necessary integrity or update rules to automatically enforce the Rule of Precedence for classifications.)

If this classification were defined as pro forma, and implemented using a type-code, the resulting model would appear as follows.

Diagram 2.34

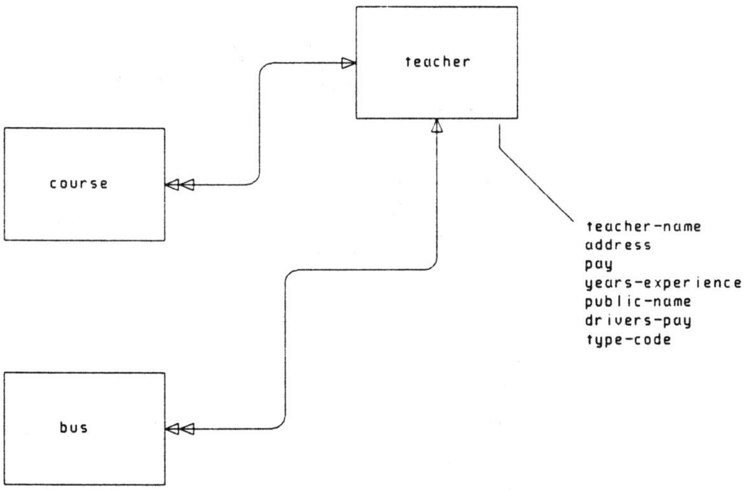

This would be the exact structure that users or programmers "see" in interacting with this database. Notice the appearance of type-code, whose values presumably could be inspected to ascertain which teachers are also bus-drivers.

The negatives associated with this implementation include the following.

- **Update anomalies.** The accuracy of this database will depend on users and programmers consistently and correctly coordinating the values of the type-code at all times. First they must always use only permissible values of the type-code and always in the correct manner. Errors in this regard, of course, may not be easily captured and explained. Beyond that, values for the attribute types years-experience, public-name, and drivers-pay, and instances of the relationship to bus, can only be legitimately offered to the database if the value of type-code is simultaneously updated to denote "bus-driver." (Otherwise, they should be null.) Should anybody (or any program) at any time ever "forget" this rule, the database immediately loses its integrity. (Some teacher, not officially marked as a bus-driver, will nonetheless possess bus-driving information.) A similar situation could occur if an existing bus-driver is discontinued in that role (the type-code value is correctly altered), but the other bus-driving information is not simultaneously deleted (or archived). The reverse is also possible. All of these anomalies create an open invitation to errors and possible contamination of database content.
- **Semantic clarity.** The type-code implementation strategy hides information about the meaning of the data, essentially burying it in the content of the database itself. Users and programmers must be subsequently prepared to operate procedurally in order to extract

it. (The "meaning" of the data is bound up in the definition and closed domain of type-code. During actual interaction with the implemented database, class membership must be ascertained by individual inspection of every record occurrence and its type-code value.) For example, the following questions cannot be answered by simple examination of the above model. Do all teachers potentially drive buses? Do all teachers potentially receive drivers-pay? What does years-experience mean, if anything, in the context of teaching? What special types or roles of teacher does this school recognize? The information needed to answer these questions is simply unavailable without additional explanation or insight.

- **User-friendliness.** Because the information needed to interpret the meaning of this database is not explicit in the model, users need to know something more than the model tells them in order to successfully interact with the database. They must know what the valid type-code values are, what they mean, and what other related rules for updating (as illustrated above) simultaneously apply. This lowers the user-friendliness of the design significantly. It may also significantly complicate the logic of requests or programs operating against the database.
- **Modification.** The issue of database change is a complex and subtle one, and it is impossible to state that one approach is always clearly superior to another on this point. However, the factor almost always missed in such assessments is the ease of broadcasting changes to programmers and to users, and to re-educate them about a modified classification scheme. Clearly, the "direct" implementation has significant advantages in this important area.

2.4 Table Handling

In any data resource, certain types of data exist whose primary function is to edit, control or even provide the values associated with attributes of other object types. In traditional methodologies, such data is commonly defined in "tables," a name consequently used to describe the form of the data itself. The labels "editing table," "validation table," or "look-up table" are also commonly used.

The concept of "table" is not formally necessary in the entity modeling approach. Indeed a "table" can always be modeled using one or more entity types, with the appropriate determinants and attributes. The entity types so identified, however, often have little seeming correspondence to the real external entities of the enterprise, nor few, if any, "normal" business interactions—i.e., relationship types. Often, the only real connections to the rest of the model are those involved with integrity constraints. (The reader may wish to review Section 3.1-1 on integrity constraints before examining the present discussion.)

Since the notion of "table," however, is relatively familiar to professionals and others, and since it can be simulated quite easily using entity modeling constructs, practitioners may find its use to be convenient and worthwhile in their more detailed enterprise modeling activities. For these reasons, the handling of tables is explored more fully in the present section.

2.4-1 Basic Table Representation

Tables are generally used for closed domains whose values are nonetheless too numerous to list individually. An example is zip code.

Diagram 2.35

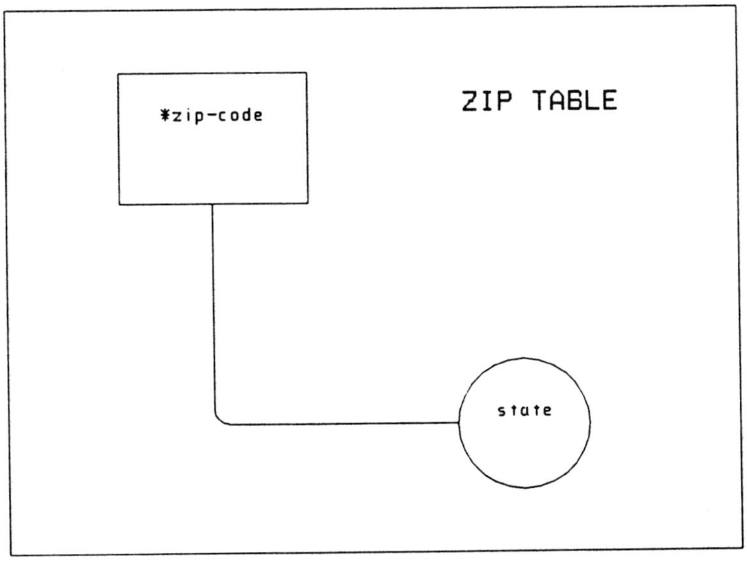

"Zip table" is defined as an aggregate object. (The use of the aggregate object permits the bounds of the table to be identified and named.) The determinant of the single entity type in the table is zip-code (this is the field used to "enter" the table), and this entity type has one attribute, state. Upon implementation, this table would contain all valid zip codes, and the state where each is located.

The utility of this table is primarily for editing the attribute values of other object types—namely, anywhere zip-code is used. This is represented using a "mandatory" integrity constraint.

Diagram 2.36

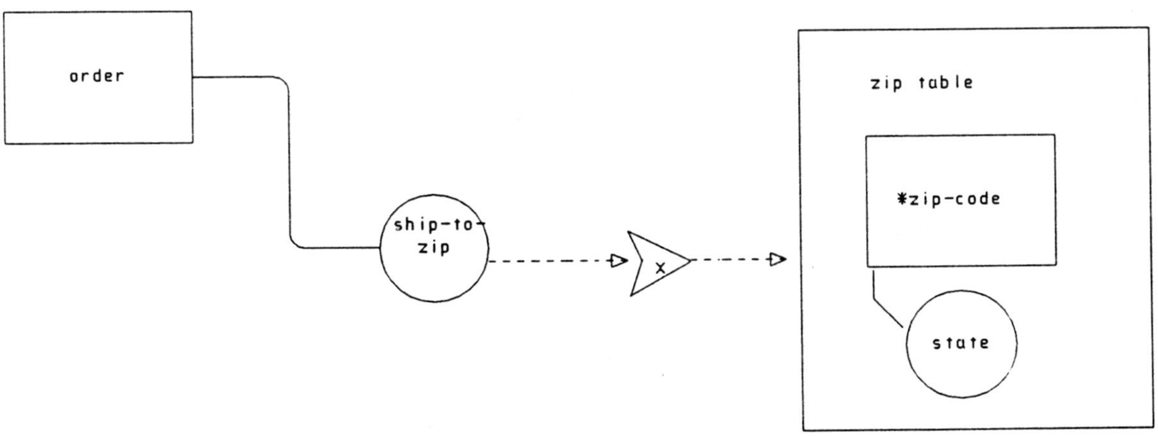

In this example, for the given value of an order's ship-to-zip to be correct, it must always be among the valid zip-code values "listed" within the table.

A somewhat more powerful "editing" constraint would be the following.

Diagram 2.37

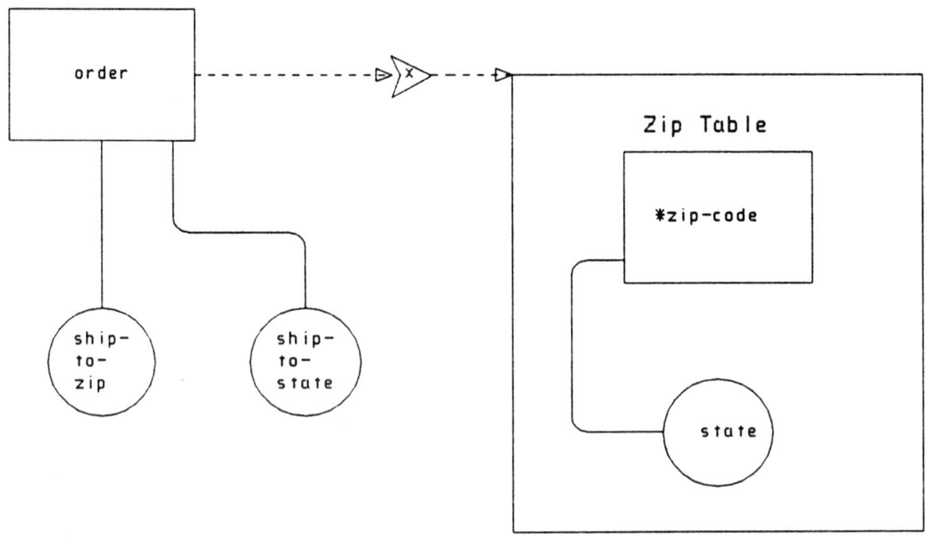

In this version, the former constraint remains in effect—that is, ship-to-date must be among the valid "entries" in the table. But now, the given ship-to-state value must (continuously) agree with the "correct" value of state as "listed" for the associated table value of zip-code. In essence, the value of ship-to-zip is being used to "look-up" the correct table value of state, to ensure that the value of ship-to-state is (continuously) correct. Note: If any ambiguity exists as to which attribute types may be involved in the verification (for example, because order has several attribute types drawn from the domain of state), then either the connections should be drawn directly from the attribute types in question, or a numbered textual note should be appended to the integrity constraint. (So as to avoid clutter, the latter is recommended.)

2.4-1.1 Table Look-ups versus Relationship Types

The basic "structure" of the above examples could have been implemented in conventional entity/relationship form. That is, ship-to-zip would be foreign key to the regular entity type "zip," establishing a mandatory relationship type for "order" between the two. (Drawing this revised version is left as an exercise to the reader. What referential integrity specification would be appropriate? Refer to Section 3.1-2.) This reveals an important insight concerning tables—in essence, they are merely entity types that are not being portrayed and connected in the "normal" way.

There may be several reasons for doing this. In the first place, the given domain(s) may be closed—and perhaps essentially under control of some outside enterprise. (This is certainly the case for zip-code—unless, of course, the enterprise happens to be the Postal Service.) The associated entity types therefore may be considered "marginal"—meaning either essentially "outside" the normal scope of business activities, or difficult to interpret in the usual entity sense. (This latter point is especially true for more complex tables.)

The decision to handle modeling questions using tables (and integrity constraints) rather than conventional relationship types may also be a purely practical one, aimed at avoiding clutter and excessive numbers of relatively unimportant relationship types. (Imagine, for example, all the places where zip-code is likely to appear in an entire entity model, and the resulting number of relationship types if handled in the usual fashion!) Finally, it may be desirable to show only integrity constraints, rather than relationships, where such connections would otherwise cross implementation zone boundaries (e.g., as in subject databases or distributed systems).

2.4-1.1-1 Handling Dates

The comments on zip-code above also hold true in the case of "dates," as the following window diagram illustrates.

Diagram 2.38

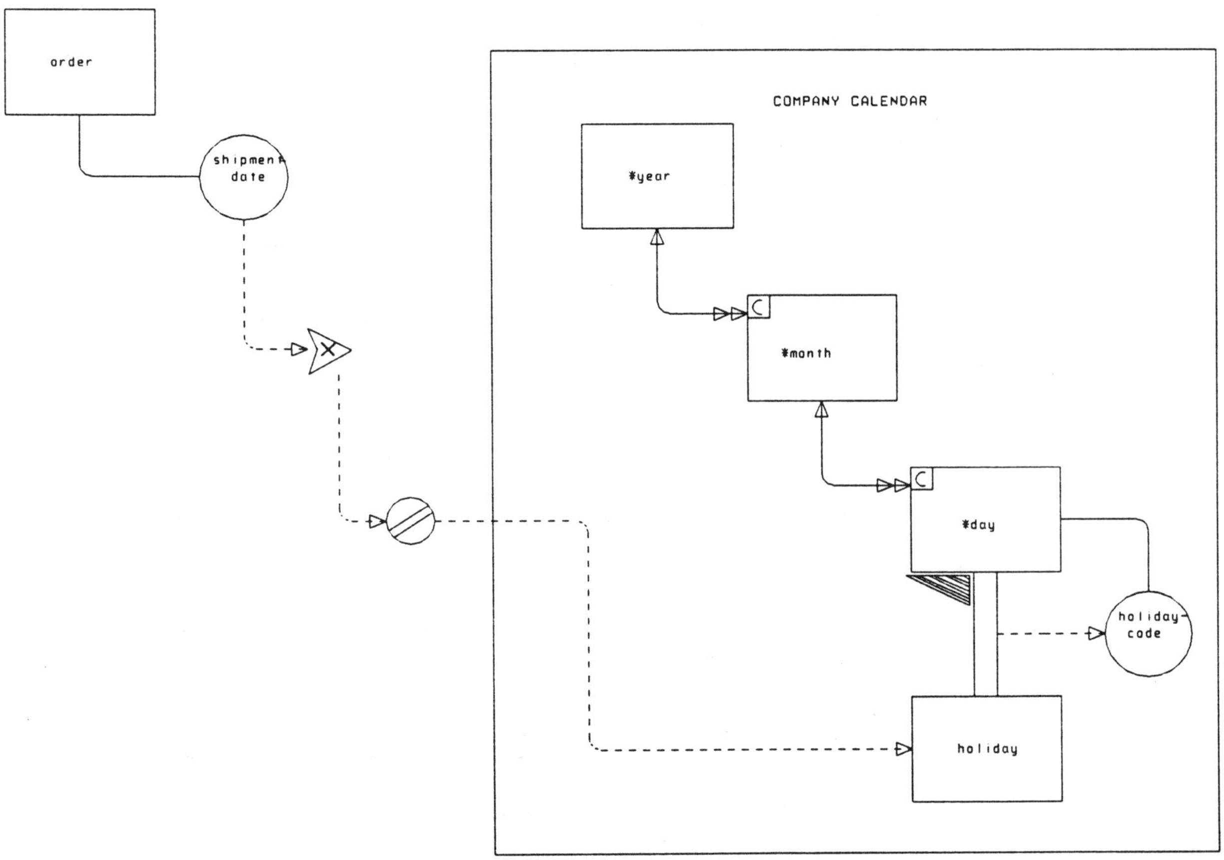

Here a table of dates has been defined called "company calendar." This table is used to identify holidays and thereby to reject any value of order shipment-date that happens to fall on such dates. (A "not" symbol is used in conjunction with the mandatory integrity constraint to define this policy. Note that the holiday classification is actually pro forma, with the attribute holiday-code—a type-code—serving as the "source.") Imagine the number of relationship types that would proliferate across an entire entity model if every appearance of date as an attribute actually produced a relationship type to the "company calendar"!

2.4-1.1-2 Handling Defined Lists

A final point on the use of tables is the following. In the case where the actual table values are few enough that they may be listed exhaustively, the use of tables may provide a convenient manner to express established business rules in the very same context as the entity model itself.

Diagram 2.39

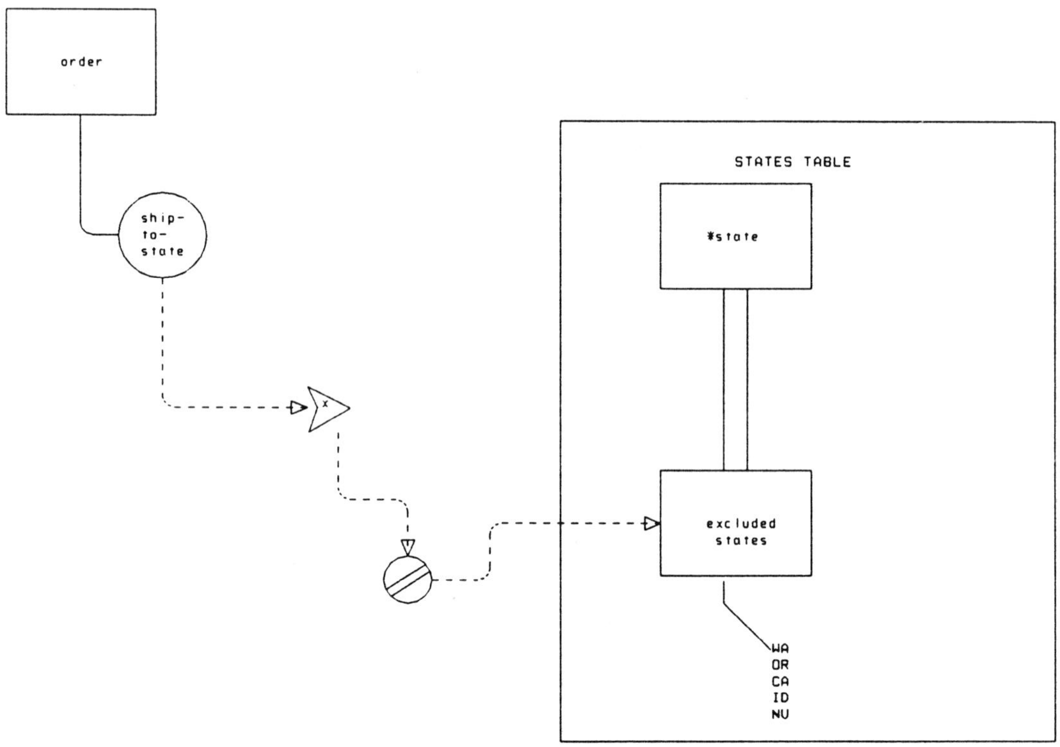

This company cannot accept orders that must be shipped to states where they do not do business—namely, Washington, Oregon, California, Idaho and Nevada.

2.4-1.1-3 Handling Ranges

Another reason for handling certain data as tables, rather than as "normal" entity types, is because the determinant values are actually ranges rather than individual (unitary) values. It is hard to visualize a "normal" entity occurrence, of course, having a range of values as its determinant.

Diagram 2.40

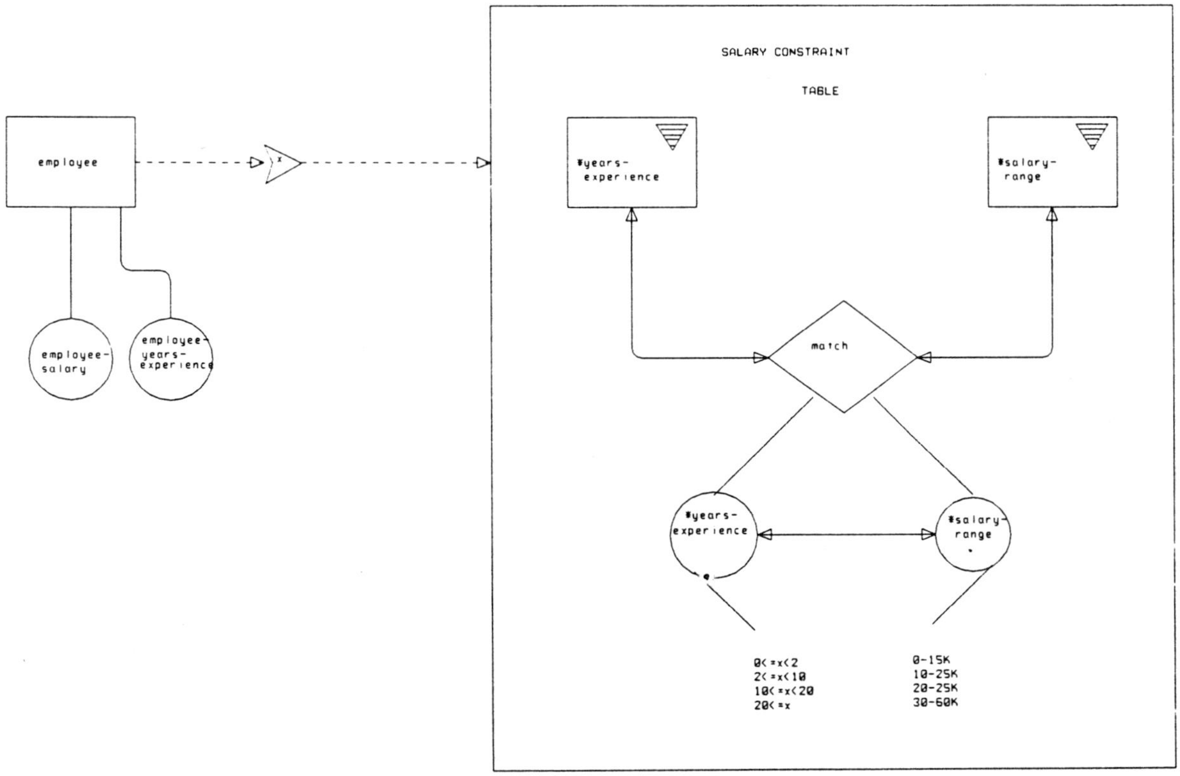

This table establishes valid salary ranges for employees, given years of experience. Note that the determinants of the table have ranges as values rather than individual, unitary values. It may be desirable to actually define these domains in this fashion, as the following permits. Such domains are called **ranging domains**.

Diagram 2.41

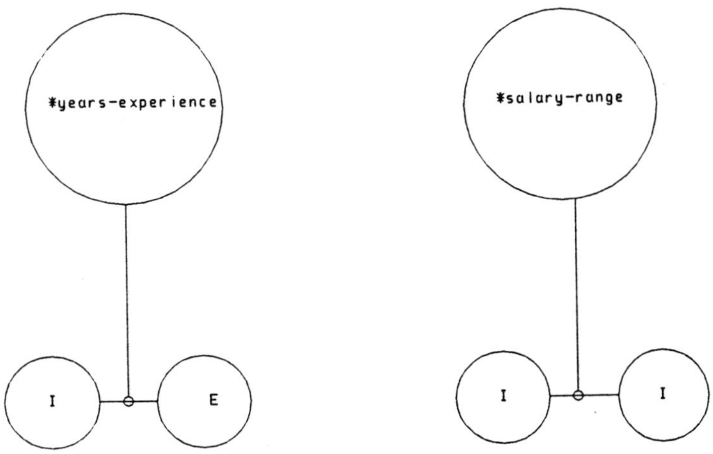

The special symbols for years-experience and salary-range define the domains as consisting of paired range values. The "I" stands for "inclusive"; the "E" for exclusive. Actually, this is a special form of composite definition, with the partition omitted. The unabbreviated forms would appear as follows.

Diagram 2.42

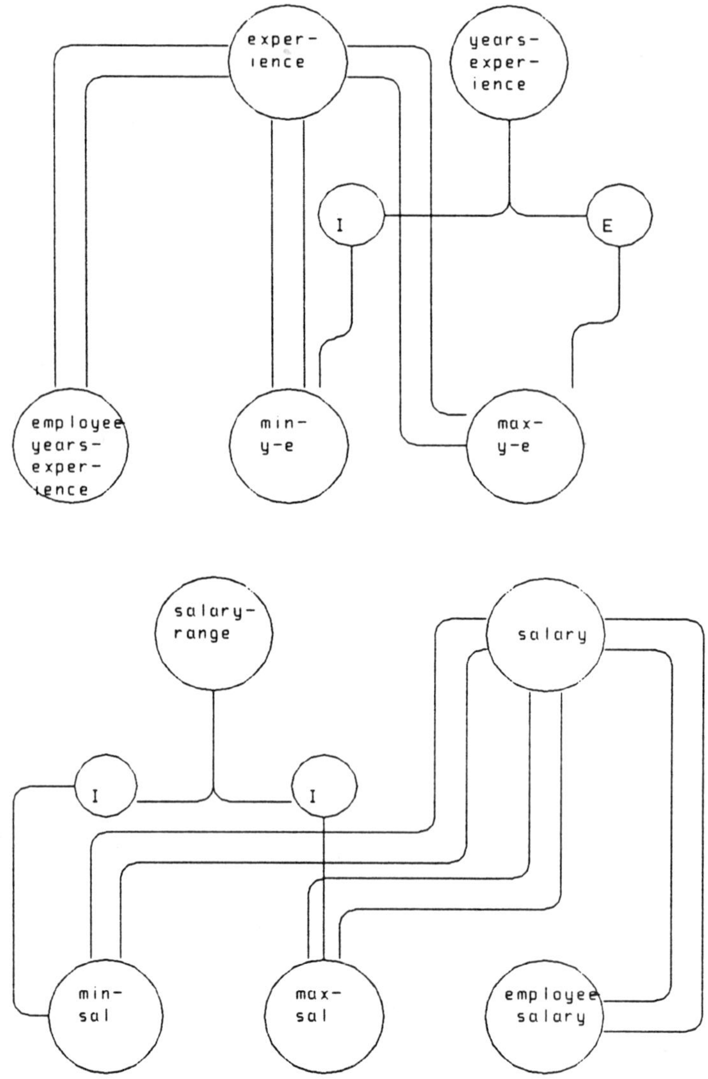

Note incidentally, that the values (i.e., range values) of salary-range overlap. This presents no problem, however, since the ranges defined are still nonetheless distinct.

The "salary constraint table" in Diagram 2.40 was defined in a more comprehensive manner than probably necessary. Specifically, both years-experience and salary-range were defined as "entry points," so that a value of either could be verified against the other. These entity types, however, were marked as "nonstored," resulting in "match" becoming the primary stored object. This could have been represented directly simply by showing "match" as a kernel entity type having two determinants.

2.4-2 Complex Table Handling

The tables needed for editing, validation, and control of any given data resource can become quite complex—as complex, in fact, as the real life businesses they support. The following sampling is offered to provide suggestions about how to handle more complex tables. It is recommended that these conventions be used only relatively late in the development of an entity model, where complete consistency of presentation technique and specification is desired.

Diagram 2.43

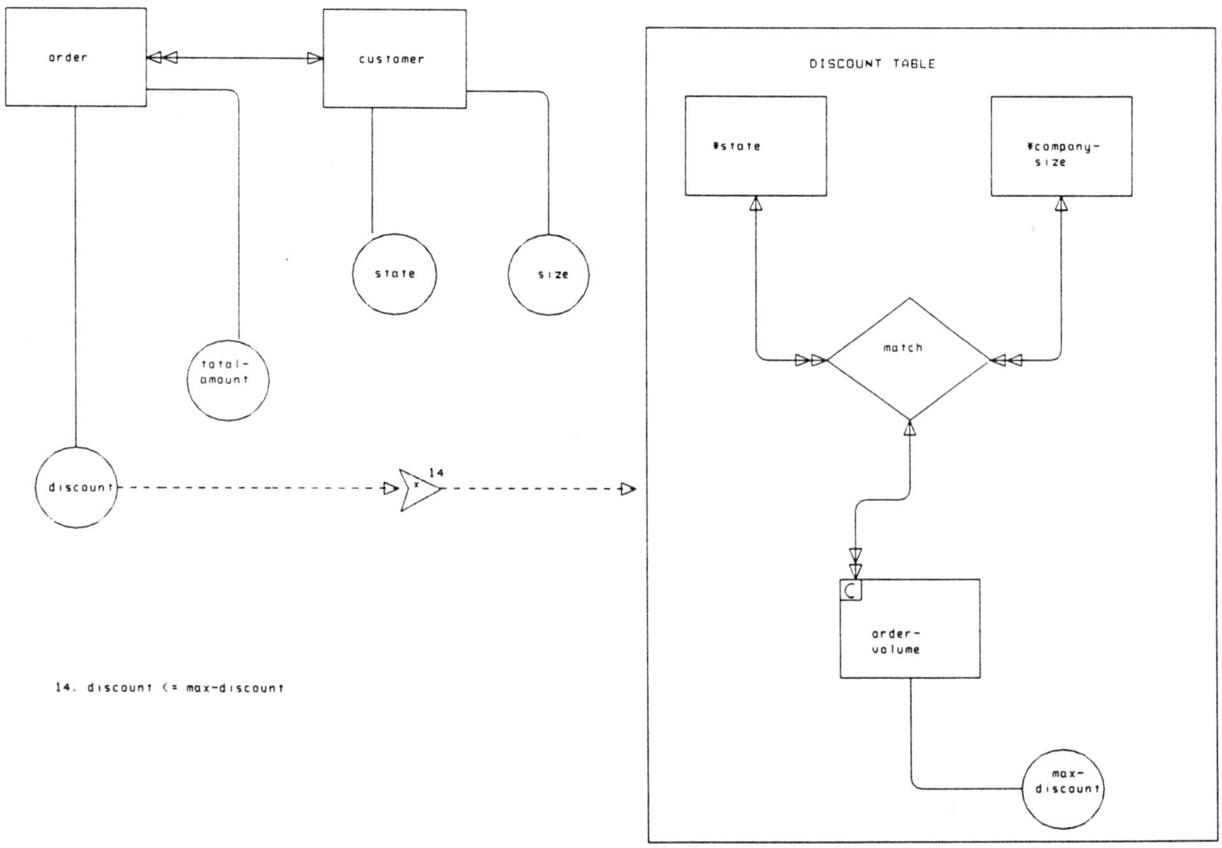

When a (new) discount value is given to an order, the amount of the discount cannot exceed a certain defined maximum value, depending on the total amount of the order, and on the state and size of the company placing that order.

2.4-2.1 The Time Dimension in Tables

Frequently, validation such as the above is time-dependent—that is, permissible discounts vary with time. For example, applicable breakdowns of company size might vary with time, as could maximum discount permitted. This could be shown as follows.

Diagram 2.44

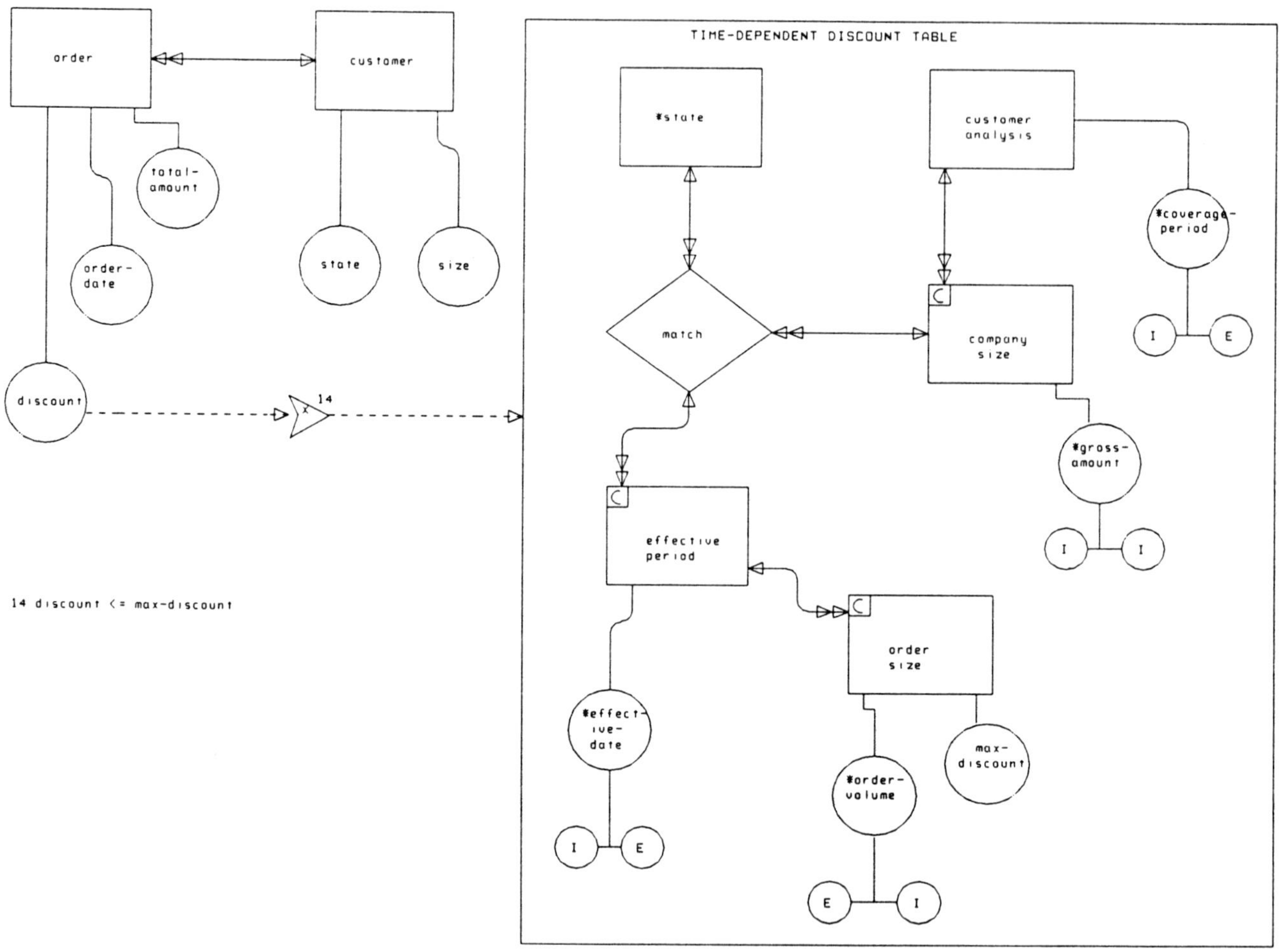

In this example, order-date is used to select a table entry for customer analysis (based on coverage-period), and then an entry for effective period (based on effective-date). These and other attributes in the table have been indicated as ranging domains. (More specifications in the integrity constraint note than shown are probably desirable to clarify this.)

2.4-2.2 Tables and Classification

Tables often provide selective values for classes of objects. This means that the classification of an object must be reflected in the composition of the table. This is illustrated in Diagram 2.45.

Customers are classified into residential, commercial, and government, and values for order discount are validated accordingly (also using order-amount and effective-date). A composite domain discount-set has been defined for the table exactly reflecting the classification of customer.

Diagram 2.45

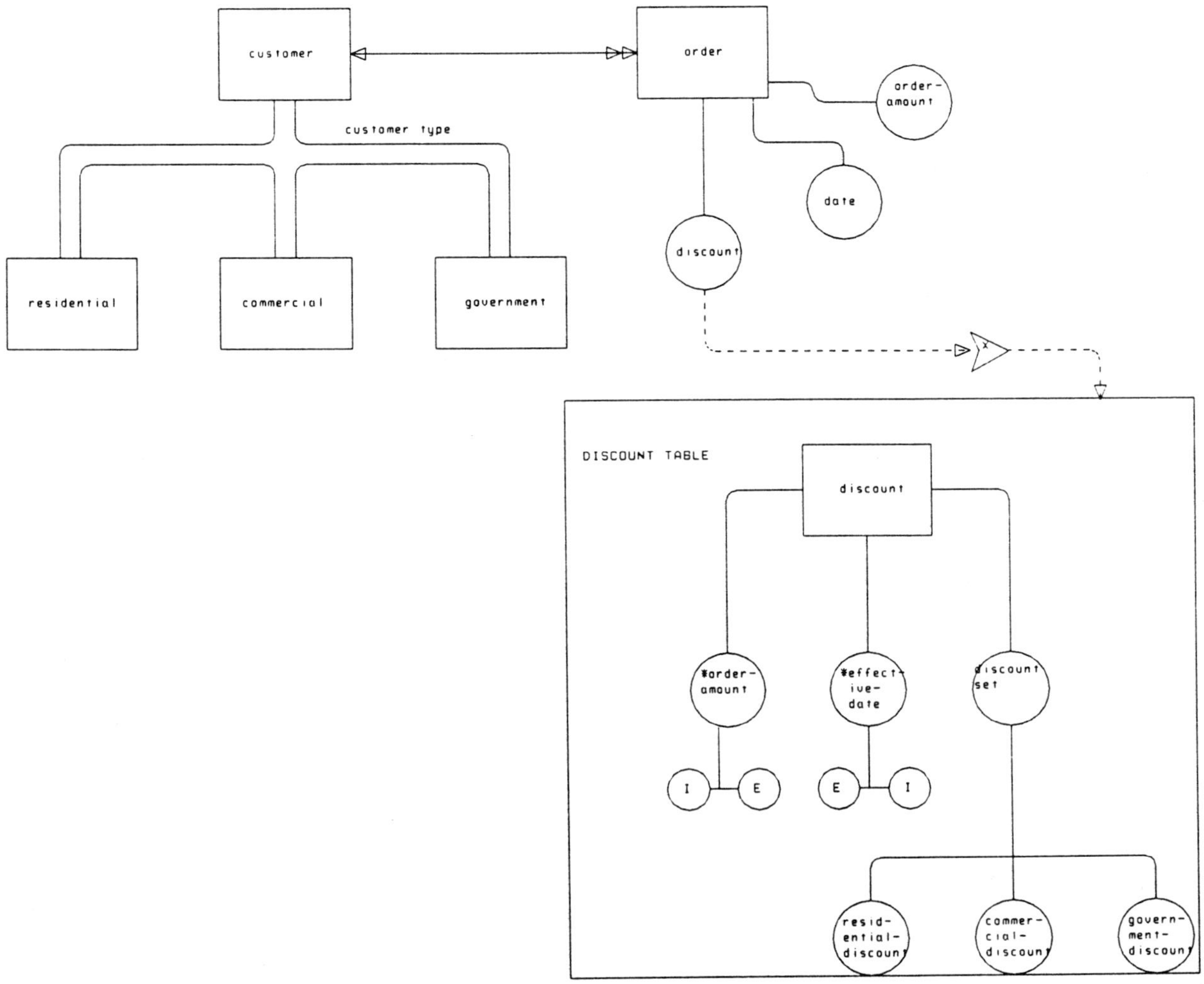

A domain such as this is called a **reflective composite domain** because its partitions match or "reflect" some classification on an exact 1-to-1 basis. For convenience, such a domain may also be defined as follows, simply using the name of the relevant classification.

Diagram 2.46

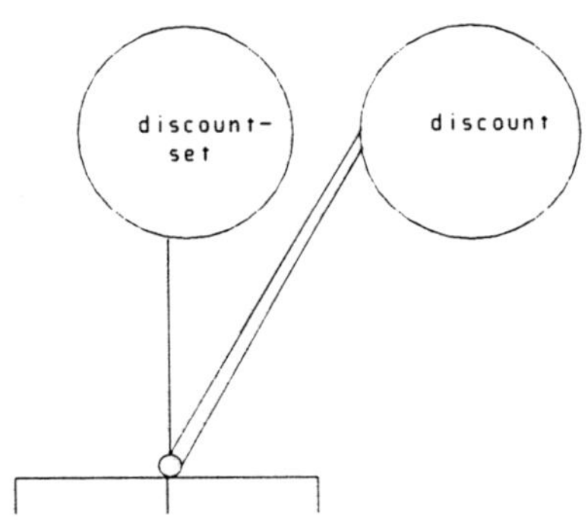

More complex reflective domains may be defined using Cartesian products. For example, suppose that orders were also classified in the following manner, and that the breakdowns were needed in "discount table."

Diagram 2.47

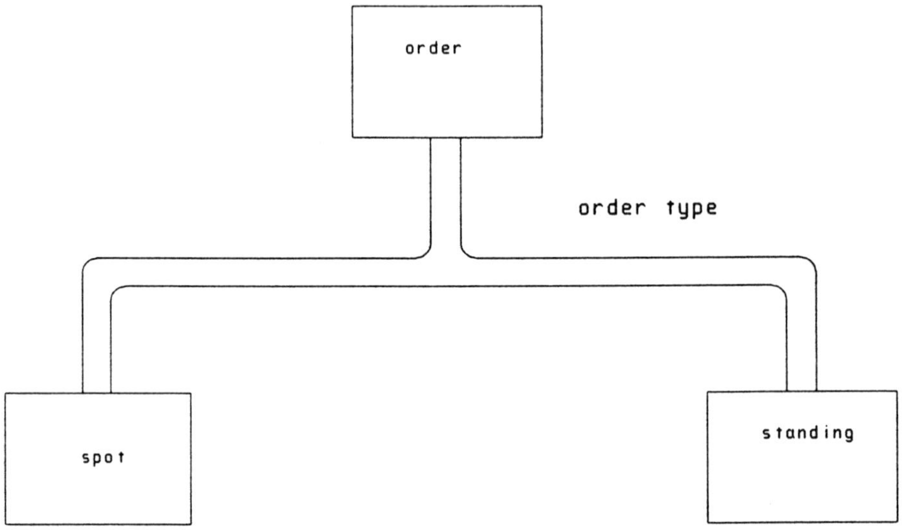

Discount-set would thus need to be defined as follows.

Diagram 2.48

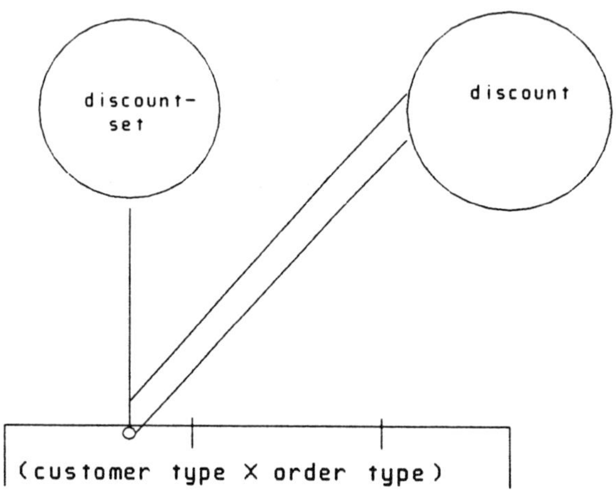

Discount-set would now consist of six partitions, one for each possible combination of customer type and order type subtypes.

An alternative to the above implementation of discount table would involve making customer type into a type-code domain, and using it as an entry point into the table. This might appear as follows. (In practice, abbreviated codes for the customer types would probably substitute.)

Diagram 2.49

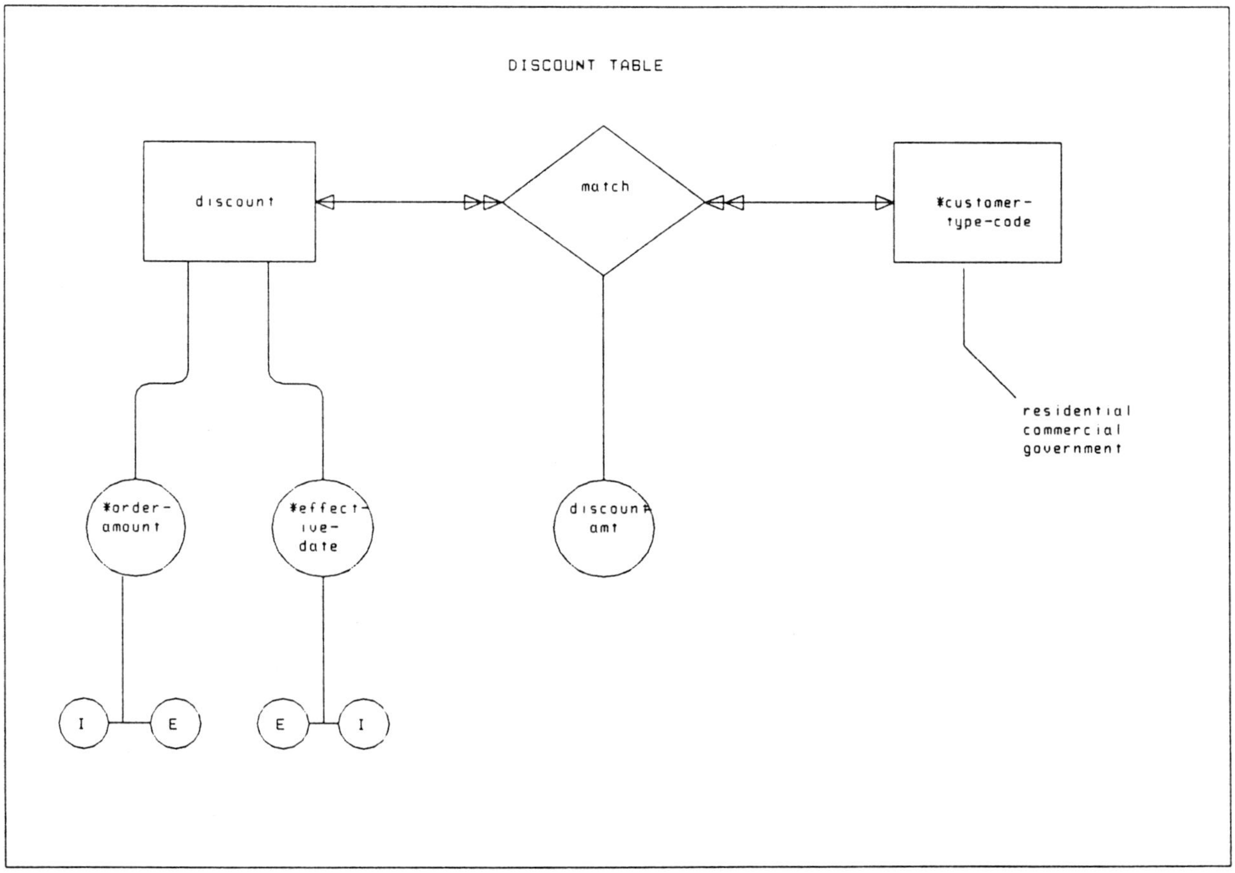

In this version, the types of customers appear as actual values in the table, rather than as attribute names. It should be noted that this invites many of the same negatives previously discussed in connection with the general use of type-codes to implement classifications. (See Section 2.3-2.) However, if the customer type classification were pro forma and implemented using a type-code, then consistent implementation within associated tables would probably be desirable.

2.4-2.3 Tables and Behavior

The analysis of behavior—rules that control updating and thus the integrity of a data resource—is the subject of Part III. Since tables are often significantly involved in defining such behavior for an entity model, several examples are previewed here.

Diagram 2.50

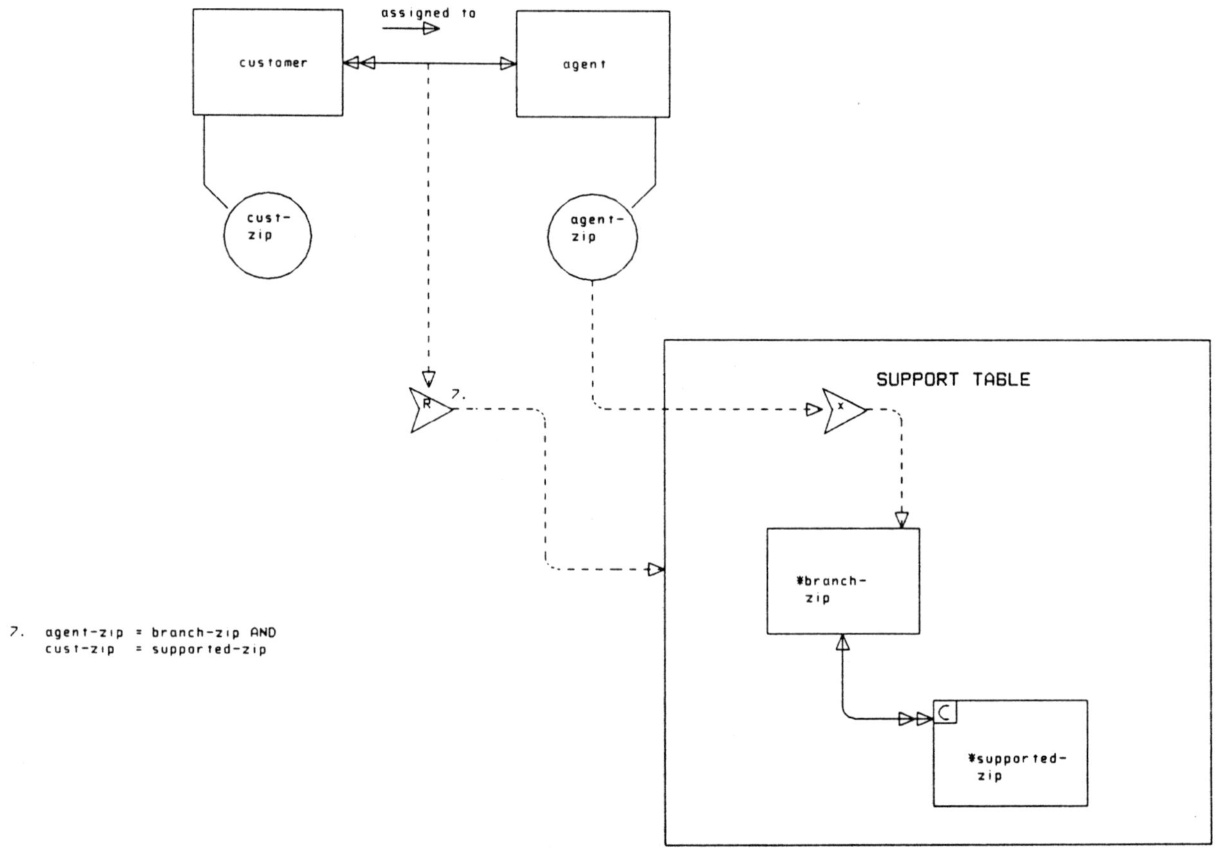

Correct instances of the indicated relationship type are restricted to cases where the customer's zip code is among those actually supported by the associated agent.

2.4-2.3-1 Automatic Table-based Updating

Automatic actions in an entity model specify when certain types of updating are to take place (see Section 3.1-3). These specifications can be used to define automatic table-based updating.

In Diagram 2.51, the value of an order's ship-to-state is provided automatically (via the "propagation" automatic action) from zip table. The provision of a new or revised value for the ship-to-zip for an order (presumably by the user) automatically triggers this update. Should the table value of state associated with the zip subsequently change (unlikely in this case), that changed value would be automatically propagated to ship-to-state. The value of est-delay is also automatically initialized in this specification (by the same trigger as above) to the current table value of avg-delay. (If the table value of avg-delay subsequently changes, however, the change is not automatically "propagated" to est-delay.)

Diagram 2.51

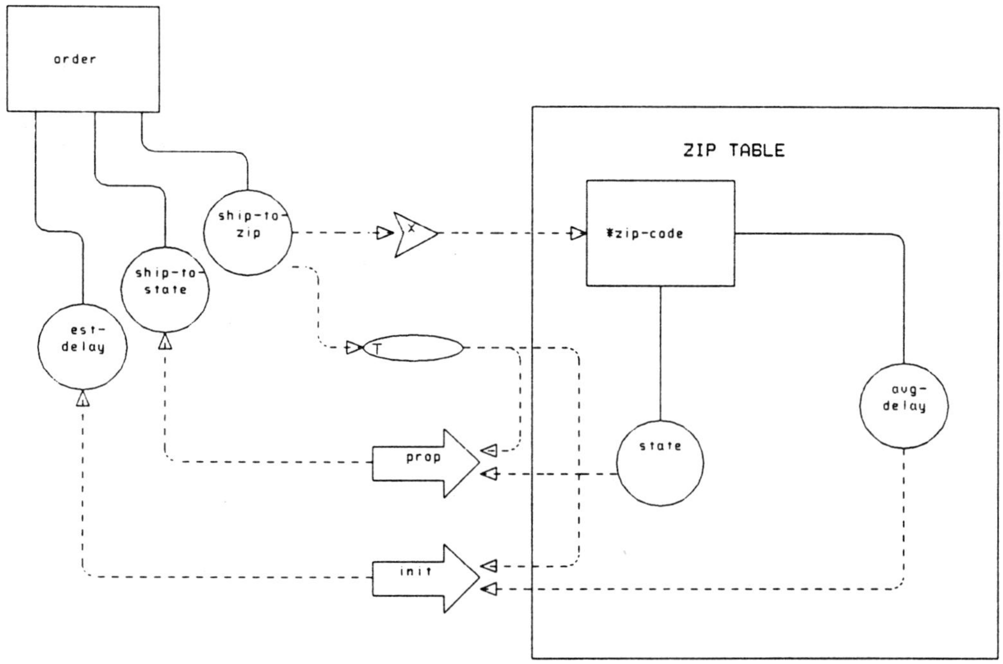

GUIDELINES AND CONVENTIONS FOR TABLES

- Use tables to establish editing and control values.
- The boundaries of a table are delineated using an aggregate object, which is named appropriately.
- Objects outside the table are bound to it by integrity constraints, rather than relationship types, even though a value basis for such relationships does exist.
- Use notes for integrity constraints to avoid ambiguity and to specify value conditions more precisely.
- Ranging domains, which have lower and upper limits defined as partitions, may be used as determinants (or nondeterminants) in tables.
- Use reflective composite domains in tables to match non-pro forma classifications within the entity model.
- Tables are especially useful for entity types that fall outside the scope of the enterprise's control; that are difficult to interpret in the usual sense; and/or that are so broadly connected across the model as to clutter it significantly. Zip codes, calendar dates, and organizational charts are frequent candidates for tables.

Diagram 2.52

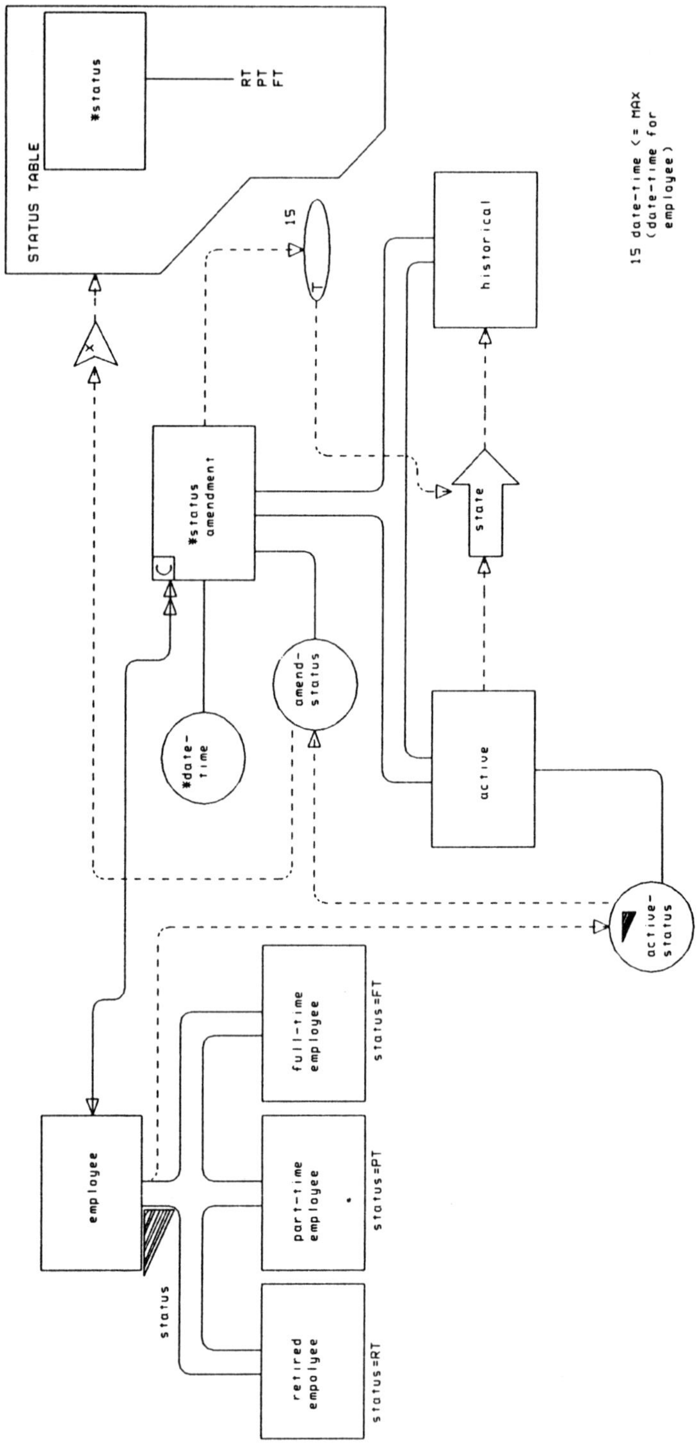

Employees are classified by pro forma "status," whose source is the active-status attribute of the most recent status amendment. (The trigger acts so as to never leave more than one occurrence of status amendment—the most recent—in the "active" subtype.) Active-status, however, is a pro forma attribute whose source is amend-status. Values of amend-status must be continuously correct according to the defined values of status table, which thereby governs the behavior of this model.

PART 3: BEHAVIOR

3.0 Behavior

An entity model has been viewed thus far in this text as more or less a static collection of objects and connections that correspond to real things and their interactions in the enterprise. This collection becomes a blueprint for implementation of one or more corresponding database(s), which provide for that collection to be populated by actual data. Throughout this population and subsequent use, the ultimate authority for interpreting the meaning of the data (i.e., its "semantics") remains the entity model itself.

Very little has been said, however, about the integrity of that data—in other words, rules that apply in keeping it correct at all times. In fact, in all only three general integrity rules have thus far been formulated (in Part I). These are reiterated below.

As these rules suggest, the correctness of database content can only be compromised when its content is being extended or modified—in other words, during updating. The rules that apply to a database during updating are therefore designated as the **behavior** of the corresponding entity model.

GENERAL INTEGRITY RULES

Integrity Rule #1 (Association Types)
An occurrence of an association type can only exist if the object occurrences it relates exist. It can only be created if each occurrence of every related object already exists. Deleting any one of the related object occurrences causes the association type occurrence to be deleted automatically.

Integrity Rule #2 (Characteristics)
An occurrence of a characteristic can only exist if the corresponding occurrence of the object characterized exists. It can only be created if the occurrence of the object characterized already exists. Deleting the occurrence of the object characterized causes the characteristic occurrence to be deleted automatically.

Integrity Rule #3 (Classifications)
An occurrence of a subtype can only exist if the corresponding occurrence of its supertype exists. It can only be created if the corresponding occurrence of its supertype already exists. Deleting the related occurrence of the supertype causes the subtype occurrence to be deleted automatically.

As opposed to a static, object-oriented view, such behavior therefore gives a dynamic view of the actual operation of the database.

An entity model, of course, is a mirror image of some particular enterprise. That enterprise naturally has dozens or hundreds of specific rules (or business policies) that govern its own behavior and distinguish it from others. Since these rules govern changes in the status of the enterprise, they translate directly into updating rules for its database(s). They thus represent specific integrity rules (i.e., behavior) that can be defined for its own entity model(s).

Such specific integrity rules, even though "shared" and universal to the enterprise (just like its data should be) have not traditionally been captured in the context of its entity model(s). Instead, they have usually been stated vaguely (if at all) in largely uncoordinated analytical and design documents, and then buried deep in the logic of application programs. Since application programs are notoriously unreliable in the consistent and correct application of such rules, this has often been the source of considerable frustration and error. It has sometimes also led, unjustly, to distrust of the database design itself.

The entity model provides a promising alternative for the analysis and specification of such universal, enterprise-specific "behavior." Its rules can be superimposed onto the existing framework of objects and relationship types, creating what is sometimes called a **conceptual schema**. (The resulting database system is also sometimes called **intelligent**.) The purpose of Part III is to explore this important opportunity as fully as possible.

3.0-1 Levels of Detail

Consideration of an entity model's behavior represents more detailed and refined analysis of a data resource than entertained in Part I. It therefore requires a new and expanded set of symbols and connections for the entity model.

In Section 0.2, five cumulative levels of detail were discussed, with new symbols and connections introduced within each. Part I primarily discussed the first two of these, **Presentation** and **Professional**.

The new behavior objects now examined fall into the latter three levels of detail, **Integrity**, **Attributes** and **Measurement**.

- **Integrity:** These specify what conditions must be examined and/or preserved in the database when updating of some particular part is requested. They may also specify what additional updates must occur.
- **Attributes:** Updating and measurement in a database often require detailed field-level conditions to be met. These may include key specifications, integrity constraint value conditions, and attribute triggers.
- **Measurement:** These specify that updates of certain database parts automatically invoke arithmetic operations (e.g., ongoing "measurement" of how many, how much, how often, etc.).

3.0-2 The Operation of Behavior

Behavior is an apt designation for what is involved in understanding and specifying rules for updating in an entity model. Specifically, a "behavior" always consists of a stimulus, something that provokes or causes a behavior to take place, and a reaction to that stimulus, the "behavior" itself. No behavior can be completely defined without definition of both the stimulus and the reaction.

In specifying behavior "objects" for an entity model (i.e., the specific updating rules that apply), the identification of both a stimulus "side" and a reaction (or behavior) "side" is therefore necessary. The definition of a behavior (a rule for updating) in an entity model thus always conceptually appears something like this.

Diagram 3.1

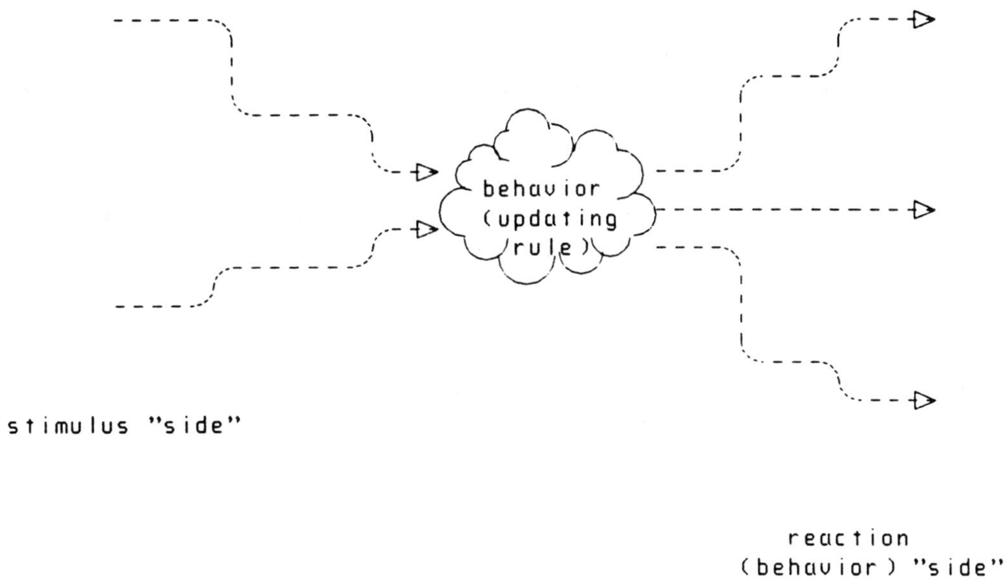

As the next section discusses, there are four different types of automatic behavior (and subclasses within each) that may be defined using behavior objects. These objects always have at least one stimulus side connector coming "into" them, and one reaction side connector coming "out" of them. (Dashed lines are recommended for showing these connectors—this clearly distinguishes them from relationship types.) The connectors link the behavior object (i.e., update rule) with other relevant portions of the database, where the actual stimuli and reactions respectively occur.

Unlike many other objects of an entity model (e.g., entity types, association types, etc.), an automatic behavior object is seldom selectively named by the creator of the entity model. Instead, a specific behavior object is identified by a coded, arbitrary number (not meaningful in itself), which may be used to link it with explanatory text or more precise specification in some associated document.

Diagram 3.2

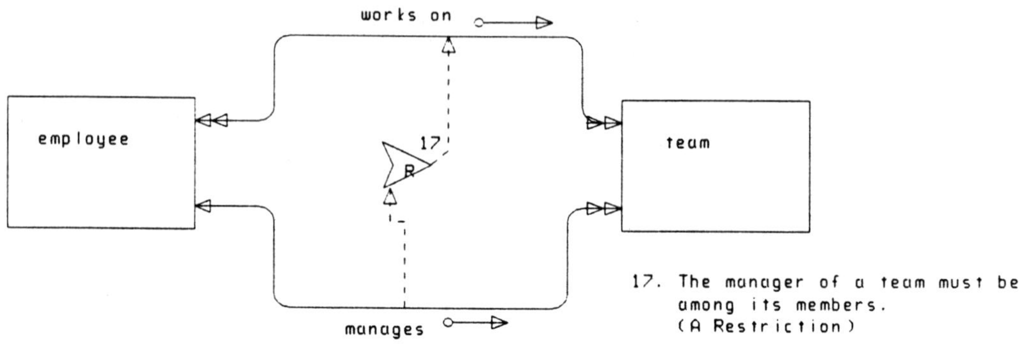

Because of the "clutter" factor, liberal use of "zoom" window diagrams to specify all forms of automatic behavior is strongly recommended.

3.0-3 Types of Behavior

There are four general types of automatic behavior that can be specified for an entity model. Each has its own specific object type. As the remainder of this Part explains, there are numerous subclasses for each behavior type (except triggers). A designation for the appropriate subclass generally is placed inside the behavior object defining the behavior, as the above example illustrated (i.e., "R").

The four general types of behavior are enumerated opposite along with definitions of the relevant stimuli and reactions for each. See Appendix IV for a complete set of rules governing stimulus and reaction connections.

Diagram 3.3

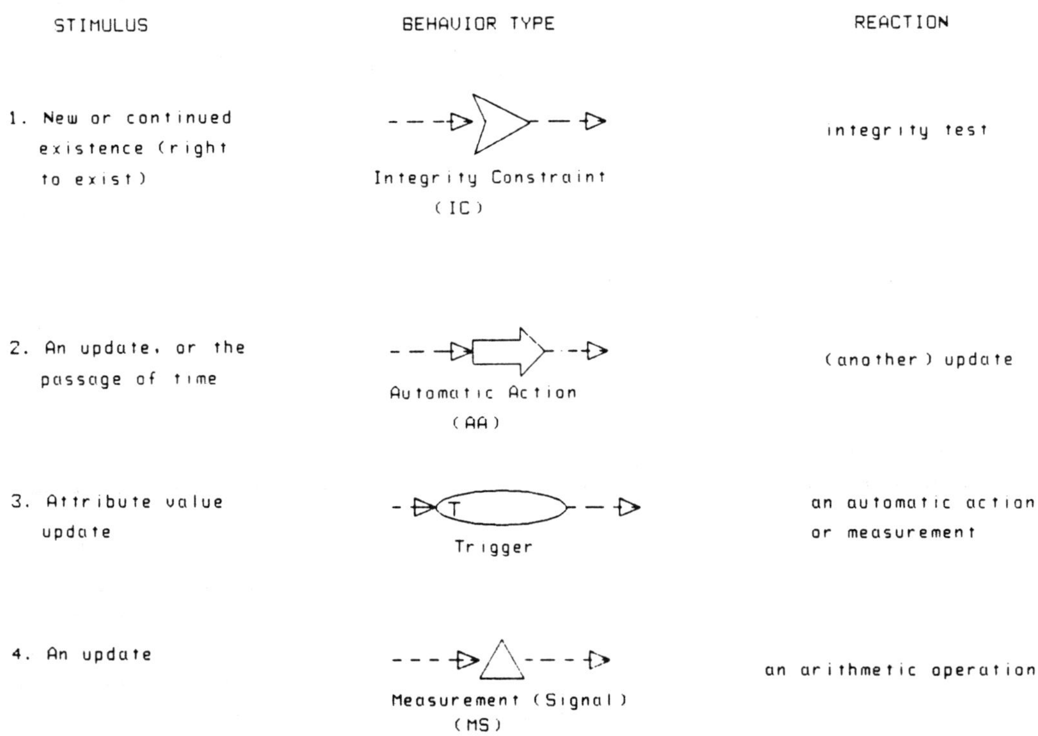

3.0-4 Implementation

Unfortunately, existing DBMS (including relational) do not support most of the forms of automatic behavior discussed below. The practitioner is therefore reminded that the associated graphic representation techniques are primarily intended for requirements definition (i.e., capturing "business rules") and for analysis. There are obvious implications for application implementation architectures; however, these are not discussed in this text.

SECTION 1 Integrity-Level Objects and Connections

Various enterprise-specific updating rules are necessary to maintain the ongoing integrity of database content. These rules specify what conditions must exist in the database for the updates to occur, or certain additional updates that must automatically take place whenever some specific update is desired.

3.1-1 Integrity Constraints (ICs)

These rules for updating specify conditions in the database that must be met (and checked continuously) for something to exist. This "thing" is on the stimulus side (since its right to exist must be continuously checked), whereas the things actually checked in the behavior are on the reaction side. In a sense, the IC actually becomes a property of the "thing," although not a property in the sense of attributes.

An integrity constraint generally answers these three questions:

- Can an occurrence of the thing be added? (This stimulates a check of relevant conditions on the reaction side.)
- Can an occurrence of the thing continue to legitimately exist if established conditions (on the reaction side) are changed?
- Can an occurrence of the thing continue to legitimately exist if something already established (on the reaction side) is deleted? (This also stimulates a re-evaluation on the reaction side.)

Integrity constraint subclasses are listed below. Each of these subclasses is individually discussed in the remainder of this section.

Integrity Constraints (ICs)

R	**Restricted**	Existence of instances of one or more relationship types is contingent on the existence of instance(s) of one or more other relationship types.
X	**Mandatory**	Existence of an object is contingent on the existence of one or more other objects and/or connections.
ME	**Mutually Exclusive**	Existence of an object precludes co-existence of two or more other objects and/or connections.

(Continued)

LIM	**Limited**	Existence of an object places defined limits on the number of some other object(s) and/or connections.
FIX	**Frozen**	Existence of one or more objects and/or connections requires discontinuation of updating for certain other objects and/or things.

3.1-1.1 Restricted

Occurrences of certain relationship types in an entity model can only exist so long as occurrences of certain other relationship types or objects continue to exist. The existence of such relationship types is therefore **restricted**. An appropriate IC behavior object is used to define such restrictions.

Diagram 3.4

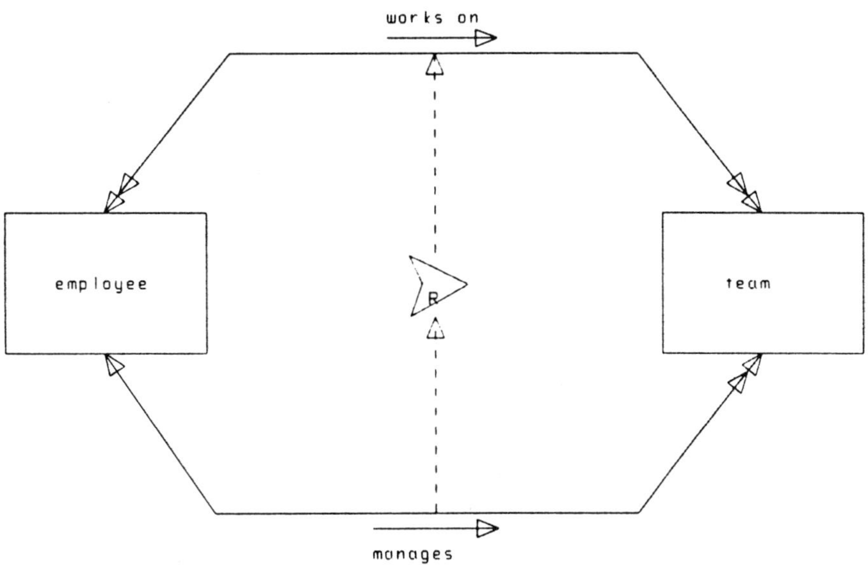

In this example, the manager of a team must also always be a member of that same team. In other words, there must always exist an instance of "works on" that is identical to each instance of "manages."

The integrity constraint object marked "R" has been introduced to specify this rule. It is connected from the relationship type so restricted ("manages") to the relationship type restricting ("works on"). (Incidentally, exactly the same restriction as above could be defined even if an association type is placed into "works on." The reaction side connector would then merely point to the new association type.)

Diagram 3.5

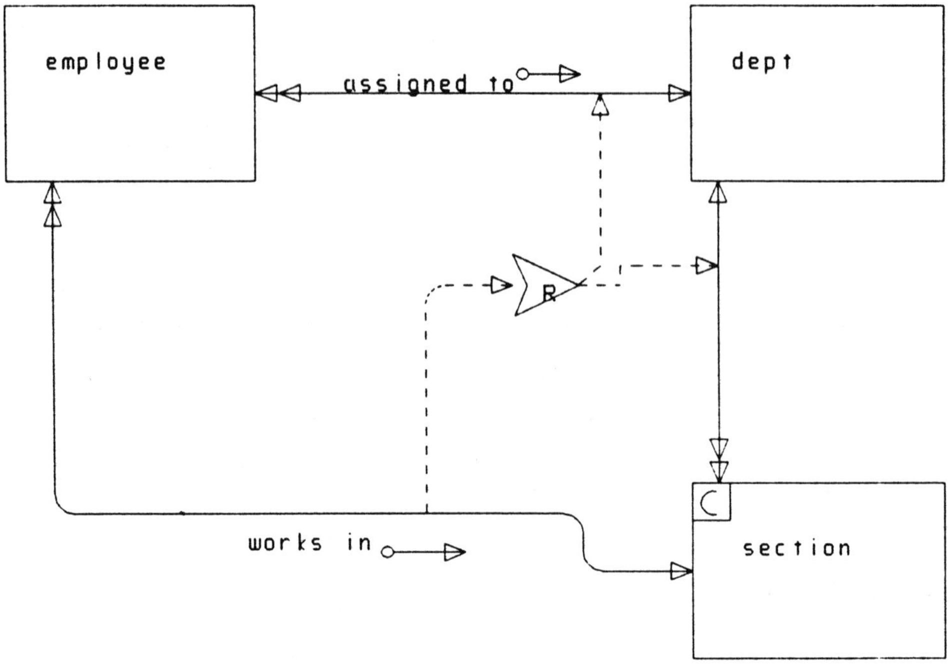

In this example, an employee can only work in a section of a department to which he or she is assigned.

Diagram 3.6

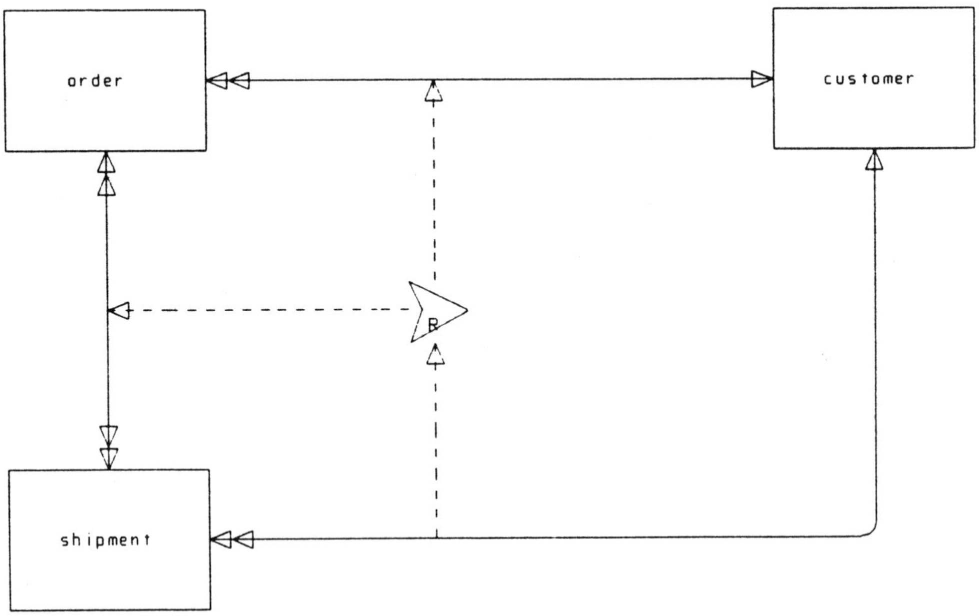

This example shows that a shipment cannot be sent to a customer who did not order it.

3.1-1.1-1 "Not" Restrictions

It is often desirable to indicate that existence of occurrences of a relationship type is contingent on equivalent occurrences of one or more other relationship types not existing.

Diagram 3.7

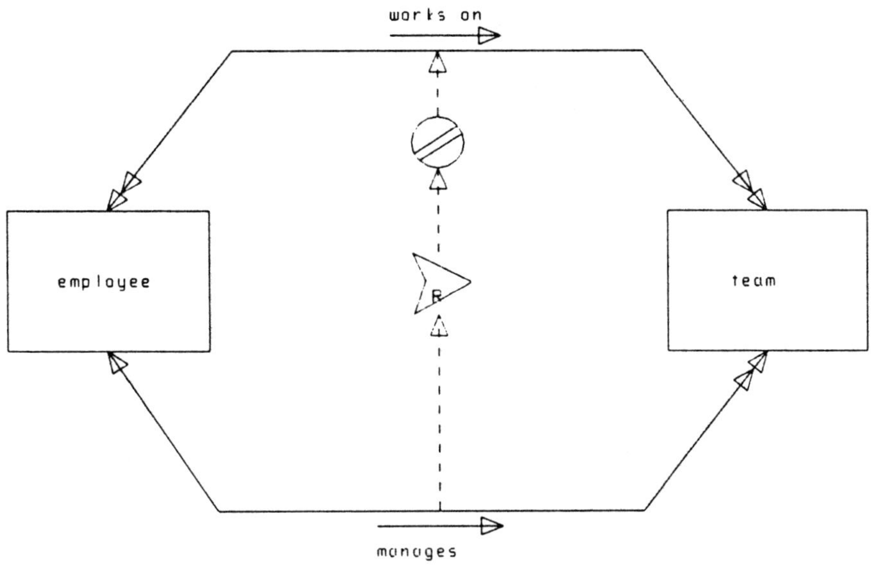

In this alternative, no "manages" instance is ever permitted to be the same as any connection instance of the "works on" relationship type. (This is indicated by the newly inserted "not" or "prohibited" symbol.) In other words, no employee will ever be recorded as both working on and managing the same team. This specification provides an important alternative to the earlier version where, in essence, relationship type instances would have been stored "redundantly" (albeit with specified control). In this new version, no such redundancy exists.

Diagram 3.8

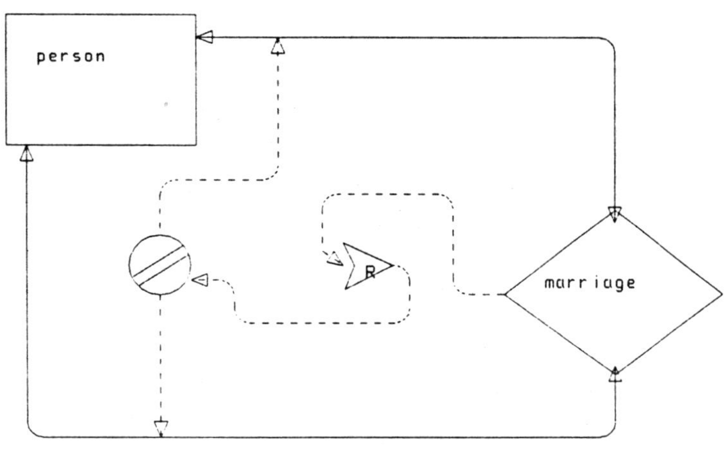

This restriction shows that a person cannot marry himself or herself. (Note that the restriction IC symbol has been omitted in this example. This is a shorthand version for "not" specifications which may be cautiously used to avoid clutter.)

The "not" symbol is called an **Integrity Constraint Qualifier** (ICQ). A list of valid ICQs for restrictions is presented in the diagram below. (See Appendix V for a complete list of valid ICQ use for all ICs.) As their name suggests, ICQs are only used with integrity constraints (not any other type of automatic behavior). More than one ICQ may be used for a given IC as necessary, but they all may only be used on the reaction side.

Diagram 3.9

Valid Integrity Constraint Qualifiers (ICQs) for Restrictions

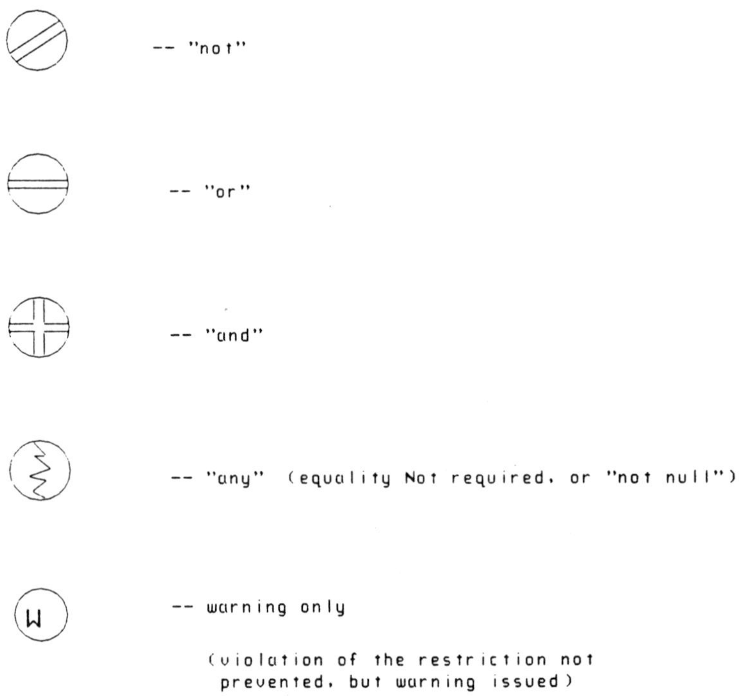

3.1-1.1-2 Restrictions and Classifications

The "not" specification is a particularly useful ICQ, especially in conjunction with classifications.

In Diagram 3.10, an employment counselor may not be assigned to any person who is retired. Another way of saying this is that the "counsels" relationship type is general to all subtypes of people except those who are retired. This specification avoids having to redefine the "counsels" relationship type for each of the other subtypes individually.

Diagram 3.10

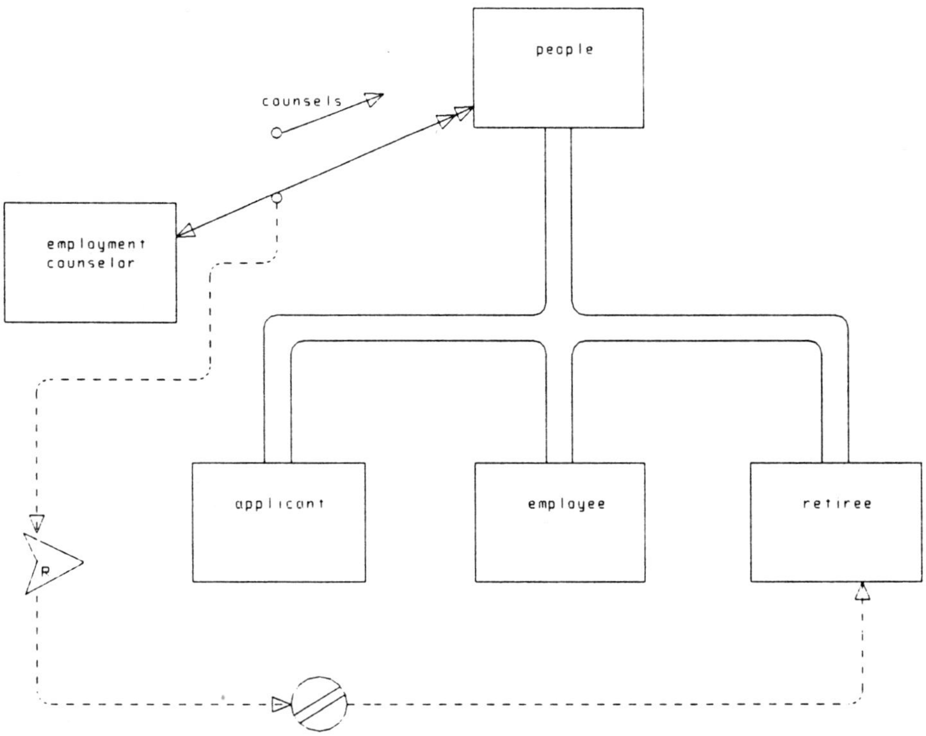

3.1-3.1-3 "Any" Restrictions

The usual sense of a restriction is "equal," or "same," or "identical to." This sense can be changed to "any" (as in "any will do, even if not equal") by use of the appropriate "any" ICQ symbol. An example illustrates.

Diagram 3.11

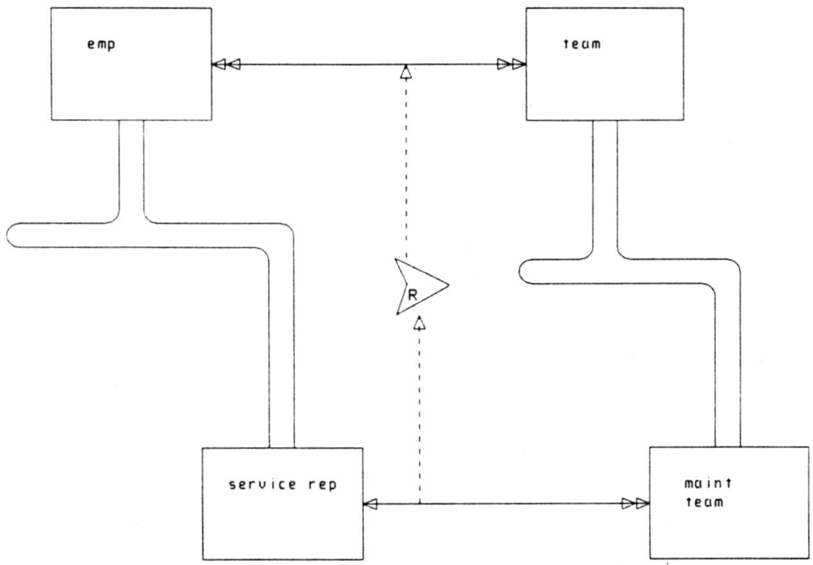

This example shows that service representatives on a maintenance team must presently be among the members of that same team.

Suppose the policy of this enterprise were changed slightly, such that a service representative on a maintenance team had to be a member of some team, but not necessarily that particular maintenance team. This could be shown as follows.

Diagram 3.12

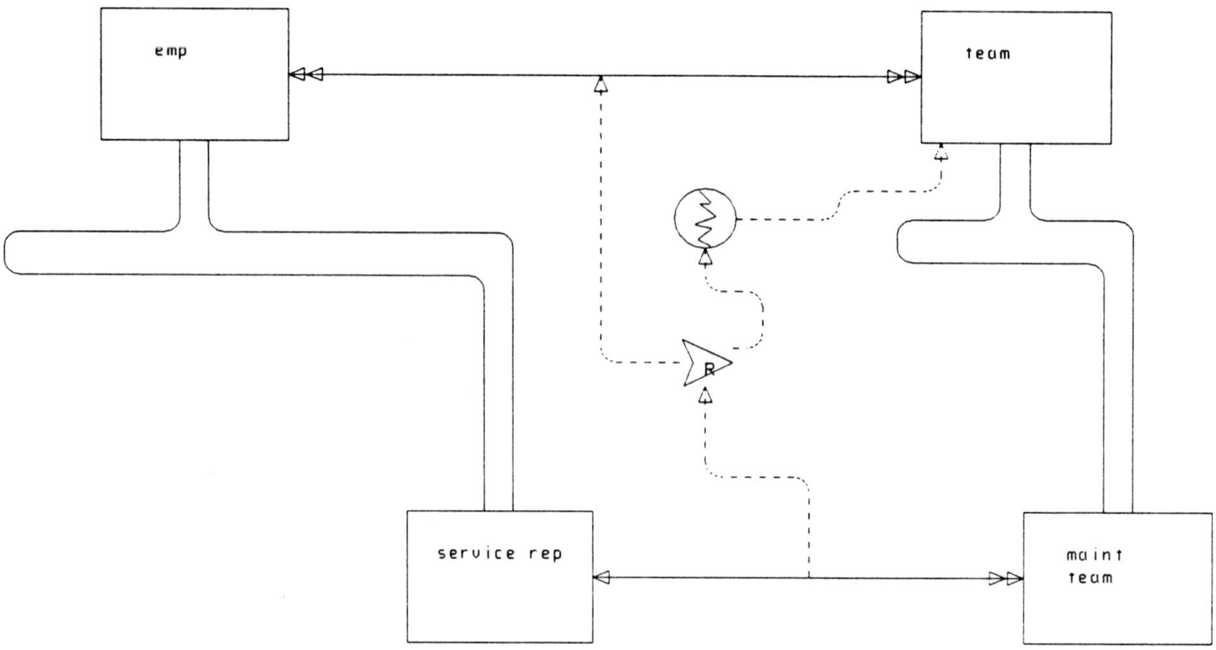

This alternative specifies that membership on *any* team will do. The "any" symbol essentially breaks or nullifies the "equal" constraint on the "team" side. (If the service representative had to be a member specifically on at least one *maintenance* team, then an additional reaction side connection from the IC to "maintenance team" would be shown.)

In a slight variation of the above, suppose the policy were the following. For a maintenance team to have a service representative, it has to be a team with members, but not necessarily including the particular employee acting as the service representative. This could be shown as in Diagram 3.13. This new specification would show that "any" team member will do. ("Equality" constraints on the "employee" side are "broken.")

Suppose that no service representative could be assigned to a team unless at least one team (not necessarily *that* team) has at least one member (not necessarily that service representative in particular). This would be shown as in Diagram 3.14.

Diagram 3.13

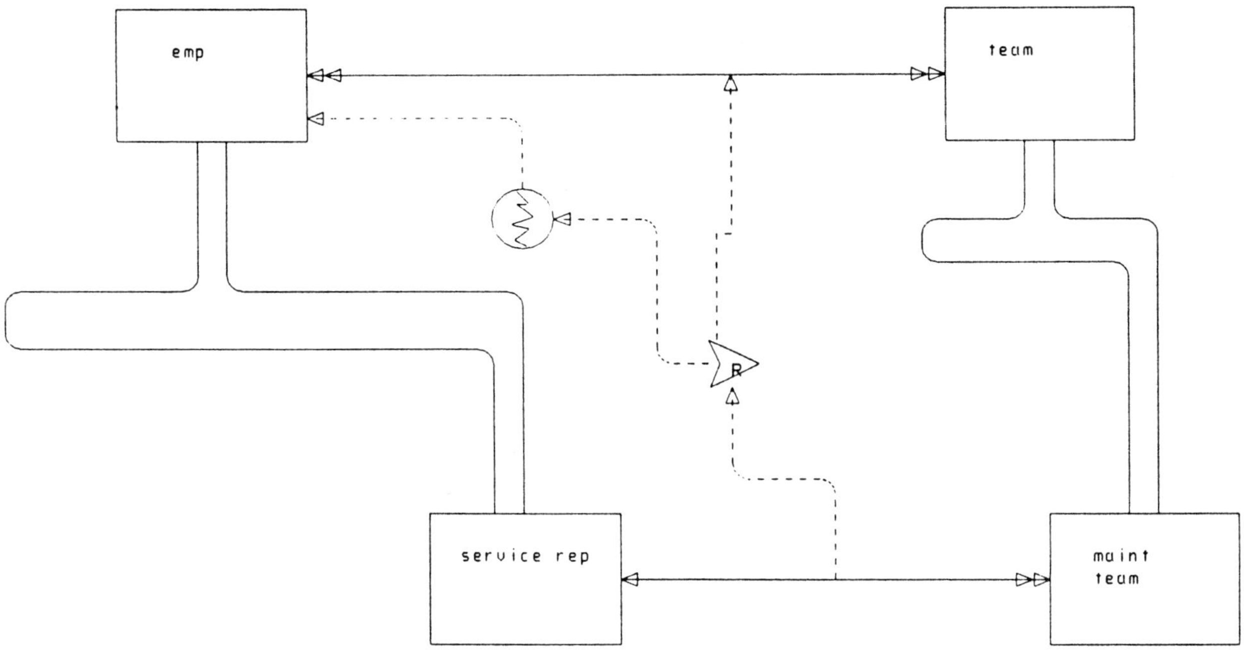

Diagram 3.14

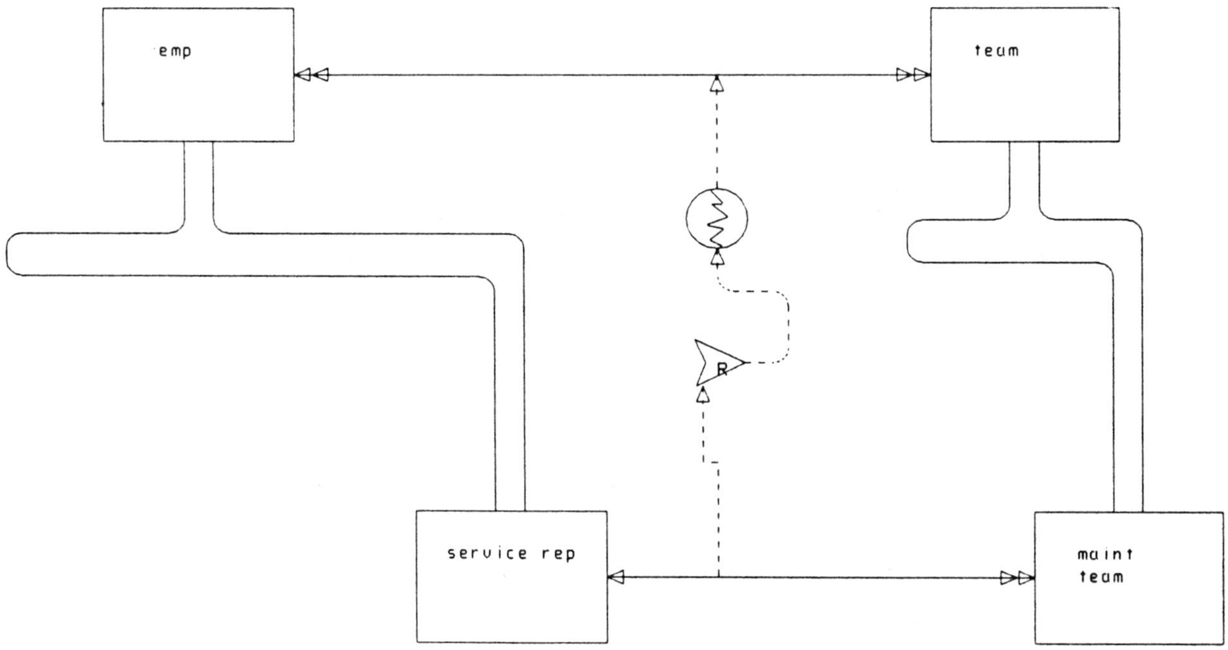

Here, "any" team membership will do because all "equality" is "broken" by the any symbol. This particular specification, of course, would be unusual.

The "not" ICQ is also useful with "any." Suppose, for example, that the service representatives can only be assigned to maintenance teams *without* any members. This more complex rule would be shown as follows, in Diagram 3.15.

Diagram 3.15

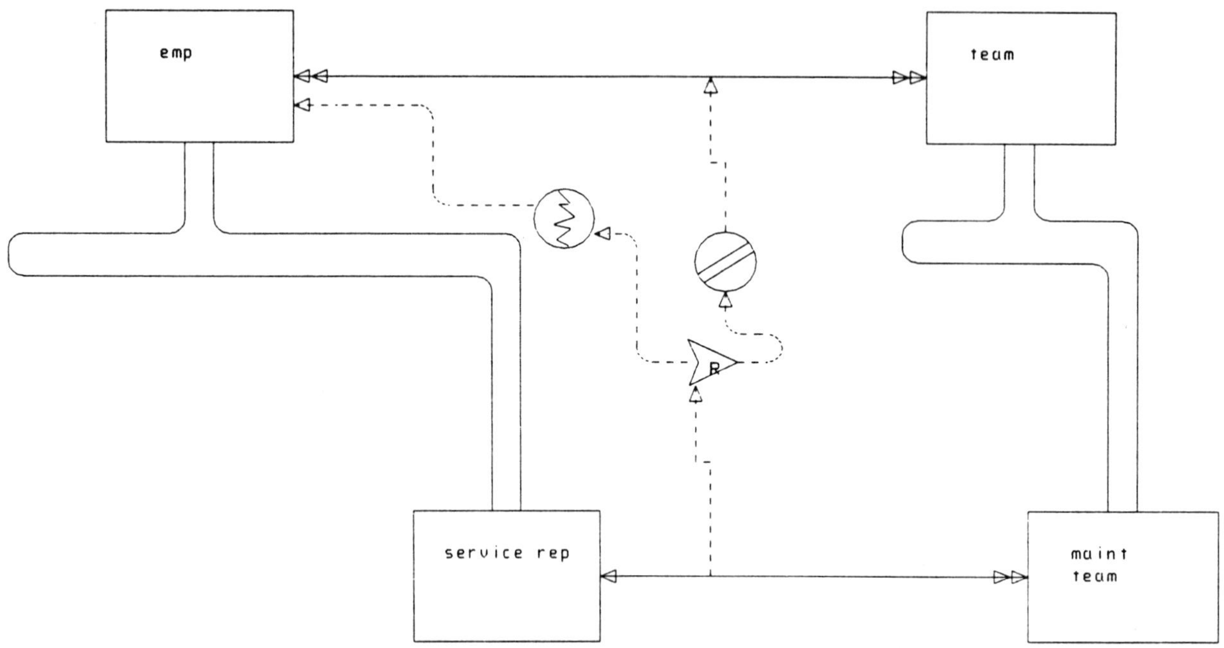

The "any" causes a "match" with *any* employee on the left. Therefore an instance of the lower relationship type will "match" any instance of the upper relationship type for the same team. Since the restriction's "not" ICQ says "matches" are always disallowed, a service representative can effectively only be assigned so long as the team has no members whatsoever.

GUIDELINES AND CONVENTIONS FOR INTEGRITY CONSTRAINT QUALIFIERS (ICQs)

- ICQs are used only for integrity constraints, not other forms of automatic behavior.
- ICQs logically refine the meaning of the associated integrity constraint.
- One or more ICQs may be used for any given integrity constraint, but always on the "behavior" side only.
- An ICQ always has one connection coming into it, and one or more leaving it.
- Selection of ICQs is dependent on the type of integrity constraint—not all ICQs are available for all ICs. (See Appendix V.)

3.1-1.1-4 Restrictions and Aggregate Relationship Types

Aggregate relationships, named collections of other relationship types, were introduced in Section 1.2-4.2. These were previously treated as "not to be stored."

If "stored," the "redundancy" of relationship type instances must be controlled. Several examples of such control for "stored" aggregate relationship types are shown below. In these examples, the users must create and manage instances, although the "correctness" of these instances is controlled by restrictions. (Refer to the section on automatic actions for system-managed alternatives.)

Diagram 3.16

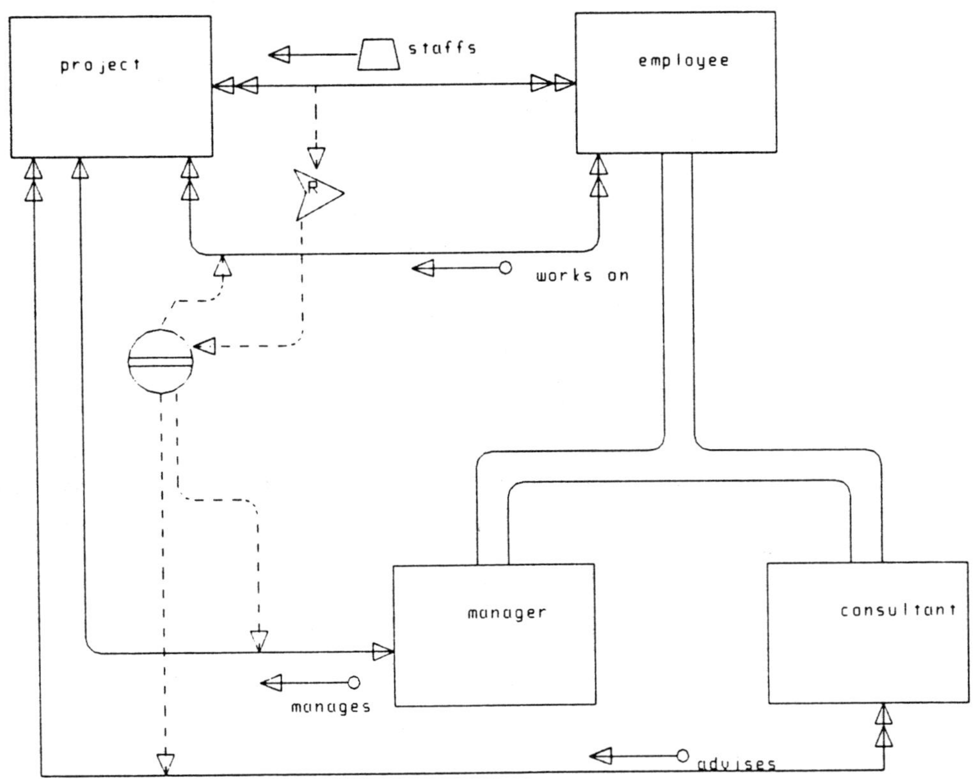

In this example, an "or" ICQ has been given for the restriction indicating that instances of "staffs" must correspond to instances of either "works on," or "manages," or "advises." (The "or" ICQ, however, is never "exclusive." For example, should equivalent instances of these latter relationship types co-exist, the restriction above is still nonetheless satisfied.)

In the series aggregate relationship type shown in Diagram 3.17, instances of "sells" are restricted to any indirect relating of an agent to a product via the "path" designated. Note that the total number of valid "sells" instances may be less than the total number of "path" instances since different manufacturers may sometimes sell the *same* product(s).

GUIDELINES AND CONVENTIONS FOR RESTRICTIONS

- Restrictions are used only for relationship types.
- A restriction should never be connected from an object on the "stimulus" side.
- A restriction is defined by placing an "R" inside an integrity constraint symbol and connecting it from one or more relationship types (on the stimulus side).
- The restriction specifies the conditions under which occurrences of the relationship type can be created and allowed to exist, and also when changes or deletions to other parts of the database are to be prevented.
- Connect the restriction (on the "behavior" side) to other relationship types and/or objects as appropriate in specifying the associated business rule.
- Use integrity constraint qualifiers (ICQs) on the behavior side (only) to refine the specification.
- A "not" ICQ means instances of the relationship type will be dependent on occurrences of other objects or connections *not* existing.
- An "any" ICQ nullifies the implicit "equal to" meaning of an IC. The "any" ICQ essentially means "any instance will do" (to satisfy the restriction).
- Use subtypes on the "behavior" side to clarify which types of objects specifically apply to the restriction.
- Use integrity constraint value conditions (ICVCs) to specify attribute-level conditions for restrictions.
- Use a recursion ICVC to extend restrictions for cyclic or recursive structures.
- Use a clock symbol, with a note, to show any effective or discontinuation date.

3.1-1.1-5 Value Conditions

Certain restrictions involve checking value conditions defined on the reaction side of a behavior. These conditions, called **Integrity Constraint Value Conditions** (ICVCs), must be continuously met for a stimulus-side relationship type instance to exist. ICVCs always refer to actual attributes on the reaction side (even when the actual connections point to other objects). Valid ICVCs are shown in Diagram 3.18. (Refer to Appendix V for complete rules of usage.)

Diagram 3.17

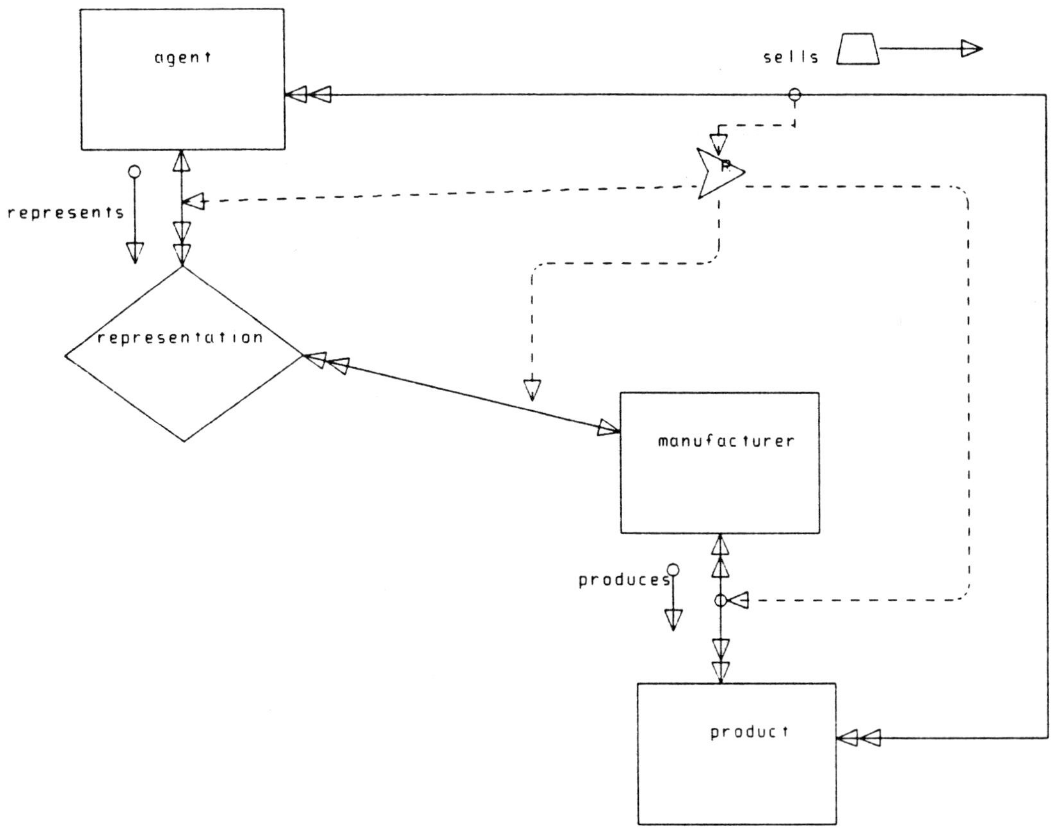

Diagram 3.18

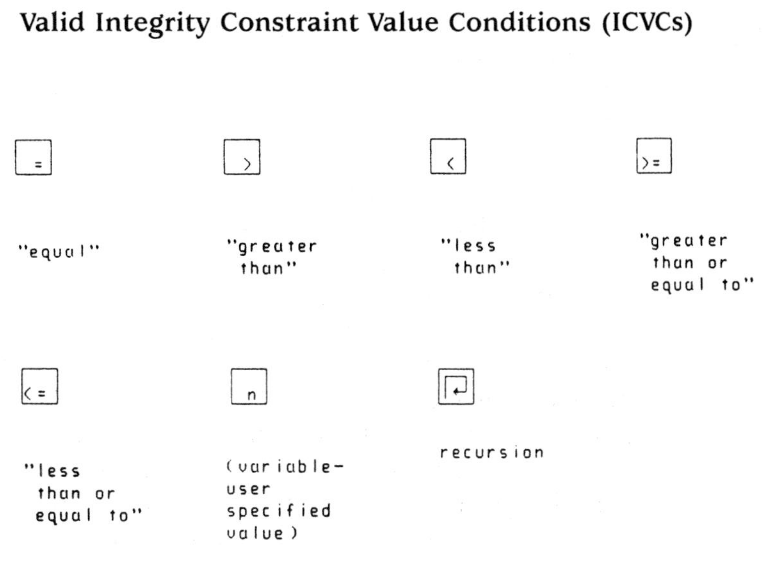

Diagram 3.19

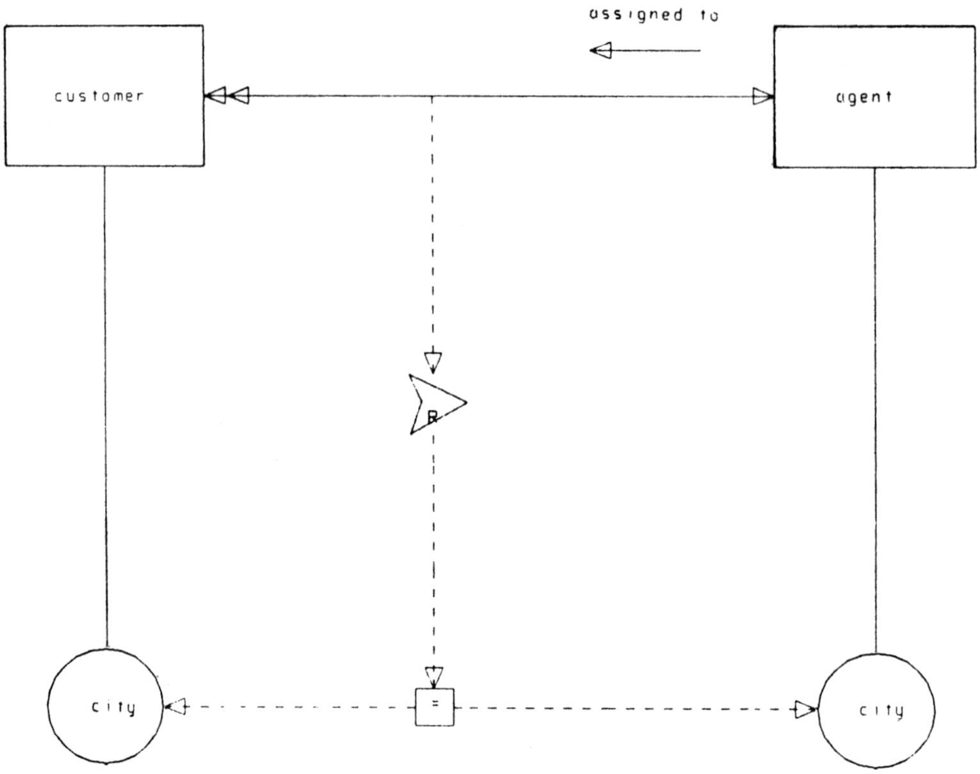

This example specifies that the agent assigned to a customer must be located in the same city as the customer (i.e., that their respective city values must be "equal"). If this "equal" value condition does not hold true, then the relationship instance cannot be created. Furthermore, any update to the city value of any customer or agent is prevented so long as an "assigned to" relationship instance continues to exist that depends on (i.e., is restricted to) that condition's remaining true. This implies that when a customer or agent relocates, any and all assignments currently in effect must first be removed or modified. (Note: Because of the presence of attribute types in the diagram above, it is not officially at the "integrity" level of detail, but is actually lower. It is included here, as are subsequent diagrams, for consistent illustration.)

Diagram 3.20 indicates a student can only register for a seat in a class (via the "assigned to" relationship type) where the course is offered during the same semester as one for which the student is registered. Note that the "semester" objects on the reaction side are not specifically attribute types. When an ICVC points outward to non-attribute objects, as in this case, the value comparison is understood to be for the *determinants* of the objects. In this example, both "semester" characteristics would presumably be determined by the partial determinant, semester-no; thus the IC defined restricts instances of "assigned to" to "equal" instances of semester-no. (Determinants of the objects characterized—i.e., "student" and "course"—are excluded for this particular comparison.)

Diagram 3.20

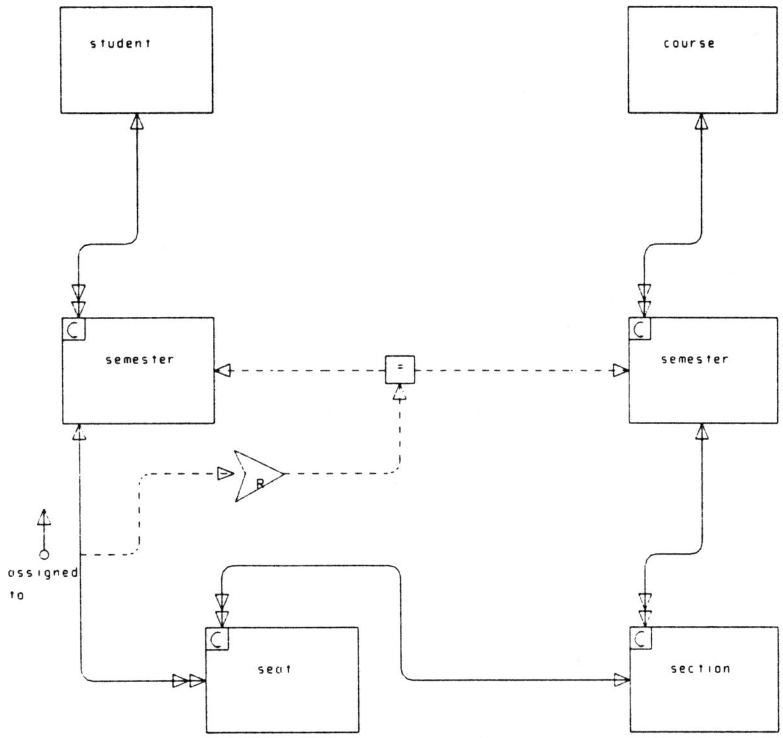

Diagram 3.21

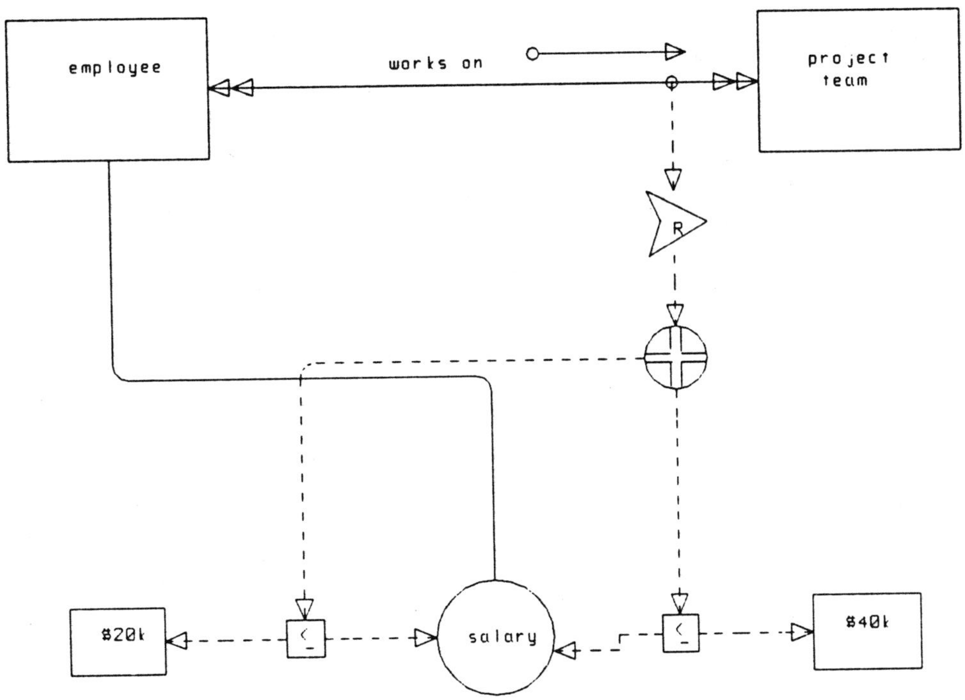

Diagram 3.21 expresses non-equal value conditions for instances of the relationship type "works on." Specifically, the salary range of any employee working on a project must fall between $20K and $40K (inclusive). Note that the directionality of value conditions for non-equal ICVCs is significant.

The above expression is somewhat clumsy. The modeler may prefer the following annotated alternative.

Diagram 3.22

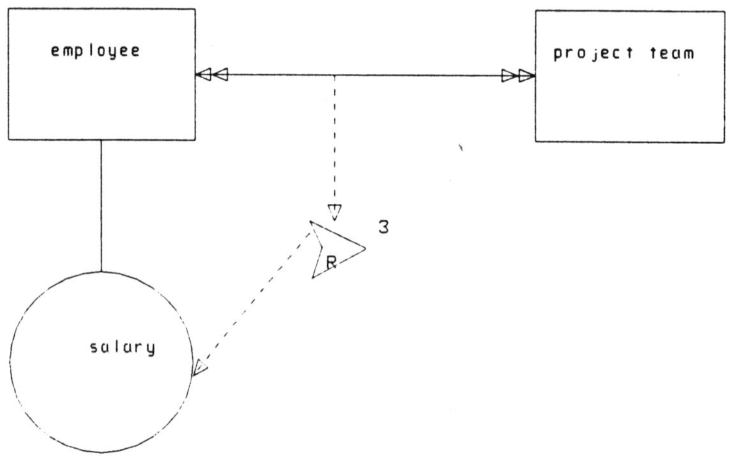

3. $20k <= salary <= $40k

Use of ICVCs may be commingled with ICQs in the same restriction, as illustrated by the following example.

Diagram 3.23

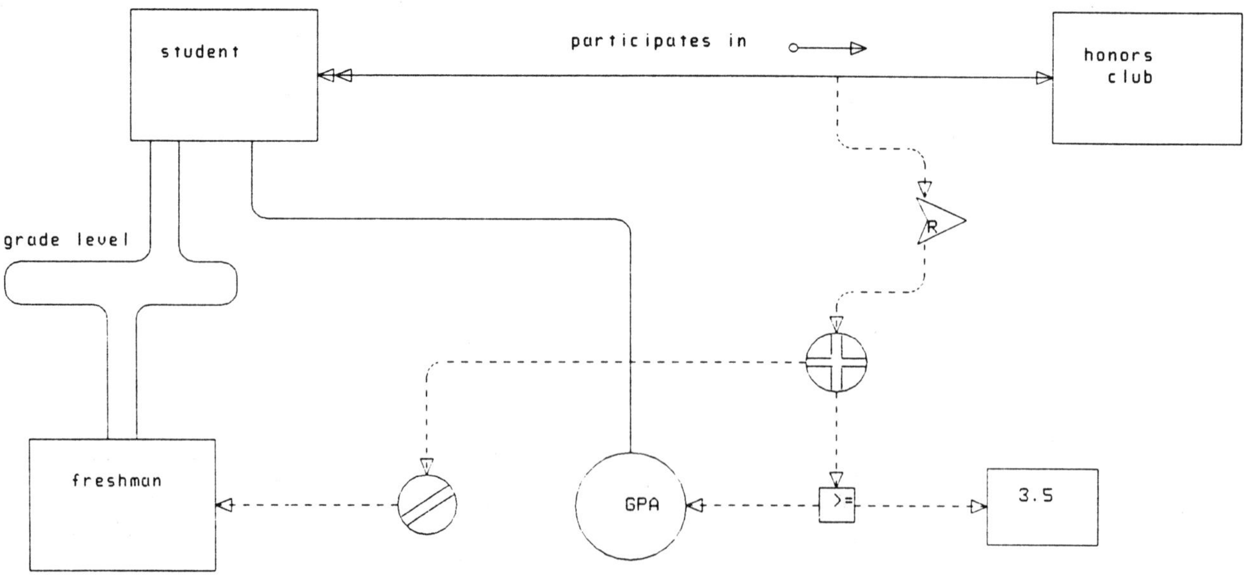

This specification indicates that for a student to participate in an "honors club," that student must not be a freshman and must also have a grade point average (GPA) of 3.5 or better. As this example properly shows, use of an ICVC must appear after (or "beyond") any ICQ—that is, farther to the reaction side than any ICQ to which it is directly connected.

GUIDELINES AND CONVENTIONS FOR INTEGRITY CONSTRAINT VALUE CONDITIONS

- ICVCs are only used in conjunction with integrity constraints—not any other type of automatic behavior.
- ICVCs may only be used for restricted ("R") and mandatory ("X") ICs.
- ICVCs always indicate a comparison of attribute values for attribute types that are always on the reaction side of the IC. The indicated condition must be met for instances of the relationship type(s) indicated on the stimulus side to exist.
- The ICVC is designated by a small square box containing the appropriate value comparison symbol (e.g., =). User-defined comparison values may also be specified as appropriate.
- An ICVC containing a value comparison symbol must always have two or more reaction side connectors coming out of it.
- If an existing ICVC connector connects to an object other than an attribute type, than the comparison is understood to be for the determinants of the object. (For characteristics, only the partial determinant is included.)
- When used in conjunction with an ICQ, the ICVC must always appear after the ICQ on the reaction side.

3.1-1.1-6 Recursion

Recursive or cyclic structures (objects that relate back to themselves through one or more relationship types) present special requirements for integrity constraint specification. The following example illustrates.

In Diagram 3.24, employees manage other employees. Using a "not-equal" ICVC, version one specifies that no employee can directly manage himself. This leaves open the question, however, of whether an employee is permitted to manage any employee (including indirect subordinates) who manages him either directly or indirectly. Version two specifies that this is not permitted, by inserting a "recursion" ICVC after the "not equal."

The effect of the recursion ICVC is to extend automatically the not equal restriction through all "loops" of the recursive relationship type in both directions. This ensures that no "matches" can be made even after cycling as many times as possible.

Diagram 3.24

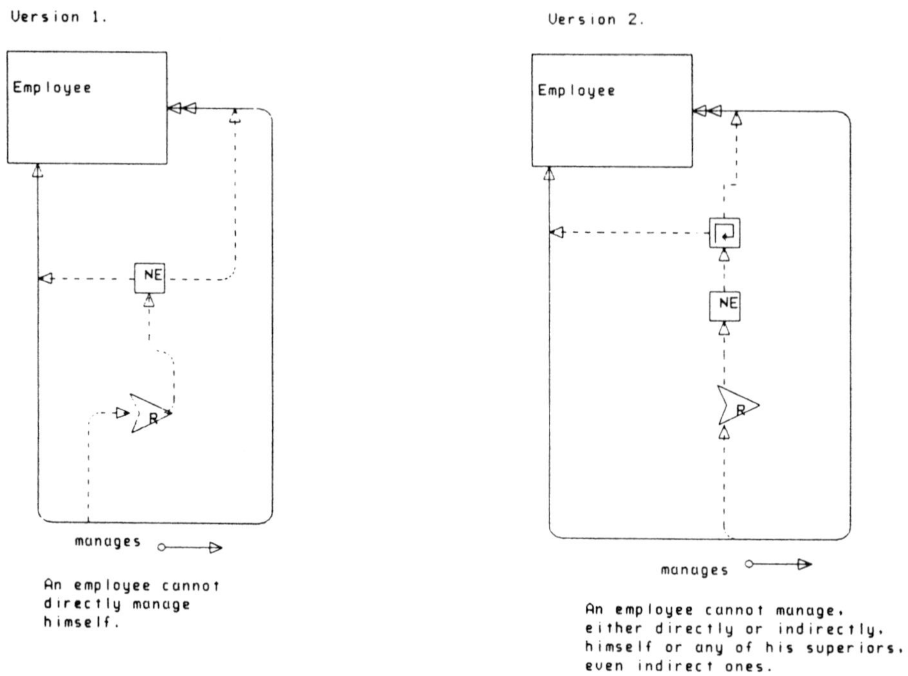

3.1-1.2 Mandatory

The integrity constraint "mandatory" (abbreviated "X") is to objects as "restricted" is to relationship types. A "mandatory" specification means that the valid existence of an object is contingent on the existence of one or more other objects and/or connections. A "mandatory" IC is therefore always connected on the stimulus side from an entity type, characteristic type, or association type, *never* a relationship type.

In Diagram 3.25, the mandatory IC states that no order can ever exist in the database without designating the customer placing it. (The lower version is a shorthand form that may be used [cautiously] to reduce clutter.) Specifically, this mandatory IC dictates that no instance of order can exist without a related occurrence of the relationship type "places" also existing. Note that since no mandatory IC has been defined for customer, instances of customer can apparently exist without related orders.

Mandatory ICs raise interesting questions about specific update consequences. For instance, in the example above, what happens if a new order designates a particular customer that does not (already) exist? This topic is fully explored in the section on *Referential Integrity*. (See Section 3.2-3).

In Diagram 3.26, a credit application can only be made by customers who have already placed orders. The existence of a credit application occurrence is thus generally constrained by the existence of these other things.

Diagram 3.25

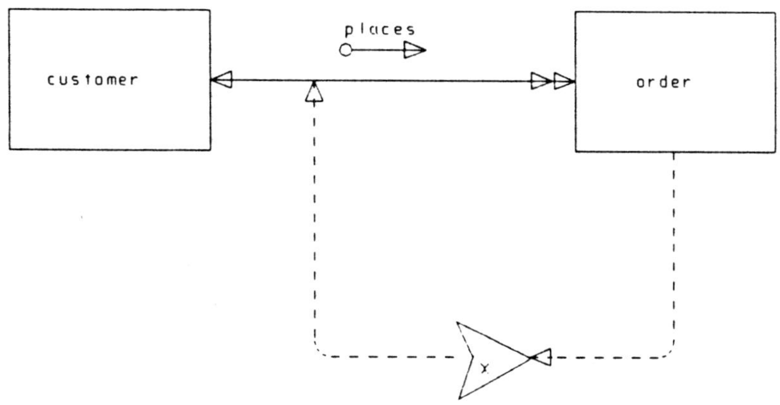

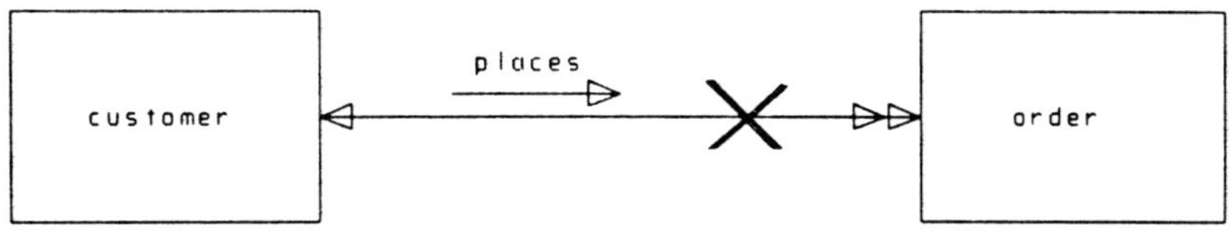

Diagram 3.26

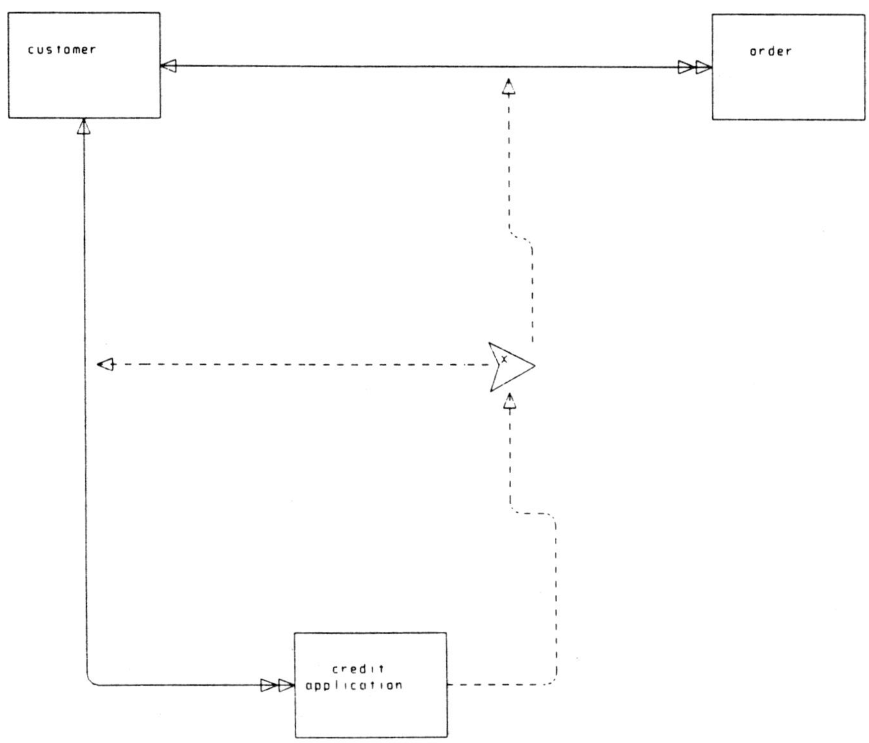

Diagram 3.27

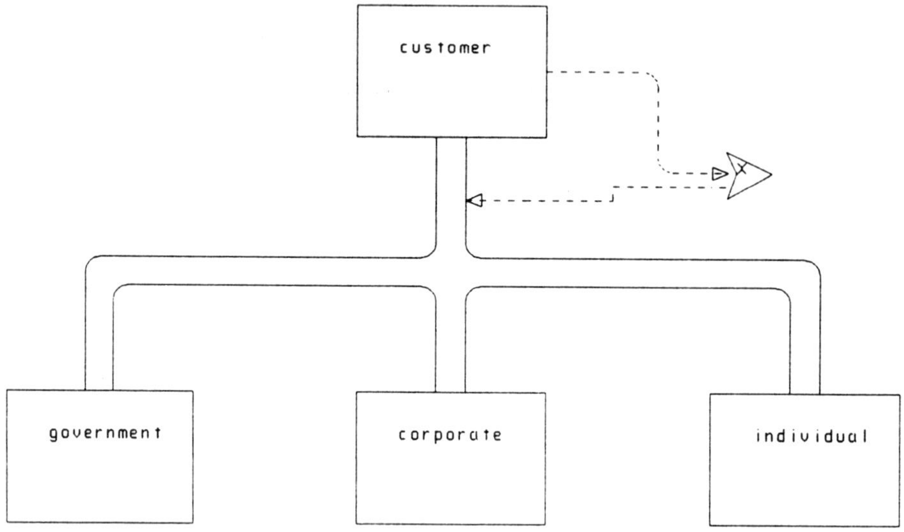

This mandatory specification indicates a customer must be classified according to its type, of which there are three choices. (Note: To avoid clutter, the IC symbol and connections are sometimes omitted, and an "X" is placed either near the branching of the classification relationship type, or close to the mandatory subtype(s).)

Diagram 3.28

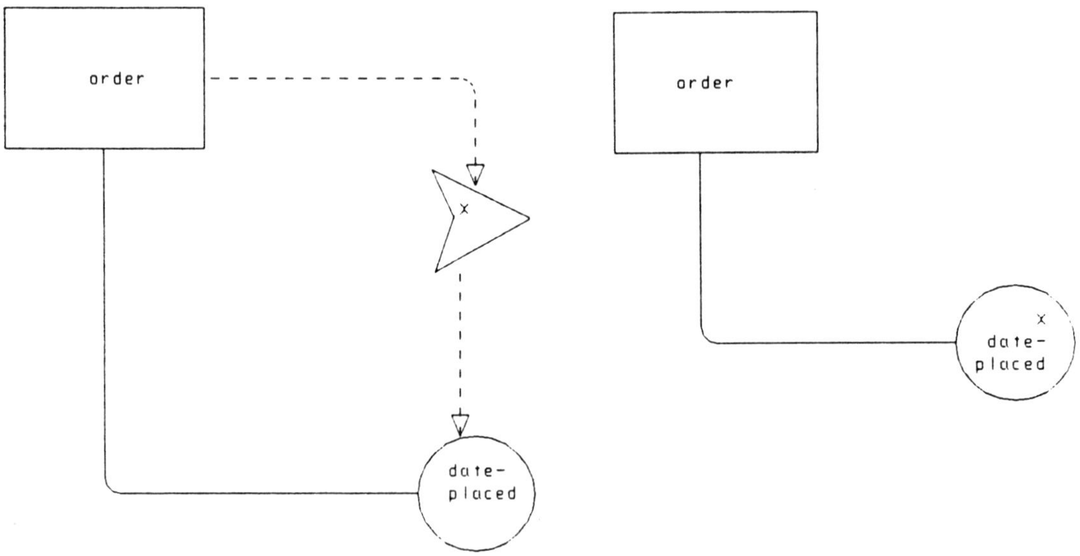

This mandatory specification shows that every order must always have some value of <u>date-placed</u>. (The shorthand form on the right may be used to reduce clutter.)

3.1-1.2-1 "Mandatory" and Integrity Constraint Qualifiers (ICQs)

"Mandatory" specifications may also use ICQs. Such use is often quite helpful for precisely defining business rules.

Diagram 3.29

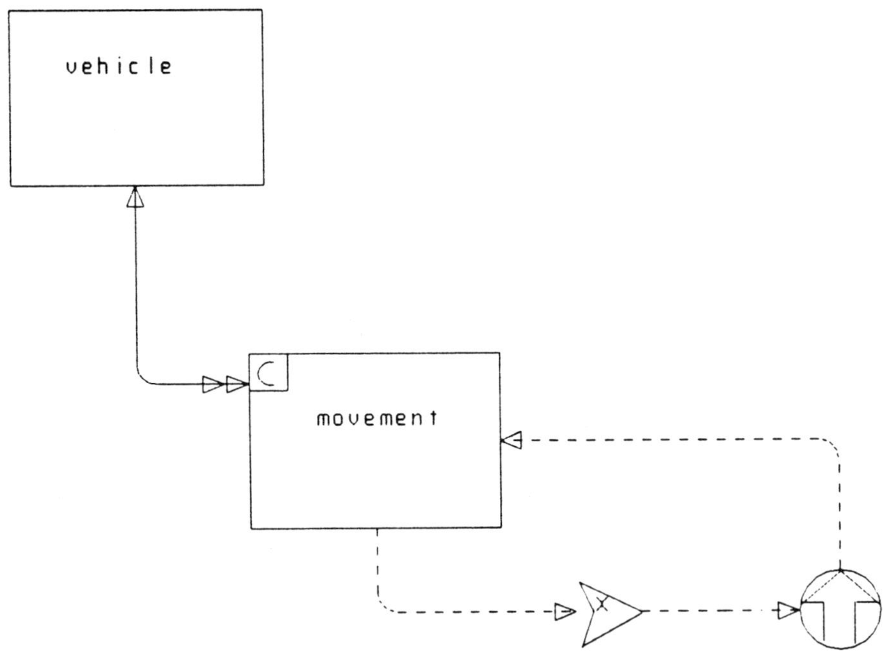

This special "ascending" ICQ specifies that each new occurrence of "movement" must have a determinant value greater than the last (i.e., those for all occurrences entered previously). Since movement would probably be partially determined by date-time, this means each movement "event" must happen after the last one recorded. (As this example suggests, a mandatory IC using the "ascending" ICQ must always connect both to and from the very same object. Because of this, the mandatory IC and connections are often omitted from the diagram, and the "ascending" ICQ is simply placed inside the object of interest.)

In Diagram 3.30, the "not" mandatory constraint (shown in abbreviated form, without the mandatory IC object per se) indicates that this (betting) enterprise does not accept markers from bookies. Note that the "not" symbol does not connote the sense of "optional" (i.e., *not* mandatory), but rather that it is mandatory that certain other things not exist. Also note that reaction side connectors have been used to show a "path" (via relationship types) to the "bookie" subtype, so that no ambiguity exists concerning which instance of bookie (if any) may be of interest for correct evaluation of the IC. Since there is another "path" to bookie in this diagram (via the "sold to" relationship type), such ambiguity might have otherwise arisen.

Diagram 3.30

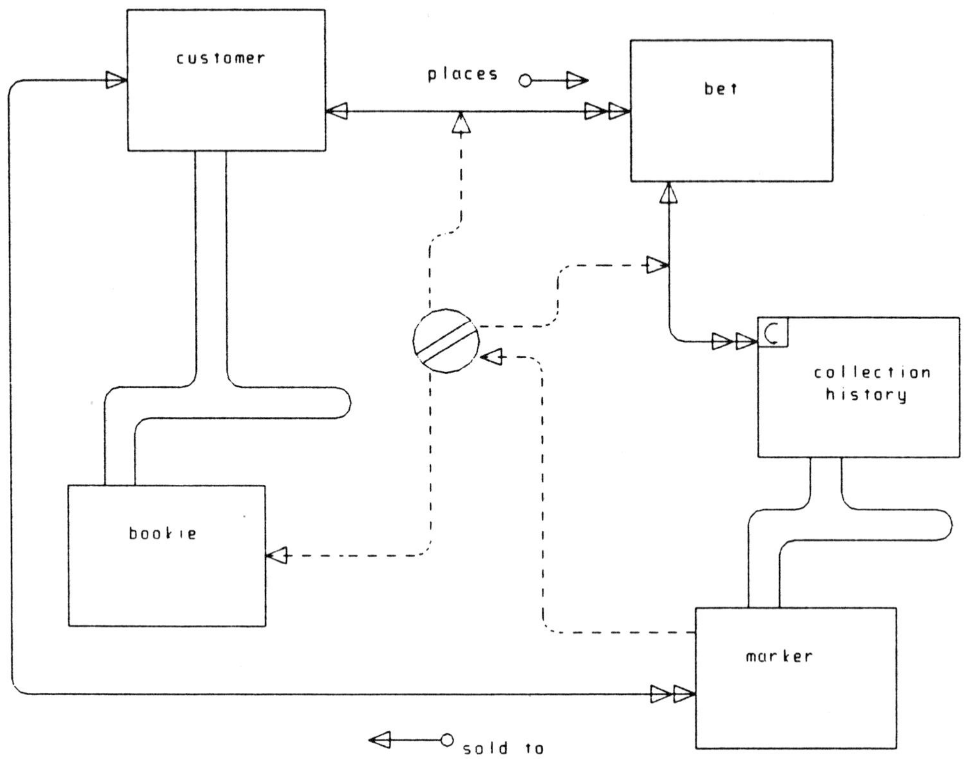

Diagram 3.31

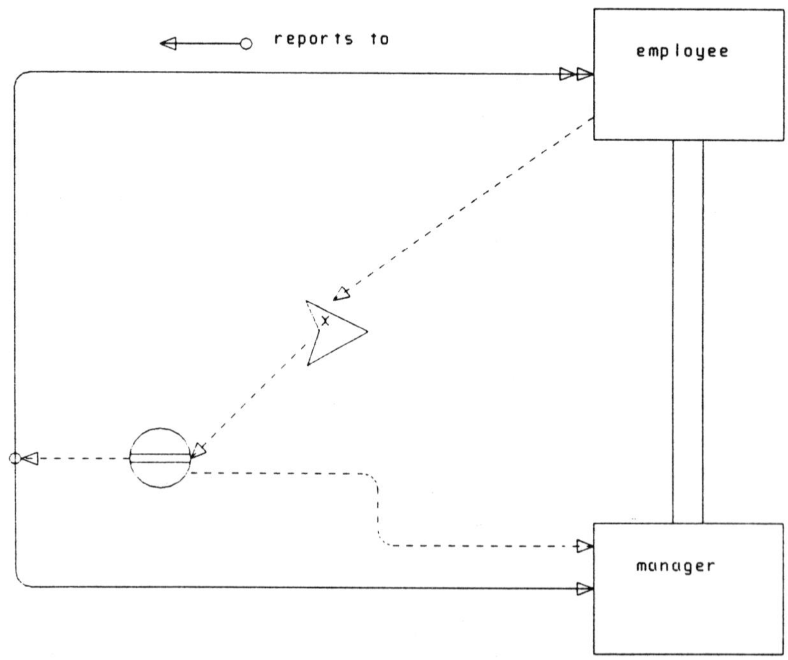

In Diagram 3.31, every employee must be a manager or have a "reporting to" relationship to some (other) manager. At least one of these assertions must be true. (*Both* may also be true since the "or" ICQ is not "exclusive.")

Diagram 3.32

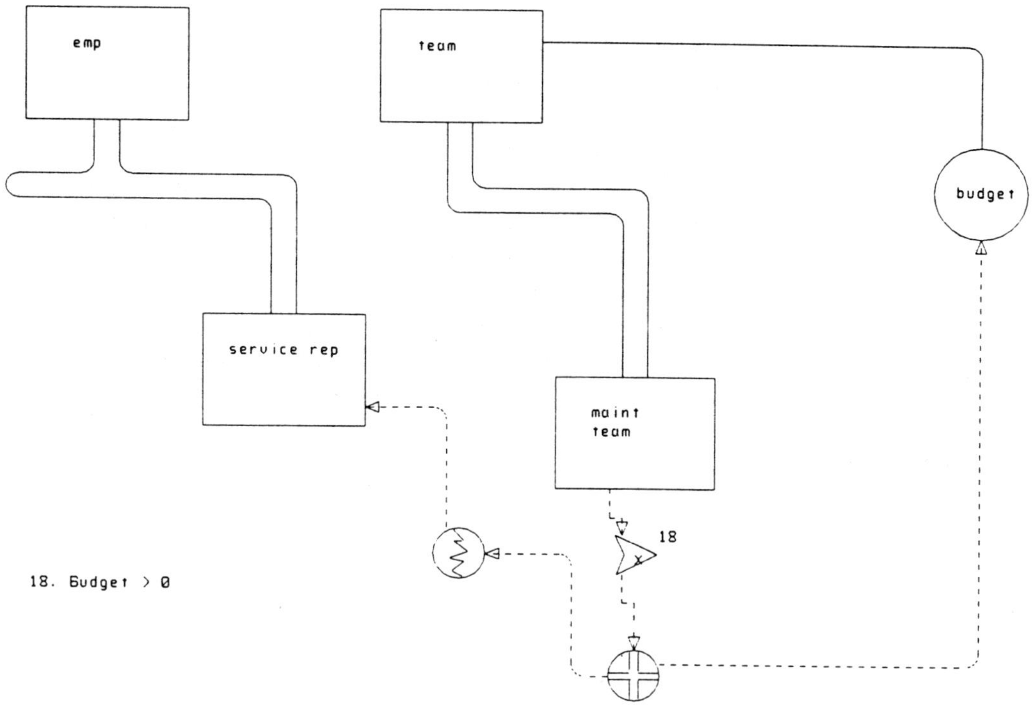

A team can only be designated as "maintenance" if it has some non-zero budget value, and if some (any) service representatives have been designated (for the enterprise as a whole). (Note: The meaning of the integrity constraint would have been the same even without the "any" ICQ in this case; it is included here for the sake of clarity.)

Diagram 3.33

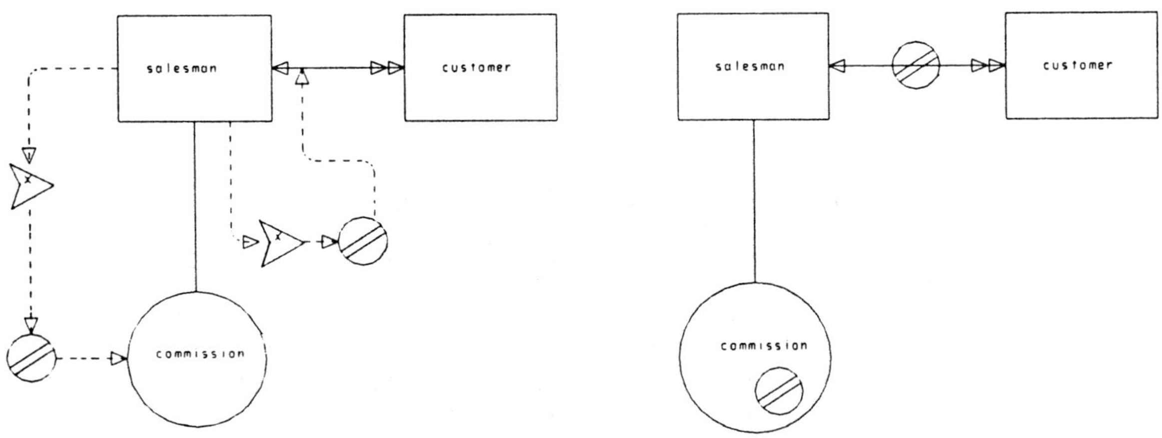

In Diagram 3.33, salesmen are never permitted to have either relationships to customers or values of commission. (The version on the right is a shorthand form which may be used to avoid clutter.) This is equivalent to saying that this relationship type and attribute type are prohibited for salesmen, and that they are not legitimate for this data resource.

That being the case, why include them in the model at all? There may be several reasons for doing so. One is simply to remind the modelers that these particular items have been examined and decided to be inappropriate. Another is to emphasize that these are common mistakes or misconceptions concerning business policies. (This enterprise, for example, may assign customers and commissions to salesmen based strictly on region. Presumably some larger segment of the entity model than the above would show this correctly.)

A third reason concerns transitions in business policy and timed changes that affect the structure of the entity model. Suppose, for example, that the enterprise *has* permitted customers or commissions to be directly assigned to salesmen in the past, but now wishes to discontinue this practice effective some given date. This "clocked" integrity constraint may be shown as follows. The clock symbol acts as an implicit trigger in "firing" the constraint.

Diagram 3.34

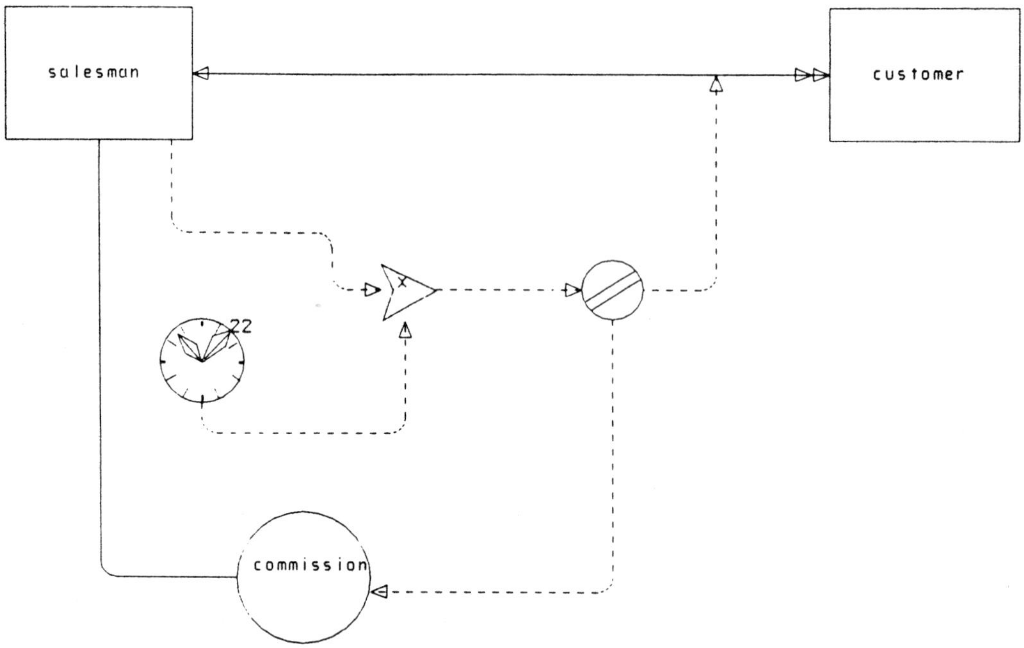

3.1-1.2-2 "Mandatory" and Integrity Constraint Value Conditions (ICVCs)

Like restrictions, "mandatory" ICs may also involve attribute type value conditions on their reaction side. All the previously discussed implications and conventions remain the same. (Refer to Appendix V for complete rules of usage.) Several examples follow.

Diagram 3.35

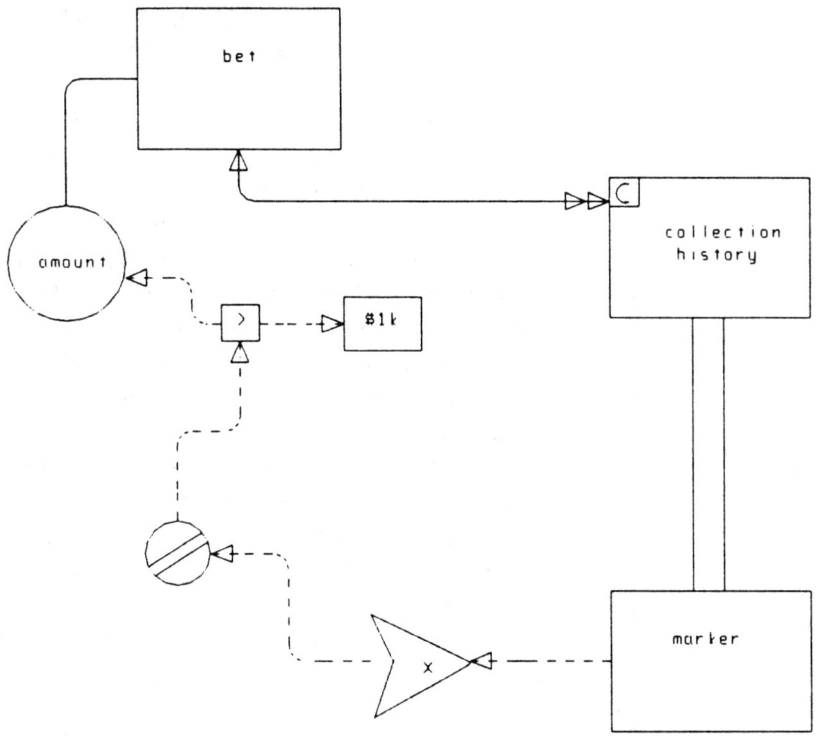

Markers will not be accepted for bets in excess of $1000.

Diagram 3.36

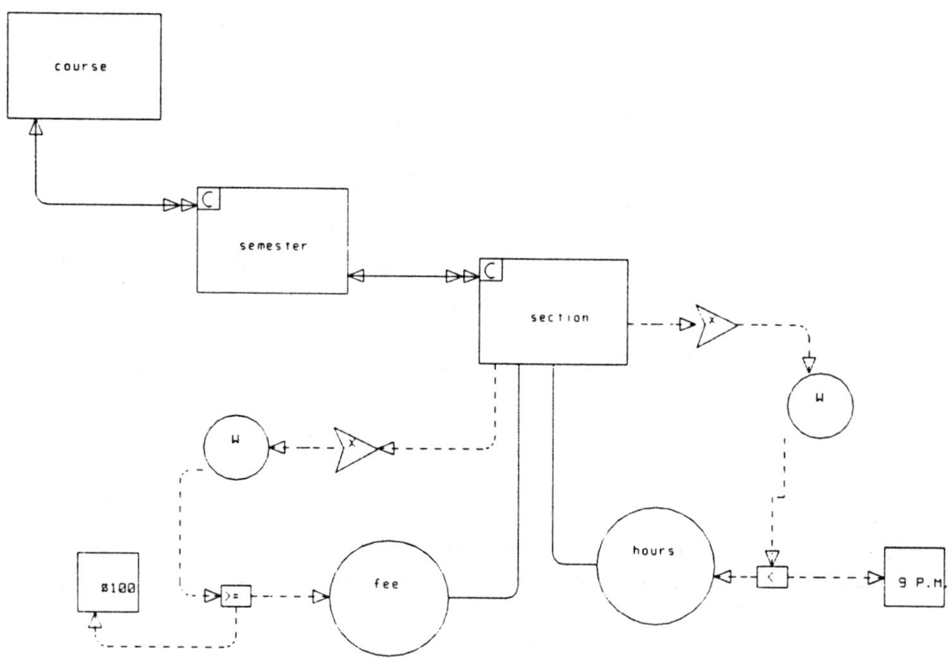

A warning is given upon creation of a class if its fee exceeds $100, or if it meets after 9 p.m.

GUIDELINES AND CONVENTIONS FOR MANDATORY

- "Mandatory" is used for objects rather than relationship types.
- A mandatory IC should never be connected from a relationship type on the stimulus side.
- A mandatory integrity constraint is defined by placing an "X" inside an integrity constraint symbol and connecting it from exactly one object (on the stimulus side).
- "Mandatory" specifies conditions under which occurrences of the object type can be created and allowed to exist, and also when changes or deletions to other parts of the database are to be prevented.
- Mandatory should generally not be used for aggregate objects or aggregate association types.
- Connect the mandatory constraint (on the "behavior" side) to other objects and/or relationship types as appropriate in specifying the associated business rule.
- When a mandatory IC is connected to a relationship type, null values are automatically precluded for any associated foreign keys.
- Use integrity constraint qualifiers (ICQs) on the behavior side (only) to refine the specification.
- A "not" ICQ does not mean not mandatory (i.e., optional), but rather that occurrences of the object type will be dependent on occurrences of other objects and/or connections *not* existing.
- Use an "ascending" ICQ to show that each new occurrence of an object must have a value for its determinant greater than the last.
- Use a "not" ICQ to show prohibited properties and relationships for an object.
- Use subtypes on the "behavior" side to clarify which types of objects specifically apply to the constraint.
- Use ICVCs to specify attribute-level conditions.
- Use a clock symbol, with a note, to show any effective or termination date for the constraint.

3.1-1.3 Mutually Exclusive

Like "mandatory," a **mutually exclusive integrity constraint** is always defined for an object rather than a relationship type. It precludes coexistence of two or more other objects and/or connections defined on the "reaction" side of the IC. In this sense, it always acts as an "exclusive" or.

Diagram 3.37

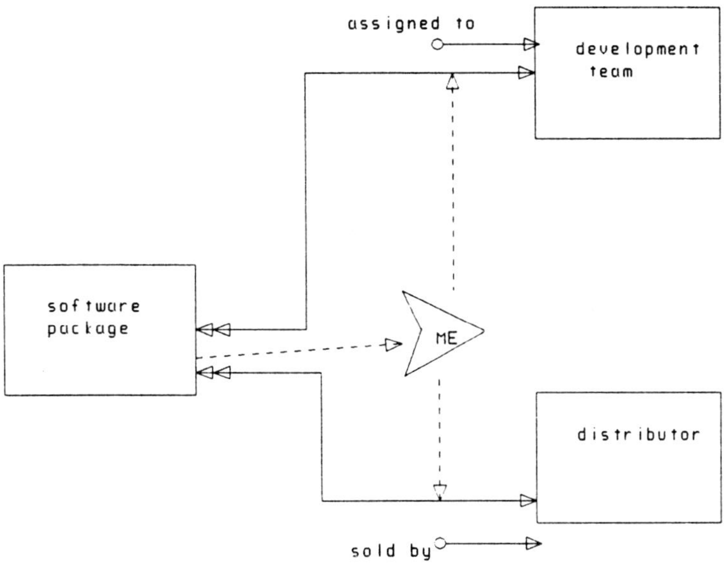

A software package may be assigned to a development team, or sold by a distributor, but according to this mutually exclusive IC specification, not to both at the same time. Instances of these two relationship types are thus mutually exclusive for any given software package at the same point in time. (Note that as in the above, there should always be at least two reaction-side connectors coming out of any mutually exclusive IC behavior object.)

Diagram 3.38

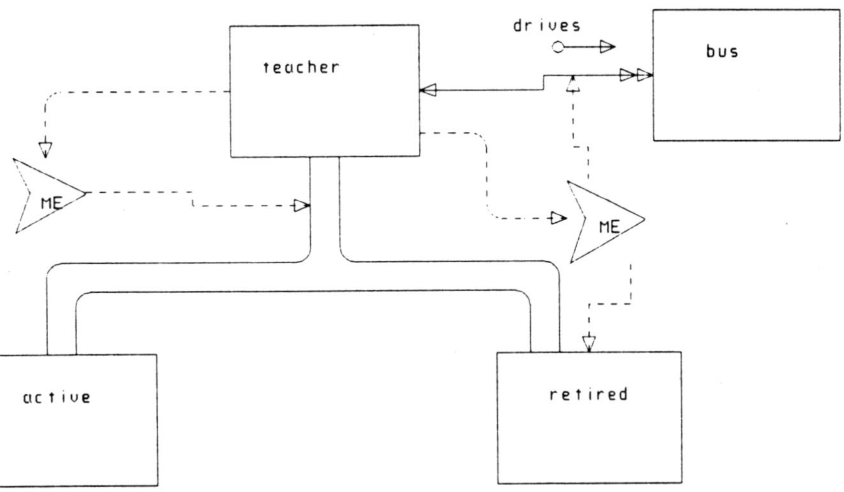

This diagram shows that a teacher cannot be both "active" and "retired" simultaneously. (The classification is mutually exclusive.) It also shows that retired teachers cannot drive buses.

To avoid clutter, the integrity constraint symbol and the connectors are sometimes dropped in specifying a classification as mutually exclusive, substituting an "ME" near the "branching" of the classification relationship type instead. The following diagram (also showing the classification as mandatory) illustrates.

Diagram 3.39

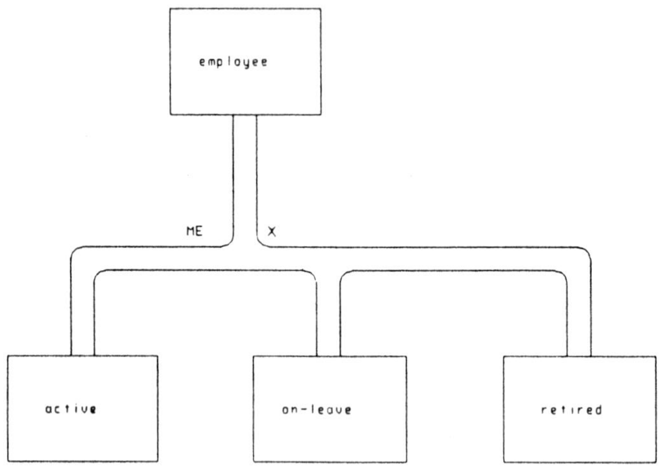

3.1-1.3-1 Mutually Exclusive and the "Any" ICQ

Like the restriction IC, "mutually exclusive" has the sense of equality or sameness.

Diagram 3.40

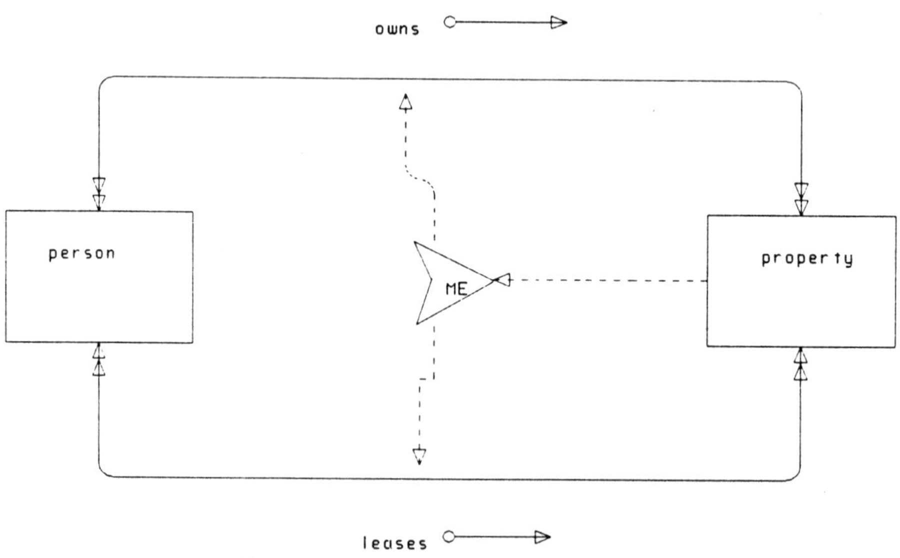

This example specifies that a particular property may not be owned and leased by the same person at the same point in time. (In other words, this IC precludes equivalent instances of both "owns" and "leases" from co-existing.) It does not, however, preclude the same property from being owned by one person and leased by some other person simultaneously.

If the property could never be leased and owned simultaneously, an "any" ICQ should be included, as follows.

Diagram 3.41

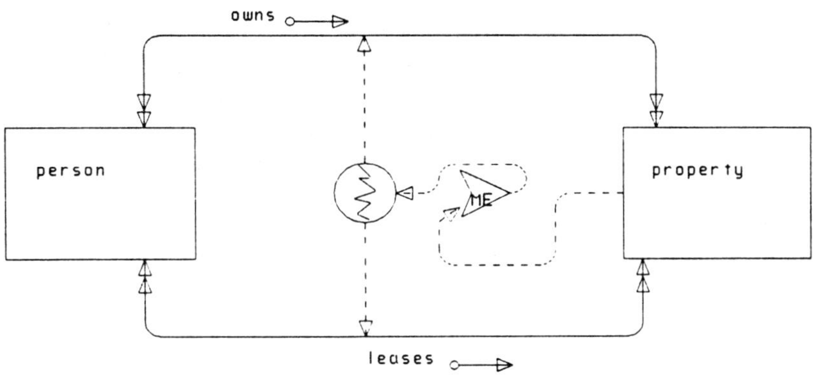

The "any" ICQ in this specification breaks or nullifies the "equality" on the reaction side. Any relating of person is now considered to satisfy the constraint. Under this specification, a property is either leased or owned—but never both simultaneously, even by different people.

The above situation is somewhat unique. It only arises where there are two or more "many" paths to the same entity type on the reaction side including supertypes or subtypes. If the two or more paths lead to completely different entity types, then ME is sufficient for precluding all simultaneous instances, since equality can be ascertained only on the stimulus side.

Diagram 3.42

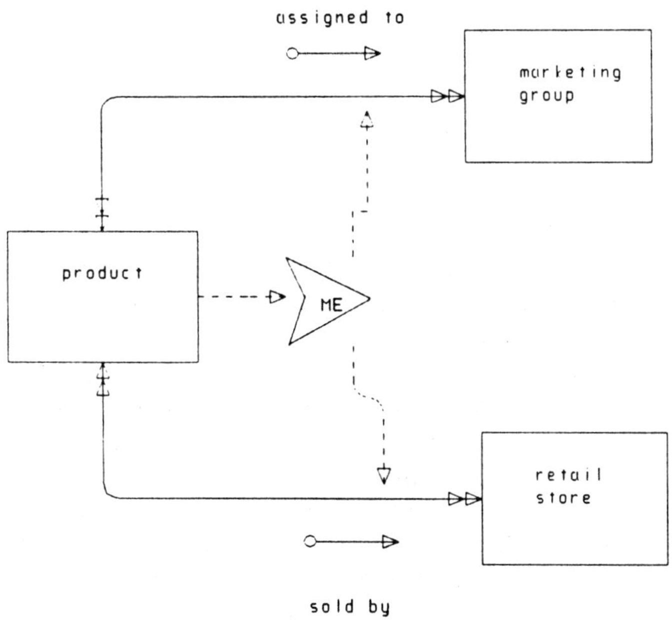

A given product will not have any instances of "assigned to" if it has any instance of "sold by," and vice versa.

3.1-1.3-2 Vectored Mutually Exclusive

All mutually exclusive integrity constraints denote situations where instances of the designated objects and/or connections are mutually exclusive. Sometimes, however, there is also a specific order (a "vector") in which these mutually exclusive objects and/or connections must be created. This ordering should never be violated.

Diagram 3.43

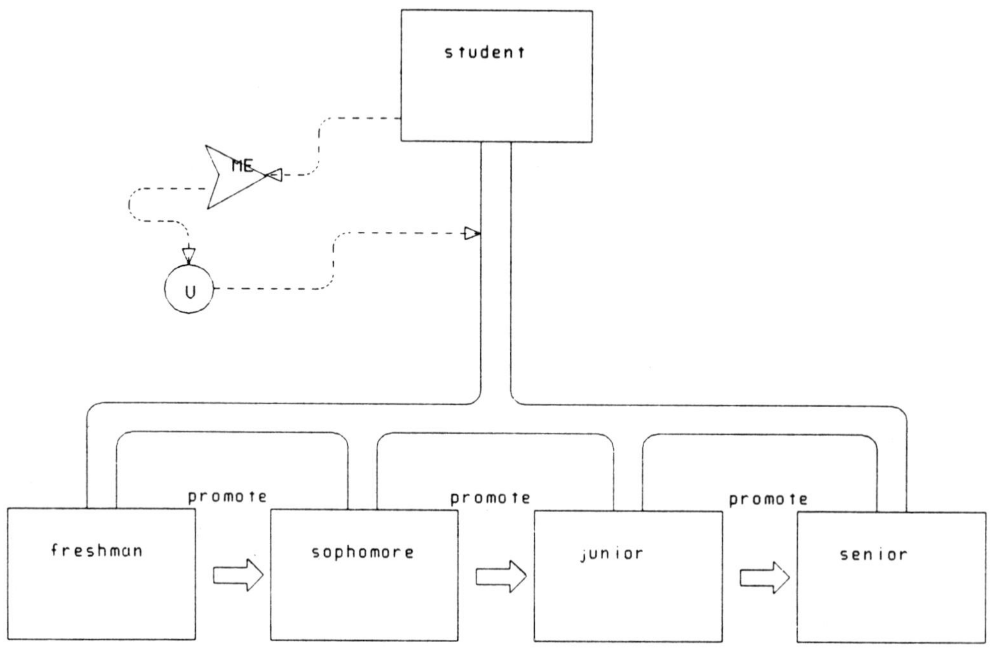

This classification has been denoted as mutually exclusive, and by means of the appropriate ICQ, is also vectored. (When defined as vectored, an ETH is always understood by convention to be directional toward the right.) This specification simply states that no student is ever (officially) demoted; therefore the student's single subtype occurrence must always only move to the right. Vectored mutually exclusive ETH are often also presented with state change(s) (shown above in shorthand form), and often triggers and archives as well. (These types of specifications are discussed in the subsequent section on automatic actions.) Mutually exclusive classifications, with either automatic or user-specified vectoring, are especially important in the analysis of entity life cycles (see the Design Supplement).

GUIDELINES AND CONVENTIONS FOR MUTUALLY EXCLUSIVE

- "Mutually exclusive," like "mandatory," is used for objects rather than relationship types.
- A mutually exclusive IC should never be connected from a relationship type on the stimulus side.
- A mutually exclusive integrity constraint is defined by placing "ME" inside an integrity constraint symbol and connecting it from exactly one object (on the stimulus side).
- "Mutually exclusive" specifies that the co-existence of related instances of two or more relationship types and/or objects is prohibited.
- Mutually exclusive is not meaningful for classifications having only a single subtype, or for aggregate objects or aggregate association types.
- Connect the mutually exclusive constraint (on the "behavior" side) to two or more other objects and/or relationship types as appropriate in specifying the associated business rule.
- Use an "any" ICQ to prevent the simultaneous existence of instances of two or more relationship types to the same object even when related to different occurrences of that object.
- Use a "vectored" ICQ if there is a defined order in which occurrences of the mutually exclusive objects and/or relationship types should be created.
- A classification defined as mutually exclusive never has more than one occurrence for all subtypes at a time. If "vectored," this subtype occurrence can only correctly move to the right.
- ICVCs are not generally used for ME.
- Use a clock symbol, with a note, to show any effective or termination date for the constraint.

In Diagram 3.44, a given software package may have many leads, prospects and customers. The mutually exclusive specification indicates, however, that the same company may only be a lead, or a prospect, or a customer (not more than one of these) for the same software package at the same time. The vectoring specifications additionally show that a particular company must first be a lead for a given software package, then and only then a prospect, and then and only then a customer.

Note that use of the "any" ICQ is permitted after the "vectoring" ICQ. Establishing the implications of such use in the above example is left as an exercise for the reader.

Diagram 3.44

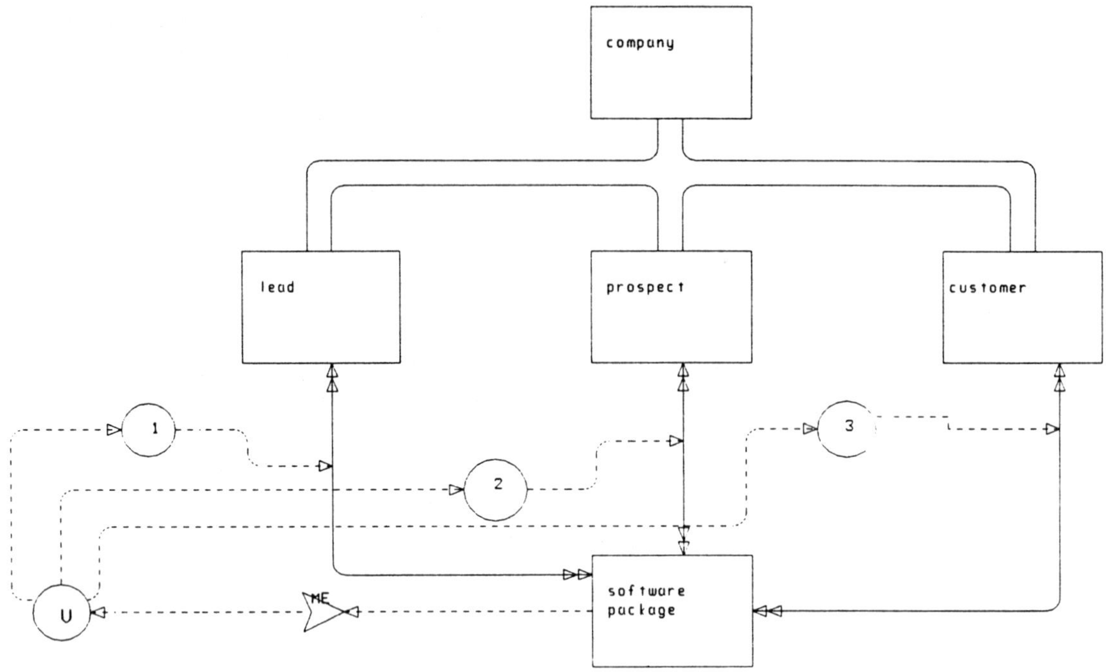

3.1-1.4 Limited

The "limit" IC places constraints on the number of instances of some relationship types(s) and/or object(s) that may exist for some other designated object.

Diagram 3.45

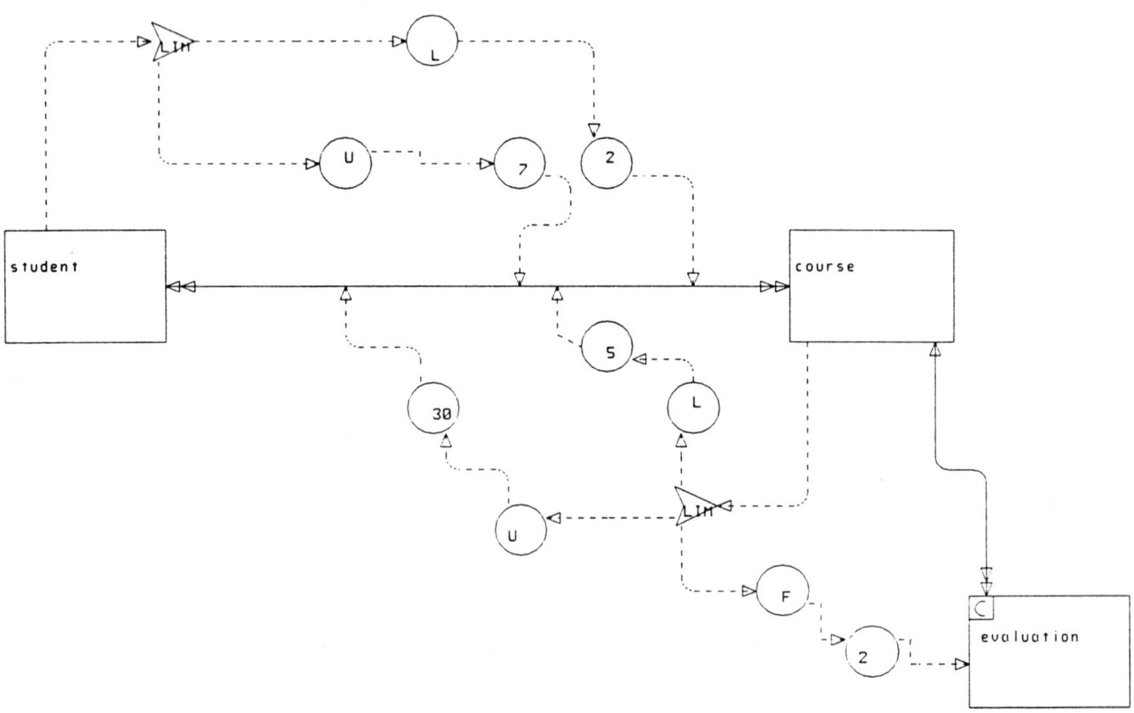

The various limits placed on the model above are as follows:

- A student may not take less than 2 courses (lower limit).
- A student may not take more than 7 courses (upper limit).
- A course must have at least 5 students (lower limit).
- A course may have no more than 30 students (upper limit).
- A course must have two fixed evaluations (fixed limit).

Diagram 3.46

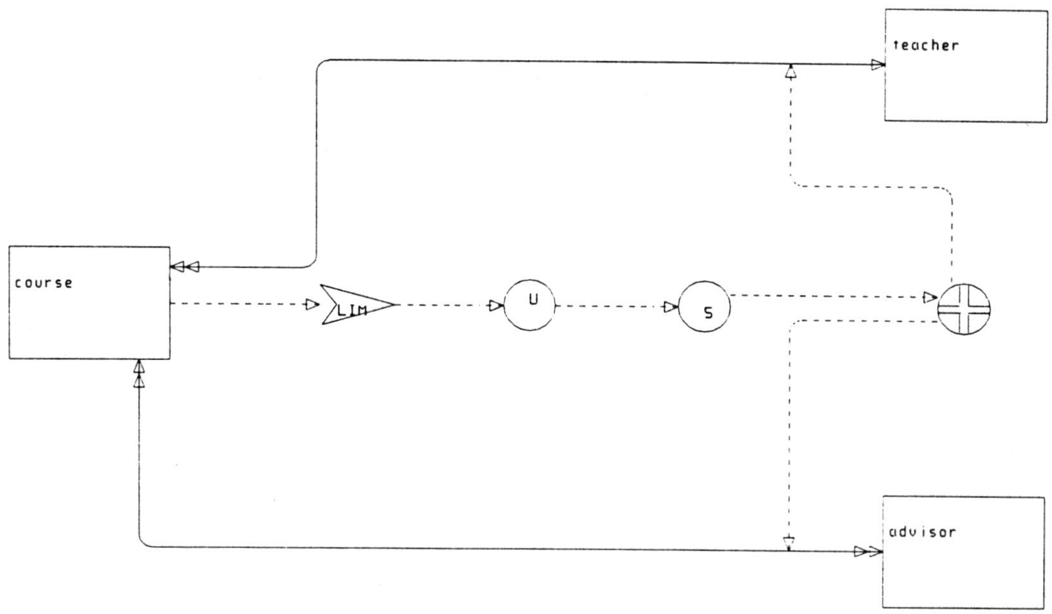

In this example, a course may have a total (upper limit) of 5 teachers and advisors combined.

Diagram 3.47

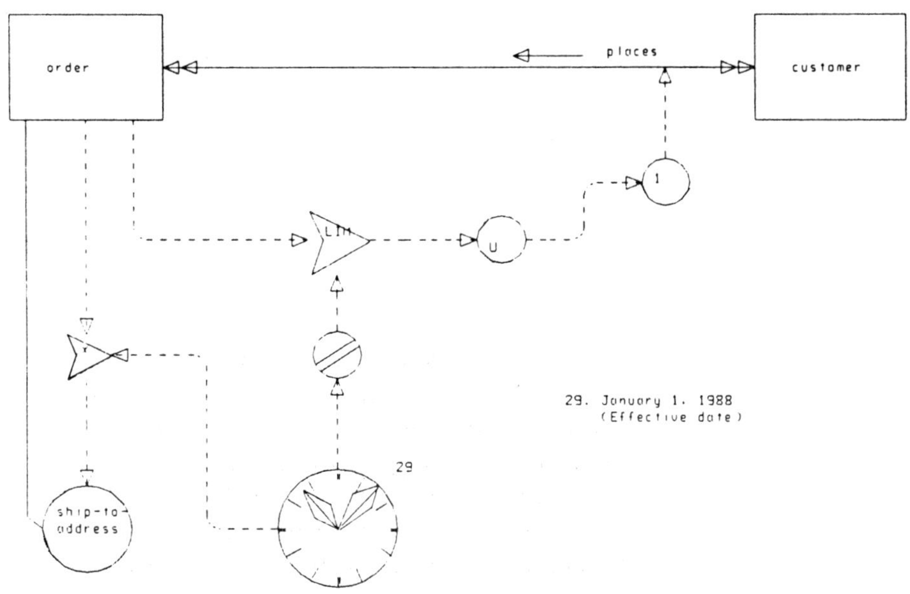

According to the clocked integrity constraint in Diagram 3.47, on the given effective date, the enterprise will cease enforcing a current limit of only one customer per order, but will begin requiring a value of ship-to-address for every order. (Note that the entity model has presumably facilitated this future change by supporting a "many" relationship type to customer, even though currently limited to "one.")

When used between a clock and an IC, the "not" ICQ's usual sense of "prohibited" translates into "terminate" or "cancel," as above.

3.1-1.4-1 Handling Exceptional Cases

Real-life operation of enterprises is full of possible exceptions to standard practices. Whereas these exceptions may occur relatively infrequently, they still must nonetheless be accommodated within information systems. Entity models provide important opportunities to capture and record such cases in a timely and succinct fashion.

Diagram 3.48

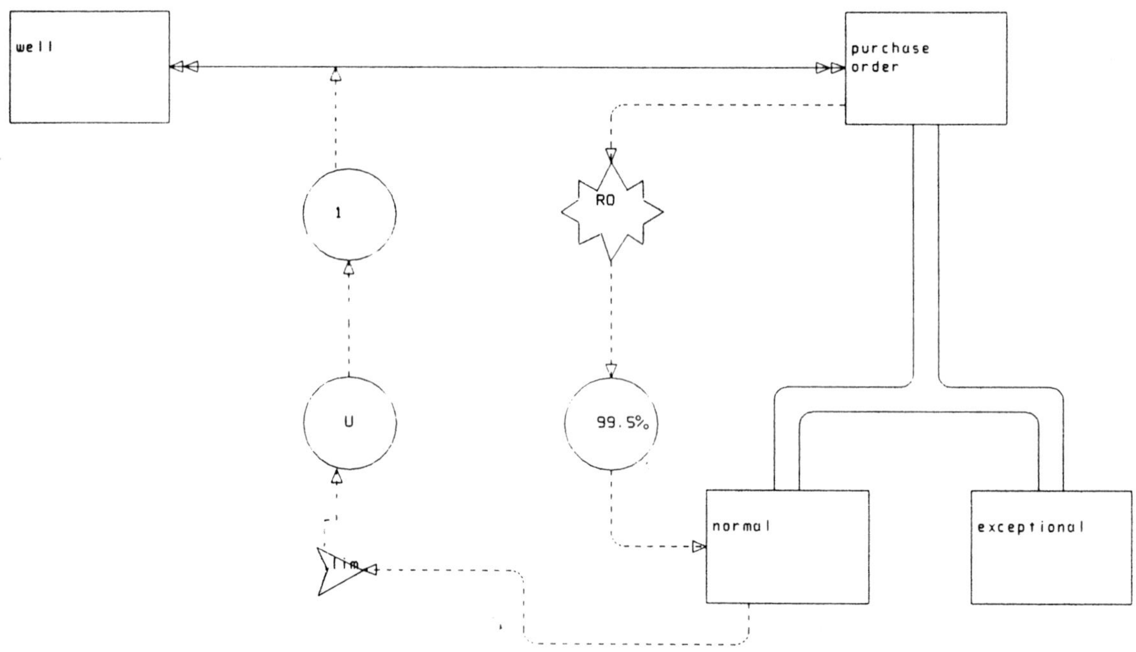

In this petroleum company, over 99% of all purchase orders are "normal." (This is indicated by a relative occurrence frequency estimate.) All normal cases pertain to only one well. There are, however, exceptional circumstances (e.g., natural disasters and storms) where a single purchase order may pertain to "many" wells. The relationship type between purchase order and well has therefore been defined as "many," and the subtype "exceptional" excluded from the "normal" limit.

GUIDELINES AND CONVENTIONS FOR LIMITATIONS

- "Limited," like "mandatory," is used for objects rather than relationship types.
- A limited IC should never be connected from a relationship type on the stimulus side.
- A limited integrity constraint is defined by placing "LIM" inside an integrity constraint symbol and connecting it from exactly one object (on the stimulus side).
- "Limited" places upper, lower, or fixed limits usually on the number of relationship type occurrences some object is permitted to have. Connect to these relationship types on the "behavior" side.
- Define the type of limit, and the numerical quantity, using ICQs.
- "Limited" is not generally meaningful for aggregate objects and aggregate association types.
- Use limitation constraints to differentiate the implications of normal and exceptional business cases.
- ICVCs are not generally used for LIM.
- Use a clock symbol, with a note, to show any effective or termination date for the constraint. (Effective dates are often especially desirable for lower and fixed limitations.)

3.1-1.5 Frozen

The very existence of some specified object(s) and/or connection(s) may preclude any updating to other objects and/or connections. In such an integrity constraint, instances of these other objects and/or connections are frozen—i.e., their current values are fixed.

Diagram 3.49

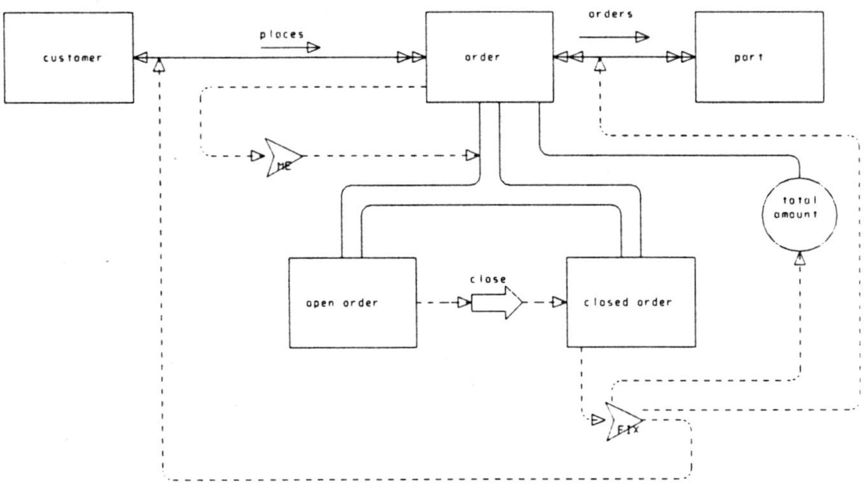

In this diagram, when an order passes to the "closed" subtype (i.e., upon the state change "close," which is shown here in the abbreviated form), the current instances of the relationship types "places" and "orders" for the order are frozen, as is the current value of total-amt, one of its attribute types.

Diagram 3.50

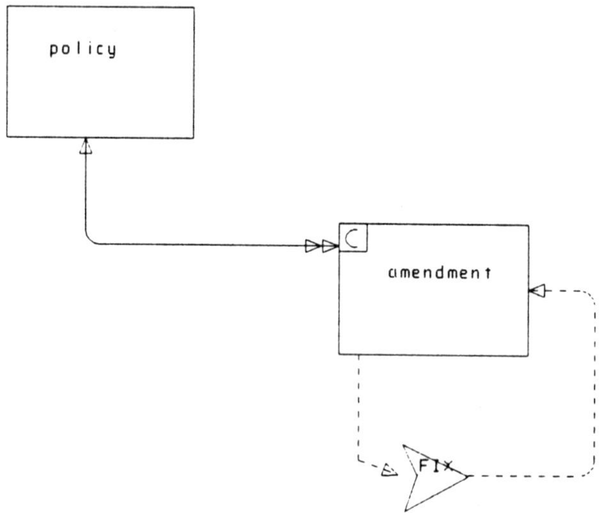

Upon creation, an occurrence of a policy "amendment" is frozen. No updates to that amendment are subsequently permitted.

CONVENTIONS AND GUIDELINES FOR FROZEN

- A frozen constraint is defined by placing a "FIX" inside an integrity constraint symbol.
- Identify what object(s) and/or relationship type(s) whose existence of occurrences causes the current values of other object(s) and/or relationship types to be frozen.
- Identify the former on the stimulus side, and the latter on the "behavior" side.
- ICQs and ICVCs are not generally used for frozen.
- Use a clock symbol, with a note, to show any effective or termination date for the constraint.

3.1-2 Automatic Actions

Certain updating actions can, or should be translated automatically into certain other update actions that are executed within the same time-frame. Since the correctness of the database depends on these **automatic actions** occurring as defined, they too fall under the category of "integrity." As behavior, their stimulus is one update and their reaction is another (set of) update(s). From an analytical point of view, they can always be described in the sense of business rules or operational policies.

Defining automatic actions (AAs) is accomplished by invoking an **action** (or process) object, specifying the type (or subclass) of the automatic action, and connecting the object correctly on both the stimulus side and the reaction side to other objects and/or connections. A list of AA subclasses is given below. It should be noted that the detailed operation or invocation of AAs can be controlled or qualified by triggers.

Diagram 3.51

Automatic Actions (AAs)

PROP	**Propagation**	An update causes one or more other updates.
INIT	**Initiation**	An update causes initiation of values for specified objects or connections.
REPL	**Replacement**	An update causes substitution of one thing for another.
PAIR	**Pairing**	An update causes 1-to-1 pairing of two occurrences.
AGREL	**Aggregate Relationship Type**	An update to a relationship type instance is automatically coordinated with an aggregate relationship instance.
STATE	**State Change**	An update precipitates a state change for an object.
ARCH	**Archiving**	An update, or the passage of time, causes automatic archiving.

By convention, if an action object has a user-defined name (rather than an automatic action name) and no specified trigger, the object is assumed to be a user-defined process. This is especially significant in the definition of state changes during entity life cycle analysis, which supports discovery and identification of transactions and processes on a data-controlled basis. (See the Design Supplement.)

3.1-2.1 Propagation

The propagation of an update permits automatic recording of some additional event(s) or interaction(s).

Diagram 3.52

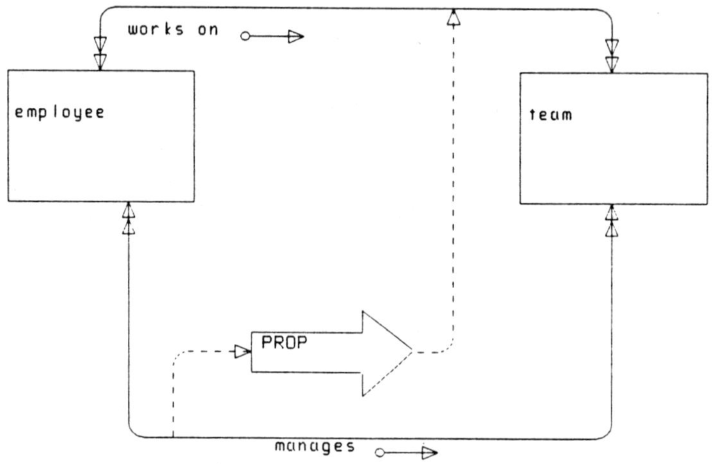

In this model, the manager of a team must also be included among workers for that team. The above propagation for the "manages" relationship type implies the following:

- Whenever an instance of "manages" is added to the database, it will also automatically be added as a "works on" instance.
- Whenever an instance of "manages" is changed, the corresponding instance of "works on" is changed.
- Whenever an instance of "manages" is deleted, the corresponding instance of "works on" is also deleted.

Furthermore, in order to avoid disintegrity, the propagated instances for "works on" are **locked into** the propagation. In other words, those particular instances (but only those instances) cannot be directly updated by users on the "works on" side.

These rules generally hold true for all propagations. Incidentally, the propagation above would work exactly the same had association types been added into the M:N relationship types.

In Diagram 3.53, the cars on a particular running of a train must also be recorded as moving. A propagation has been defined to record such movement. These car movement instances, of course, are "locked into" the propagation as previously described. There are several noteworthy features of this example:

- One "run" instance translates into multiple "move" instances.
- "Run" and "move" are defined equivalently—both are characteristics with the same type of determinant (e.g., date-time). Such

Diagram 3.53

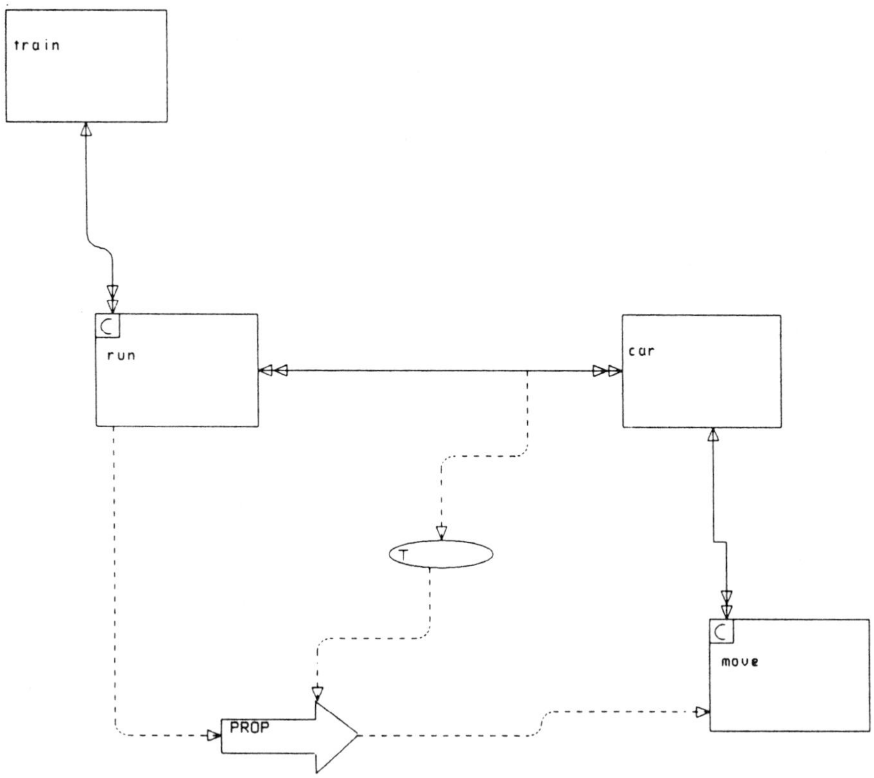

equivalence on the stimulus and reaction sides is necessary in all propagations.

- This propagation has a defined trigger, which designates which cars are relevant to the propagation (i.e., those on the particular running of a train). The trigger thus acts as a qualification (i.e., *only* those cars on a particular run are of interest).

GUIDELINES AND CONVENTIONS FOR PROPAGATION

- The object or relationship type on the reaction side must be equivalent to the one on the stimulus side.
- Updates to the reaction side object or relationship type will be echoed to the reaction side.
- Updates to the echoed instances on the reaction side are inhibited for users. (This distinguishes propagation from initiation.)
- Triggers may be used to qualify the propagation; that is, to narrow the instances to be propagated.
- Use clocks to specify time-based propagations.

3.1-2.2 Initiation

Updates to certain objects or connections can, or should, cause automatic initiation of one or more other objects or connections. The instances of the latter objects or connections, which are on the reaction side of this automatic action, are not, however, locked into it. Thus, unlike propagation, subsequent user updates to them are permitted. In essence, after initiation, the particular instances produced by the AA are completely uncoupled from the instances from which they originally derived.

Diagram 3.54

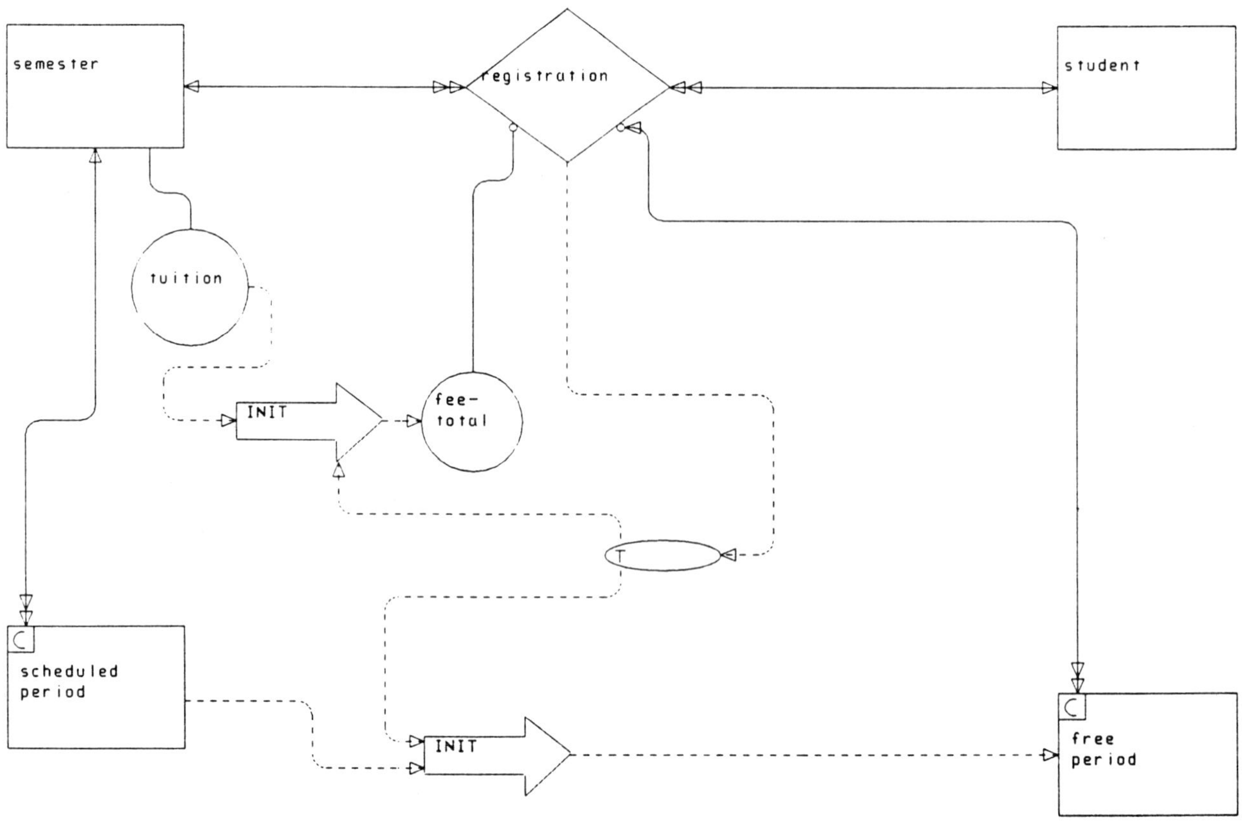

Upon registering for a semester, two initiations are automatically triggered. First, the students' semester fee-total is initialized to the standard semester tuition value. Second, a list of free-periods (a characteristic) is initiated for the student in that semester based on the semester's scheduled periods. Note that in both these cases, the objects on the stimulus and reaction sides are defined in equivalent fashion.

Once initiated, both the student's fee-total as well as his or her free periods may be updated freely by the user. For example, the fee-total may be incremented for other charges. No further automatic actions will occur for those particular instances.

GUIDELINES AND CONVENTIONS FOR INITIATION

- The objects or relationship types on the reaction side must match the ones on the stimulus side.
- Values, occurrences or instances on the stimulus side are echoed once, and only once, to the corresponding objects and/or relationship types on the reaction side.
- Updates to the echoed instances on the reaction side are not inhibited for users. (This distinguishes initiation from propagation.)
- Subsequent updates to the things on the stimulus side will not be echoed to the corresponding things on the reaction side.
- Triggers may be used to pinpoint and qualify the precise event that causes the initialization to occur.
- Nonautomatic updates to echoed instances on the reaction side can be inhibited, if desired, by use of a prohibited qualifier for an appropriate integrity constraint defined for the given object or relationship type. (In such case, automatic archiving is probably also desirable, in order to provide some means for removal of instances from the database.)
- Use clocks to specify time-based initiation.

3.1-2.3 Replacement

Replacement is a special class of automatic action wherein a specified type of update causes an instance of an object or connection to be deleted and replaced by an instance of another equivalent object or connection. This more or less constitutes an automatic "move."

GUIDELINES AND CONVENTIONS FOR REPLACEMENT

- The stimulus side and reaction side objects in a replacement AA must be equivalent.
- A trigger should be defined showing what specific type of update causes it to occur.
- Replaced instances of the reaction side object may not be added or deleted by users, nor their determinant values altered. (They are "locked into" the replacement.)
- Use clocks to specify time-based replacement.

Diagram 3.55

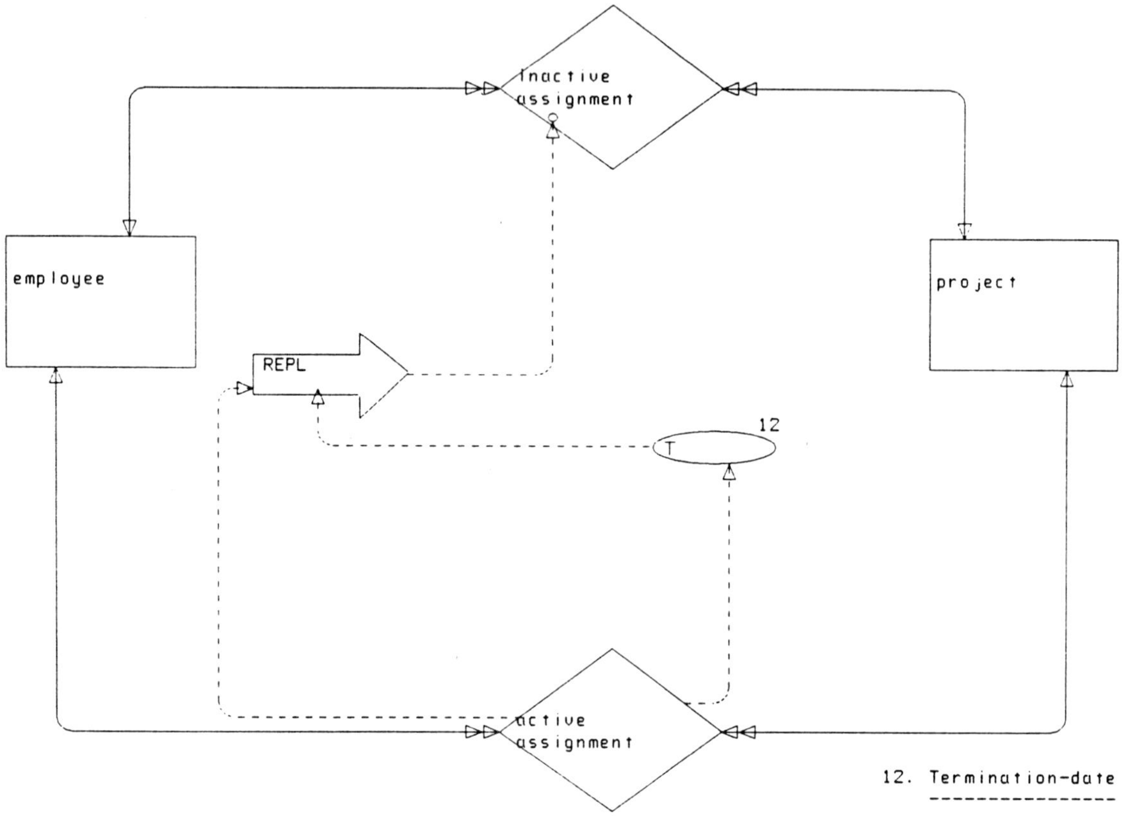

In this example "active assignment" and "inactive assignment" are equivalent association types. The replacement AA prescribes that an instance of the former will be replaced by an instance of the latter (which is "locked into" the replacement) based on the defined (attribute-level) trigger. This trigger prescribes that the replacement is to occur whenever a value for termination-date is supplied (i.e., it is nonnull). Naturally, termination-date must be a defined attribute of both association types.

In Diagram 3.56 (continued from a previous one), the student's free periods in a semester are initiated from the "scheduled period" characteristic of semester. Whenever a student subsequently "takes" a seat in some class, a replacement is automatically triggered that eliminates the free period from the student's registration and substitutes an instance of "committed period." This latter instance is "locked into" the AA.

Note that in this model, "committed period" has been defined as "not stored." This means instances are not actually stored. (If a list of committed periods is required, it can always be produced by accessing all the class periods for courses taken.)

In essence, replacement without restorage is simply deletion. This can be denoted in shorthand fashion as the following example illustrates.

In Diagram 3.57, after a train completes a run, its cars may be individually "placed into" a holding area until assigned to a new running of a train. As soon as such new assignment is made, however, the existing

Diagram 3.56

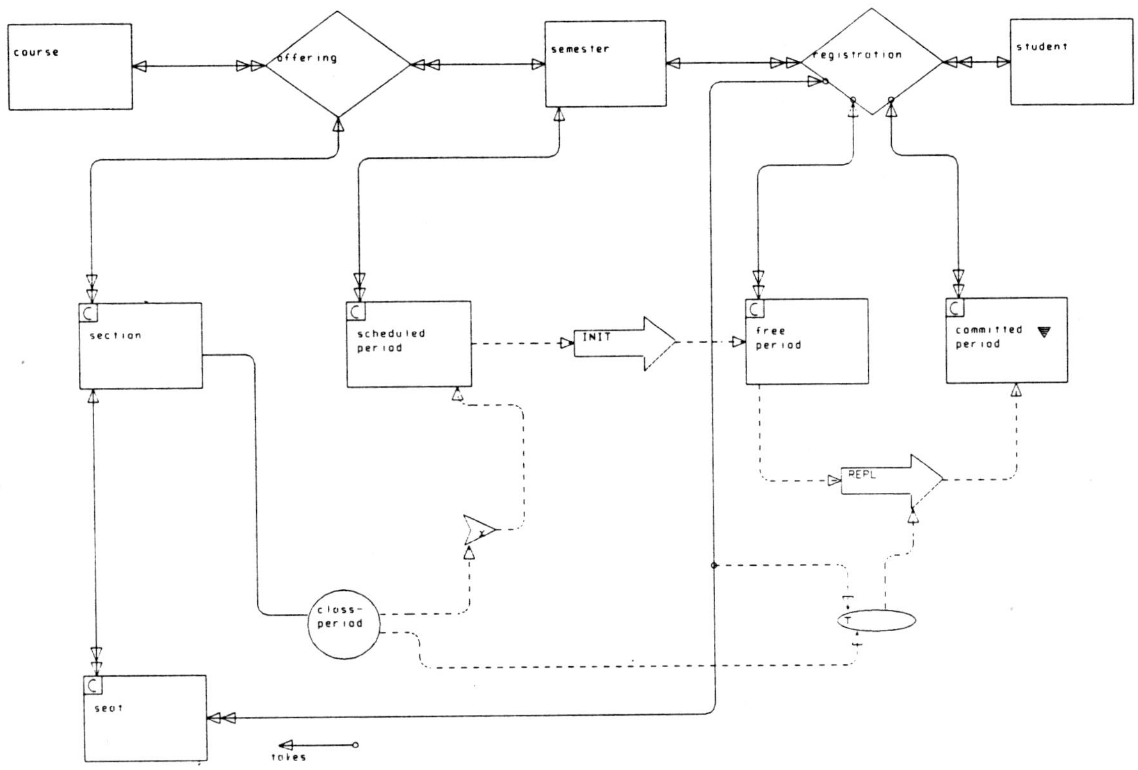

Diagram 3.57

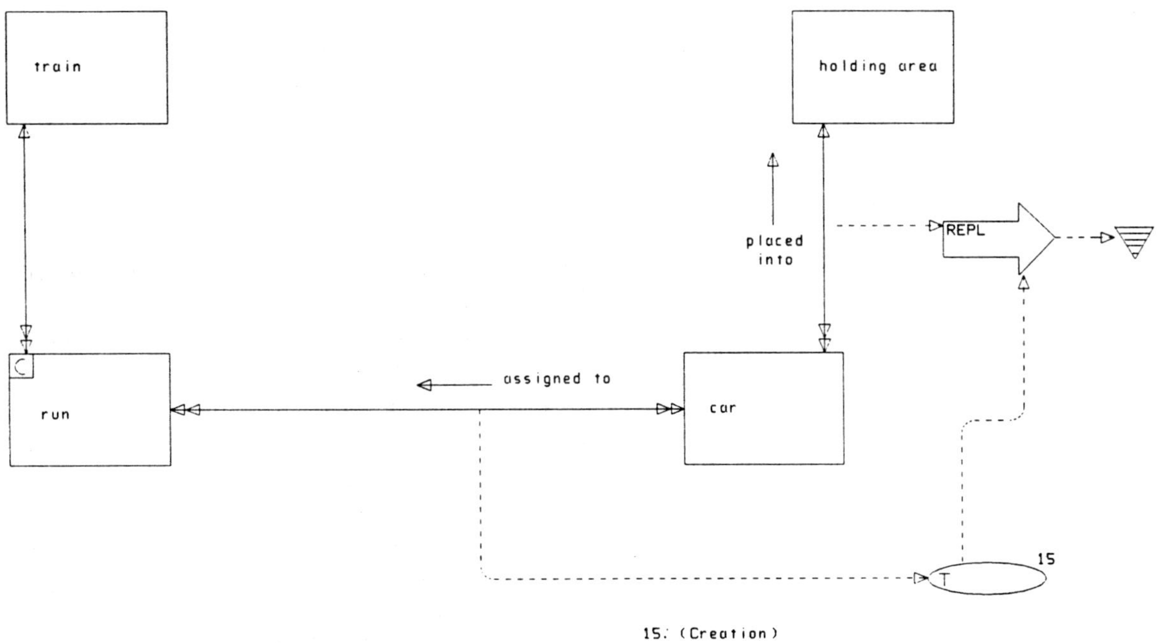

relationship instance to "holding area" can be discarded. Note that since this instance is discarded, and cannot be reconstructed in any fashion, it is not in any meaningful sense "locked into" the AA.

3.1-2.4 Pairing

Pairing is another special type of automatic action. In pairing, every instance of one object type, which must be either a characteristic or a kernel entity type, must be paired upon creation with exactly one instance of another object type. This latter instance is generally the most recent.

Diagram 3.58

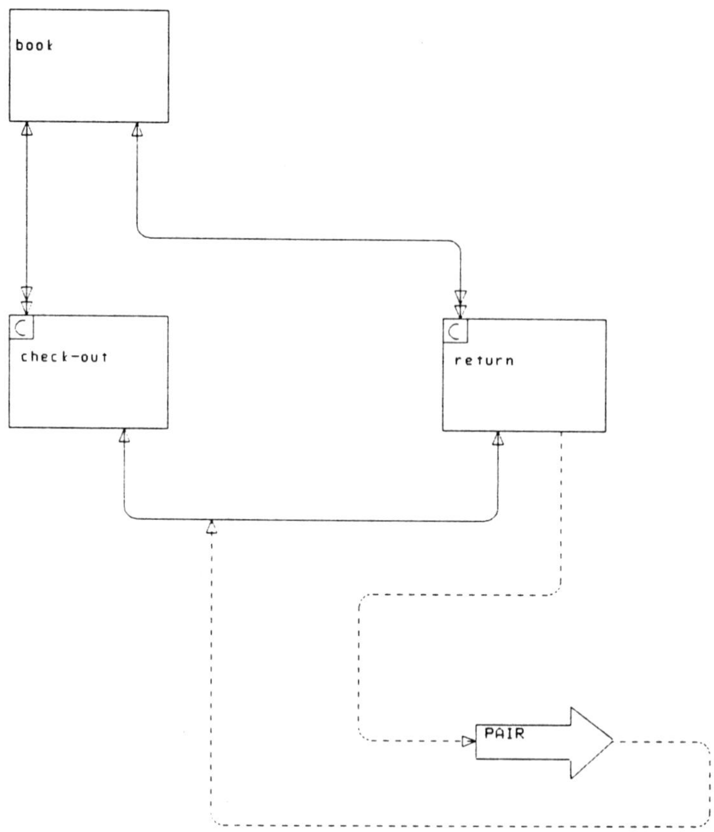

In this library enterprise, every "return" of a book (determined by date-time) must be paired with the single, most recent "check-out" of the book (also determined by date-time). Naturally a "return" (called the **pairing object**) that cannot be "paired" is cause for special user action. Note that a 1:1 relationship is required between paired objects. Note also that new instances of "check-out" (called the **paired object**) cannot be created until all previous instances have been successfully paired.

In Diagram 3.59, every railroad car "departure" must be paired with the (most recent) arrival at a station.

Normally in pairing, the determinants of the respective object types are defined on the same domain. In this case, pairing automatically requires that the determinant value of the pairing object be greater than, or equal to, the determinant value of the paired object. (Also, the determinant value of each new instance of the paired object must be greater than, or equal to, the last instance of the pairing object.) These rules permit automatic

Diagram 3.59

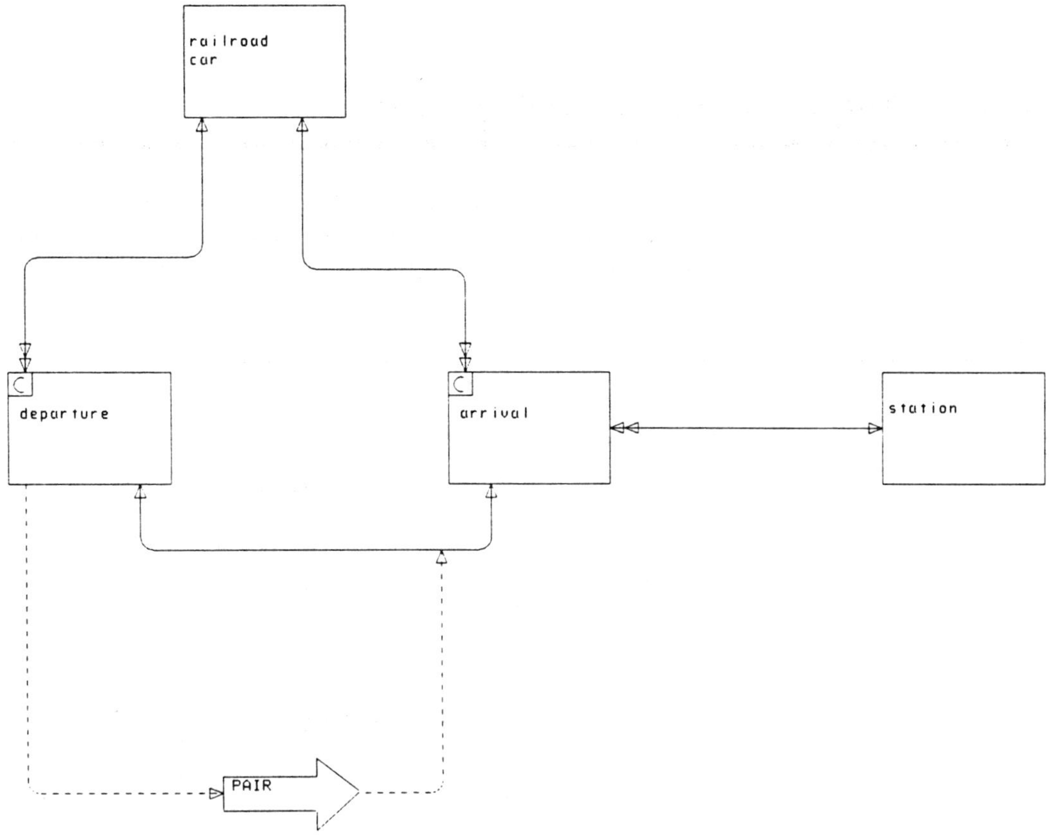

GUIDELINES AND CONVENTIONS FOR PAIRING

- Pairing is always defined for two equivalent characteristics and/or kernel entity types.
- The determinants of the two respective object types are normally defined on the same domain, so that instances can be automatically co-sequenced.
- The paired objects must be connected by a 1:1 relationship type.
- An instance of the stimulus-side object (the pairing object) can only exist if paired with an instance of the reaction-side object (the paired object). (This is generally the most recently created object instance.)
- Failure of an instance to pair is cause for error and rejection.
- New instances of the object on the reaction side cannot be created until all prior instances have successfully paired.
- Clocks should generally not be used with pairing.

mutual sequencing of the objects' occurrences. For example, if the determinants represent date-time, these rules require that every new instance of the two objects be mutually sequenced according to time.

3.1-2.5 Aggregate Relationship Type

This automatic action automatically manages all aspects of instances of an aggregate relationship type, including creation and deletion. Users may not update these instances.

Diagram 3.60

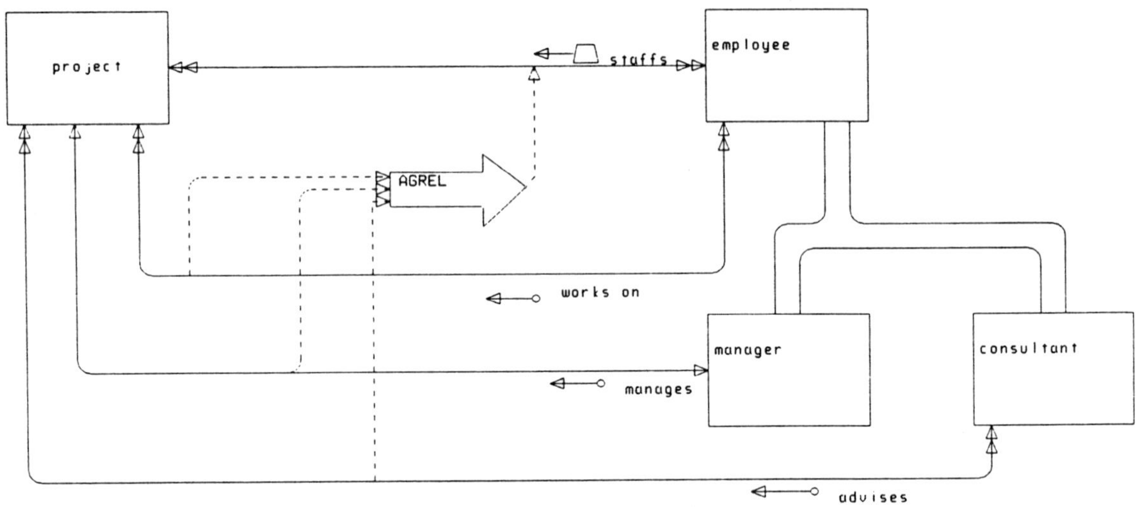

In this example, instances of "staffs" (defined as an aggregate relationship type) will always be "automatic" (i.e., system-managed), based on the replication of update actions for "works on," "manages," and "advises." Users may "read" or "traverse" instances of "staffs," but never update them. (If "propagation" had been specified, updates to "locked-in" instances only would have been inhibited.) This AA provides an important alternative to earlier approaches to aggregate relationship types, including the original nonstored version, as well as the integrity-controlled, but user-managed version discussed under "restriction" ICs.

Note that "staffs" above is an M:N relationship type. Since association types are generally desirable and/or necessary for M:N relationship types, "staffs" should probably be modified to include one.

However, since aggregate relationship types are out-of- bounds to user updating, use of the regular association type symbol (a diamond) may not be desirable. Therefore a new symbol is introduced for specific use under AGREL, called an **aggregate association type**. As illustrated below, it has the shape of a trapezoid. In all other respects, the aggregate association type acts just like a regular association type, including compliance with General Integrity Rule #1.

Diagram 3.61

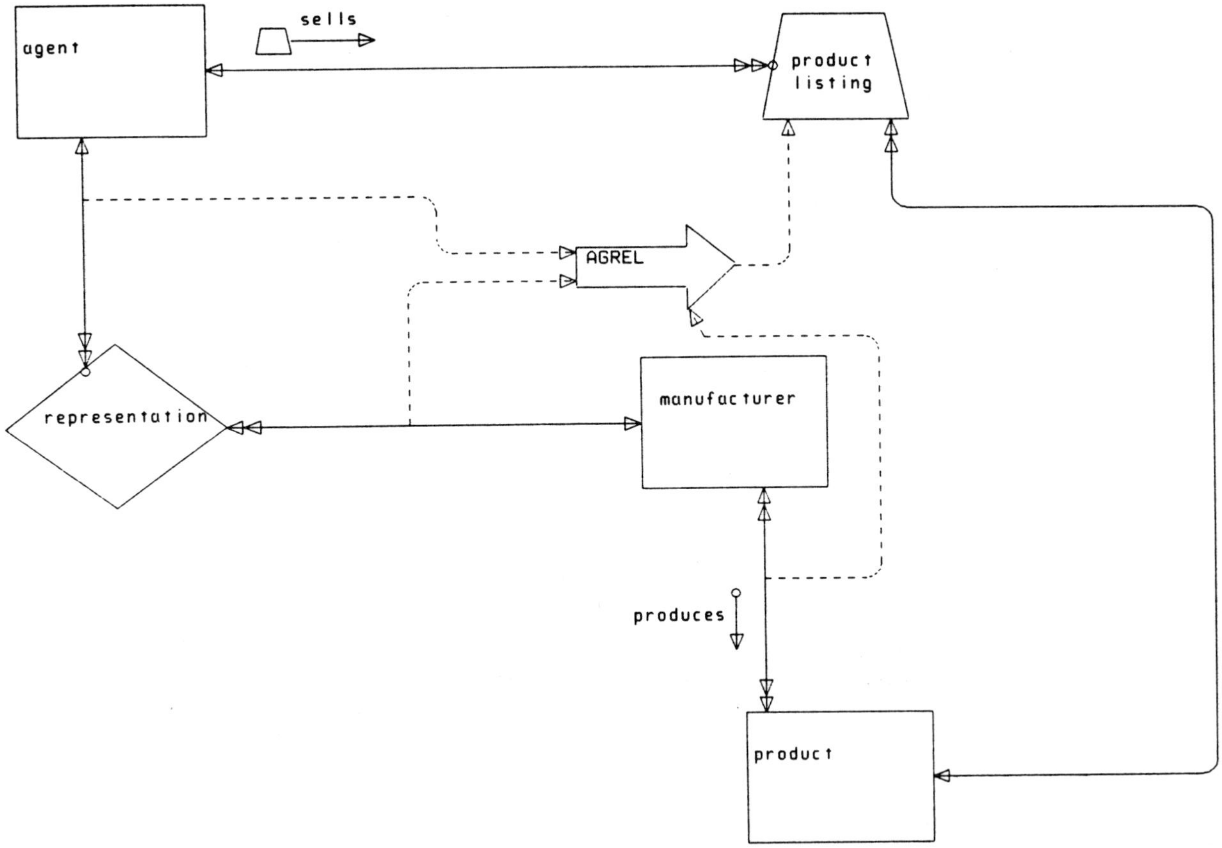

In this example, an AGREL AA has been defined for the designated stimulus-side relationship types. The reaction side points to the "sells" aggregate relationship type, where an aggregate association type (called "product listing") has been inserted. (See the section on Measurement for insight into the types of automatic intersection data that might be managed therein.) Users will not be permitted to update instances of either "sells" or "product listing" itself.

As with any association type, the aggregate association type borrows the determinants of the objects it relates (i.e., "agent" and "product") to also use as its own. As previously discussed, there may be fewer instances of "product listing" than total "traces" on the stimulus side since an agent may represent multiple manufacturers who nonetheless "produce" the very same product. One important function of AGREL is to consolidate such repetitions automatically.

The reader may want to try the following modification to the above model as an exercise. Suppose agents may sell some, but not necessarily all of the products of each manufacturer they represent. (They still may sell the same product for multiple manufacturers.) Adjust "product listing" to reflect this new selectivity. (Hint: first introduce a new association type.) Note: This particular problem is often presented to illustrate "fifth normal form" in discussions of normalization.

GUIDELINES AND CONVENTIONS FOR AGREL

- AGREL may be defined for any aggregate relationship type.
- Users may not update any instances of the aggregate relationship type.
- Updates to instances of the stimulus-side relationship types are automatically reflected on the reaction side.
- Consolidation of "redundant" traces is performed automatically.
- For M:N aggregate relationship types, a special aggregate association type should be used, which by convention, is a trapezoid.
- Aggregate association types obey all rules for regular association types.
- Clocks should generally not be used for AGREL.

3.1-2.6 State Change

This automatic action provides the opportunity, usually via triggers, to specify precisely what conditions cause a state change to occur. State changes are particularly significant in the analysis of entity life cycles which may be used for the discovery of transactions and processes. (See Design Supplement.)

Diagram 3.62

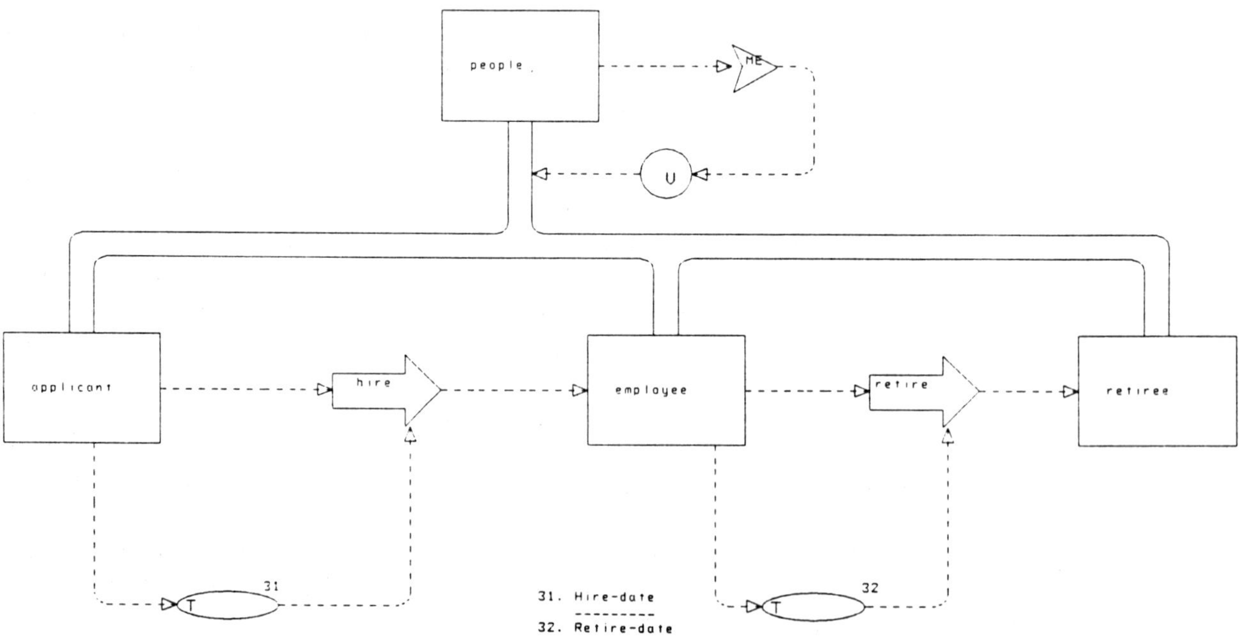

In this classification, which is vectored mutually exclusive, the state change (of a person) from "applicant" to "employee" ("hire") is caused by supplying a value for hire-date (an attribute type). The state change "retire" from "employee" to "retiree" is caused by supplying a value of retire-date, another attribute type.

Note that user-defined action names (i.e., "hire" and "retire") have been used in the diagram above for the state change action objects, rather than the official AA name "STATE." (Such selective naming is recommended practice.) The state changes shown in this example are still automatic, however, since sufficient attribute triggers have been specified.

GUIDELINES AND CONVENTIONS FOR STATE CHANGE

- The automatic action STATE may only be used in mutually exclusive classifications. Such classifications are often vectored.
- A state change may be defined between subtypes (often adjacent), or for the ETH as a whole.
- Only one state change, always moving to the right, should be defined between any given pair of subtypes.
- Use a user-specified action name to identify a state change wherever possible. This name may have aliases.
- A trigger must be defined for the state change to be automatic.
- The trigger may state one or more conditions that cause the state change to occur.
- Use clocks to specify time-based state changes.

3.1-2.7 Archive

The archive automatic action provides an opportunity for stating the conditions, usually via triggers, under which the archiving of appropriate instances of specified objects and/or relationship types is to occur. Archived data is presumed outside the control of the entity model, but not necessarily lost to the enterprise. Archiving criteria are presumed "weaker" than for any other IC or AA.

Diagram 3.63

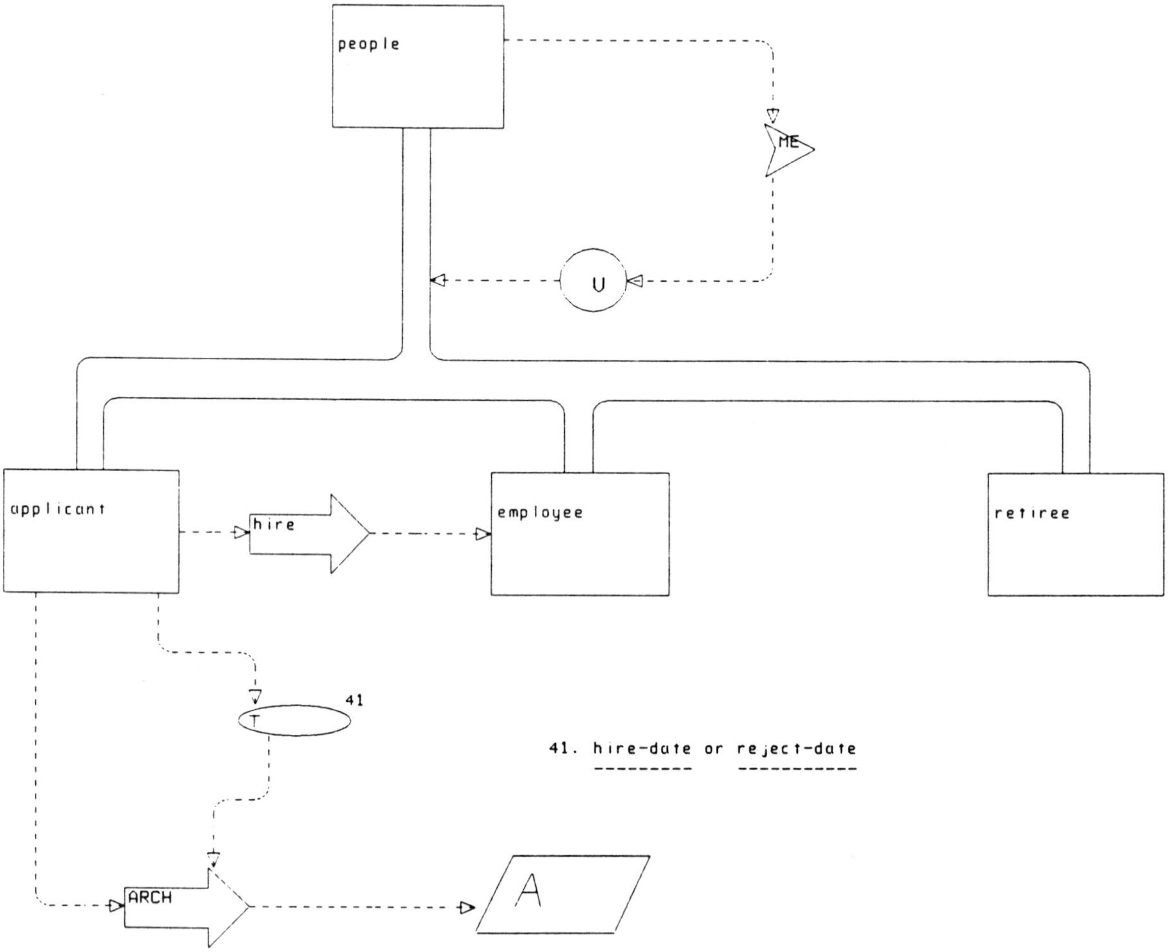

In this example, which continues the previous, information about applicants is designated for automatic archiving. A special symbol, by convention a parallelogram, has been introduced for this purpose. (Since there is no selective notation for the archive itself, everything about applicants is presumed designated for archiving.)

Archives have the special sense of data for which updating is discontinued or disallowed (i.e., "frozen"). The data is presumed stored (for example, on tape, microfilm, paper, or even direct access devices), but outside the normal scope of the entity model and the associated database. (To avoid clutter, the ARCH AA object is often omitted, showing only the archive itself. In this usage the trigger connects directly to the archive.)

Note that the trigger above includes hire-date, the same as for the previous state change. Since the classification is defined as mutually exclusive, the archiving thus may "save" applicant information (for the enterprise) that could not have otherwise been retained or passed forward. (This is a common usage.) Note also that the trigger includes a reject-date, at which point the person is no longer of "active" interest to the enterprise.

Diagram 3.64

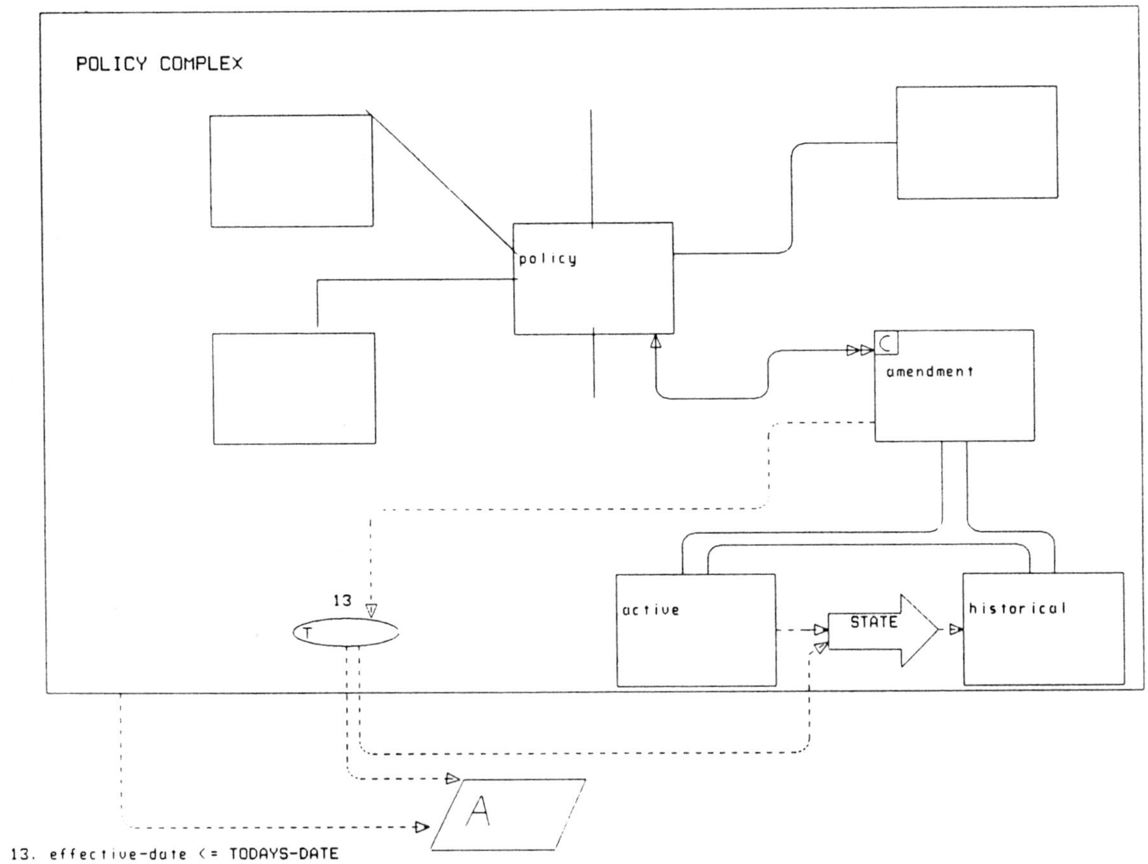

An aggregate object called "policy complex" is used in this example to define all the objects (and connections) appropriate for automatic archiving in this triggered behavior. Use of aggregate objects to define archiving boundaries whenever larger than a single object is recommended practice.

Upon the effective date of an amendment, a "snapshot" of the relevant portion of the database is made in order to record "before images" of the changes to be applied. Such snapshot archives may be subsequently used to reconstruct or audit existing conditions at a given point in time. (Note: It may be desirable to "freeze" amendments once they pass into the historical state so as to avoid possible inconsistency with the archived information. To do this, the business policy of the enterprise must permit retroactive corrections to be made as new amendments.)

"Snapshot" archives are frequently used where complicated or sensitive modifications are being made to data, or where complex outputs (e.g., reports, documents, communications to customers, etc.) are being produced. This is especially useful if the DBMS-supplied audit trail or recovery log is inadequate for supporting easy reconstruction and inspection.

GUIDELINES AND CONVENTIONS FOR ARCHIVES

- An archive is designated by a special parallelogram.
- The archive may appear only on the reaction side of an ARCH AA.
- The ARCH AA may connect on the stimulus side from one or more data objects, which define the information to be archived.
- The ARCH AA object itself may be dropped from an entity model to avoid clutter.
- At least one trigger should normally be defined for each archive. (For convenience, this trigger can be omitted if the trigger simply covers creation and any modification of the exact same information as to be archived.)
- This trigger may specify one or more conditions under which archiving is to occur.
- An archive is often a better choice than an active/historical classification of some objects, especially if the "historical" information is unlikely to be ever used or changed subsequently.
- If the archive does not specify what particular items are to be archived, then "everything" (within the bounds of the specification) is assumed.
- Archiving may not violate other ICs or AAs.
- Use archiving to "save" information that cannot otherwise be passed forward in state changes of mutually exclusive classifications.
- Use aggregate objects to specify complexes of objects and connections to be archived.
- Archiving triggers defined without additional specifications automatically produce "after" images.
- In cases where changes are prerecorded as pending amendments, effective dates defined for triggers can be used to automatically produce "before" images.
- Use the codes "BI" or "AI" within an archive to clarify the need for either "before" or "after" images in modification-triggered archives.
- If the same trigger is defined for both a state change and an archive involving the same subtype, the archiving occurs first.
- Use clocks to indicate time-based archiving.

SECTION 2
Attribute-Level Objects and Connections

Automatic behavior at the attribute level primarily involves triggers, determinants and foreign-keys, and referential integrity.

Triggers, which always operate at an attribute level even when connected from other types of objects, are important devices for specifying many types of automatic behavior in detail. Such usage (which was suggested by several examples in the previous section) is explored more fully here. Triggers are also useful in the important problem of handling the time dimension of entity models (i.e., time-sequenced data). Several opportunities in this regard are also discussed in this section.

Determinant and foreign key specifications were discussed in Part II, in connection with defining attributes, and are not discussed further here. This section does, however, examine in depth Referential Integrity, a topic which is much discussed in conjunction with the relational model. Because Referential Integrity has to do with update inhibitions and propagations based on foreign key values, it also constitutes important attribute-level behavior.

3.2-1 Triggers

Triggers are needed to fully define certain relevant types of automatic behavior in an entity model. Even though they often connect from other objects on their stimulus side, they nonetheless always involve some sort of update action by attribute value. They may be therefore considered attribute-level objects.

As their name suggests, triggers may be used to control the "firing" of certain automatic actions (and measurement signals). They are always used in conjunction with these two behaviors, never for integrity constraints.

A trigger may be viewed in two ways, both correct:

- As a statement of the specific updates that cause other updates or arithmetic operations to occur.
- As a means to limit these other updates or arithmetic operations to cases where specific conditions hold true (i.e., as qualifications).

In Diagram 3.65, all employees are either staff members or executives (a mutually exclusive, vectored classification). The deciding factor (trigger) is salary. As defined, a salary of $30,000 or greater automatically moves an employee into "executive" status. The trigger is thus both the cause of the state change (salary becomes $30,000 or more) as well as its *qualifier* (no state change occurs *unless* salary reaches this level).

Diagram 3.65

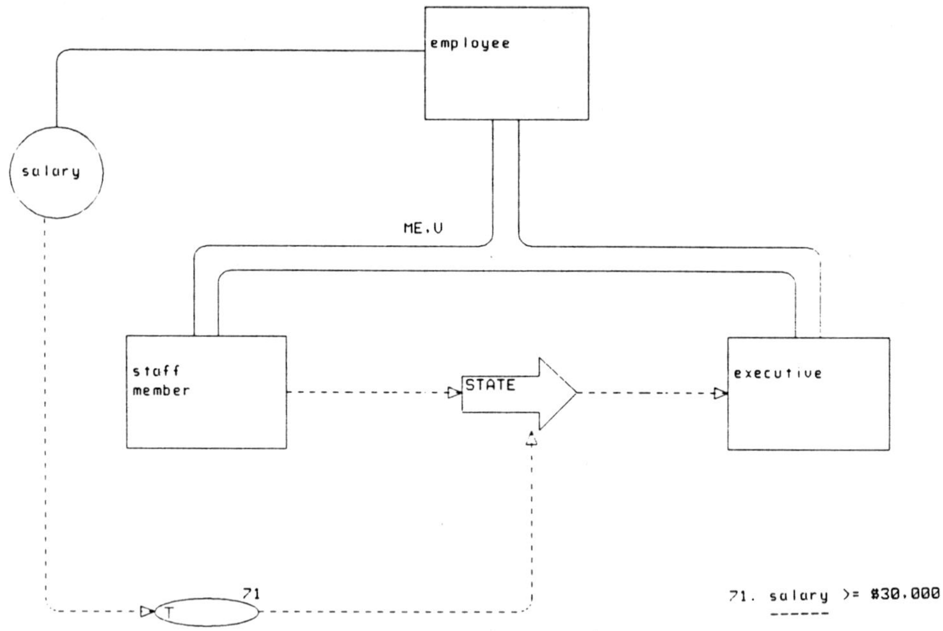

A trigger is always understood as involving update actions for attribute types. This is true even if the stimulus side connects to another type of object. In this case, updates for the object's determinants are considered decisive for the trigger unless other conditions are specified.

Additional examples of more complex triggers are given in the following.

Diagram 3.66

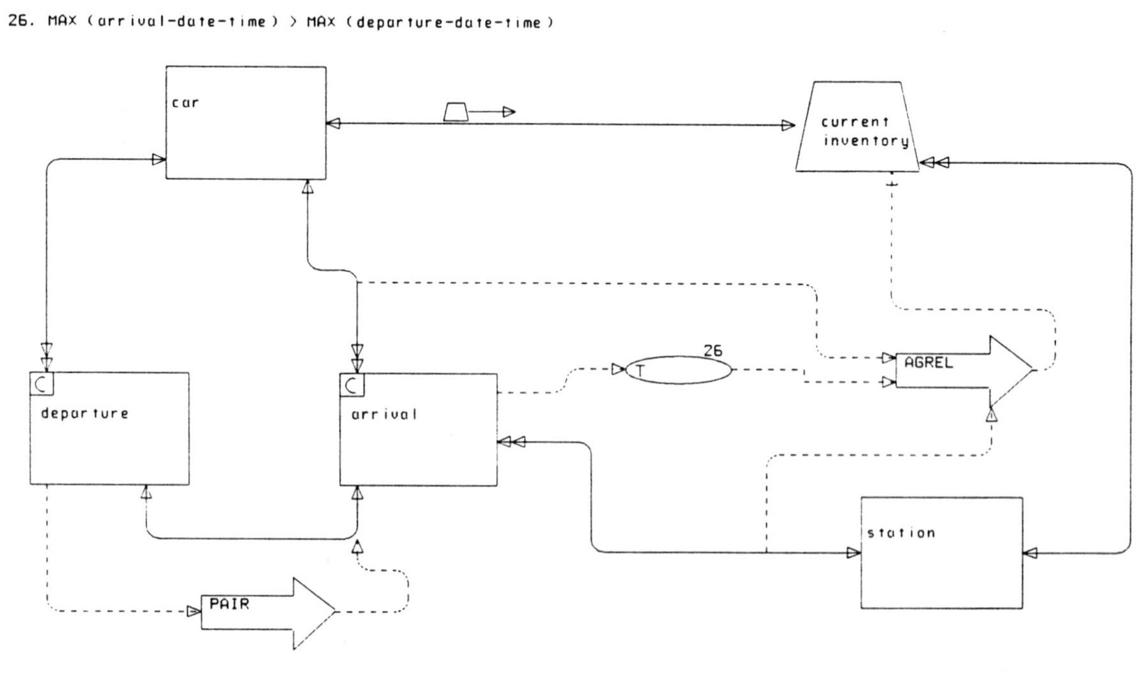

In this example, this "railroad" enterprise keeps track of all car movements historically. This makes quick access to an up-to-the-minute car "inventory" for some particular station problematic. To solve this difficulty, an aggregate relationship type has been established. The trigger essentially says that only an "arrival" not paired with a later "departure" may produce instances for the aggregate association type.

Diagram 3.67

21. MAX (return-date-time) >= MAX (checkout-date-time)
23. MAX (return-date-time) < MAX (check-out-date-time)

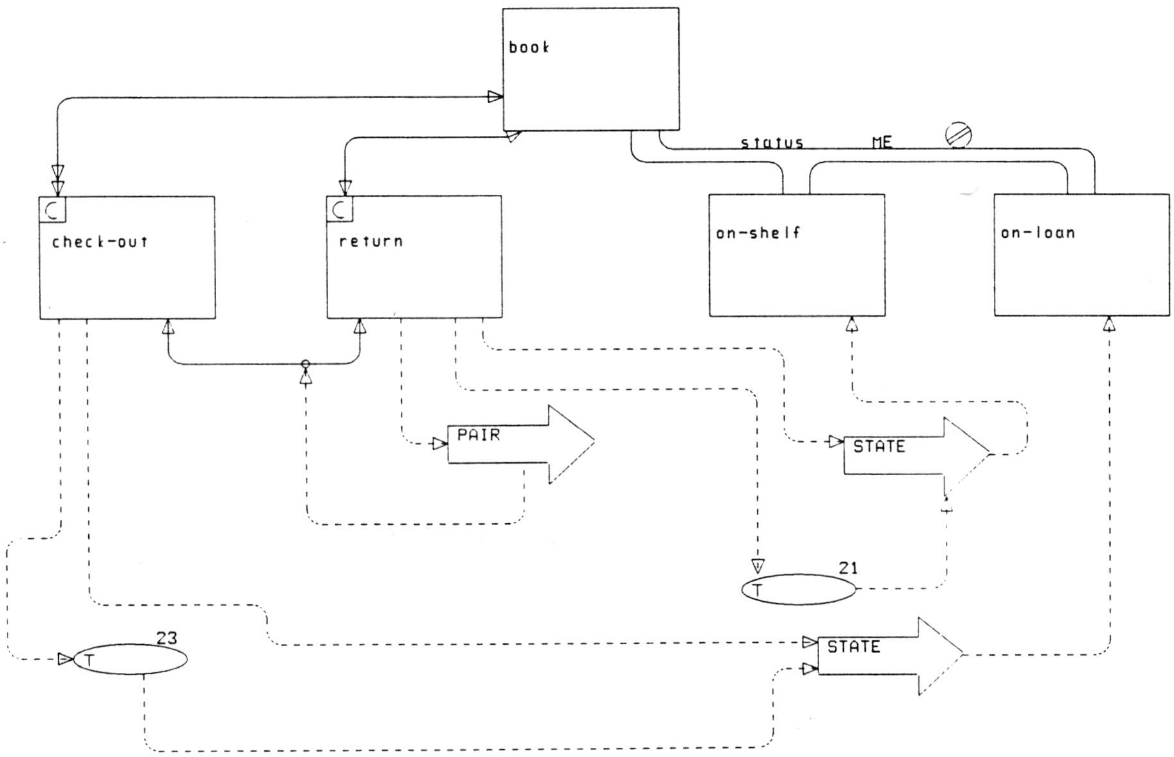

This example automates a library "enterprise" system. A "return" propagates to an "on-shelf" subtype occurrence, whereas a "check-out" propagates to an "on-loan" subtype occurrence. The triggers provide relevant attribute-level conditions for the propagation.

Note that since these triggers are defined as the inverse of each other, one properly "unlocks" before (or simultaneously as) the other. (Exercise for the reader: Show "status" as a pro forma classification using a "source" type-code in "book." Do any of the AA or trigger definitions change?)

In Diagram 3.68, triggers are used via propagation AAs to create appropriate instances of measurement points for the defined automatic measurement. (Measurement is discussed in Section 3.3.1.)

Diagram 3.68

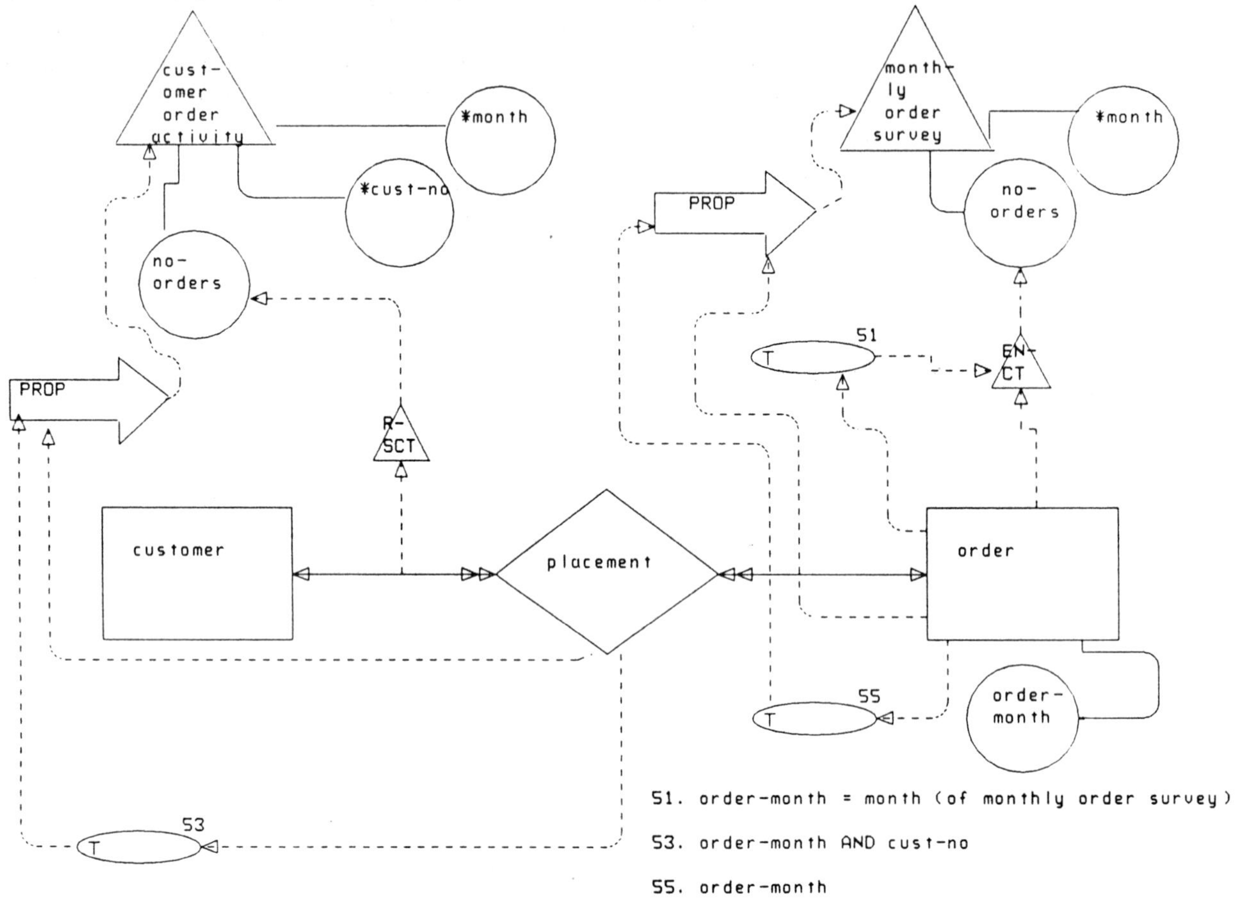

GUIDELINES AND CONVENTIONS FOR TRIGGERS

- Automatic triggers are defined using special ovals specifying "TRIGGER" (or "T" for short).
- A trigger may be used only for automatic actions (AAs) and measurement signals (MSs), not integrity constraints (ICs). One of these behavior objects must always appear on the reaction side.
- A trigger may connect on the stimulus side from one or more objects, normally including one or more attribute types.
- A trigger is always understood as involving update actions on attribute types on the stimulus side, even if connected to other object type(s).
- Multiple conditions may be expressed for each trigger, using ANDs or ORs as necessary. Any Boolean expression is valid, along with MIN and MAX. These conditions "fire" the trigger.
- The attribute conditions that "fire" the trigger are given as a special note associated with the trigger.

3.2-1.1 Clocked Triggers

The stimulation for many triggers includes not only attribute updating but time factors as well. This is indicated using a clock symbol.

Diagram 3.69

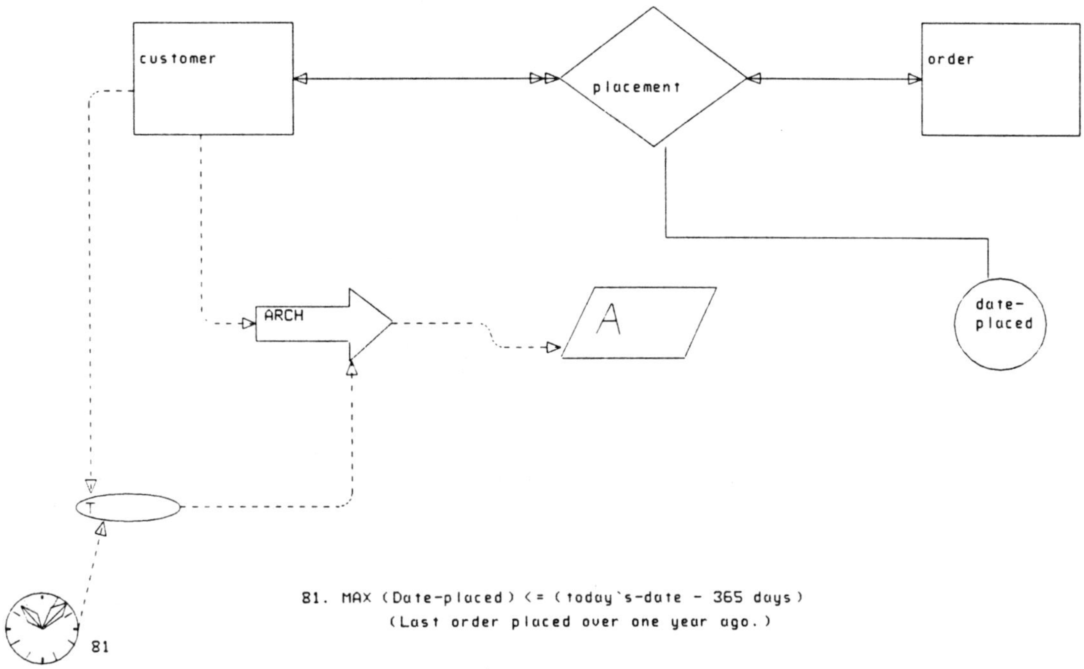

Clocked triggers are especially common for periodic business events reflected in "batch" processes. They are especially useful for communication and illustration purposes.

3.2-2 Keeping Track of Current Events

One of the most common problems in entity modeling is keeping track of "current" or "active" event occurrences when also maintaining a stream of historical or previously active events of the same type. The following ideas, simplified subsequently, are suggested for attacking this important problem.

In Diagram 3.70, an employee may have many statuses in his or her career, but only the most current is active. This is shown as follows.

Diagram 3.70

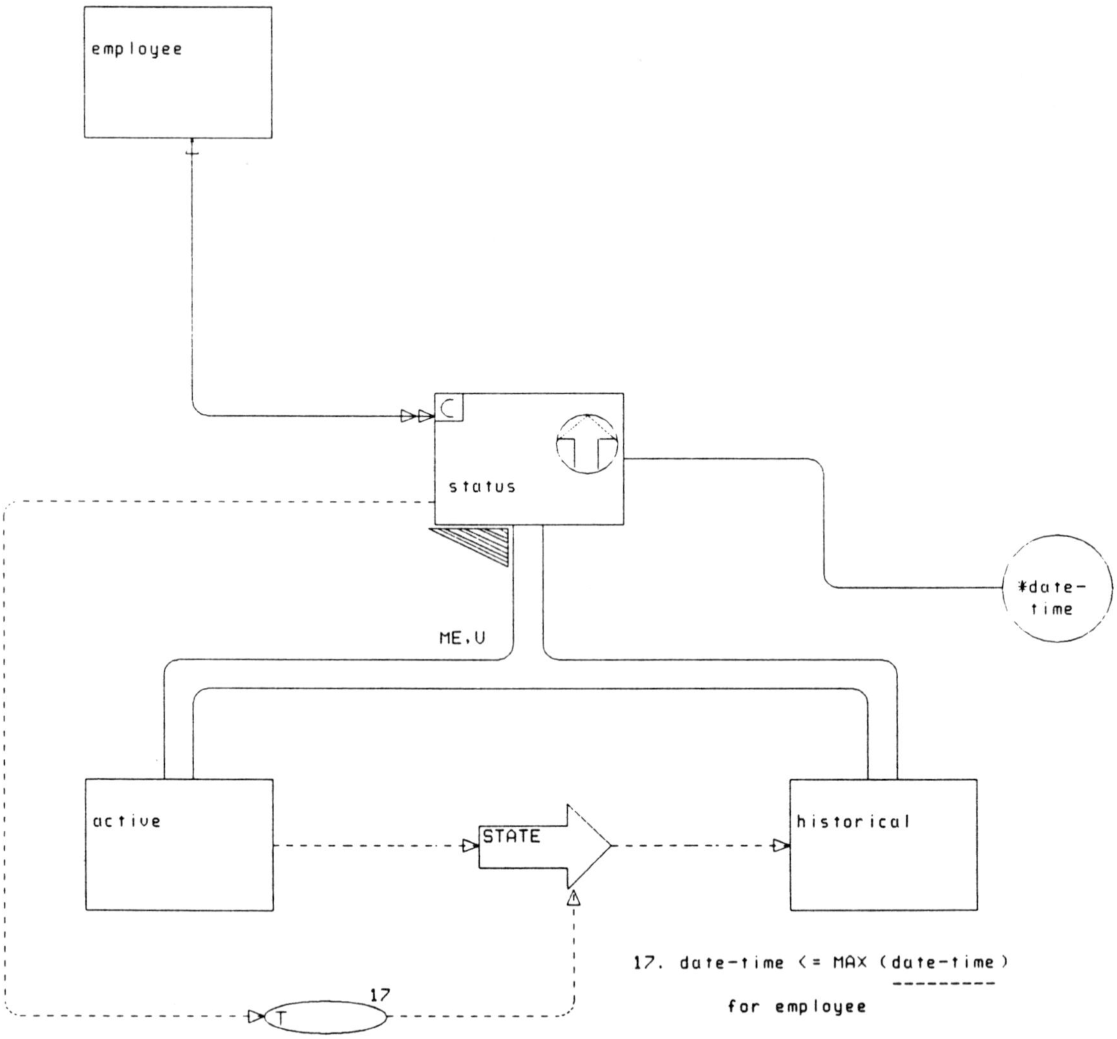

- ▸ Status is classified by "active" and "historical." This classification is mutually exclusive, and vectored toward "historical."
- ▸ Status is determined by <u>date-time</u>, whose values must always be created in ascending order.
- ▸ The state change between "active" and "historical" is triggered by MAX (<u>date-time</u>) for that employee (i.e., the most recently created status is always active). Note that as defined, there is at most ever only one "active" status.
- ▸ This classification has been defined as pro forma (i.e., not to be implemented as shown). However, there is no need for a "type-code" attribute in "status" as the "source" of the classification since the "active" status can still always be determined by "most recent" (i.e., MAX (<u>date-time</u>) for employee).

The above set of declarations is so common that a special shorthand notation is offered for defining it as follows.

Diagram 3.71

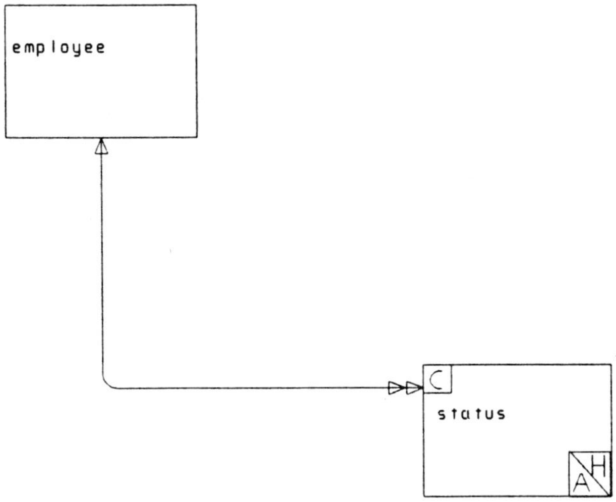

This declaration is exactly equivalent to the former. It is up to the modeler, of course, to ensure that such declaration is appropriate and consistent in all respects. Especially important is ensuring that a strictly ascending order for values of the particular determinant is meaningful.

There are often very stringent business rules concerning "historical" occurrences—namely that all updates are frozen. This may be shown as follows.

Diagram 3.72

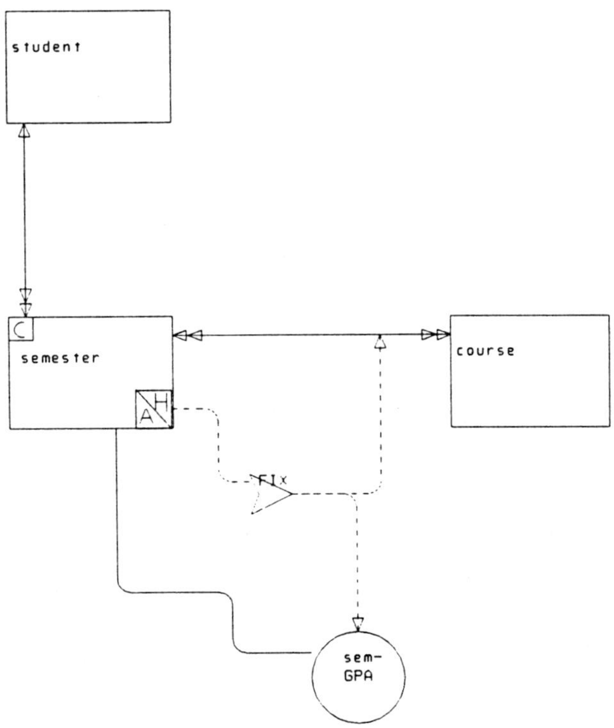

A student's semester-by-semester registration has been defined as above. For all historical occurrences, a "FIX" IC has been declared such that no new courses may be added (or existing ones dropped) and no changes to the semester's GPA (grade point average) will be tolerated. Note that the IC exits "semester" at the "H" of the special A/H symbol, thereby signaling "historical" only. If the "FIX" pointed back to "semester," then *all* properties and relationships of all historical occurrences would be understood as "frozen."

Also worth noting is that the above declarations can be modified by redefining the trigger.

Diagram 3.73

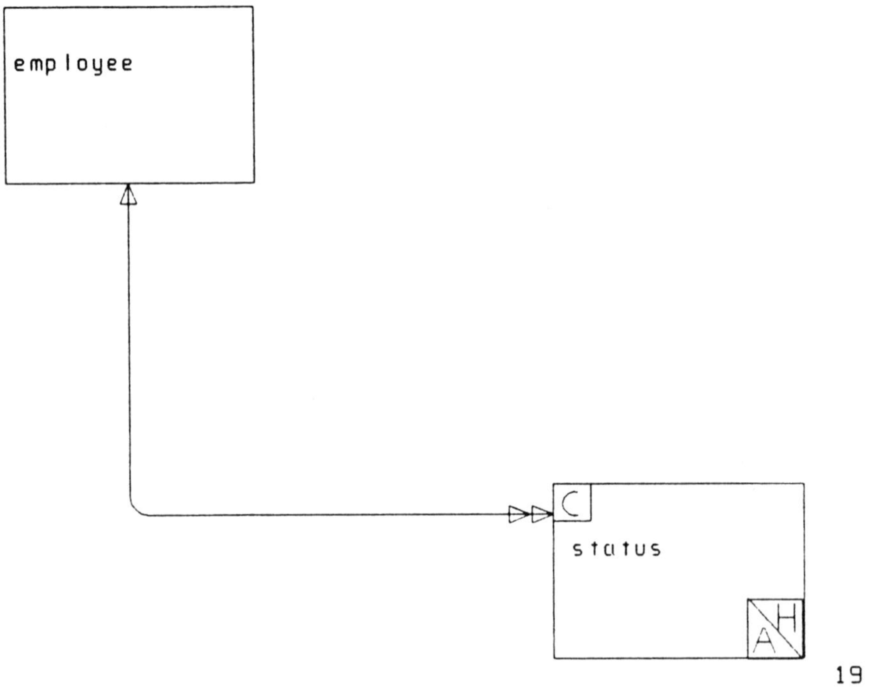

19. date-time < TODAY'S-DATE

Now there may be many "statuses" in the implied active subtype, all of whose date-time values are not yet "historical" (i.e., not yet less than today's date). This violates none of the rules specified earlier.

3.2-2.1 Pending Events

The problem of modeling "pending" (or scheduled) events versus active events is essentially the mirror image of the historical versus active problem. The following is suggested for handling it. As before, this structure is simplified subsequently.

Diagram 3.74

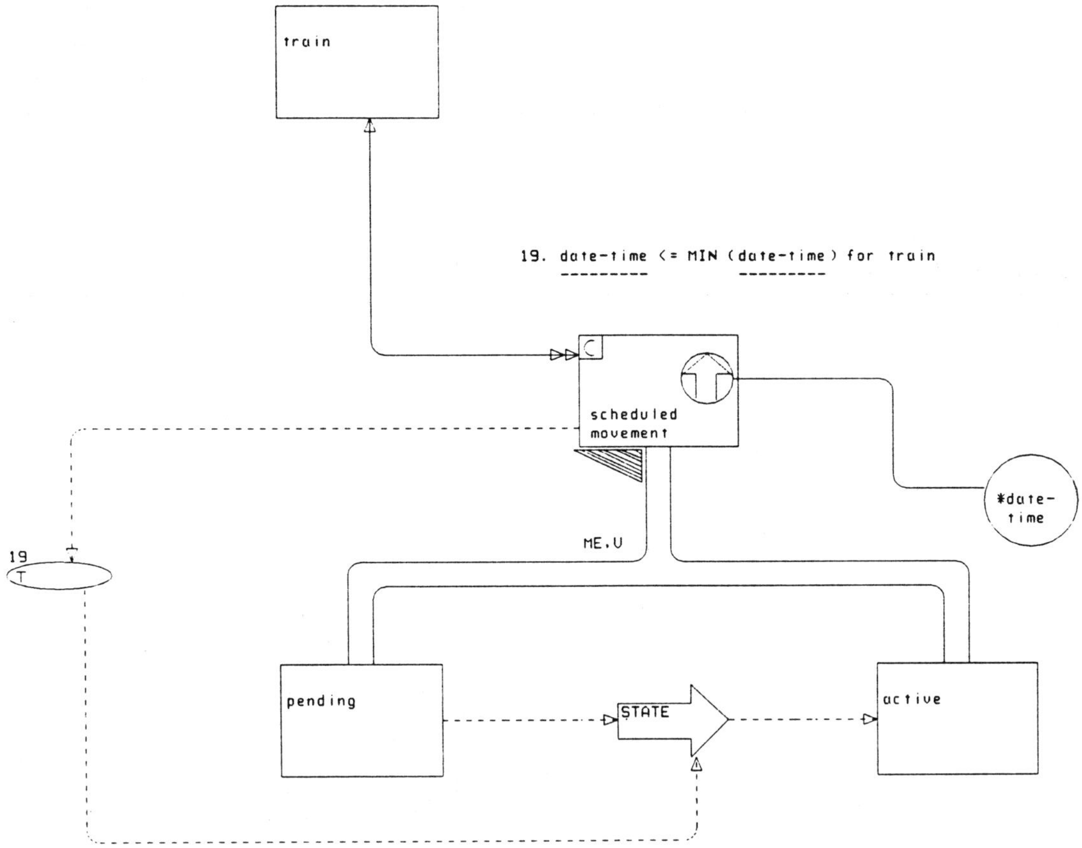

This can be abbreviated simply to the following.

Diagram 3.75

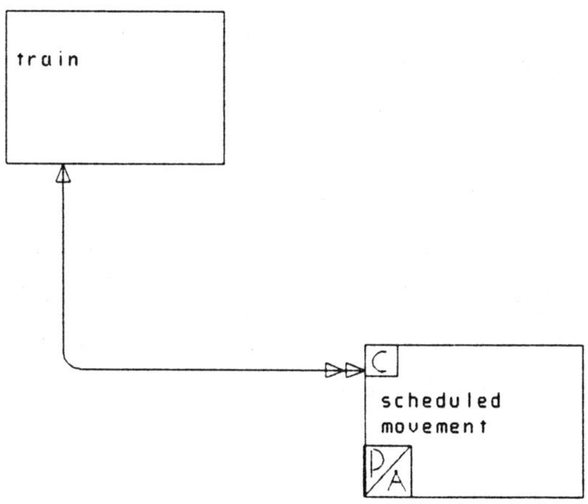

Analogous comments to the historical/active case apply.

3.2-2.2 Commingled Events

It is possible (but not always desirable) to handle both scheduled and historical events together. Such declaration always requires explicit triggers, since distinguishing "active" instance(s) from both pending and historical instances using MIN or MAX for the same determinant, is obviously impossible.

Diagram 3.76

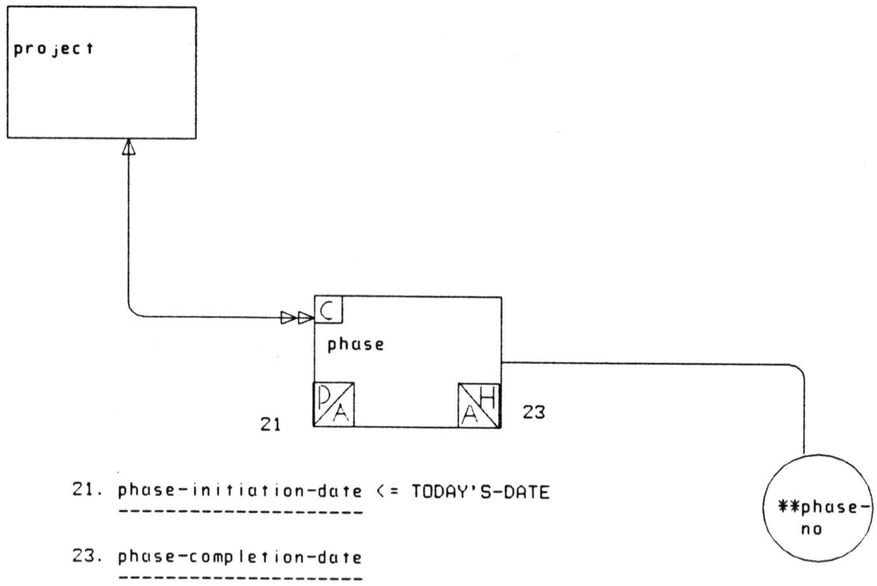

This is equivalent to the model in Diagram 3.77. Note that the triggers are defined for the "actual" phase-initiation-date and phase-completion-date, not the corresponding "scheduled" dates (if any).

To ensure that each and every phase always has its own nonoverlapping time slot, the following ICVCs for "phase" would also be necessary:

phase-initiation-date ≥ phase-completion-date
phase-initiation-date ≤ PRIOR (phase-completion-date)

These specifications, incidentally, would also ensure that there was never more than one "active" phase at a time.

Diagram 3.77

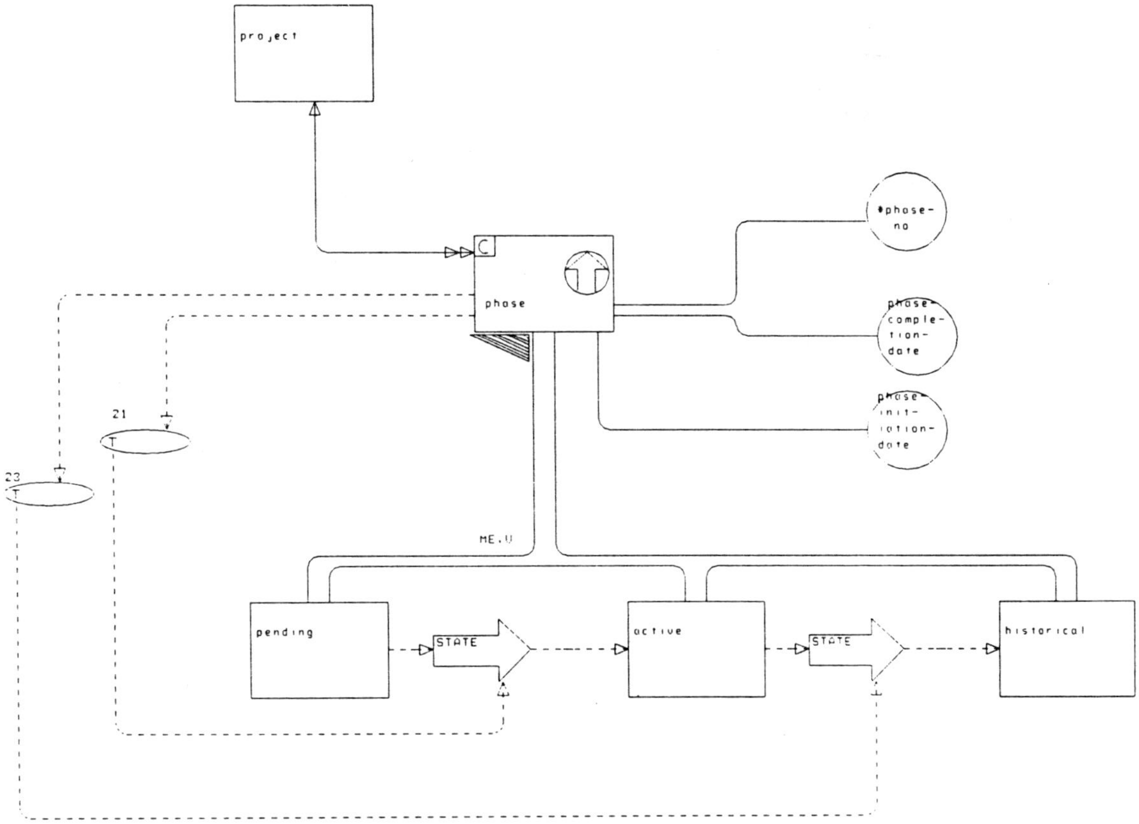

3.2-3 Referential Integrity

According to the relational model, when a thing (e.g., an occurrence of an entity type) is referred to in another object using the values of its determinants (i.e., as "foreign keys"), that thing ought to exist. This is called **referential integrity**. In the context of entity modeling, this rule applies specifically to relationship types. This section examines detailed specifications for referential integrity in an entity modeling context.

3.2-3.1 Referential Integrity and Foreign Keys

Examples of foreign keys in an entity model are given in Diagram 3.78. In both versions cust-no is a foreign key for "customer." In the latter instance, order-no is also a foreign key (in the association type) to "order." Naturally, any detailed blueprint for actual database implementation should show all foreign keys as a basis for establishing relationships.

Especially in the former of the two models below, however, no specific information is given about the integrity of the indicated relationship type. For example, there is no explicit statement that the customer referred to

Diagram 3.78

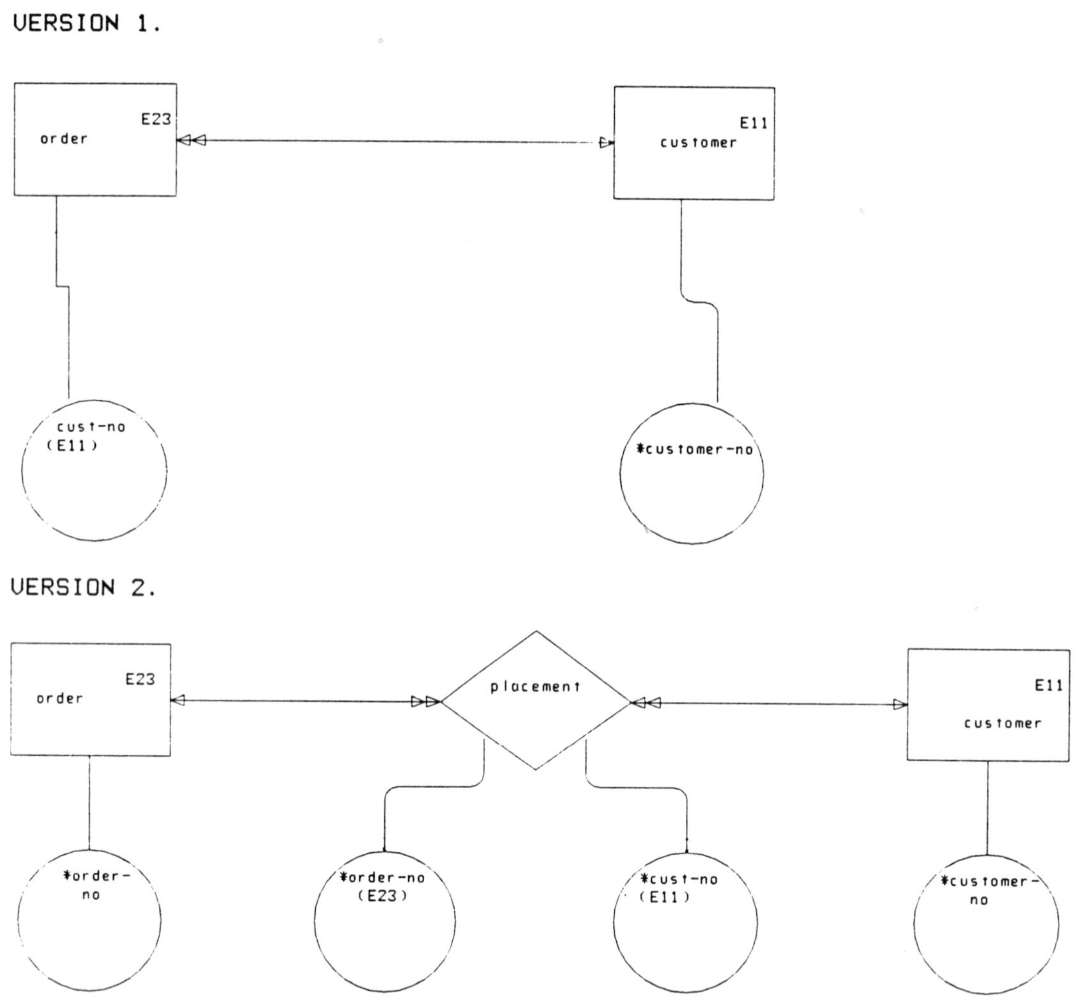

by cust-no (in "order") must actually exist as an occurrence of "customer." Similarly, there is no explicit statement about what should (or should not) happen if a customer is deleted, but some order (by virtue of its value for cust-no) still refers to it. In either case there therefore exists the potential for disintegrity. This is called **open** (or unspecified) referential integrity.

In the latter of the two examples, the general rule of integrity for association types (Integrity Rule #1) precludes loss of integrity as above. However, in practice, association types may be implemented under some DBMS that either does not support this rule or provides additional options for its operation. There is therefore still often a need for closer specification.

3.2-3.2 Referential Integrity and the "Mandatory" Integrity Constraint

One effect of the "mandatory" IC for a relationship type is to "close" open referential integrity. "Mandatory" precludes null foreign key values, and also says that all values must be legitimate.

Diagram 3.79

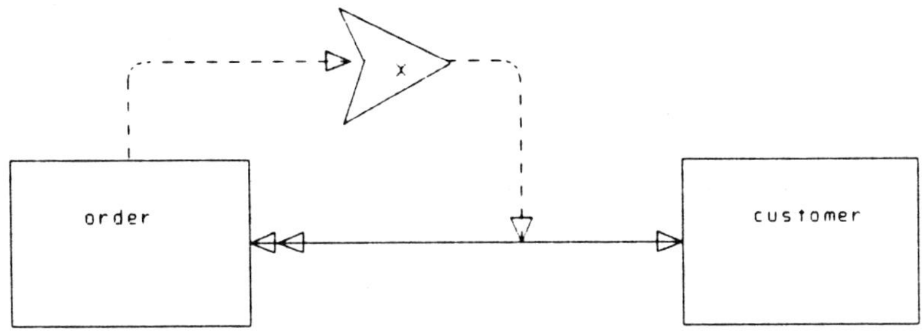

This specification insists that every occurrence of "order" must have a valid customer relationship (instance). Its effect is also to specify that every order must have a valid value for cust-no, its attribute type (not shown) that is the foreign key of "customer." (A mandatory IC for cust-no, by itself, would only specify that a value must exist, not that it would also always have to be valid as a foreign key into customer.)

Whereas this specification "closes" the referential integrity, it does not prescribe what should actually happen when some updating event would violate the rule. The possibilities are comprehensively presented in the diagram below.

Diagram 3.80

Options for Referential Integrity

	Possible Update Actions			
Desired result	**create an order (and provide customer reference)**	**relate existing order to a different customer**	**delete customer**	**delete a particular order from a customer**
Automatically take whatever other update actions are necessary to complete the update, satisfying referential integrity as appropriate	Automatically create customer occurrence if it does not already exist PROPAGATE ADD: PA (Also called CASCADE)		Automatically delete any related order occurrences PROPAGATE DELETE: PD (Also called CASCADE)	Automatically delete the order
Reject the update on the grounds of referential integrity	Reject creation of the order if customer does not exist REJECT ADD: RA (Also called RESTRICT)	Reject modification of the order if the customer referenced does not exist	Reject delete of customer if still related to any order REJECT DELETE: RD (Also called RESTRICT)	Reject modification (order must be deleted first)
Accept the update but force null values for foreign keys (Not valid for mandatory relationship types)	Accept creation of the order, but force null values for invalid customer reference ASSERT NULL VALUE: ANV (Also called NULLIFY)	Force null value for the customer reference if new customer does not exist	Accept delete and force null values in all orders that reference that customer (but do not delete them) PROPAGATE NULL VALUE: PNV (Also called NULLIFY)	Permitted; null value forced for order's customer reference (do not delete the order)

The six alternatives, PA, PD, RA, RD, ANV and PNV are called **referential integrity options** (RIs). On each end of a relationship type, PA, RA or ANV may be chosen, and PD, RD or PNV may be chosen. Representation of RIs for relationship types in an entity model is accomplished in conjunction with action directional arrows. An example illustrates.

Diagram 3.81

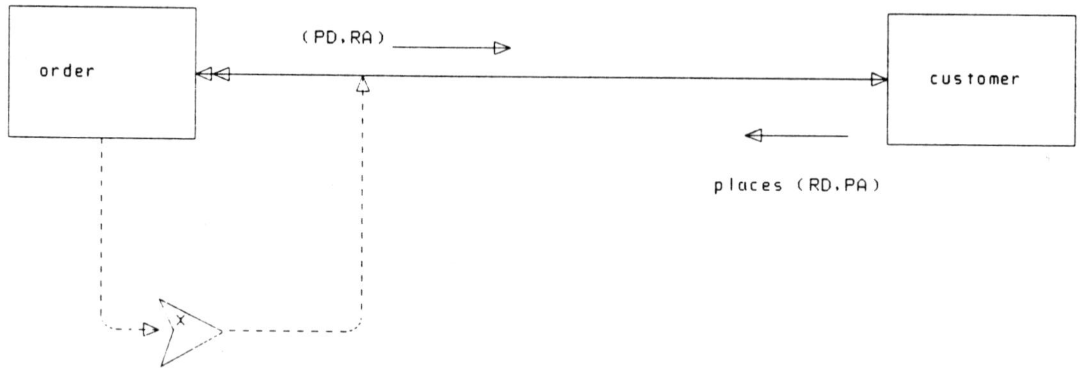

In this example, the following rules for referential integrity will hold true:

1. Creation of an order (or new customer reference) will always be rejected unless that customer already exists.
2. Deletion of an order will always automatically cause deletion of the customer (probably not desirable).
3. Creation of a customer, or addition of order references, will automatically cause creation of referenced orders, if any.
4. Deletion of a customer will be rejected if any orders still refer to it.

These results would be exactly the same had the relationship type been M:N instead of M:1, and/or had an association type been included. (When association types exist, the RI reads "through" to the objects(s) at the far end.) RIs are not desirable for a relationship type joining a characteristic to the object characterized, since general Integrity Rule #2 governs updating in that circumstance.

ANV and PNV are not valid for a mandatory relationship type, which automatically prohibits null values. When PA, RA, PD and RD are used for relationship types that are not mandatory, their effect is to ensure that any foreign key value given is valid, but not to preclude null values. PD should be used sparingly since automatic deletes may cascade extensively.

Generally, RIs should be employed only for very detailed and stable entity models.

3.2-3.3 Conflict Identification

Certain sets of "mandatory"/RI specifications are logically inconsistent or impossible. Identification of such instances is called **conflict identification**.

Diagram 3.82

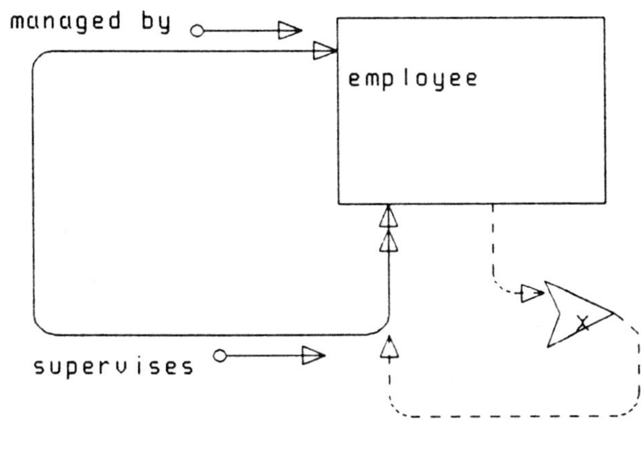

With or without RIs, this specification is inappropriate. (For example, how would the first employee be entered into the database?) RA or PA without the mandatory IC might be more appropriate.

Diagram 3.83

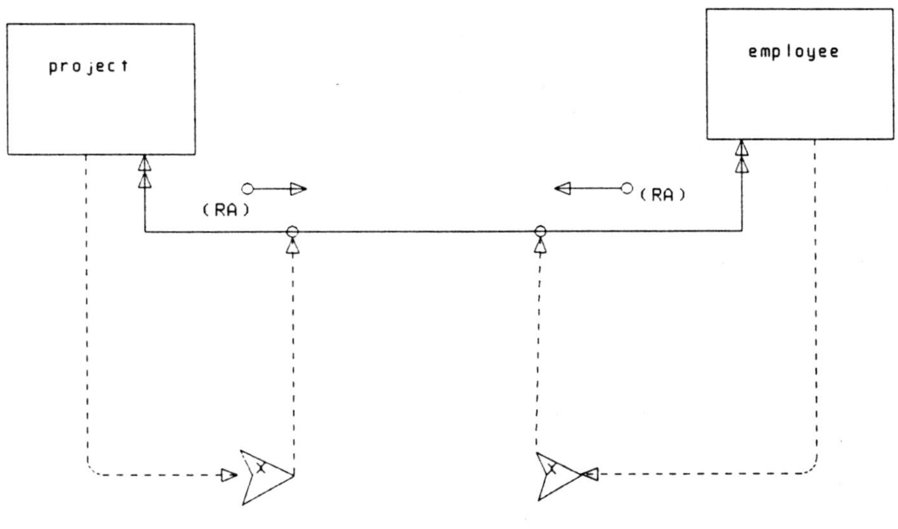

This specification is also impossible (also for the same reason as above). "RD" on both ends would also be impossible. (Would PA on both ends? PD?)

Diagram 3.84

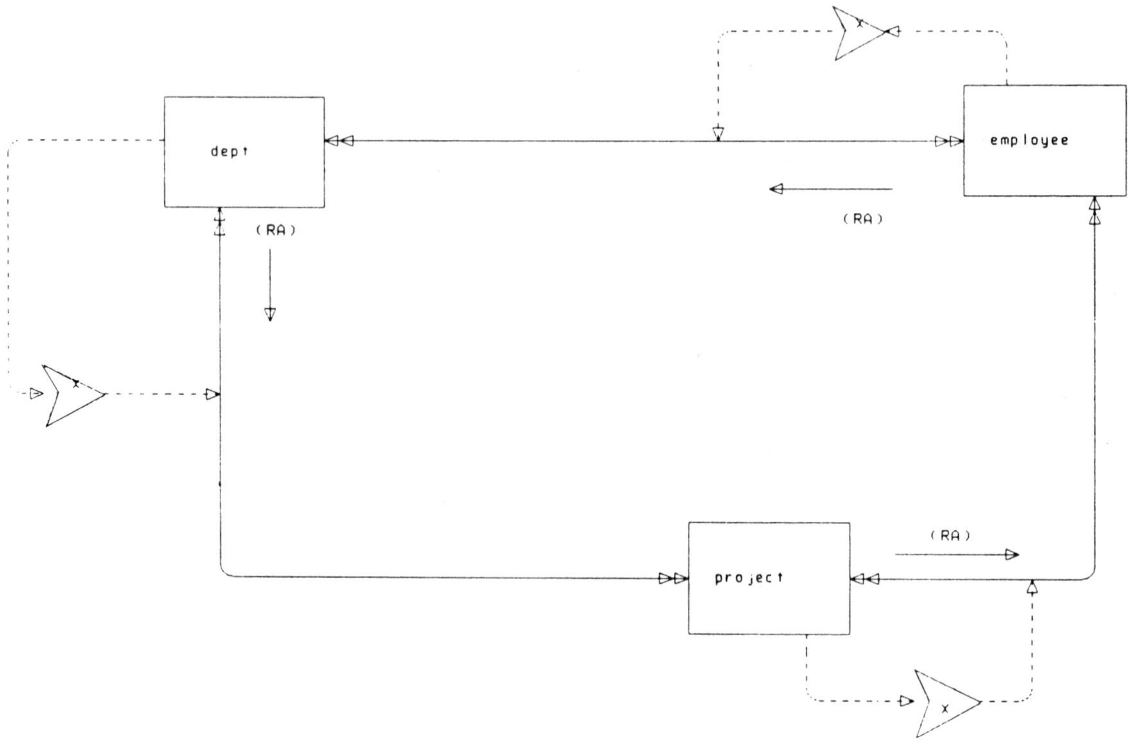

This specification is also impossible (also for the same reason as above). "RD" on each locale shown, also pointing as shown, would likewise be impossible.

GUIDELINES AND CONVENTIONS FOR REFERENTIAL INTEGRITY OPTIONS

- RIs should be used only in very detailed and stable entity models.
- RIs generally say how referential integrity is to be enforced.
- RIs apply only to relationship types, not including those joining a characteristic to the object characterized.
- RIs read "through" association types.
- Even without RIs specified, "mandatory" precludes violation of referential integrity (but without saying how). A mandatory specification automatically precludes null values from any foreign keys.
- PD, RD, RA and PA may be used for either mandatory or non-mandatory relationship types.
- For nonmandatory relationships, the effect of RA, PA, RD and PD is to ensure that every nonnull value of the foreign key(s) is valid, but not to preclude nonnull values.
- ANV and PNV may be used only for nonmandatory relationship types since mandatory relationship types automatically preclude null values.
- Every relationship type may have one set of RI specifications at each end.
- At either end of a relationship type, PA, RA or ANV may be specified, and PD, RD or PNV.
- PD should be used cautiously.
- If no RI is specified for relationship types not specified as mandatory, updating may violate referential integrity (i.e., invalid foreign key values may be allowed as per the DBMS).

SECTION 3
Measurement-Level Objects and Connections

In any data resource, higher forms of information are synthesized from lower forms. When this synthesis involves arithmetic operations defined for the properties and connections of the corresponding entity types, it is called measurement.

Pseudo-measurement, such as before-the-fact estimates of size for the future database, is also often desirable. These various types of measurement necessitate additional objects and connections to describe the relevant entity model behavior.

3.3-1 Measurement

Certain objects, which might otherwise be considered entity types, exist primarily to hold highly synthesized or statistical information (i.e., measurement data). This makes these entity types, which are called **measurement points**, distinct from the six types of entity types previously discussed—people, places, things, organizations, concepts and events.

These other six kinds of entity types are really more fundamental to the data resource than measurement points since they contain the data from which "measurement" is produced. Measurement points also generally appear later during the analysis of the enterprise than the others, as "higher" forms of information are being identified and accommodated. Sometimes they may refer to the very same entity occurrences as occurrences of other "basic" entity types, and exist merely to separate "tactical" or "strategic" information from basic operational attributes of those very same things. For all these reasons measurement is at the lowest and final level among the five levels of detail in entity modeling.

3.3-1.1 Measurement Points

To provide for these distinctions, a new object (called a **measurement point**) is introduced. By convention, it is represented by a triangle. In all other respects, a measurement point looks and acts like a regular entity type—it has a set of one or more determinants, possesses attributes, is named, may participate in relationship types, etc. (So as not to clutter an entity model, however, relationship types to the measurement point are often omitted.) In fact, in ascending conversion, it may be actually converted to a regular kernel entity type.

3.3-1.2 The Measurement Signal (MS) Object

To connote synthesis of information, or some arithmetic process that must be consistently executed, a new behavior object called a **measurement signal** (MS) is introduced. Like all behavior objects, it has stimulus-side connections and behavior-side connections.

Diagram 3.85

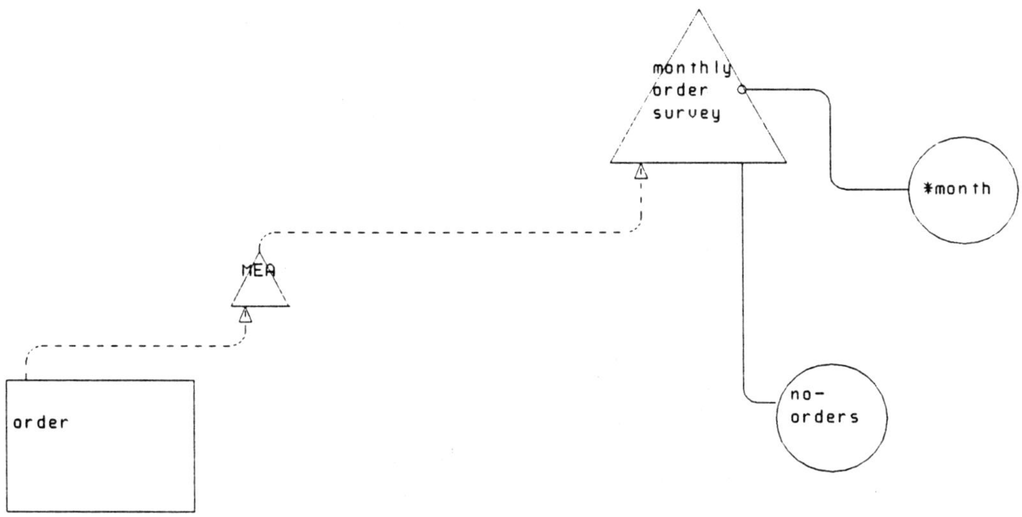

In this example, a measurement point "monthly order survey" is connected on the reaction side of an MS that connects on the behavior side to "order." The determinant of the measurement point is month, and an attribute no-orders is presumably used to count how many orders have been placed during any given month. Note that "order" and "monthly order survey" are not connected by any *relationship type*, but merely by this defined "measurement" behavior.

A complete list of MSs is given below.

Diagram 3.86

Measurement Signals (MSs)

MEA	**Measurement**	an arithmetic operation, synthesis, or derivation between objects.
FT	**Format Transform**	an automatic conversion from one domain's format to another, possibly with computation.
RSCT	**Relationship Count**	an automatic count of relationship instances for some object.

(Continued)

ENCT	**Entity Count**	an automatic count of entity occurrences for some object.
VLCT	**Value Count**	an automatic count of values across some object.
SPEC	**User-specified**	a processing behavior that is user-specified.

GUIDELINES AND CONVENTIONS FOR MEASUREMENT POINTS

- Measurement points are used for highly synthesized or statistical data, often strategic or tactical in nature and usually produced arithmetically from lower forms of data.
- Measurement points are represented by triangles.
- They otherwise look and act like regular kernel entity types.
- They have one or more determinants and may have attributes and relationship types.
- They should be named using a noun.
- Relationship types to a measurement point are often dropped to avoid clutter in the entity model.
- Every measurement point should generally be connected on the reaction side of a Measurement Signal (MS).
- Use AAs and triggers to govern creation and existence of instances of a measurement point.
- Use clocks to supply timing or replenishment criteria for measurement.

3.3-1.2-1 The MEA MS

The MEA MS is used to signify synthesis or measurement between objects, without defining its specific form or operation. MEA is thus a loose measurement indicator without "hard" meaning or implications.

Diagram 3.87 broadly outlines the ongoing derivation of information about "order" activity. (As in the above, the MS "MEA" is often dropped from diagrams in order to reduce clutter.) Specifically, the previously defined measurement point "monthly order survey" appears, along with a new measurement point, "order volume." This latter measurement point, which loosely connects to an aggregate object ("order placement") on the stimulus side, has the determinants <u>cust-id</u> and <u>month</u>. It is apparently used to keep monthly totals for each customer.

Diagram 3.87

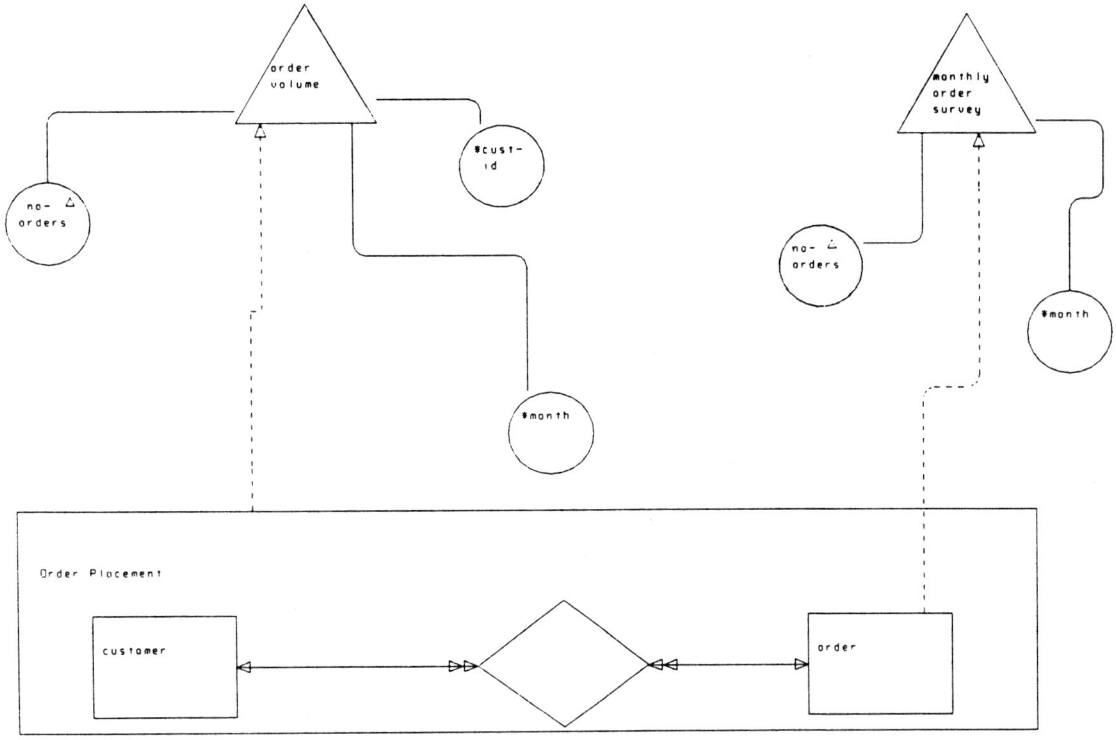

Diagram 3.88

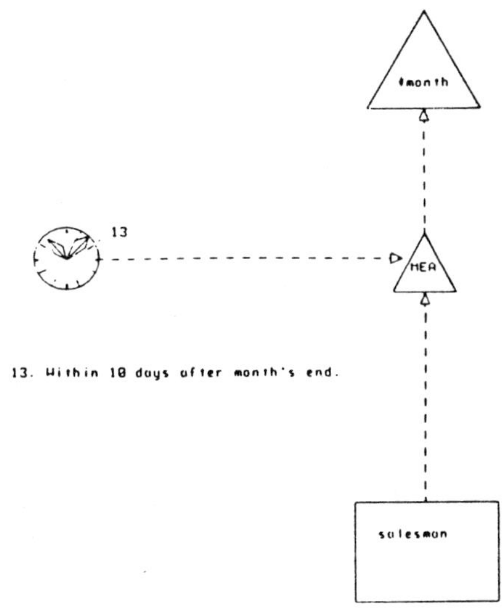

Monthly measurements are maintained for salesmen. A timing criteria has been supplied for this measurement using a clock, specifying that this measurement must be completed by a certain (relative) date. Presumably, this criteria reflects the users' tolerance for availability of the synthesized information.

3.3-1.2-2 Format Transform

The values of one domain are often calculated or reformatted from the values of another. Properly specified, this transformation represents a form of automatic synthesis.

Diagram 3.89

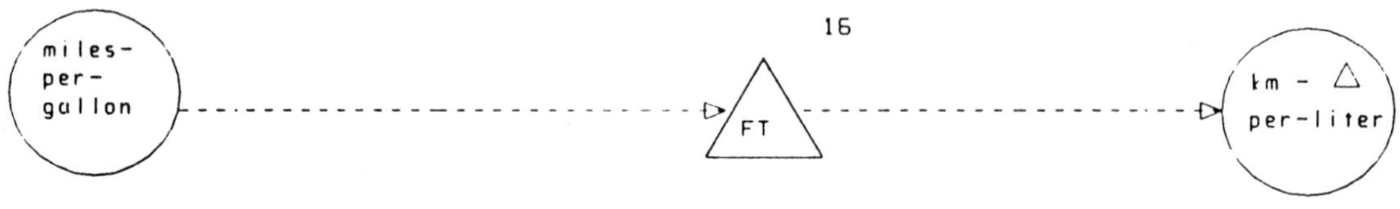

In this example, values of km-per-litre are specified as always calculated from miles-per-gallon. A formula is presumably given for this purpose. Naturally, the rules of formation (i.e., formats) of the respective domains must be compatible.

The implications of this specification are the following.

- Values of the derived domain km-per-litre are always automatically calculated from miles-per-gallon anywhere they are used.
- Whenever km-per-litre is used as an attribute of some object, miles-per-gallon must also appear as an attribute in order to supply its values.
- Values of km-per-litre are "locked into" the MS. They cannot be created or modified by users.

The FT MS may also be used between attributes of an object. In contrast to such specification for domains, this implies that the derivation is not universal to the entity model, but only operates within the context of the associated object.

3.3-1.2-3 Relationship Count

This automatic measurement is used to keep a running tally of relationship type instances for some object. It connects from a relationship type to an attribute (or object) type.

In Diagram 3.90, two tallies are kept for "student": the (total) no-semester-enrolled and the (total) no-course-taken (across all semesters). The purpose of these tallies would generally be to provide quick and on-line availability of the information. (Question for the reader: How could the number of courses taken by a student *each semester* be shown? Hint: an association type is needed.)

In Diagram 3.91, one type of "intersection data" for the aggregate association type, "product listing," is produced automatically using RSCT. No-manuf-for-product in essence tells how many different manufacturers produce some given product that some given agent sells.

Diagram 3.90

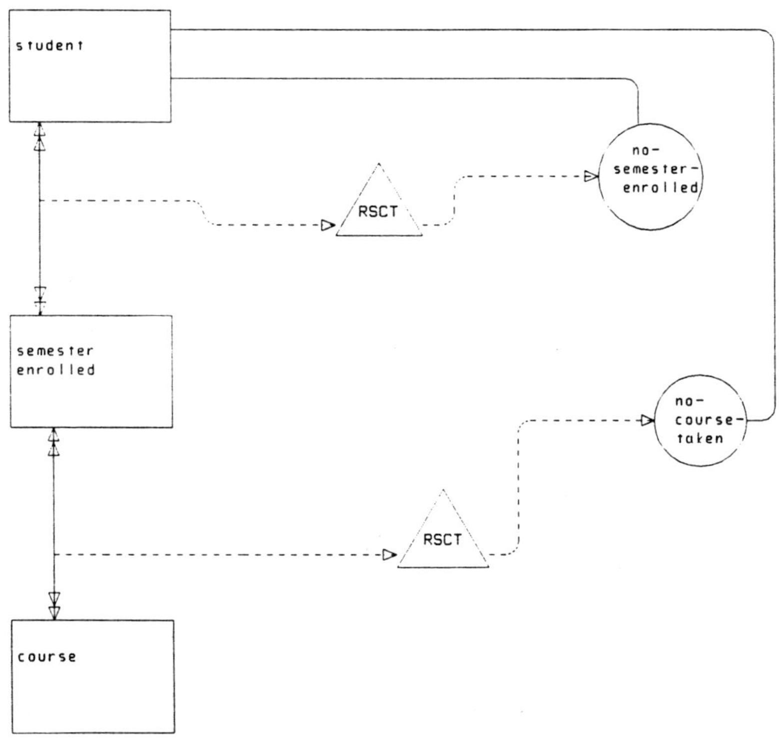

Diagram 3.91

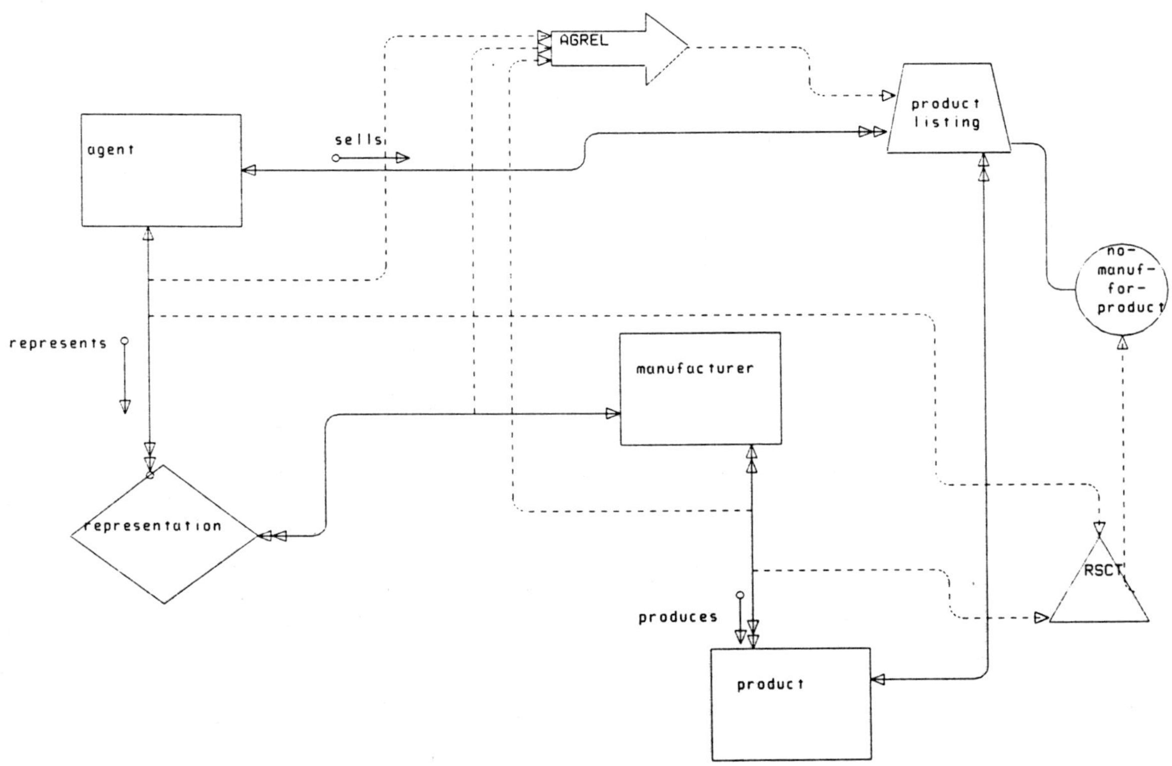

3.3-1.2-4 Entity Count

This automatic measurement is used to keep a running tally of object occurrences, often for a measurement point.

Diagram 3.92

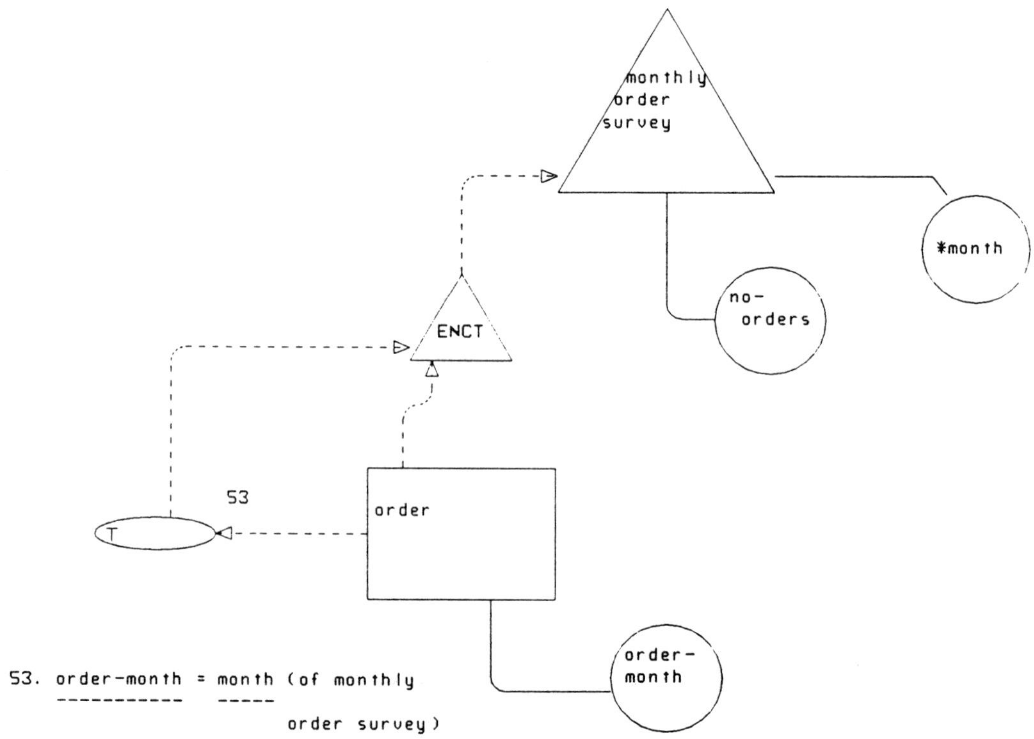

In this example, a tally of orders placed during each month is kept using a measurement point. A trigger defined for the MS specifies the relevant attribute condition for the automatic accumulation.

In the variation in Diagram 3.93, a classification is used to refine the count to filled orders only.

3.3-1.2-5 Value Count

This automatic measurement is used to keep a running tally of the number of different values an attribute has taken. Such information may also be useful for certain physical DBMS decisions.

An example is given in Diagram 3.94. Note the special introduction of an "enterprise" measurement point. Since this entity type can only have one occurrence, it needs no determinant.

Diagram 3.93

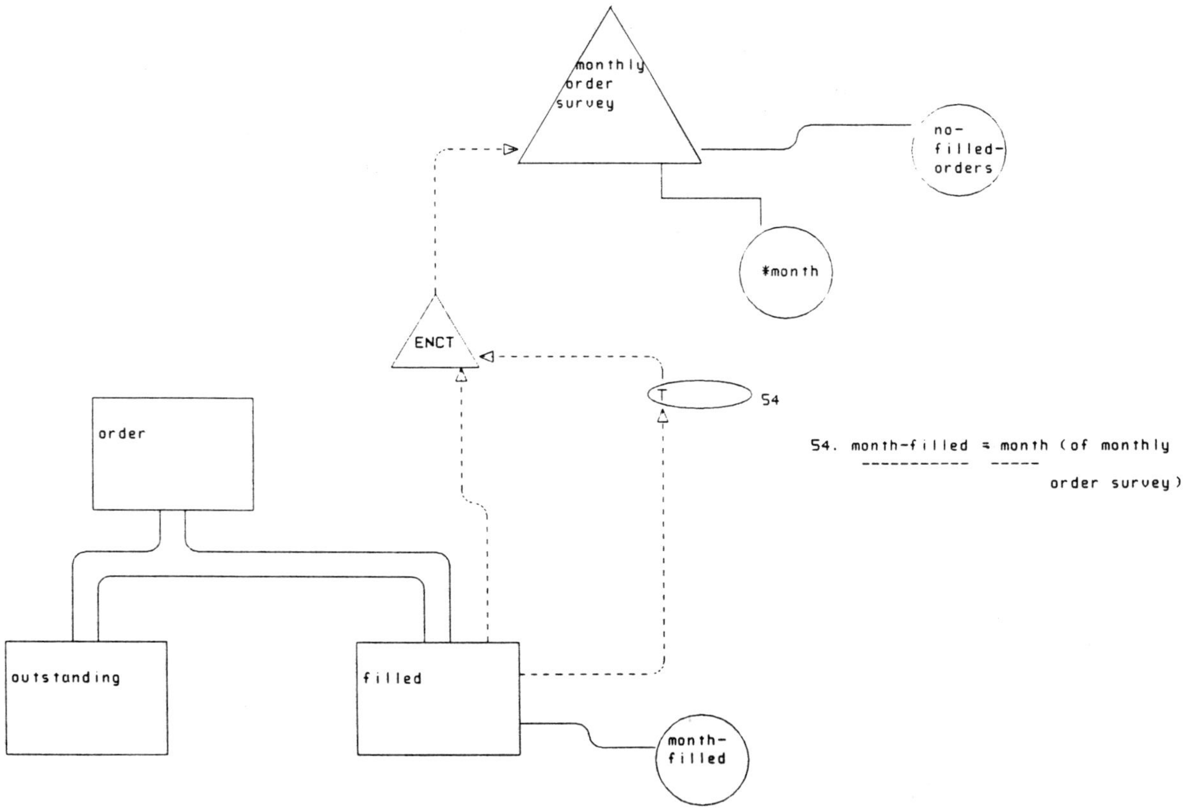

Diagram 3.94

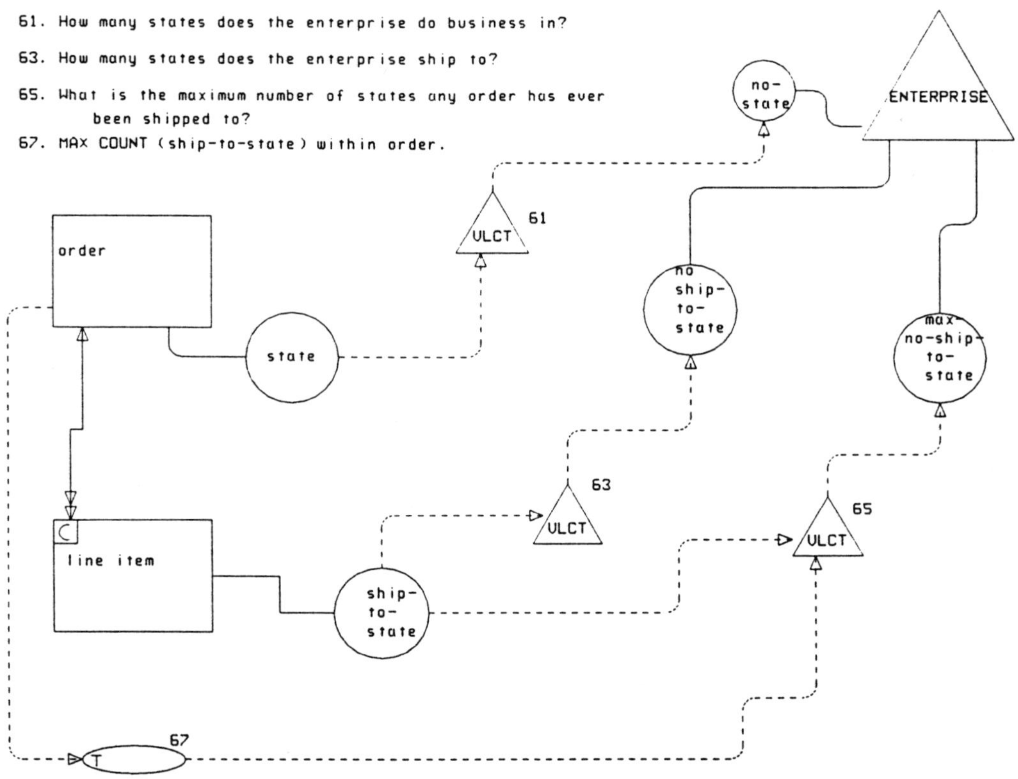

3.3-1.2-6 User-Specified MS

Any set of objects and/or connections can be linked to other objects via the SPEC MS behavior object. This simply says that some computational connection exists between the objects that will be specified as a formula using a textual note. This connection should never be used in the place of relationship types, or other formal behavior objects.

3.3-2 Frequency Estimation

It is often important to capture best estimates for the future dimensions of a database to be implemented. These are pseudo-measurements and pseudo-behavior, since they are rendered before the fact.

The entity model provides a convenient place for the precise recording of various types of such estimation. These various types are listed opposite. Normally, such estimates are not gathered until relatively late in the entity modeling process, after the enterprise has already been thoroughly analyzed and modeled and the entity model has become relatively stable.

Diagram 3.95

Frequency Estimates (FEs)

VOL	**Volume**	the number of instances expected for some object.
MO	**Multiple Occurrence**	the number of instances of some relationship type that some object is expected to have.
MAX	**Maximum Occurrence**	the maximum number of instances of some relationship type some object is expected to have.
RO	**Relative Occurrence**	the percentage of instances of some object that are expected to have a value for some attribute, or an occurrence for some classification, or an instance of some relationship type.
VAL	**Values**	the number of values expected in some domain.
DIS	**Discrimination**	the number of instances of some object expected for the typical value of some attribute type.
XDIS	**Exceptional Discrimination**	the number of instances of some object that have an unusual or atypical value for some attribute type.

3.3-2.1 Frequency Estimates (FEs)

A new object is introduced to capture frequency estimates. This object has a source-side, and an enumeration-side, connected to objects and/or relationship types as appropriate.

3.3-2.1-1 Volume (VOL)

This FE estimates how many instances of some particular type there are projected to be. The source side and enumeration side for this FE are always the same.

Diagram 3.96

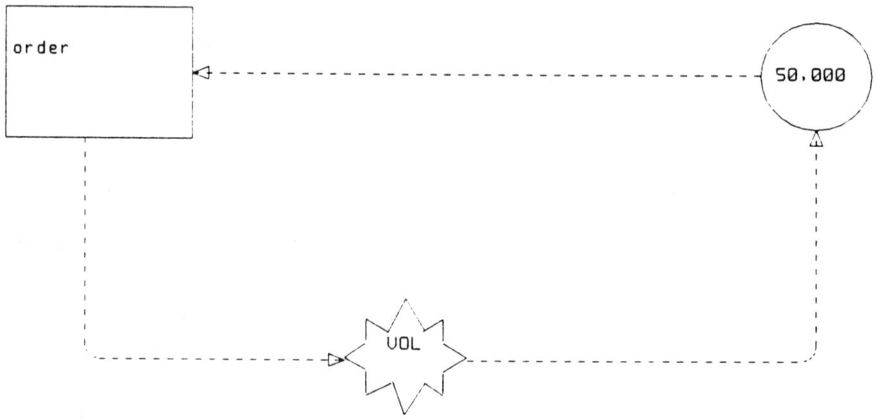

The projected number of (non-archived) orders is 50,000 at any given time. (The estimate value is given inside an "enumerator.")

3.3-2.1-2 Multiple Occurrence (MO)

This FE estimates how many instances of some relationship type for an object are normally expected.

Diagram 3.97

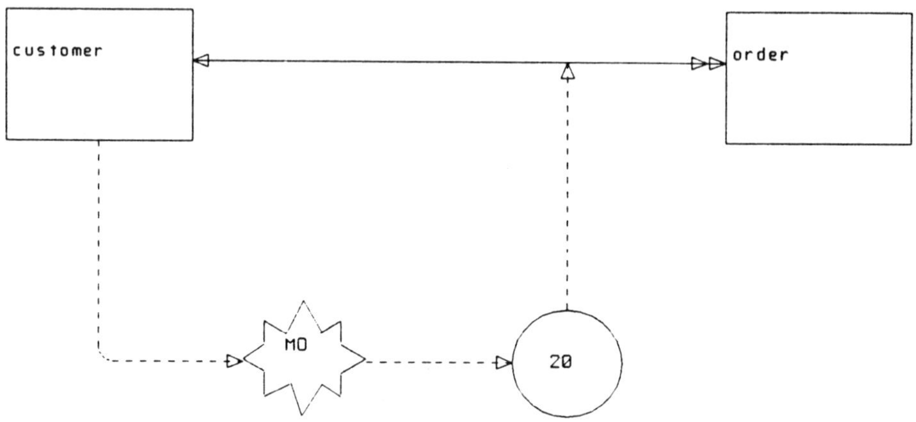

Each customer may be normally expected to place 20 orders. Note that the source for this FE is an object, whereas the enumeration side points to a relationship type.

3.3-2.1-3 Maximum Occurrence (MAX)

It is often important to know that the maximum multiple occurrence anticipated differs significantly from the "normal."

Diagram 3.98

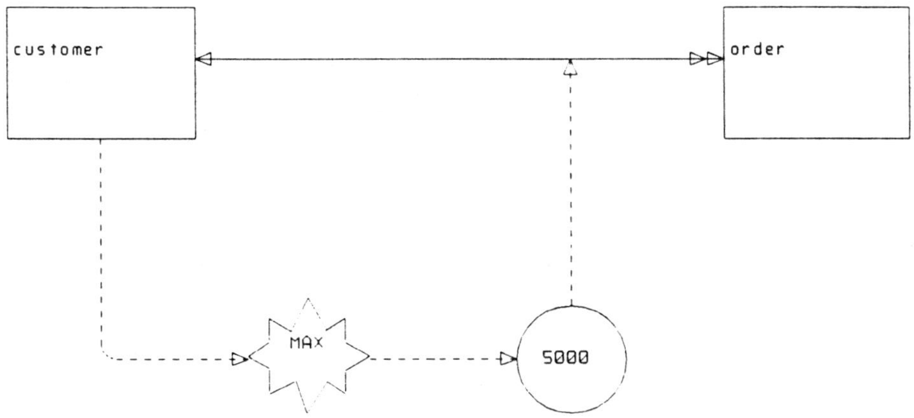

In this continuation of the previous example, where the MO FE was 20 orders per customer, the MAX is found to be 5000—a significantly larger value. This may indicate that some special class or type of customer exists. If so, and if that subtype can be defined explicitly, the above MAX specification may become an MO for the subtype.

3.3-2.1-4 Relative Occurrence (RO)

This FE may be used to specify what percentage of occurrences of some object can be expected to have values for some attribute. (Note that the RO for a mandatory attribute would naturally be 100%.)

Diagram 3.99

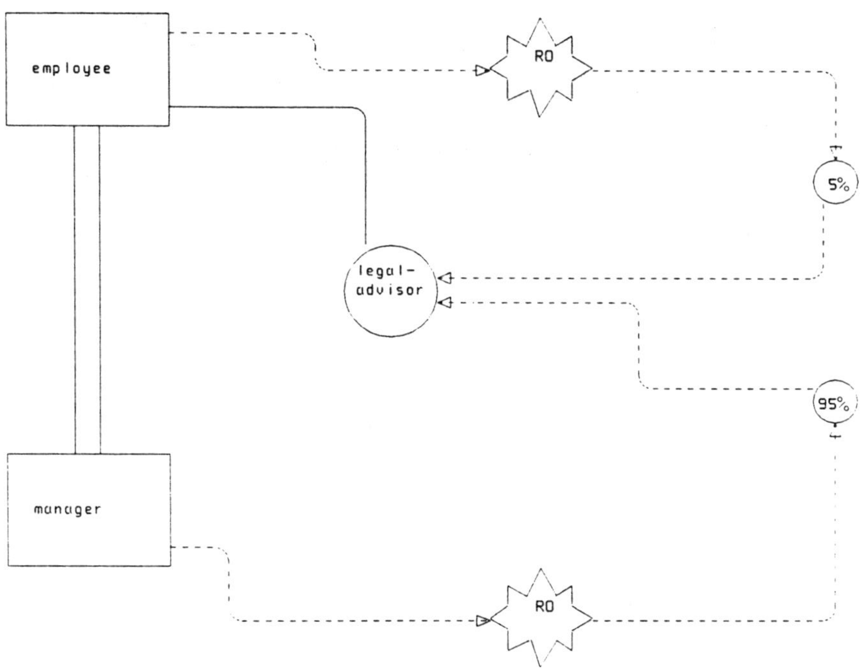

Here, the RO for legal-advisor, an attribute of "employee," is indicated as 5%, whereas for the subtype "manager" it is indicated as 95%.

Relative occurrence (RO) may also be used to specify what percentage of occurrences of some object can be expected to have occurrences for a particular classification or subtype, or a particular relationship type. Again, all "mandatory" classifications, subtypes, or relationship types must always show 100%.

Diagram 3.100

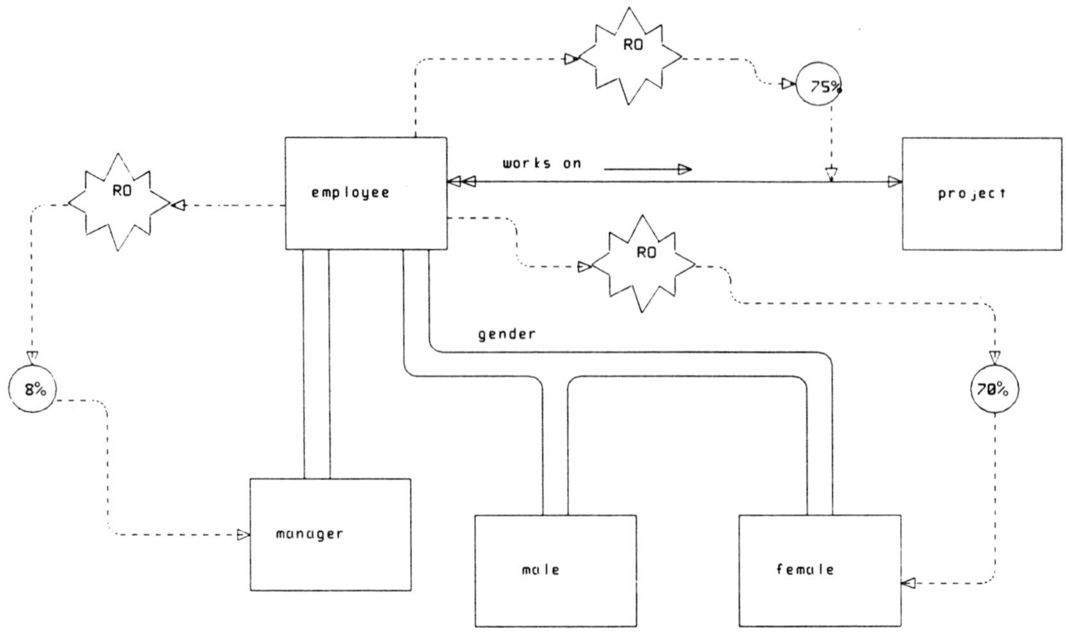

In this enterprise, the following estimates are made:

- 8% of all employees are managers
- 70% of all employees are female
- 75% of all employees are assigned to a project.

3.3-2.1-5 Values (VAL)

This FE is used to estimate how many values will ever appear for some given domain across all uses.

Diagram 3.101

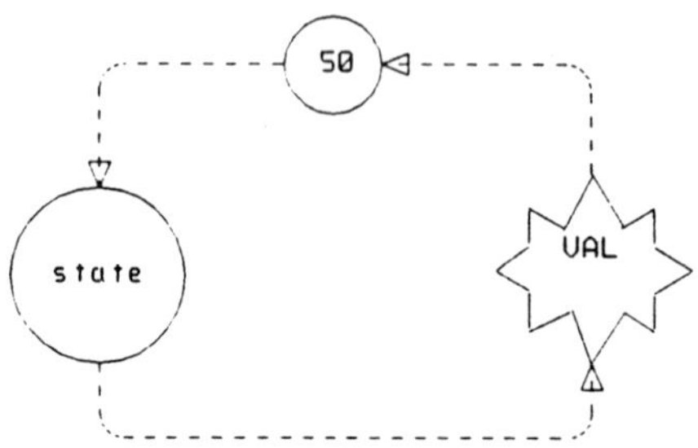

There are fifty anticipated values of state.

3.3-2.1-6 Discrimination (DIS)

This FE projects how many instances of some object are likely to have the same value of some attribute.

Diagram 3.102

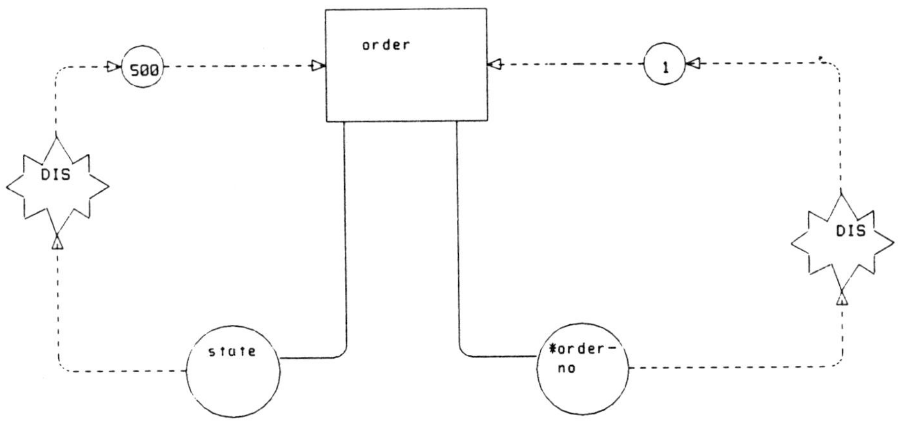

According to the above, each state (value) is likely to be associated with (i.e., discriminate) 500 orders. Values of the determinant order-no, as expected, only discriminate 1 order (for each value).

3.3-2.1-7 Exceptional Discrimination (XDIS)

This FE is used to highlight unusual cases of discrimination.

Diagram 3.103

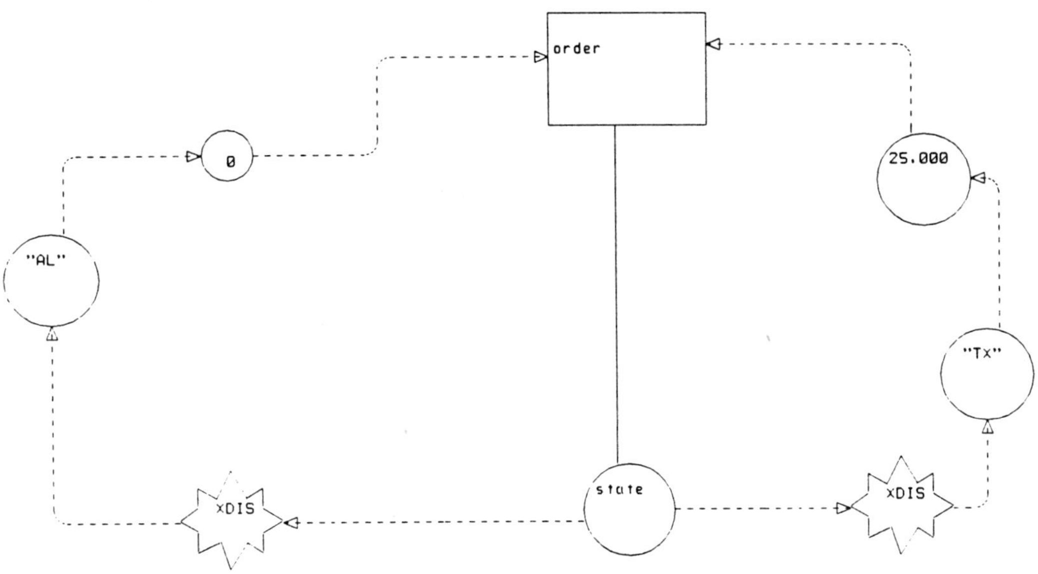

This information may be useful in eliminating certain values from indexing schemes.

DESIGN SUPPLEMENT

S.0 Data-Controlled System Design

Any information system exhibits extensive behavior, only some of which can be defined as truly automatic. The rest simply consists of user-controlled processing.

One of the most significant components of database system analysis and design is discovery and definition of these "other" processes lying within the user-controlled portion. These processes are triggered by specific, well-defined transactions, which are entered by users or other agents performing information-related actions in the enterprise. Building successful information systems to support that enterprise requires comprehensive and exhaustive sets of well-defined transactions that satisfy the operational needs of the organization in a data-friendly fashion.

This requirement has a very practical side. In many database system development efforts, the "data" side has been almost totally separated from the "process" side, making communication and coordination between the two at best difficult, and sometimes virtually impossible. In part, traditional analytical techniques are to blame for this. Normalization, a popular data design technique, for example, has no direct fit whatsoever with any "process" analysis techniques, including structured analysis and flow charting. This is a great gap that needs to be filled.

Fortunately, modest extensions to some of the entity behavior modeling techniques discussed in this book have great potential in this regard. These extensions produce powerful analytical tools capable of producing not merely data-driven designs, but truly **data-controlled** designs. The purpose of this Supplement is to introduce and briefly discuss these leading-edge ideas in a preliminary fashion. It is not intended to be comprehensive or complete.

Whereas these new tools are relentlessly data-oriented, the following important point should be emphasized. They are not intended to *replace* more traditional "process" or "flow" analysis techniques, but rather to complement them. Specifically, they should be looked upon as a *front-end* for these other techniques, aimed specifically at discovering where these latter techniques should be focused.

S.1 Entity Life Cycles

Many classifications actually represent a well-defined **life cycle** for occurrences of the classified object. Each subtype is actually a stage or **state** through which occurrences pass as they age. Return movement to a previous stage in a life cycle is often inappropriate and may be prohibited. Entity life cycles are also sometimes called **entity life histories** (or merely

entity histories). Entity life cycle analysis may be performed for kernel entity types, characteristics and association types.

S.1-1 State Changes and Transactions

The analysis of entity life cycles provides an important basis for discovering the transactions (processes) that govern "movement" of data through its history.

Diagram S.1

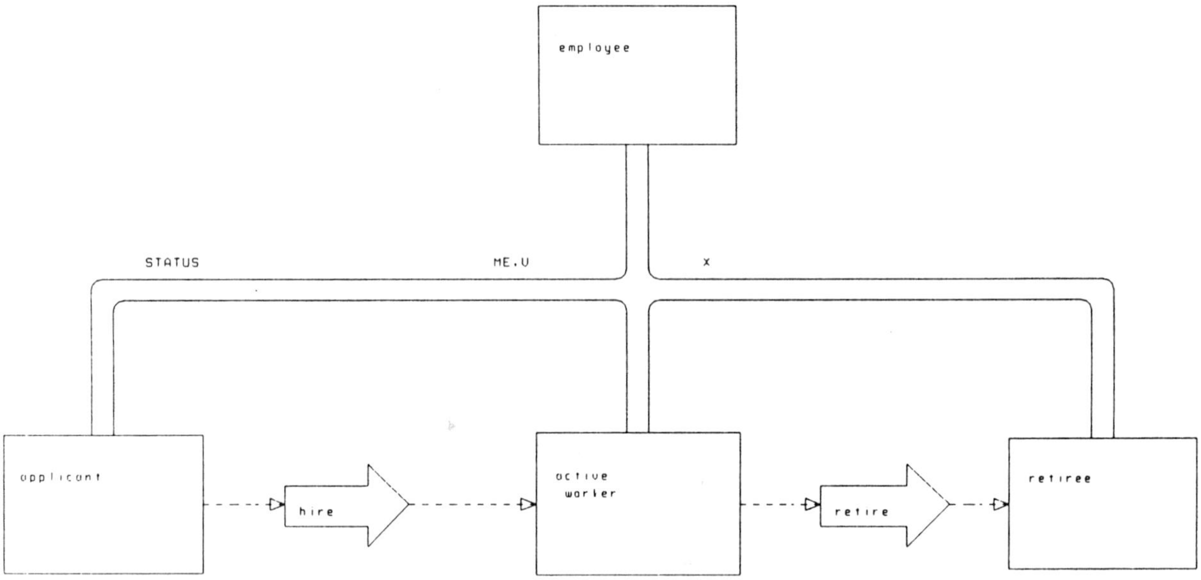

In this simple employee status classification, an employee must be either an applicant, an active worker or a retiree. Logically, a given person is first an applicant, then an active worker, and then, and only then, a retiree. In other words, there is orderly movement to the right among the subtypes of employee, reflecting the natural "history" of employees in this enterprise.

The mutually exclusive, vectored classification shows this appropriately. In general, defining any mutually exclusive, vectored classification for an object automatically indicates that a life cycle or life history exists for that object. Each of the subtypes in the classification represents a meaningful stage or state within that life cycle.

Given precise definition of the valid states for the object in this fashion, an orderly set of transactions (or processes) can be identified that propel and control an occurrence's fixed journey across the life cycle. Indeed, several such transactions have been identified above (namely, "hire" and "retire"). These transactions are merely state changes of the object. In general, *all* transactions governing an entity life cycle actually represent state changes.

Notice, however, that the state changes in the diagram above cannot be considered automatic. This is because no attribute-level triggers have been defined for them. Something else must be initiating the actions.

S.1-2 Agents

Especially early in requirements analysis and design for some information system, it is probably not desirable to define automatic triggers. Instead, it may be preferable to indicate that some particular part of the organization, or some person within it (called an **agent**), can do something (i.e., take some action) that "triggers" the state change. Such an agent would be shown as follows.

Diagram S.2

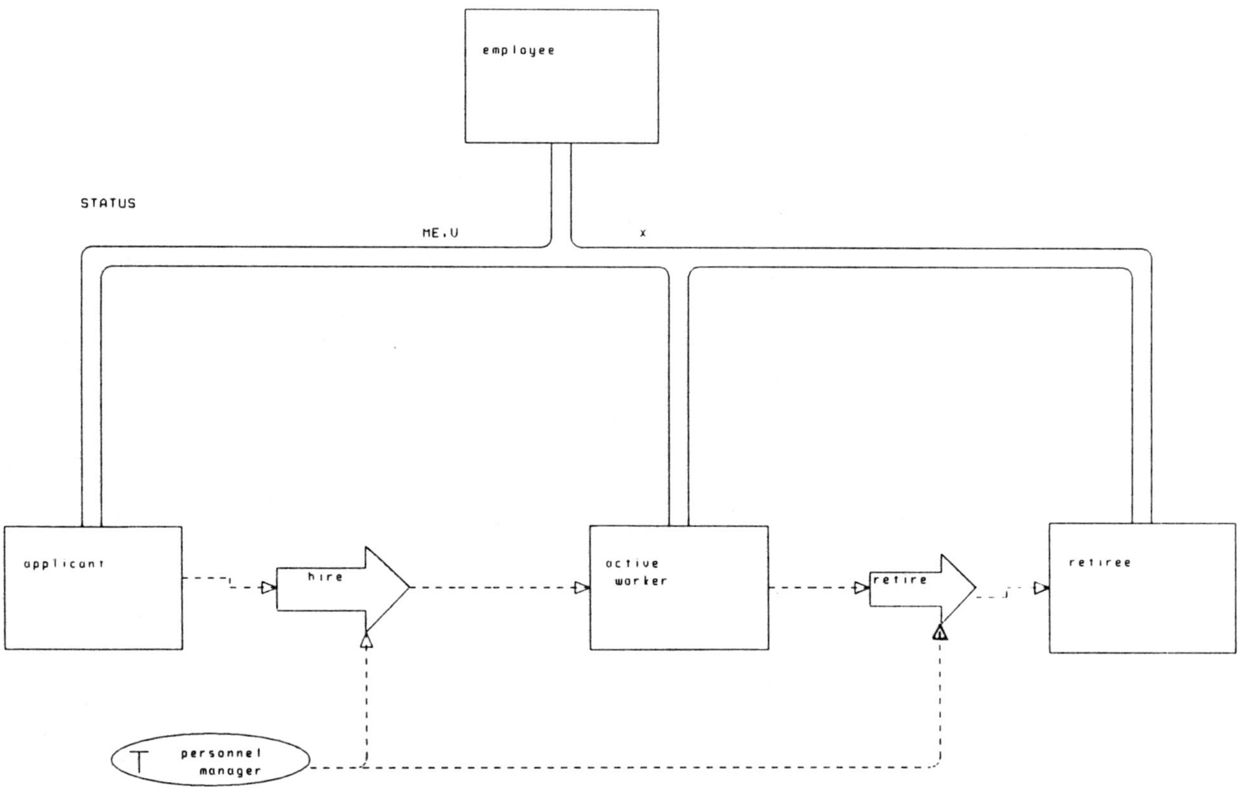

Here the "trigger" is simply the personnel manager, who can take the proper action (i.e., invoke the proper transaction) to cause changes of state for given occurrences of employee. As above, agents should be shown in entity life cycle diagrams using the oval previously reserved for truly automatic triggers.

S.1-3 Variable Outcomes and Iteration

Often, user-specified state changes may be repeated more than once and have more than one outcome. The following illustrates.

Diagram S.3

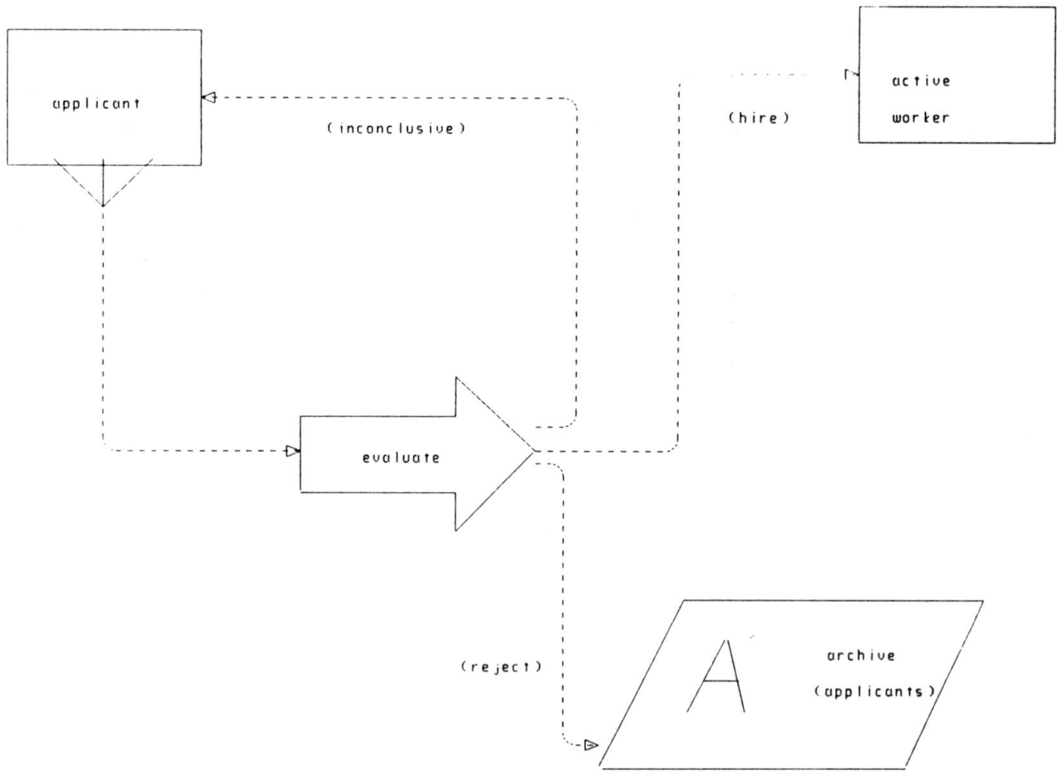

In this diagram, which is an example of **user-defined vectoring**, the previous state-change "hire" has been refined to show a more complete set of actions for moving an occurrence out of the "applicant" state. The three possible results (labelled appropriately) are "hire," "reject" and "inconclusive." These lead to the **terminating states** of the state change.

"Applicant" is called the **originating subtype** for the state change. Defining any originating subtype that is to the right of any terminating subtype for the same state change is generally inappropriate (especially for "vectored" classifications) and should be avoided without due consideration.

Note that "inconclusive" leads back to its own originating subtype. As long as there are other outcomes of the state change, this is not inappropriate. It simply identifies one valid result the state change may have.

Ending back at the originating subtype after a state change occurs implies **iteration** of the transaction (process) for the very same object occurrence. This potential iteration is shown using a special "crow's-foot" symbol at the point that the connection exits the originating subtype. (Iteration also means an indeterminant number of evaluation events for the originating subtype; this suggests the need for an associated characteristic—under "applicant"—in order to keep track of repeated evaluations.)

Note the use of the **archive** at the termination of the transaction's "reject" outcome above. As always, archives represent a means to "keep" (historical) data when no longer of active interest, or when it would violate mutual exclusivity in the classification if kept under the control of the model itself. Archives are thus very useful devices in conjunction with entity life cycle analysis and support.

S.1-4 Mandatory and Prohibited Antecedents

For a valid occurrence of a certain subtype to exist in a life cycle, that occurrence must sometimes have previously existed in one or more prior states. These prior states are called **mandatory antecedents**. (Unless explicitly designated as such, however, all prior states are always considered "optional.") The originating subtype of any state change that terminates in a given state is always considered a mandatory antecedent for that state.

It is cumbersome to show mandatory antecedents graphically using connections. Use of an **antecedents matrix** is therefore generally recommended. An example is provided in the next section. (The states in an entity life cycle may also be numbered, and prohibited antecedents identified for any given subtype in the model by coded references.) Mandatory antecedents may also be defined for individual state changes.

Generally, every state change in a life cycle should have one and only one originating subtype. If a state change needs *more* than one, this indicates that the state change applies to some more general entity type. When this more general object is identified as the originating subtype (this is recommended practice), identification of **prohibited antecedents** (disallowed originating subtypes) for the state change may be required. This is illustrated below. Prohibited antecedents for individual states may also be defined. Naturally, the originating subtype for a state change can never be defined as prohibited for either the state change itself, or its terminating subtypes.

Diagram S.4

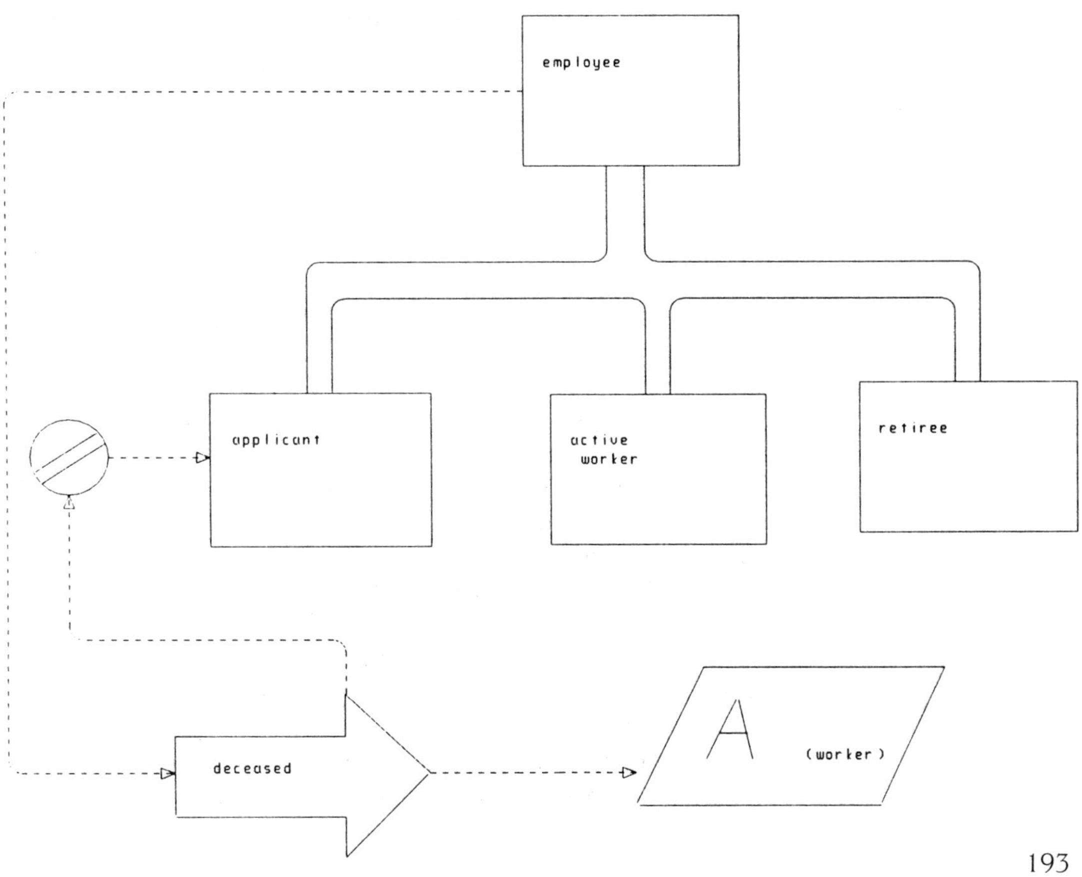

The "not" symbol has been used to show that special processing for deceased workers is inappropriate for applicants.

Prohibited antecedents may also be defined in an antecedents matrix (which may also show mandatory antecedents) or by coded references on the model itself. If an antecedents matrix is for state changes, then it is laid out state change vs. state; if for states themselves, then states appear along both axes. For completeness, antecedents matrices should generally include archives even though they are not proper subtypes.

S.1-5 Mandatory State Change Constraints

Certain state changes cannot be allowed until specified conditions exist in the database. These conditions are called **mandatory constraints**. An example follows.

Diagram S.5

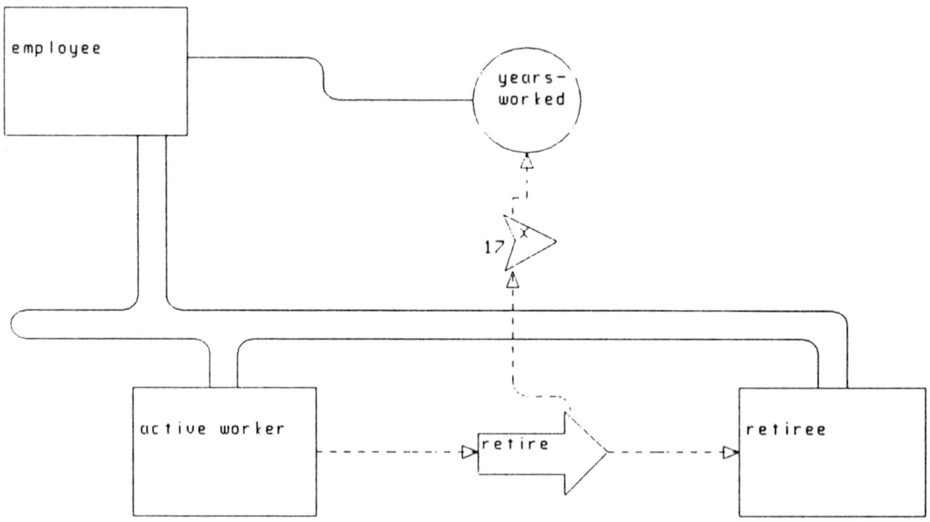

17. years-worked >= 5

An employee cannot officially retire until accumulating five years of service.

Note that the constraint above has been defined for the state change itself, rather than the "retiree" state. This presumably means that it *is* possible to be a "retiree" in this enterprise without having five years of service. This may suggest that some other state change (perhaps "abnormal") has not yet been discovered. If no such additional state change exists, then the mandatory constraint probably belongs to the "retiree" state itself rather than to the state change "retire," since the associated business policy is therefore general for all workers.

Often, mandatory state change constraints are too complex to express easily in graphic form. In such cases, textual notes may substitute.

GUIDELINES AND CONVENTIONS FOR ENTITY LIFE CYCLES

- An entity life cycle is shown using a mutually exclusive classification (normally mandatory). (This classification may have subclassifications, as needed.) Each subtype is an ordered stage, or state of the life cycle.
- A specification of "vectored" is recommended (at least initially) for any classification supporting a life cycle. This specification reconfirms the general rule that no state change should ever terminate in a subtype to the left of the originating subtype.
- Entity life cycle analysis may be performed for kernel entity types, characteristics, and association types.
- The classification used for an entity life cycle may be pro forma.
- Show the user-defined state change using an action symbol, appropriately named and connected to the subtypes of interest. Each state change represents a transaction or process.
- Identify the agent capable of, or responsible for, invoking a state change using an empty "trigger" symbol, appropriately named.
- A state should generally never have more than one state change leaving it. A state change should always have at least one, but never more than one connection, coming into it.
- An originating state is not required for the first state in a life cycle, and a terminating state is not required for the last one.
- If a state change seems to have more than one originating state, then identify some supertype as the originating state.
- A state change (transaction) may have more than one result or outcome (but always at least one). Each distinct outcome should lead to a separate subtype and be shown with an appropriately labeled connection.
- One of the outcomes of a multi-outcome stage change may lead to the same subtype as the originating subtype. (This represents possible iteration, which is shown with a crow's foot at the originating subtype.)
- Use a characteristic to record information about a possibly iterative state change.
- All life cycles must have at least as many state changes as there are states.
- Use archives where the data resulting from the conclusion of a state change is of no subsequent interest to the life cycle as a whole.
- Use a "not" symbol where a state change is specific to some, but not all the subtypes of a classification. This identifies prohibited states.

(Continued)

GUIDELINES AND CONVENTIONS FOR ENTITY LIFE CYCLES
(Continued)

- The originating state for any state change is always a mandatory antecedent for that state change and all of its terminating states.
- Mandatory and prohibited antecedents for states or state changes are best shown using an appropriate antecedents matrix.
- Show mandatory constraints for state changes either graphically or using textual notes.
- If there is no state change to reach a terminating state other than one having a mandatory constraint, then the constraint belongs to that state.
- Use zoom diagrams liberally for defining entity life cycles.

S.2 Data-Controlled Design: An Example

The following example illustrates suggested steps of life cycle analysis and transaction discovery for a typical object. The entity type "order" is chosen for this analysis.

Step 1. Any entity type may always have at least two potential states, "available" and "unavailable" (for processing).

Diagram S.6

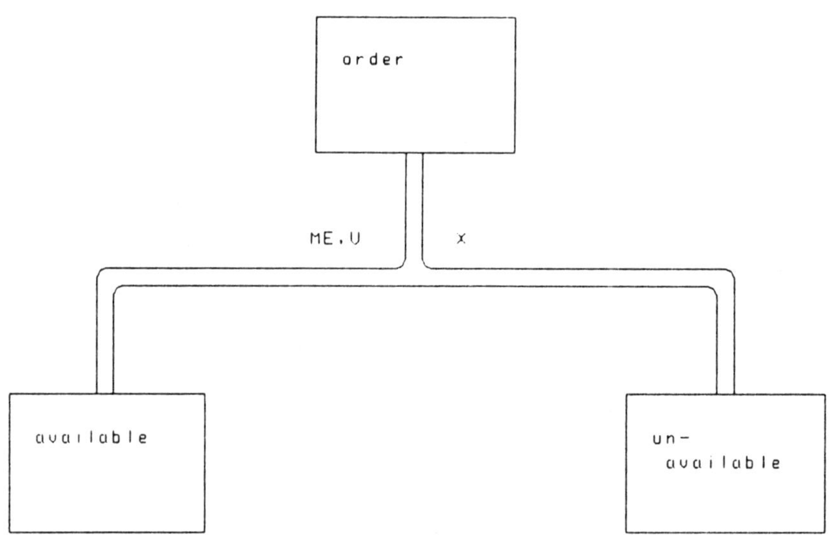

This produces two proto-processes, "receive" and "deactivate," one to arrive at each state in this mandatory (and exhaustive) classification.

Step 2. There are generally several reasons why the final state in any prototype life cycle can be reached. "Unavailable" can therefore be subclassified.

Diagram S.7

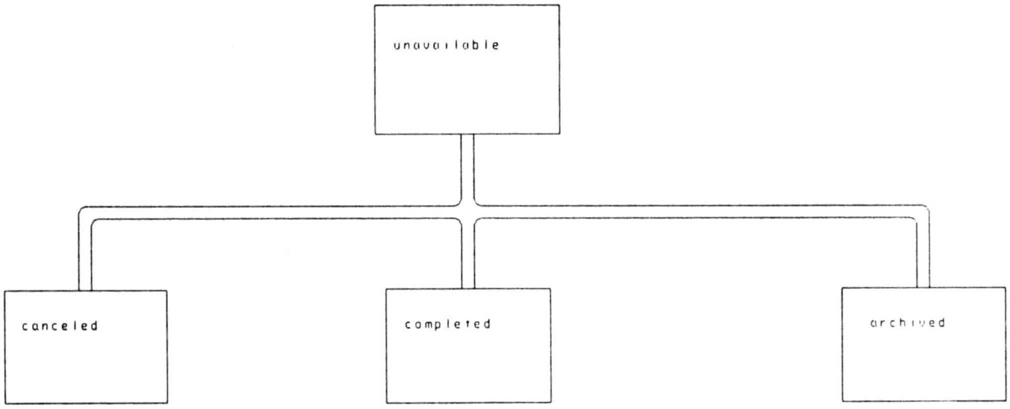

This produces three more proto-processes, one for each additional subtype (state).

Step 3. Select the most normal or successful end-result among these states and analyze further. In this example, "completed" would be the appropriate choice.

Ask the question, what is necessary to arrive at any additional states to the right of this subtype?

Diagram S.8

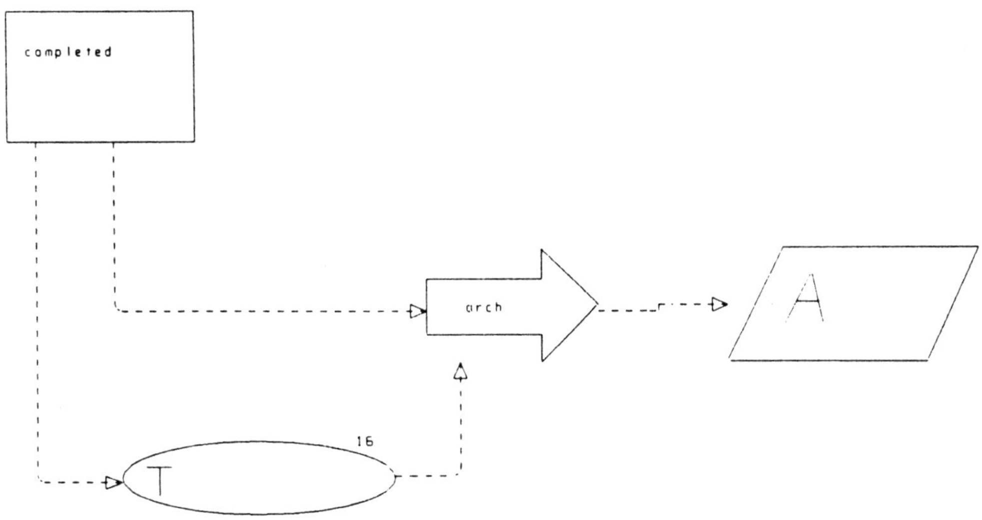

16. Aged six weeks from completion.

This behavior is automatic. Note that the archive cannot be considered to be a subtype.

Step 4. Then ask, what stages are necessary to arrive at the selected subtype during normal operations (i.e., what subtypes exist to the left)? The following steps, all subtypes of order (not shown), are identified.

Diagram S.9

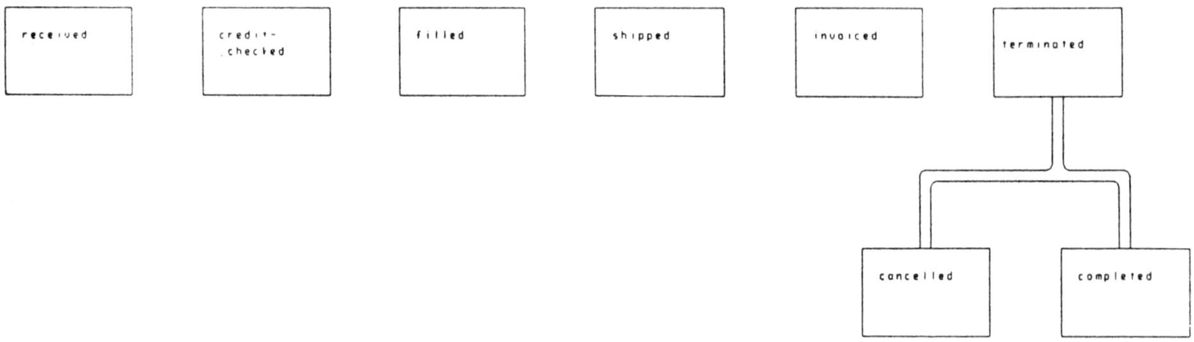

Six states are identified, with two additional subtypes for "terminated." Note that these latter subtypes (along with the archive) replace the earlier "unavailable." "Received" also substitutes for the earlier "available." Continue subclassification as required. ("Filled," for example, may have two subtypes, "back-ordered" and "filled-in-full.")

Step 5. For each state, examine the state change needed to move an occurrence forward in the life cycle. For "received," this produces the following.

Diagram S.10

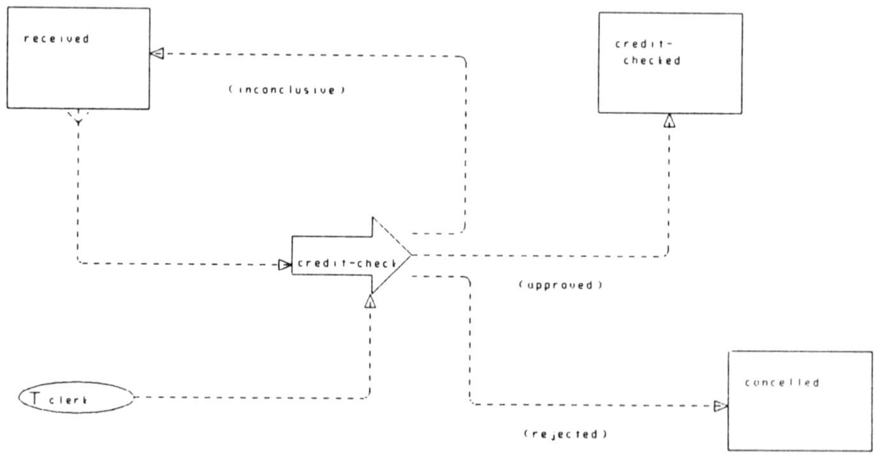

In performing a credit check, a clerk (the initiating agent) may produce any one of three outcomes ("inconclusive," "approved," or "rejected"), each terminating in a different subtype. Credit check may be performed iteratively if "inconclusive."

Step 6. Identify actions that cause the normal flow to be terminated prematurely. Also identify states for which such actions are disallowed (i.e., prohibited antecedents).

Diagram S.11

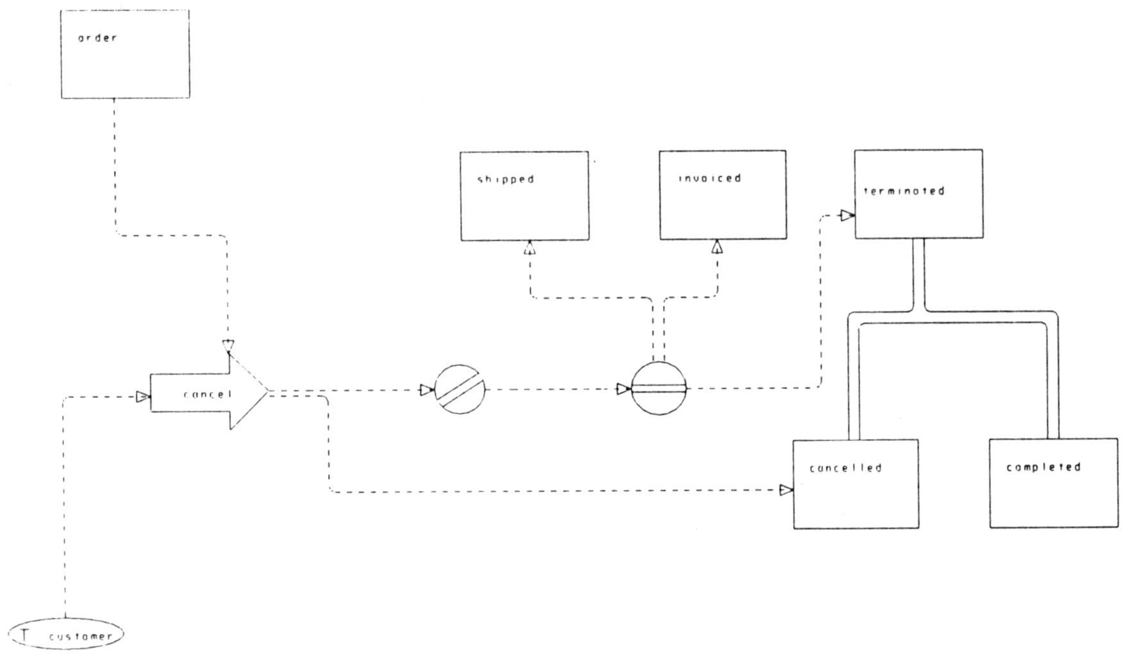

A customer may cancel an order, but not if it has already been shipped, invoiced, or terminated.

Step 7. It is often useful to identify all mandatory and all prohibited antecedent states in an *antecedents matrix*.

Diagram S.12

ANTECEDENTS MATRIX

States:	1	2	3	4	5	6	7
1. Received	-						
2. Credit-checked	x	-					
3. Filled	x	x	-				
4. Shipped	x	x	x	-			
5. Invoiced	x	x			-		
6. Cancelled	x			p	p	-	
7. Completed	x	x	x	x	x	p	-

(all generally prohibited)

x - mandatory antecedent

p - prohibited antecedent

Step 8. Identify mandatory state change constraints for each state change (transaction).

Diagram S.13

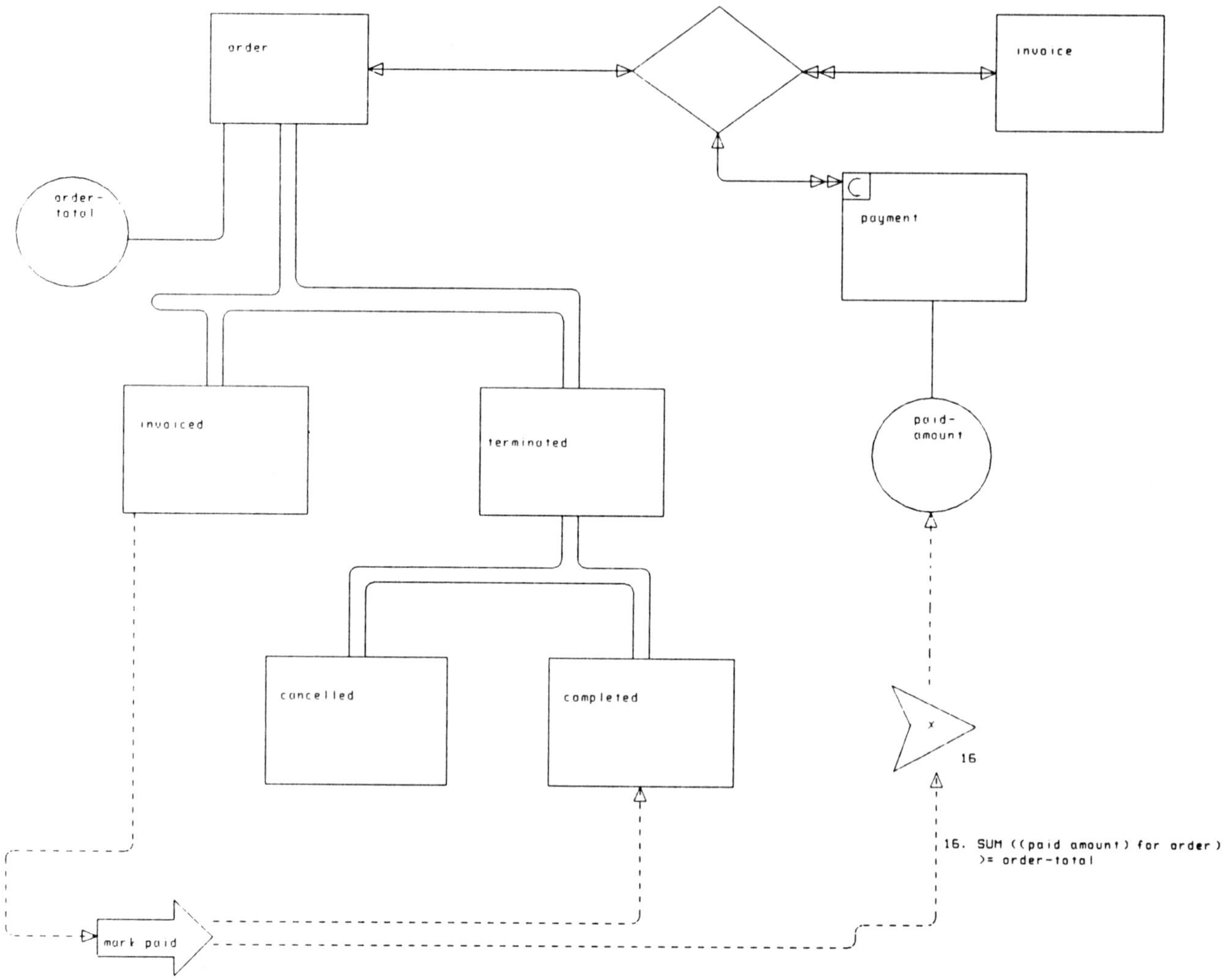

An invoice cannot be "completed" until paid in full.

Also, inspect all terminating states for state changes having mandatory constraints (as above) to determine whether there may be other, as-yet-undiscovered state changes to reach them for which the constraint would not apply. (If not, the mandatory constraint belongs to the terminating state, rather than the state change.)

Step 9. Inspect final subtypes missing archive criteria. Note that the previous archive criteria was specified for "completed," but not for "cancelled." This leaves a subtype of "terminated" without archiving criteria.

Step 10. Define *suspense criteria* for each state, as appropriate.

Diagram S.14

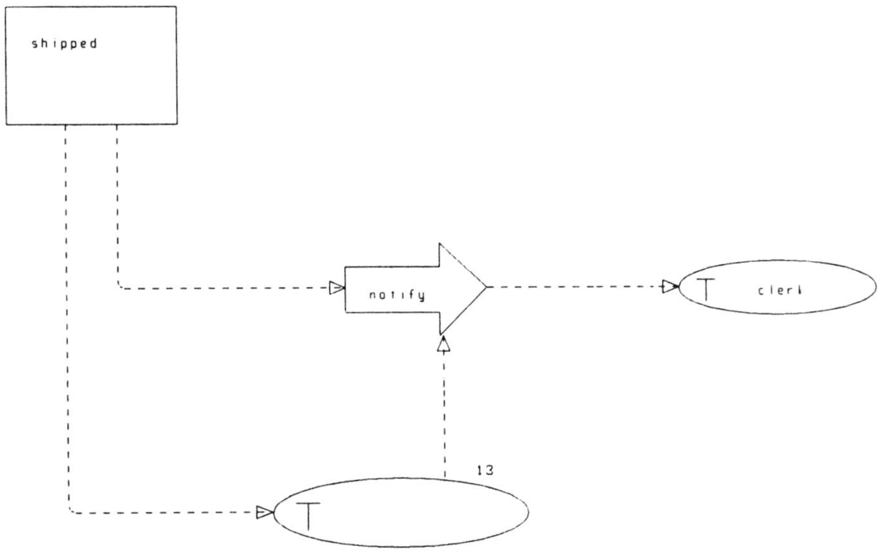

13. Aged two weeks.

If an order stays in the "shipped" state for more than two weeks without being invoiced, a clerk is automatically notified. (To avoid clutter, the action object "notify" above may be dropped. More complex "suspense" criteria and notification agents may be documented in tables.)

Step 11. Define the preferred implementation. Many life cycles are implemented as pro forma, using type-codes. At least one type-code per classification, including subclassifications, is deemed most appropriate.

Alternatively (or additionally), a pro forma life cycle may be supported using a series of dates, one for each state, which remain null until the object occurrence reaches that state (if ever). This may prove desirable even for nonpro forma life cycles—for example, as a check against stages missed. Note, for example, that the states "filled" and "shipped" were not defined as required antecedents for "invoiced." Customer satisfaction, of course, demands that these crucial steps not be overlooked! A clocked mandatory integrity constraint for the appropriate date attribute types would therefore be desirable.

Generally, dates and other historical information concerning the passage of an occurrence through a life cycle may be placed either in the supertype, or cumulatively, in each of the subtypes. To avoid problems with null values, the latter is preferred in nonpro forma classifications.

APPENDIX I

Namable Objects and Connections

Objects	May be named (and have aliases)	Named objects or connections whose names must be unique in one entity model
entity type (kernel)	yes[6]	yes
aggregate object type	yes[6]	yes
association type	yes	no[1]
characteristic type	yes[6]	no[1]
domain type	yes[6]	yes
attribute type	yes[6]	no
aggregate association type	yes	no[1]
measurement point	yes	no[1]
archive	yes	no
integrity constraint	no	—
automatic action	no[2]	—
nonautomatic action (process)	yes	no
measurement signal	no	—
automatic trigger	no	—
agent	yes	no
zone	yes	yes
frequency estimate	no	—
alias	yes[6]	no[7]

Connections		
relationship type	yes[3]	no
classification relationship type	yes	no
alias	no	—
attribute	no	—
partitioned domain	no	—
subsetted domain	no	—
aggregate relationship type source	no	—
pro forma source[4]	no	—
behavior[5]	no[8]	—

1. If two or more instances have the same name, then they must have a different set of determinants (and vice versa).
2. State changes may be individually named, but to be truly automatic, require that a trigger be defined.
3. Multiple action names are permitted for the same relationship type, each using a directional indicator.
4. Including classifications, relationship types, and attribute types.
5. Including integrity constraints, automatic and nonautomatic actions, measurement signals, triggers and agents, and frequency estimates.
6. Name is mandatory.
7. Must be unique for entity type (kernel), aggregate object type, domain type, and zone unless marked as prohibited.
8. The outcomes of a state change may be named.

APPENDIX II

Part I: Objects and Connections by Levels of Detail for Entity Models (Cumulative)

Levels of Detail	Objects	Connections	Special Designators
1. **Presentation** (basic objects connections)	entity types (kernel) zones	relationship types aliases	directional indicators (for relationship types) aliases "not" (for prohibited aliases)
2. **Professional** (refined objects and connections)	characteristic types association types aggregate objects	classification (ETH) aggregate relationship type sources pro forma relationship type sources	"stored" "not stored" "pro forma" "pro forma" directional indicators aggregate relationship type directional indicators clocks
3. **Integrity** (entity-level behavior rules for updating)	integrity constraints (ICs) automatic actions (AAs) triggers archives aggregate association types	behavior	integrity constraint qualifiers (ICQs) integrity constraint value conditions (ICVCs) crow's foot (iteration) "pending/active" "active/historical"
4. **Attribute** (attribute-level detail, including properties, key specifications, referential integrity, table handling, pro forma attributes, etc.)	attributes and domain types	attributes pro forma classification sources pro forma attribute sources partitioned domains subsetted domains	determinants foreign keys referential integrity pro forma domains and attributes prohibited domains and attributes derived domains and attributes ranging domains and attributes reflective domains and attributes
5. **Measurement** (data derivation and synthesis, and frequency estimates)	measurement points measurement signals (MSs) frequency estimates (FEs)		

Part II: Objects and Connections for Special Definition Tasks (Not Cumulative)

Definition Tasks	Objects	Connections	Special Designators
Domains	domain types measurement signals (MSs) frequency estimates (FEs)	partitioned domains subsetted domains behavior (for MSs) aliases attributes (for coupled domains)	aliases determinants "not" (prohibited domains) "pro forma" "derived" ranging domains reflective domains
Entity Life Cycles	entity types (kernel) zones characteristic types association types integrity constraints (ICs) actions (state changes) triggers (agents) archives attribute types	relationship types aliases classification behavior attributes pro forma classification sources	directional indicators aliases "stored" "not stored" "pro forma" clocks integrity constraint qualifiers ("not," "or," "and," "vectored," "ascending" crow's foot (iteration) determinants derived domains

APPENDIX III

Rules for Connections (Excluding "Behavior" Connections)

Connection Type	From	To
Relationship type	exactly one entity type, characteristic type, association type, aggregate association type, or measurement point (any object with determinants)	same, but not necessarily of the same *type*
Classification		
... entity type hierarchy (ETH)	exactly one kernel or characteristic entity type (the supertype) on top	one or more of the same of the *same* type, on bottom [the subtype(s)]
... Domain subsetting	exactly one domain on top (the superdomain)	one or more of the same on bottom [the subdomain(s)]
Source connection		
... for aggregate relationship type for pro forma ...	exactly one (aggregate) relationship type	two or more other relationship types
... relationship type	exactly one relationship type	exactly one other relationship type
... attribute	exactly one attribute type	exactly one other attribute type
... ETH	exactly one ETH or subtype	exactly one attribute type (a type code used to distinguish subtypes)
Attribute/alias		
... attribute	exactly one entity type, characteristic type, association type, aggregate association type, measurement point or archive (any object with attributes)	exactly one attribute type
... alias	exactly one named object or connection	exactly one alias (banner)
partitioned domain	exactly one domain type (the composite)	two or more domain types (the partitions)

APPENDIX IV

Rules for Behavior Object Connections

Note:

proper objects: Include entity type, association type, characteristic type

data objects: Include proper objects, aggregate objects, aggregate association types, and measurement points

Rules for Integrity Constraints (ICs)

	Stimulus Side	Behavior Side
R restricted	from one or more relationship type(s) and/or association type(s), and optionally a clock	To (same), or data objects
X mandatory	Version 1. From exactly one data object, except aggregate object or aggregate association type, and optionally a clock	To one or more relationship type(s), ETH(s), and/or attribute type(s), or to itself
	Version 2. From exactly state change (Entity life cycles only)	To one or more relationship type(s), ETH(s), and/or attribute type(s)
ME mutually exclusive	From exactly one data object except aggregate object or aggregate association type, and optionally a clock	To one ETH; two or more sets of relationship types; or two or more sets of attribute types
LIM limited	From one or more data objects except aggregate object or aggregate association type, and optionally a clock	To one or more relationship type(s)
FIX frozen	From one or more data object(s) or measurement point(s), relationship (types), ETH(s), archive(s), or attribute type(s), and optionally a clock	To one or more relationship type(s), attribute type(s), aggregate object(s), or ETH(s)

Rules for Automatic Actions (AAs)[1]

	Stimulus Side	Behavior Side
PROP[2] "propagation"	From exactly one proper object or relationship type	To one or more proper object(s) or relationship type(s) (not necessarily of the same type)
INIT[2] "initiation"	From exactly one proper object or relationship type	To one or more proper object(s) or relationship type(s) (not necessarily of the same type)
REPL "replacement"	From exactly one data object or relationship type	To exactly one other data object or relationship type equivalent to the one on the stimulus side
PAIR "pairing"	From exactly one kernel or characteristic entity type	To exactly one 1:1 relationship type, connected to an object of the same type as the one on the stimulus side.
AGREL "aggregate relationship type"	From two or more relationship types	To one aggregate association type or aggregate relationship type
STATE "state change" (automatic)	Version 1. From exactly one subtype in a mutually exclusive classification	To one or more subtypes, which must generally be to the right in a classification for the same entity type.
	Version 2. From exactly one supertype in a mutually exclusive classification	To exactly one classification for which it is the supertype
ARCH "archiving"	From one or more data objects	To exactly one archive object

1. Connection from a trigger on the AA's stimulus side is always permitted.
2. Connection from a state change on the AA's stimulus side is permitted for entity life cycles.

Rules for Automatic Triggers

Stimulus Side	Behavior Side
One or more proper objects* or measurement points* or attribute types; or "clock"; or association type* or relationship type(s)	One or more behavior objects (AA or MS type only)

*Note: These are also associated with either determinants and/or foreign keys.

Rules for Measurement Signals (MSs)[1]

	Stimulus Side	Behavior Side
MEA "measurement"	From exactly one data object or attribute (Note: aggregate objects should be used for "more than one.")	To one or more measurement points
FT "format transform"	From exactly one domain or attribute type	To exactly one other domain or attribute type
RSCT "relationship count"	From one proper object and one or more relationship types	To one attribute type (Note: The "path" should be continuous and/or unambiguous)
ENCT "entity count"	From one data object, which may not be an aggregate	To one attribute type
VLCT "value count"	From one domain or attribute type	To one domain or attribute type
SPEC "special"	From one or more data object, which may not be aggregate, and/or one or more attribute type	To one measurement point, or one attribute type

1. Connection from a trigger on the MS's stimulus side is always permitted.

Rules for Frequency Estimates (FEs)

	Source-Side (Origin)	Enumeration-Side
VOL (volume)	From exactly one data object, except an aggregate	To itself
MO (multiple occurrence)	From exactly one data object, except an aggregate	To exactly one relationship type coming from it (should be 1:M)
MAX (maximum MO)	From exactly one data object, except an aggregate	To exactly one relationship type coming from it (should be 1:M)
RO (relative occurrence)	From exactly one data object, except an aggregate	To exactly one attribute type of its own, or of a supertype
VAL (values)	From exactly one domain	To itself
DIS	From one or more attribute types	To exactly one data object, except an aggregate
XDIS	From one or more attribute types	To exactly one data object, except an aggregate

APPENDIX V

Valid Integrity Constraint Qualifiers (ICQs) and Integrity Constraint Value Conditions (ICVCs) and Rules of Usage[1]

ICQs:

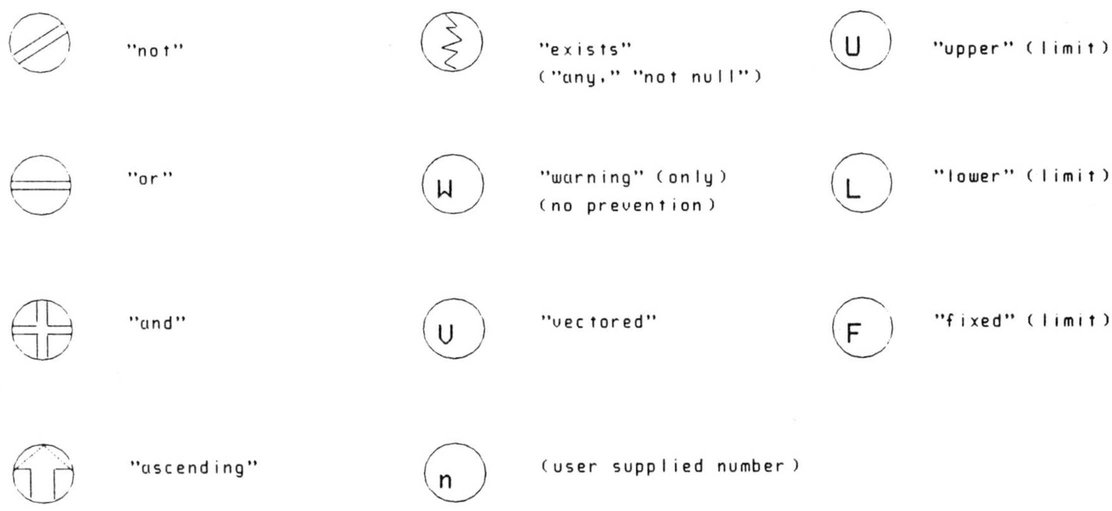

ICVCs:

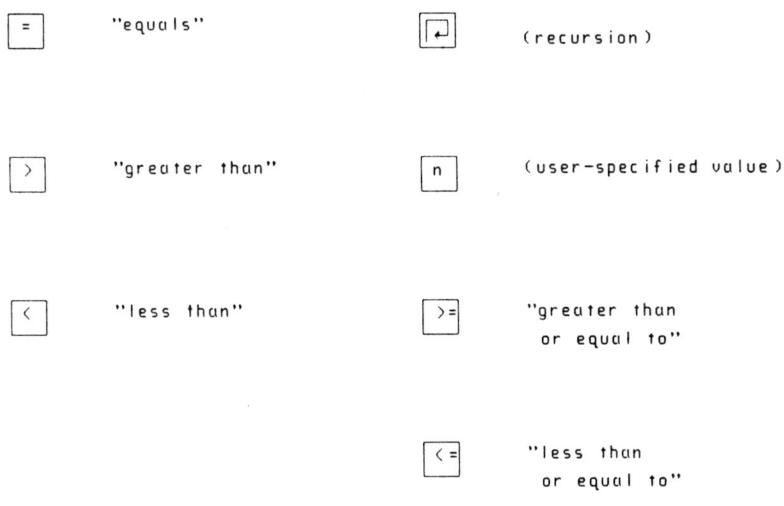

1. ICQs and ICVCs are generally only valid in conjunction with Integrity Constraints (ICs).

Rules of Usage

Rules of Usage	IC	Valid ICO	Valid ICUC[2]
R (restricted)		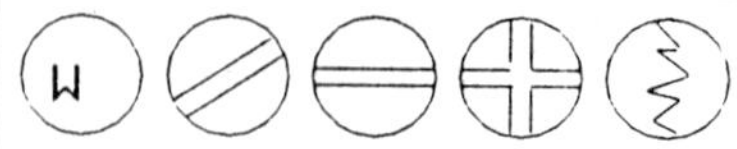	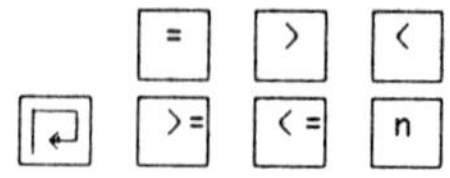
X (mandatory)		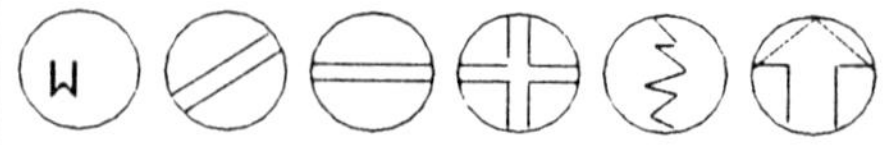	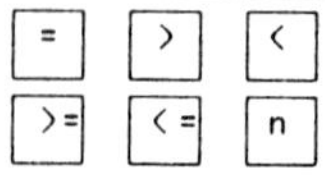
ME (mutually exclusive)		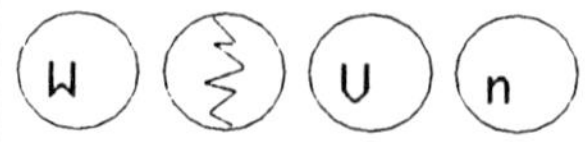	———
LIM (limited)		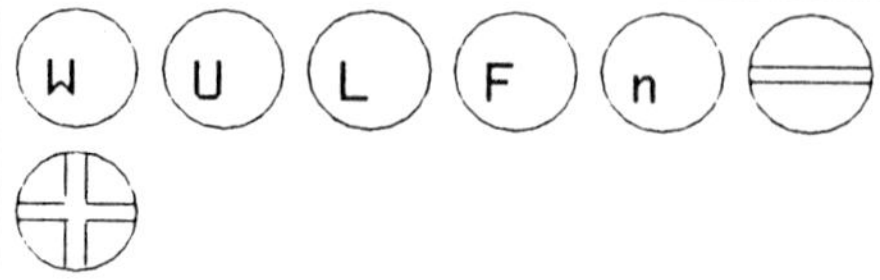	———
FIX (frozen)			———

2. Never valid for use with  or 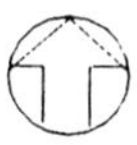

GLOSSARY

AA: See automatic action.

abstract classification: An entity type hierarchy in which the determinants of the supertype and the subtype do not correspond to the same domain.

action: A process (or transaction). Actions are the specific behaviors of an information system.

action name: A verb that describes a business action between the object types connected by a relationship type.

actor: See agent.

agent: The person, organization unit, or machine that is capable of, and responsible for, initiating a user-defined state change.

aggregate: A named collection of objects and/or relationship types within an entity model.

aggregate association type: An association type appearing in an aggregate relationship type, whose updating is controlled by an automatic action.

aggregate object: A named collection of other objects and their connections.

aggregate relationship type: A named collection of relationship types, represented as a relationship type.

aggregation hierarchy: See aggregate object.

alias: Another name by which an object or connection is known.

anomaly: See update anomaly.

antecedent (state): Any prior state in a life cycle.

antecedents matrix: A matrix listing either states by state changes, or states by states, and showing all mandatory and prohibited antecedents.

archive: A repository where the enterprise can save data about some object(s) and/or relationship type(s), but place it outside the scope or control of the entity model per se. Data in an archive is generally not subject to updating.

ascending conversion: Transformation of an entity model to some less detailed form.

association type: An object that holds information (attributes) that describe a relationship (type) between two or more other objects—rather than either of the objects individually. An association type "borrows" the determinants of the objects related to also use as its own.

atomic (domain): A domain that has no partitions and is therefore not composite.

attribute: A domain used to give some specific property of an object (i.e., a "field").

automatic action: A behavior whereby one type of update is defined to invoke or cause one or more other updates automatically.

behavior: Update processing in an information system.

behavior (automatic): Rules in an entity model that will apply to the corresponding database during updating in order to maintain integrity. Behavior specifications generally reflect business policy or rules.

bill-of-materials relationship type: See recursive relationship type.

binary association type: An association type that "borrows" the determinants of two and only two related objects to also use as its own.

cardinality: The maximum number of instances of some relationship type that an object type is permitted to have.

characteristic (entity type): An entity type that is tightly coupled to some other object, for which it provides information about some related repetitive event, or some multivalued set of properties. Occurrences of a characteristic can only exist so long as the related occurrence of the characterized object continues to exist.

characterized object: The object to which a characteristic is coupled.

characterizing relationship type: The relationship type that connects a characteristic to the object it characterizes.

classification: The breaking down of a more general thing into special types of things (i.e., classes) of the same thing. (See also entity type hierarchy.)

classification aggregate relationship type: An aggregate relationship type where the defined collection of other relationship types all exist between the members of one or two classifications.

classification relationship type: The connection between a supertype and a subtype in an entity type hierarchy.

clocked integrity constraint: An integrity constraint with a defined effective or discontinuation date.

clocked trigger: A trigger for which a time component (e.g., event date, time window, elapsed time, etc.) is defined.

closed domain: A domain whose valid member values are (or can be) listed beforehand. This list of values may supplant the rules of formation for the domain.

CO: See characterized object.

composite (domain): A domain that does not have its own rules of formation but rather assembles two or more other domains (called partitions) into a larger unit.

composition: See composite (domain).

conceptual schema: A definition or model for a data resource that contains specifications for domains and behavior, as well as objects and relationship types.

conflict identification: Identification of logical inconsistencies or impossibilities in the definition of integrity constraints.

connections: Interactions between objects in the real world, as represented in an entity model.

cyclic structure: See recursive structure.

data-controlled: An information system, or architecture, wherein transactions are comprehensively defined as either automatic or user-controlled state changes.

data element: In conventional usage, an atomic data type roughly corresponding to a domain.

data model: See entity model. data resource: A collection of data, generally to be stored, supporting some portion, or all of an enterprise.

derived (domain): A domain whose values are produced by an algorithm, procedure, or set of calculations.

determinant: A domain whose values may be used in uniquely distinguishing between occurrences of some entity type.

directional indicator: A small arrow accompanying an action name for a relationship type indicating the subject and object of the action.

discrimination: The expected number of instances of some object having a typical value of some attribute type.

domain: A set of values whose formation conforms to a common definition (i.e., format or syntax, and meaning). Domains are used as attributes to give properties of entity types and certain other objects.

enterprise: An organization or company that needs to store data about its activities, resources and/or environment in a controlled, sharable fashion.

entity life cycle: The stages, or states, through which an occurrence of an object passes as it ages. An entity life cycle may be shown using subtypes of a mutually exclusive classification (with vectoring), and used to identify the transactions or processes that move the occurrence from one state to the next.

entity (life) history: See entity life cycle.

entity model: A model of an enterprise, or some portion thereof, which is based on the objects of that enterprise, and their interactions, rather than on its dynamic processes or functions. An entity model is a blueprint for database implementation.

entity/relationship approach: An analysis technique aimed at creating a purely logical model of an enterprise that identifies the things (entity types) within that enterprise, and how they interact, without respect to its dynamics or process "flow." The ER approach (sometimes called ERA approach—"A" for attributes) is generally credited to Peter P. Chen, who created it in order to satisfy needs for DBMS-independent data structuring.

entity type: A thing that exists, or that gives some focal point in understanding or organizing the real world. An entity type is something that is meaningful to the enterprise, about which information is collected and maintained.

entity type hierarchy: The association of one or more entity types with a more general entity type, of which they are merely special classes, types or kinds.

enumeration side: In a frequency estimate, the ending point (i.e., object or connection) whose future number of instances is being estimated.

enumerator: An estimate or sequencing value relevant to some specification of behavior.

ER approach: See entity/relationship approach.

ER diagram: See entity model.

ETH: See entity type hierarchy.

exceptional discrimination: The expected number of instances of some object having an unusual or atypical value for some attribute type.

exhaustive classification: A classification in which all possible subtypes have been identified.

FE: See frequency estimate.

field: In conventional usage, the use of a data element to hold actual values in some particular record type. (A "field" is roughly equivalent to an attribute type in entity modeling.)

foreign key: The appearance of the determinant(s) of some entity type or characteristic in some other object (as attributes), thereby establishing the actual basis for a relationship type between that object and the former. Values for the determinant in this other object are called "foreign keys."

frequency estimate: An estimate for a dimension of some specified portion of a yet-to-be-implemented database.

frozen: An integrity constraint defined for some object(s) and/or relationship type(s), whereby the mere existence of occurrences precludes any updating to certain other designated objects and/or relationship type(s).

generalization: The identification of a thing of which other things are simply special classes, types or kinds.

generalization hierarchy: See entity type hierarchy.

homonym: A name that is used to refer to two or more conceptually distinct things (e.g., domains).

hybrid aggregate relationship type: An aggregate relationship type defined as having both classification and series components.

IC: See integrity constraint.

ICQ: See integrity constraint qualifier.

ICVC: See integrity constraint value condition.

identifier: See determinant.

imaginary classification: Any classification of an imaginary entity type.

imaginary entity type: An entity type that may exist, but for which the enterprise can produce no controllable or unique identifier.

implementation zone: Some zone (of an entity model) that will be implemented as a unit, apart from other (implementation) zones.

inheritance: The availability of all properties and/or relationship types of a supertype to all subtypes thereof.

initiation: An automatic action wherein an update causes certain objects and/or connections to be initiated based on the current status (i.e., values) of others.

instance: See occurrence.

integrity: Correctness (of database content).

integrity constraint: A rule for database updating, in order to maintain database integrity.

integrity constraint qualifier: A specification that refines or modifies the meaning of an integrity constraint.

integrity constraint value condition: A comparison of values for attribute types all defined on the reaction side of a "restricted" or "mandatory" integrity constraint. The condition must be continuously satisfied for an instance of an object or relationship type defined on the stimulus side to continue existing.

intelligent database system: A database system that is built and operates on the basis of a conceptual schema.

intersection data: Attributes that belong to an association type.

ISA: See classification relationship type.

kernel (entity type): Any entity type that is not a characteristic. Kernel entity types are central to an entity model, and their occurrences can generally exist without reference to any other object.

kernel determinant: A determinant whose values by themselves can uniquely and unambiguously distinguish between occurrence of an entity type. Kernel entity types always have kernel determinants.

limitation constraint: See limited.

limited: An integrity constraint defined for some object that places a limit on the number of other specified objects and/or connectors that may exist.

locked into: Instances of objects and/or relationship types that are controlled on the reaction side of an automatic action. Since such instances cannot be updated by users, they are said to be "locked-into" the behavior.

mandatory: An integrity constraint that specifies an occurrence of some object can only validly exist if occurrences of one or more other objects, connections, or attributes exist and meet any specified conditions.

mandatory antecedent: Any antecedent state in a life cycle through which an occurrence must have passed to participate validly in a state change or to exist in some other state.

mandatory classification: A classification in which an occurrence of a subtype must exist for each occurrence of the corresponding supertype.

maximum occurrence: The expected maximum number of instances of some relationship type for some object.

measurement: Arithmetic operations defined for an entity model that automatically and continuously monitor "how many," "how much," "how often," etc.

measurement point: An entity type whose primary purpose is to maintain synthesized, derived or statistical data, generally produced arithmetically from other data.

measurement signal: A behavior that specifies or defines some type of measurement between connected objects and/or relationship types.

mixed model: An entity model that also contains domain definitions.

MS: See measurement signal.

multiple occurrence: The expected number of instances of some relationship type for some object.

mutually exclusive: An integrity constraint defined for some object that precludes the coexistence of occurrences of two or more other objects and/or relationship types.

mutually exclusive classification: A classification in which there can be at most one subtype occurrence for the whole classification, no matter how many subtypes it may have.

named domain subset: Any named proper or improper subset of values in a domain.

n-ary association type: An association type that "borrows" the determinants of multiple related objects (more than two) to also use as its own.

nested aggregate object: An aggregate object so defined such that it is completely contained within another.

normalization: A series of tests and rules for database design aimed at eliminating update anomalies. Normalization was originally developed as a theory complementary to the relational model.

normalized (data): See normalization.

object: Something about which information is to be recorded in a database system, or which permits specification of relevant rules or behavior.

occurrence: Any specific member of the set of instances belonging to, and defined by, the same object or connection type.

open domain: A domain for which it is not feasible or meaningful to list all possible values beforehand.

open referential integrity: A database model or implementation where referential integrity may be violated in a specific relationship type. In such a relationship type, referential integrity is unspecified.

originating state: The state (or subtype) of an occurrence before a state change is applied.

pairing: An automatic action wherein each instance of one object must be paired with one and only one instance of another, equivalent object, generally the most recent.

partial determinant: A determinant whose values cannot by themselves uniquely and unambiguously distinguish between occurrences of an entity type, but must instead always be coupled with the values of at least one other determinant, including a kernel, to do so. Characteristics have at least one partial determinant.

partition: Any of the domains assembled in a composite domain.

precedence: Dependence of occurrences of a subtype in a classification on the existence of corresponding occurrences of a supertype. The supertype therefore has "precedence."

primary name: The preferred name for an object or connection.

pro forma attribute: An inherited property nonetheless shown for the subtype (but not to be stored therein).

pro forma classification (or subtype): A classification or subtype included in an entity model that is not to be implemented (i.e., stored per se).

pro forma relationship type: An inherited relationship type nonetheless also shown for the subtype (even though not to be implemented in connection with the subtype).

prohibited: Any object or connection that is not permitted in the entity model. (Since an object or connection must first be defined to be prohibited, this really means "not acceptable in this model," or "users not permitted to create or delete instances.")

prohibited antecedent: Any antecedent state in a life cycle through which an occurrence must not have passed to participate validly in a state change or to exist in some other state.

prohibited name: An unacceptable name that might be used to refer to an object or connection.

propagation: An automatic action that translates one update into one or more others within the same timeframe, and that also continues to seek all subsequent opportunities to coordinate additional updates between those same object(s) or connection(s).

property: Describable characteristics of some object. The values of some attribute type are used to specify the property.

range: A set of values defined by an upper and a lower bounds.

ranging domain: A domain whose member values consist of ranges defined in a consistent manner.

reaction: The consequences or actions of a behavior as invoked or produced by a stimulus (e.g., an integrity check, another update, an arithmetic operation, etc.). In a sense, the reaction is the behavior itself.

recursive relationship type: A relationship type where both ends point to the very same object type. An implication may be that the object type is made up of other instances of itself.

recursive structure: A collection of one or more relationship types connecting continuously back to an object from which they started.

reduction: Substitution of an entity type box for an aggregate object during simplification, or removal of all relationship types comprising an aggregate relationship type.

referencing zone: Some zone defined in order to designate the preferred aliases (vocabulary) of some corporate group.

referential integrity: An integrity constraint in the relational model that prescribes that whenever foreign key values exist, then instances of the object(s) to which they refer (i.e., for which they are determinant values) must also exist.

referential integrity option: A specification of what specifically should happen if an update is attempted that would otherwise violate referential integrity.

reflective domain: A composite domain whose partitions match some classification on a one-to-one basis.

relational model: A prescription (theory) for the optimum construction of a DBMS, developed by E. F. Codd at IBM in the late 1960s.

relationship type: Connections between entity types, (and sometimes other types of objects) in an entity model, reflecting interactions, especially business actions, between them.

relative occurrence: The expected percentage of occurrences of some object expected to have either a value for some attribute, or an occurrence of some classification (or subtype), or an instance of some relationship type.

replacement: An automatic action that translates an update into the replacement of an instance of an object or a connection by an instance of an equivalent object or connection.

restriction: An integrity constraint that specifies that occurrences of one or more relationship types can only validly exist so long as occurrences of one or more other relationship or object types exist and meet specified conditions.

RI: See referential integrity option.

role: See subordinate entity type.

rules of formation: Rules specified to control the creation of member values in some domain (i.e., formatting rules).

semantics: Meaning (of data).

series aggregate relationship type: An aggregate relationship type where the defined collection of other relationship types are continuous between any series of objects.

source: In a pro forma specification, the attribute or relationship type actually supplying the referenced data.

source side: In a frequency estimate, the starting or reference point for which the estimate is made.

state: A stage in the life cycle of an object, represented by a subtype in a mutually exclusive classification, which is often vectored.

state change: The movement of a subtype occurrence to the right in a vectored mutually exclusive classification (i.e., entity life cycle). A state change reflects some specific response to a given set of conditions, or the overt action of some agent.

stimulus: In an automatic behavior, any event or condition (e.g., an update, the passage of time, certain value conditions, the continued existence of something, etc.) requiring a rule of updating to be applied so as to cause a reaction.

subdomain: See named domain subset.

subordinate entity type: A more specific entity type (on bottom) of an entity type hierarchy.

subtype: See subordinate entity type.

superdomain: The domain against which a named domain subset (subdomain) is defined.

superior entity type: The more general entity type (on top) in an entity type hierarchy.

supertype: See superior entity type.

terminating state(s): One or more possible states (subtypes) of an occurrence after a state change is applied.

timed integrity constraint: See clocked integrity constraint.

timing criteria: Usually used in conjunction with measurement to specify replenishment or recalculation timing, and generally reflects users' requirements for the availability of current information.

trigger (automatic): Attribute-level conditions defined for an entity model that automatically invoke certain updates and/or measurement to take place.

type-code: An attribute whose values are used to distinguish between special types, kinds or classes of an entity type.

update anomaly: Something unexpected and undesirable that occurs in updating a database that if unmanaged, leads directly to loss of integrity.

user-defined state change: The nonautomatic (i.e., agent- controlled) transaction or process that moves an occurrence of an entity type from one state to another in a life cycle.

user-specified vectoring: In a mutually exclusive classification that is used to define the life cycle of an object, the transactions (state changes) and their results that govern the movement of an occurrence through the classification as it ages.

value: One entry or member of a domain. Values are used for specific attribute types of an object to give some actual property.

value condition: See integrity constraint value condition.

vectored classification: A mutually exclusive classification where the single subtype occurrence can only move to the right between the subtypes.

vectored mutually exclusive: A mutually exclusive specification that also has a defined order of existence for occurrences of the objects and/or relationship types on the reaction side.

volume: The expected number of instances of some object.

window zone: Some zone (of an entity model) defined for special presentation or specification purposes (e.g., for definition of behavior).

zone: Some specified subset of an entity model.

zoom diagram: See window zone.